Advanced Technology for Road Transport

IVHS and ATT

For a complete listing of the *Artech House Telecommunications Library*,
turn to the back of this book

Advanced Technology for Road Transport

IVHS and ATT

Ian Catling

Editor

Artech House
Boston • London

Library of Congress Cataloging-in-Publication Data
Catling, Ian
Advanced Technology for Road Transport: IVHS and ATT/Ian Catling
Includes bibliographical references and index.
ISBN 0-89006-613-2
1. Intelligent Vehicle Highway Systems. 2. Telematics. I. Catling, Ian.
TE228.3.A38 1993 93-38272
388.3'12–dc20 CIP

A catalogue record for this book is available from the British Library

685 Canton Street
Norwood, MA 02062

International Standard Book Number: 0-89006-613-2
Library of Congress Catalog Card Number: TE228.3.A38 1993

10 9 8 7 6 5 4 3 2 1

Contents

Chapter 1
Introduction to ATT, IVHS, and RTI

Ian Catling

1.1 WHAT IS ADVANCED TRANSPORT TELEMATICS?

The automobile is over a hundred years old. For most of us, life without it would be very different, and for some of us it has changed our lives dramatically. On the whole, we tend to think that its benefits, in terms of our increased independence and mobility, outweigh the drawbacks in terms of increased stress, environmental pollution, and the risk of accidents. But these drawbacks are very real, and with the inexorable growth in the vehicle population, they are becoming harder to live with.

In some ways the experience of driving today is quite different from what it was 20 or 30 years ago. Although traffic speeds in city centers have not changed significantly, we have been squeezing more and more vehicles into our cities and onto our highways. Greater sophistication in our traffic control systems and in traffic management techniques in general has helped us to do this without catastrophic results, although in many cities it is already clear that the process of increasing traffic volumes cannot continue much further. The overall management of traffic—both in the onstreet control and in the wider context of transport in general—is an area where advanced technology is having an increasingly important effect and will continue to be vital into the next century for the management of our transport systems. On the other hand, the process of driving has really changed very little. Research shows that most drivers setting out on a journey do not have a clear idea of the route they will follow, and the dependence on maps, signs, and the driver's own—usually imperfect—knowledge of the road network has changed little in decades.

Our vehicles have an increasing amount of electronic systems, which contribute to the ease of driving, the comfort and convenience of travelers, greater efficiency, and improved safety. The development of the microprocessor has affected many walks of modern life, but its influence in road transport is only just beginning to have a significant impact. The potential is great for introducing increasingly intelligent systems into vehicles in order to help the driver drive more easily, more efficiently, and more safely.

In the last decade, communication systems have been the focus of many major technological developments throughout the world. In particular, the advent of cellular radio has had a major influence on the ability of the individual to remain in touch. The introduction of car phones has opened up new markets at a rate never envisaged in the early 1980s.

The coupling of information technology and communications—increasingly known as *telematics*—is harnessing technological advances in many ways that affect the day-to-day lives of all of us. Online point-of-sale systems which can automatically handle electronic funds transfers are increasingly familiar; ''notebook'' or ''palmtop'' computers now can contain their own fax or modem facilities, enabling interaction with remote databases to provide immediate, on-the-spot access to information; and the computer control of digital telephone systems has led to voice and data communication services unheard of a few years ago.

This book is about the application of telematics to road transport. In 1988 Roland Hüber, who was then the director of informatics research programs in the Commission of the European Communities (CEC), coined the phrases *road transport informatics* (RTI) and *integrated road transport environment* (IRTE). RTI is the application of telematics to road transport; if it can be implemented in a suitably integrated fashion, then we can hope to achieve the IRTE. In the U.S., Professor Kan Chen, one of the contributors to this book (see Chapter 12), coined the term *intelligent vehicle–highway systems* (IVHS), which embodies in a single concise phrase the same objective of achieving an integrated system. IVHS has become not only the accepted term for RTI systems in the U.S., but has lent its name to IVHS America—the association, described in Chapter 10, which has so successfully promoted the rapid progress of IVHS in the U.S. in the last two or three years.

In Europe, RTI was successfully promoted in the DRIVE research and development program from 1989 to 1991 (see Chapter 5). At the end of this program, the CEC rationalized several similar programs under the general heading of *telematics.* Thus, the program often referred to as DRIVE II is in fact the *advanced transport telematics* (ATT) program.

So there are now three (at least!) acronyms for the same subject—RTI, IVHS, and ATT. Each of them retains a valid currency and can be applied interchangeably with the others. For convenience, we will refer to ATT in this chapter, although the reader will find references to all three throughout the book. This book is intended to describe some of the exciting current ATT developments in Europe, America, and Japan, and by doing so to give the reader an overview of current progress and a feel for the quickening pace emerging in ATT implementation. This chapter will introduce these developments and provide the context in which the remaining chapters can be read. It provides a brief history to set the scene and explains the structure and overall content of the rest of the book by summarizing some of the key current developments.

1.2 HISTORY OF ATT

1.2.1 Driver Information

There are many applications of ATT. One of the most significant is the provision of information to the driver of a vehicle. We know from several studies (e.g., [1]) that the process of choosing a route is generally a rather potluck affair—even when the driver has a good knowledge of the road network, there is usually a lack of information about traffic conditions, and poor routing contributes significantly to the problems of congestion and environmental damage.

But this is not new—in 1910 the Jones Live Map (Figure 1.1) was advertised as a means of replacing paper maps and of eliminating the driving stress associated with route finding. Like most modern-day autonomous systems, the Live Map was based on dead reckoning; without additional inputs, dead reckoning is subject to cumulative error, and the Live Map did not become a success. However, the modern equivalents use map matching to improve the quality of the location finding and can provide the basis of many of the more sophisticated systems described in this book. Autonomous navigation systems are currently most widely installed in Japan, as described in Chapter 15.

1.2.2 Dynamic Driver Information

In the late 1970s, the Japanese CACS project [2] was innovative in implementing the first of the modern generation of route guidance developments, and in particular was the first prototype recognition of the importance of providing dynamic information. CACS

Figure 1.1 Jones Live Map.

used inductive loops to transmit guidance information to equipped vehicles and also used the important concept that equipped vehicles themselves could act as sensors for monitoring traffic conditions. These two concepts—the provision of dynamic information and its collection from equipped vehicles—are central to grasping the potential of the area of ATT that is perhaps closest to the market.

During the early 1980s, the concept of dynamic route guidance was developed further in Germany and in Britain. Siemens implemented a prototype Autoscout system in Munich using infrared beacons, which later became ALI-SCOUT and then EURO-SCOUT (see Chapter 4). The British Transport and Road Research Laboratory (TRRL) (which is now the Transport Research Laboratory (TRL)), implemented a prototype system (Figure 1.2) using inductive loops, which was given the name *Autoguide* [3]. Experience with these prototypes led to the implementation in the mid-1980s of two demonstration systems using the infrared technology—in Berlin (*Leit-und Informationssystem Berlin* (LISB)) [4] and in London. Although the London demonstration scheme was on a small scale, it was successfully demonstrated to over 1,000 people. The experience served to guide much of the further work, although a full-scale implementation in London has yet to happen.

The British Government also promoted the legislative and administrative framework in which systems such as Autoguide could be implemented by the private sector. In 1989 the Driver Information Systems Act was passed, requiring the secretary of state for transport to issue a license for any dynamic traffic information system to be provided to vehicles. The first license under the new act was issued not to an Autoguide system, as originally expected, but to the first commercially available in-car dynamic traffic information service in the world, a system called *TrafficMaster* [5]. TrafficMaster has a network of speed sensors mounted on highway bridges, which generate messages, via a control center, when there is congestion. The in-vehicle display (see Figure 1.3) shows the current status of the motorway network covered by the system. Initially, the system was installed on and around the M25 London orbital motorway, but is now being extended to the whole U.K. motorway network.

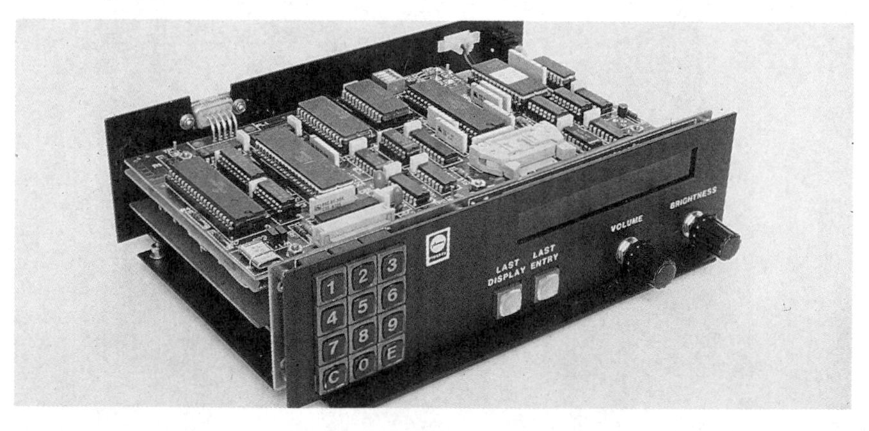

Figure 1.2 Prototype Autoguide system.

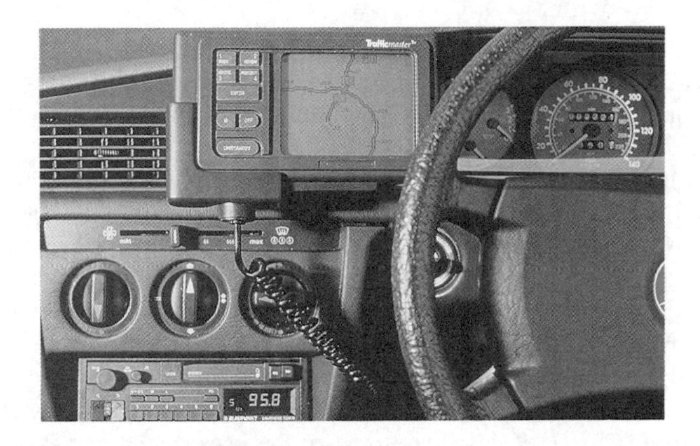

Figure 1.3 TrafficMaster in-vehicle display.

Another key development already with us is the implementation of the Radio Data System (RDS). Until recently, the only dynamic traffic information a driver was likely to receive was from the broadcast of conventional traffic messages. Systems such as the British Automobile Association's (AA) Roadwatch [6] have been built up to provide a central source of traffic information for broadcasters. In Germany, ARI and ARIAM [7] and, in the U.S., Highway Advisory Radio (HAR) are systems that can interrupt the driver's current listening when a traffic message is broadcast on another frequency. RDS provides a standard European system of digital data in the sideband of FM transmissions, which is already used for similar purposes in several European countries. RDS is being extended, however, to use a much more sophisticated capability—the traffic message channel (TMC). TMC will provide digital data describing the location and consequences of road network disturbances, which can be dealt with as the driver wishes. In the CARMINAT project [8], RDS is used to provide dynamic data directly to an on-board navigation system.

When cellular radio became widely available during the latter part of the 1980s, a new method of targeting relevant data to vehicles was opened up, which—unlike RDS—could also provide the two-way communication link necessary to provide the traffic data potential of a dynamic system. Chapter 6 describes the SOCRATES developments, which have been working to realize this potential.

In-vehicle information is a key ATT application, because when there is a communication link to the vehicle, it can be used as the basis of other functions. For example, the potential of using standardized communications is important for fleet management purposes; emergency call and emergency warning facilities can be added to some systems.

1.2.3 Automatic Debiting

A second key application area that has led to significant ATT developments is automatic debiting. Experiments in automatic toll collection began, particularly in the U.S., during the late 1970s [9] and in the last five years have led to quite widespread installation of "tag" systems in which regular users of a toll facility are billed for their usage, which is logged automatically as they drive through a toll lane (an example from Italy is shown in Figure 1.4).

Charging the use of road space—road pricing—is an idea that was first mooted in the 1920s when traffic congestion first began to be experienced. It was proposed in the U.K. in 1963 with the Smeed Report [10], and Singapore implemented an Area Licensing Scheme [11] in 1973, but it was not until the Hong Kong electronic road pricing (ERP) pilot project [12] from 1983 to 1985 that the potential was demonstrated of applying ATT techniques to demand management (Figure 1.5). The significant political factors associated with road pricing are the reason why no ERP system has yet been introduced, but growing awareness of the problems and consequences of congestion seem gradually to be bringing the prospect closer. Chapter 7 describes some of the background of automatic debiting and recent technological developments.

1.2.4 Automated Driving

In the 1960s, the first prototypes were developed of vehicles that would semi-automatically carry out some of the basic driving tasks—that is, speed and direction control. Figure 1.6 shows one such prototype developed at TRL (then the Road Research Laboratory); the rather obvious radar antenna was used to sense distances to other vehicles. This was one of the precursors of the systems that have been developed, for example, within the PROMETHEUS program described in Chapter 9.

Figure 1.4 Automatic toll collection lane in Italy (Telepass).

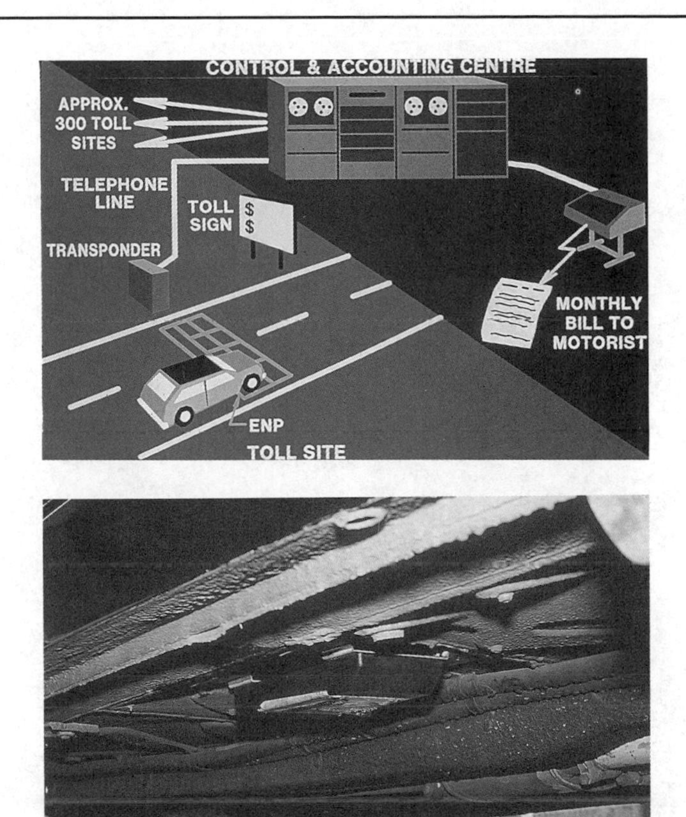

Figure 1.5 Hong Kong electronic road pricing pilot project: (a) system diagram; (b) electronic number plate.

In the same way that automatic debiting has more demanding requirements of the technology than driver information does, automated driving has even more stringent reliability needs. As is well known from recent legal history, particularly in the U.S., the onus on a car manufacturer to avoid any form of what the courts could consider negligence is paramount. Therefore, the need to include fail-safe features in such systems has meant that although the technology for demonstrating automated driving has been available for some time, realistic implementation is still some way off.

1.2.5 ATT Programs

It has been interesting to compare progress in ATT development in the three main geographic areas: Europe, the U.S., and Japan. Partly through a recognition of the potential of ATT, but also through a need to remain competitive in a worldwide environment, the European automotive industry established the PROMETHEUS program in 1986.

Figure 1.6 Prototype distance sensing equipment at the Road Research Laboratory (U.K.).

PROMETHEUS is an eight-year program which has made significant advances in ATT, particularly relating to on-board systems. The program is described in Chapter 9.

Also in the mid 1980s, the CEC was carrying out a feasibility study for the concept of a new research and development program specifically aimed at ATT. The result of this study was the DRIVE program, which formally commenced on January 1, 1988 and lasted for three years up to the end of 1991. Its sequel, often referred to as DRIVE II, was the ATT program, due to run to the end of 1994; DRIVE and DRIVE II are described in Chapter 5.

Together, PROMETHEUS and DRIVE undoubtedly gave Europe an initial edge over the U.S. and Japan in the advancement of ATT systems. These programs have been successful in promoting cooperative developments which must be the foundation on which widespread implementation of ATT systems will be based. However, there is rapid progress outside Europe. Chapter 10 describes how, in the U.S., the Mobility 2000 group was formed in 1989 and led directly to the formation of IVHS America the following year. IVHS has achieved a tremendous momentum and is spawning a number of projects whose scale will outstrip any currently being implemented in Europe (although at the time of publication the plans for DRIVE III are not yet known). One of the key features of the development of IVHS in the U.S. is the recognition of the need to establish both a universal system architecture and a strategic plan for implementation.

In Japan, although the early CACS work had a clear recognition of the importance of the total system in the development of ATT, it is true to say that the recent concentration has been on in-vehicle systems. There are currently estimated to be more than 400,000 in-car navigation systems in use in Japan, demonstrating the reality of a true ATT market, which does not yet exist elsewhere in the world. Although the evidence of the sales of autonomous units indicates a slightly different approach from that of either Europe or the U.S., there are a number of research and development programs since CACS that have investigated communication links in particular. The AMTICS and RACS programs ran until 1991—investigating Teleterminals (packet switched data via cellular radio) and microwave, respectively—when they were effectively merged into the VICS program, described in detail in Chapter 14.

A recent program introduced in Japan is the Advanced Traffic Information Service (ATIS), which is being promoted by the Metropolitan Police Department and anticipates using cellular radio for vehicles and telephone lines for personal computers in fleet management centers. At the time of publication, little information has been released about ATIS. However, it is indicative of the competitive approach in Japan that no clear system has yet been chosen. There are also developments in Japan in the field of automated driving; feasibility studies have been under way since 1990 looking into the concept of a super smart vehicle system (SSVS), which would include a number of advanced features.

1.3 ATT APPLICATIONS

Section 1.2 introduced some of the background of the range of applications becoming possible through ATT. In the U.S., these applications are categorized into five main groups, or functional areas, listed in the left-hand side of Table 1.1. This grouping of applications within the IVHS program is described in Chapter 10. Chapter 5 describes the alternative European view of categorizing ATT applications into seven areas of major operational interest. These are listed in the right-hand column of Table 1.1. There is a close match between the American and European groupings; there is an obvious one-to-one correspondence except in the area of traffic management, where in Europe the distinction is drawn between urban and interurban systems, and where the area of demand management is separately identified.

Each system of grouping ATT applications makes clear the distinction between the different user groups of the transport system. From the traveler's point of view, the benefits of a modern traffic control system may not be very apparent, but the highway authority faced with apparently ever-increasing demand for road space is concerned to maximize the capacity of the road network, and ATT can help do this.

This book concentrates on the implementation of systems in the vehicle designed to provide the driver with information. Although this is only one aspect of ATT—and the others are all included in the book—it is this one that is closest to having the greatest immediate impact in the way in which most of us travel.

1.4 ATT IMPLEMENTATION

As well as describing current developments, most of the chapters also address, at least briefly, the question of implementation. It is inevitable that in the early days of development there is a concentration on the technological aspects of new systems. However, there is an increasing awareness that the technology of ATT is probably the simplest part—there are many more complex issues that need to be addressed and solved before some of the systems can be implemented widely.

The example of Autoguide is a good one: in July 1989 it was announced that the British Department of Transport was to negotiate a license with GEC (the General Electric Company) for the provision of a dynamic route guidance system for London. The license would be in place by the end of 1989, a major pilot system would be operational by the

Table 1.1
ATT Applications in the U.S. and in Europe

U.S.	*Europe*
	Demand management
Advanced traffic management systems (ATMS)	Integrated urban traffic management
	Integrated inter-urban traffic management
Advanced traveler information systems (ATIS)	Traffic and travel information
Advanced vehicle control systems (AVCS)	Driver assistance and cooperative driving
Commercial vehicle operations (CVO)	Freight and fleet management
Advanced public transportation systems (APTS)	Public transport management

end of 1991, and commercial implementation would start in 1992. Although this ambitious timetable was not met, it does not mean that the plans have been abandoned or even curtailed; the London APPLE project, within DRIVE, and the independently funded TIGER project (see Chapter 8) are aimed at priming the full-scale commercial introduction of route guidance, and major investment plans are based on the anticipation of a large market for travel information systems.

There are a number of reasons for the apparent delay. Commercial considerations are of course a major factor, but not insignificant is the recognition of the need to integrate route guidance with other ATT applications; the interface between route guidance and traffic control is one of the major aspects of the APPLE project. A similar situation exists in Germany over the implementation of EURO-SCOUT. The Berlin LISB project was operational in 1988, and there were plans for widespread implementation of the beacon-based ALI-SCOUT, now EURO-SCOUT, system. As in the U.K., these plans are still very active, but the original timescales have had to be reviewed.

One of the reasons for the slower progression to full implementation is the continuing debate over the choice of technology for the communications infrastructure. While it is clear that the benefits of two-way communications between vehicles and control centers will be sufficient to justify significant investment, it is not yet apparent whether that infrastructure in Europe should be a new, dedicated, beacon-based system or a SOCRATES system using cellular radio. Another factor is the requirement for high-quality databases on which to base the navigation systems. The production of accurate digital maps, together with the collection of all the attributes necessary to provide unambiguous guidance to drivers, is a very substantial task.

These issues are actively being addressed, both within collaborative research projects and in individual commercial organizations. It is still confidently predicted that during the second half of the 1990s, the use of in-vehicle navigation computers linked to dynamic traffic information sources will become common, if not standard, features in new vehicles. The first fully commercial steps are already in evidence: the TrafficMaster system in the U.K., launched in 1990, is the first commercially available in-vehicle dynamic traffic information system anywhere in the world. In May 1993, TrafficMaster coverage was extended to the whole of the South of England and the Midlands, covering 70% of the national motorway flow. The first generation of Travelpilot, from Bosch, has been marketed in Germany. RDS is already operational and in use for traffic information broadcasts. In Japan, there are already nearly a half a million vehicles equipped with navigation systems.

A major feature of the European pilot projects is the recognition of the need to integrate different ATT applications. The provision of a digital communication link to a vehicle, which is likely to be financially justified on the basis of the provision of route guidance and driver information, opens up a number of other possibilities, most of which are currently under investigation.

It is now becoming widely acknowledged that ATT cannot offer solutions to over-congestion in urban networks solely through increasing network capacity, which is effectively the result of dynamic route guidance or advanced traffic control. Many transport authorities—at least within professional circles, but increasingly so outside—are recognizing the need to manage demand. One aspect of demand management is the provision of better information on public transport availability and on parking, particularly if the parking is connected to the public transport network (i.e., park-and-ride). Therefore, a number of pilot projects are actively investigating the possibility of providing information on alternative modes of travel to car drivers.

The fleet sector should benefit immediately from the introduction of ATT systems. Systems combining onboard vehicle location with two-way communication offer the fleet manager the immediate capability of automatic vehicle location in real time. In addition, the improved traffic information and potential dynamic route guidance features of these types of system should immediately produce increased efficiency of fleet operations. For these reasons, the early market for advanced in-vehicle systems is likely to be concentrated on the fleet sector.

The efficiency of operation of an urban network, particularly as it approaches saturation, is critically dependent on the techniques used for controlling the traffic signals. Urban traffic control systems such as SCOOT [13] can potentially benefit from the introduction of ATT systems by having access to more detailed data: for example, the APPLE project in London is investigating the use that can be made by SCOOT of data from a dynamic route guidance system. Similarly, and particularly in the early stages of implementation, travel and traffic information systems will potentially be able to capture real-time information from operational traffic control systems.

As pointed out in the introduction, there have apparently been some delays in the progression from early demonstration systems, such as the London Autoguide demonstration scheme, to full commercial systems. It might seem that as the need for increasing investment has increased, so the level of caution in committing resources has grown. However, the issue is more complex than that. The delay in implementation, although disappointing in some respects, has allowed a wider debate to be held about the technical, social, and political aspects of these systems. The growing public awareness and concern over environmental issues has been reflected in the recognition that implementation of systems that could be perceived as having rather narrow appeal, offering the optimum route to single vehicles without regard for community considerations, should be modified to gain wider community acceptance.

The possibility of road use charging is a relevant factor for any potential investor in ATT systems; but this possibility, with the wider recognition of the need for travel demand management in its widest sense, has also encouraged a strategy that will allow the development of dynamic route guidance systems into more broadly based information systems. These systems will offer a wider range of information, aimed not only at road network efficiency, but at providing genuinely useful, up-to-the-minute information for the traveler who, with access to these new sources of information, is more likely to see the private car as only one possible choice of transport mode.

It is encouraging that those involved in all aspects of these developments, concerned with commercial as well as technical issues, have used the intervening time well. The new generation of ATT systems is designed to lead quickly to full commercial implementation. In Europe, plans are being developed to a large extent within the DRIVE and PROMETHEUS programs. In the U.S., the IVHS Strategic Plan [14] has addressed implementation issues right from the start. In Japan, the approach of encouraging the acceptance of in-vehicle systems is complementary to the investigation of infrastructure requirements. More importantly perhaps, a considerable amount of market research has been carried out. While it is not possible to report the detailed findings of studies that are commercially protected, it is clearly true that the major companies involved in ATT are already investing significant amounts and planning to spend even more before realizing returns on their investments in order to be ready to exploit the burgeoning market once it begins to flourish. A recent Delphi study [15] investigated the views of experts on the likely dates of implementation of various ATT systems. See Table 1.2. It shows the dates at which the median response from respondents expected 5% and 50% market penetration. For example, the median view was that, by the end of the decade, 5% of vehicles will be equipped with dynamic route guidance, and that it will take until 2020 for 50% penetration. Understandably, there is a higher level of consensus on the likely timing of implementation of systems already close to the market: there is considerable disagreement over the prospects, for example, of true automated driving. Some systems might require the allocation of dedicated lanes or carriageways, which would certainly require active participation of governments.

In conclusion, the pilot projects currently under development will help significantly to establish the move towards a genuinely integrated transport environment, with travel and traffic information services playing an increasingly important part in the technology for improved transport efficiency. Implementation dates for some of the longer term ATT applications are not yet clear, but increasing concentration on the overall architecture of ATT systems is likely eventually to provide the framework in which their implementation could become viable.

Table 1.2
Median Responses for Year that Various ATT Systems Expected to Achieve 5% and 50% Penetration

System	*5%*	*50%*
Real-time traffic information	1996	2007
Static information (e.g., yellow pages)	2000	2011
Emergency call	1998	2010
Dynamic route guidance	2000	2020
Collision warning	2002	2013
Intelligent cruise control	2004	2015
Automatic backup braking	2008	2020
Autonomous lane keeping	2012	2032

Source: [15].

1.5 STRUCTURE OF THE BOOK

This book attempts to introduce the reader to all aspects of ATT and selectively goes into some detail on individual systems. It is clearly not possible to describe every ATT project in depth, but the approach taken has been to concentrate on a number of key developments. While the scope is worldwide, European developments have been given more weight. Even though the use of autonomous navigation systems is more developed in Japan and despite the recent takeoff of the IVHS program, as explained earlier in this chapter there have been more projects actually implementing prototype systems preceding commercial implementation in Europe than elsewhere.

Similarly, the reader will find some reference to most of the current developments under way within ATT, but there is a strong concentration in the book on systems that are closest to widespread implementation—those that will affect the way in which people travel over the next decade. Thus, the more specialized market sectors, such as fleet management, are described as part of overall ATT development, but not in great detail. Similarly, more advanced systems, such as those involving some form of automation of the driving task, are described, but not in the same depth as systems such as navigation and driver information.

Chapter 2 discusses the concept of ATT system architecture. This is fitting as the next chapter, because it has relevance to all the others. As pointed out earlier, there are different approaches in the three areas towards this subject: in Europe, several fundamental architectures are being worked on independently, although there are moves to bring them closer together; in the U.S., there is a positive attempt from the start to unify the overall development of IVHS within an agreed architecture; and in Japan, there is encouragement of competitive development of alternative concepts until it is clearer which will be the most successful.

Chapter 3 deals with traffic control. This is an area of ATT in which there is great potential, because the efficient use of scarce network resources is economically vital. There are a number of approaches to both urban and interurban traffic control. However, there is less need for a common approach than there is for vehicle-borne systems.

Chapters 4 to 9 deal specifically with European developments. Chapter 4 describes the EURO-SCOUT approach to dynamic route guidance and to overall traffic management. It is placed here in the book because it is the earliest significant European development in ATT, predating the DRIVE and PROMETHEUS programs. Chapter 5 presents the DRIVE and ATT programs and goes further by discussing some of the key issues for ATT implementation. Chapter 6 describes the SOCRATES concept and projects. SOCRATES can be seen as an alternative approach to EURO-SCOUT, but there are moves to try to bring together the two approaches.

Chapter 7 is a review of automatic debiting applications and of one of the major projects for developing the technology to perform both automatic toll collection and road pricing. Although there are developments in automatic debiting technology worldwide, it is currently in Europe where the most activity is taking place to address all the issues, particularly including road pricing.

A feature of the second DRIVE program, compared with the first, is its concentration on proving the viability of DRIVE I results through pilot project implementations. Chapter 8 describes the major pilot projects within the current DRIVE program in Europe. Chapter 9 deals with the PROMETHEUS program and contains separate sections dealing with an overview of the whole program, vehicle-based systems, cooperative driving, and dual-mode route guidance. This chapter includes descriptions of work on the more advanced systems such as those leading to methods of automating more of the driving tasks.

Chapters 10 to 12 describe developments in the U.S. Chapter 10 sets the scene by giving an overview of the IVHS program and describing the role of IVHS America. Chapters 11 and 12 deal with specific projects within the IVHS program. ADVANCE, described in Chapter 11, is currently the largest planned field trial, involving several thousand vehicles. Chapter 12 describes several activities and projects within the Michigan IVHS program. These two chapters clearly do not describe in detail all the projects currently taking place or planned within the IVHS program, but were selected in order to give the reader an idea of the scope of IVHS.

Chapters 13 to 15 describe the development of ATT in Japan. Chapter 13 provides an overview of recent developments and of some of the issues being addressed for the future. Chapter 14 describes the VICS program and RACS, which was one of its precursors. VICS has now become a focus for the implementation of vehicle communication requirements, although at the time of publication the recently announced ATIS project is clearly offering an alternative approach. Finally, Chapter 15 describes the development of on-board vehicle systems in Japan, currently one of the clear success stories of ATT. It describes the principles of vehicle navigation systems and some of the background of the current opening of the market to ATT in Japan.

REFERENCES

[1] Lunn, S. E., ''Route Choice by Drivers,'' SR 374, Transport and Road Research Laboratory, Crowthorne, England, 1978.

[2] Totani, S., ''Development and Current Status of CACS (Comprehensive Automobile Traffic Control System),'' *Proc. Int. Conf. on Transportation Electronics,* Dearborn, MI, 1980.

[3] Jeffery, D. J., K. Russam, and D. I. Robertson, ''Electronic Route Guidance by Autoguide: The Research Background,'' *Traffic Engineering and Control,* London, England, Oct. 1987.

[4] von Tomkewitsch, R., ''The LISB Field Trial, Forerunner of Autoguide,'' Paper Reference C391/060, Institute of Mechanical Engineers, London, England, 1989. von Tomkewitsch, R., ''LISB: Large-Scale Test Navigation and Information System Berlin,'' *Proc. ITTT Seminar P302,* PTRC, Bath, England, 1987.

[5] Abbott, J., ''Advanced Transport Systems: In-Vehicle Technology to Help Reduce Congestion: Trafficmaster,'' *Traffic Congestion Conf.,* London, England, 1992.

[6] Hoffman, S., ''AA Roadwatch: A Road Traffic Database for U.K. and Europe,'' *VNIS Conf.,* Oslo, Norway, 1992.

[7] Duckeck, R., and R. Vollmer, ''TMC (Traffic Message Channel)—Das Verkehrsfunksystem von Morgen,'' 8th ITG-Fachtagung Horrundfunk, Mainz, 1988.

[8] Challe, P., ''CARMINAT,'' *Proc. Workshop on Navigation and Planning,* Nasslingen, Sweden, 1990.

[9] Foote, R., ''Automatic Toll Systems,'' *Paying the Toll Conf.,* University of Irvine, CA, 1988.

[10] Ministry of Transport, ''The Smeed Committee Report; Road Pricing: The Economic and Technical Possibility,'' HMSO, London, England, 1964.

[11] Yee, J., ''The Area Licensing Scheme in Singapore,'' *Proc. Transpo-Asia 80 Asian Seminar,* Singapore, 1980.

[12] Catling, I., and B. Harbord, ''Electronic Road Pricing in Hong Kong—The Technology,'' *Traffic Engineering and Control,* London, England, Dec. 1985.

[13] Hunt, P. B., D. I. Robertson, R. D. Bretherton, and I. Winton, ''SCOOT: A Traffic Responsive Method of Coordinating Signals,'' Report LR 1014, Transport and Road Research Laboratory, Crowthorne, England, 1981.

[14] IVHS America, ''Strategic Plan for Intelligent Vehicle-Highway Systems in the United States,'' Report No. IVHS-AMER-92-3, 1992.

[15] Underwood, S. E., ''Delphi Forecast and Analysis of Intelligent Vehicle-Highway Systems Through 1991,'' University of Michigan, Ann Arbor, Michigan, IVHS Technical Report No. 92-17, 1992.

Chapter 2
System Architecture and Communications

Nigel Wall

2.1 INTRODUCTION

This chapter initially introduces the concept of system architecture and *open systems interconnection* (OSI) for communications. It then focuses on the relevance of the architecture projections and open communications for RTI. The communication requirements of various applications are reviewed, together with the present status and capabilities of communication systems suitable for use by RTI applications and some initiatives to standardize communication system interfaces.

The more advanced RTI systems described in this book will take advantage of a number of significant developments in technology, including:

- The use of high-power in-vehicle computer systems and road databases to produce navigation systems;
- The development of very powerful computers running road traffic congestion modeling and prediction software;
- The implementation of mobile data communications networks capable of linking these computer systems.

The equipment in the vehicle will not be a dumb terminal that simply displays messages received from a distant computer, but part of a distributed processing system. Typically, there will be one or more computers within the vehicle that are linked back to computers within the infrastructure via mobile data communications channels. In addition to the communications to the vehicle, there will be an enormous amount of information exchanged between infrastructure-based computers, which may be owned by different organizations. These organizations must agree on the basis for exchanging data. There are many issues in designing and implementing such systems, including:

1. What service is to be offered? Will the user perceive a benefit that exceeds the cost of the system?
2. How much information needs to be communicated for the system or service to operate correctly?
3. What processing should be performed in the vehicle and in the infrastructure?
4. How accurate and immediate do the data need to be?
5. Which communication systems, computer hardware, and software should be used?

These are some of the questions addressed in current development work within Europe, the U.S., and Japan. There is a clear requirement to employ some method of structuring the development of these systems; the use of a formal approach to system architecture will help. However, the concept of system architecture is subject to varying interpretations, and the benefits that can be gained from a good system architecture are often not fully appreciated.

2.2 SYSTEM ARCHITECTURE

2.2.1 Role of the Architect

The term *architecture* has been borrowed from the construction industry and applied to the field of distributed processing. The *research into advance communications for Europe* (RACE) *open services architecture* (ROSA) project defines architecture as "a set of concepts, rules and recipes (exemplified in reference object types), that can be used to specify and construct Integrated Broadband Communications (IBC) services" [1]. To explain this further, it is useful to review the role of a system architect in terms that may be equally applicable to a building's architect.

The system architect will have the same general responsibilities as a building architect. Even though a building and computer system have little in common, both need to be designed using a similar structured approach; both will "fall over" if badly designed or will cost too much if "overengineered."

In general terms, the architect has the following responsibilities:

1. Capturing the customer's requirements;
2. Designing a system that works well with other systems;
3. Ensuring that the costs are minimized and clearly understood, and perhaps redesigning part or all of the system if the costs are too high;
4. Ensuring high functionality and usability, together with an attractive *man-machine interface* (MMI);
5. Including features that will make the system more future-proof, allowing changes of use and further additions;
6. Using standard elements that will enable reuse of existing designs and facilitate competitive purchase;

7. Ensuring system integrity and performance;
8. Producing designs, plans, and specifications for each of the types of work to be undertaken, using specialist terminology (language or jargon) to generate efficient, unambiguous specifications;
9. Safety-critical considerations.

The architect will describe a building or system using a variety of techniques, languages, and projections. Although these projections may not appear to have much in common, they will all relate to the same system. Each projection focuses attention on a particular aspect of the work. These different projections interrelate, and changes to one projection may require major changes in other aspects of the design.

2.2.2 Nonarchitectural Approach

The alternative approach can be described as a tactical approach, whereby a builder or designer considers a narrower set of factors. The builder may make use of components that are already to hand, using obsolete or ''special offer'' components. While this may be a good way to save money and time in designing a prototype or one-off system, the design would not be optimal for volume production. One major problem with tactical solutions arises when the system must be extended or connected to other systems. An architectural solution will include features to cater to potential future developments, whereas a tactical solution will concentrate only on the short-term issues. Tactical designs can often be much simpler and easier to develop and put into service: their initial cost is potentially lower than for the architectural approach, but they tend to be unsuitable for onward development and will ultimately be displaced by architectural systems having the potential to accommodate enhanced capabilities.

2.2.3 Benefits of an Open RTI Architecture

While the end users of RTI systems will be pleased to see competition between operators as a means of reducing costs, there is a real danger that the customers may be confused by the development of many incompatible systems and may defer investment until a clear market leader has emerged. As with the video recorder market, people do not wish to buy a system that, while technically excellent, may be overtaken by another (incompatible) system, leaving their systems unsupported as a rival system becomes dominant. The video recorder market achieved a much higher growth rate once the dominance of VHS had been established.

It is likely that the purchaser of an RTI system will want:

1. A system that protects his original investment by enabling future service enhancements to be added;

2. Operation within any part of the world in which the vehicle is likely to travel;
3. The opportunity to access additional RTI services that become available from third parties;
4. The ability to switch to a service provider who offers a better performance or lower cost without the user having to change the installed hardware.

Ideally, RTI implementers should not develop incompatible systems, but should cooperate to develop common standards. Even with common standards, there will be enormous scope to offer quite different services. However, because of the immediate need for such systems, and a desire of each manufacturer to enter the market ahead of their competition, there is pressure to implement proprietary systems. Indeed, without some experience of practical implementations, it is unlikely that enduring standards could be produced. One of the key benefits of the CEC-directed DRIVE programs and other precompetitive activities is the stimulation of cooperation between companies with no previous history of cooperation. The results of pilot projects will need to be shared, with the objective of producing common standards.

In summary, the adoption of open architectures introduces both opportunities and threats. Among the advantages are:

- Implementations are future-proof.
- New services can be added to existing systems.
- More competition encourages lower prices.
- Customers are able to use their in-vehicle equipment with a variety of service providers.
- Customers are more likely to purchase a system with the above advantages.

Among the disadvantages are:

- Manufacturers and service providers fear the effects of competition.
- Open interfaces are often more complicated than proprietary solutions.
- The delay in the definition and agreement of the open interface delays the launch of these new services.

2.2.4 Which Parts of an RTI System Should Be Open?

The term *open* implies the use of interfaces based on specifications that have been agreed on, standardized, published, and widely accepted as the primary standard to be adopted. One of the most frequently mentioned open standards is the communications interface based on OSI. This subject will be discussed in more detail later in the chapter. However, it is not sufficient just to have an open communication system. Once communications to the distant computer has been established and data transferred, it must be understood and processed. Interfaces that need to be open include:

- Data communications;
- Databases;

- Data dictionaries;
- Operating systems;
- Safety-related aspects of MMIs.

The standardization of the road database format is essential if systems are to be used across country or state borders, where different cartographers may have produced the digital map information. There needs to be a way to obtain the appropriate information, which must be presented with an unambiguous meaning as defined by a common data dictionary. Progress is currently being made in Europe within the *Comité Européen de Normalisation* (CEN) *Technical Committee* (TC) 278 and within the *International Standards Organization* (ISO) TC 204.

2.2.5 ISO ODP System Architecture Projections

The ISO is establishing standards for *open distributed processing* (ODP) and has adopted the following approach to describing architectures. A complex system may best be described by identifying subcomponents or modules and their interfaces. There are many ways to decompose a system and many different characteristics of the interfaces between the modules that need to be understood. Several expert teams have been set up to identify the most appropriate way to handle the degree of complexity encountered. Work on European projects such as ROSA [1] and the *integrated systems architecture* (ISA) project has led to the development of the *advanced network systems architecture* (ANSA) [2], which has helped progress understanding. Similar work on ISO ODP [3] has also partitioned the architecture into five different ''projections'' or ''viewpoints'': enterprise, information, computation, engineering, and technology (Figure 2.1). The significance of each of the five architectural projections to RTI systems is explained below.

Enterprise: This projection includes the business aspects, the human interaction, and environmental elements. A system with the complexity of RTI will be provided by consortia of different specialist companies. Operation across state and national borders will typically involve many different companies, the interrelationships of which need to be understood, together with different legislation and regulation environments.

Information: It is very important to understand the nature of the information that must be passed to the end user and between the different subsystems. This leads to the production of functional requirements for the communication systems to carry application data. For instance, information about traffic problems in a small area should only be passed to travelers who are likely to benefit from that information; some types of information need to be updated more frequently than others.

The key information transfers that must be identified are those at the periphery of each individual system. These include the information presented to the end user and that exchanged with other operators and third-party information providers. This information is defined so as to meet the requirements identified within the enterprise projection.

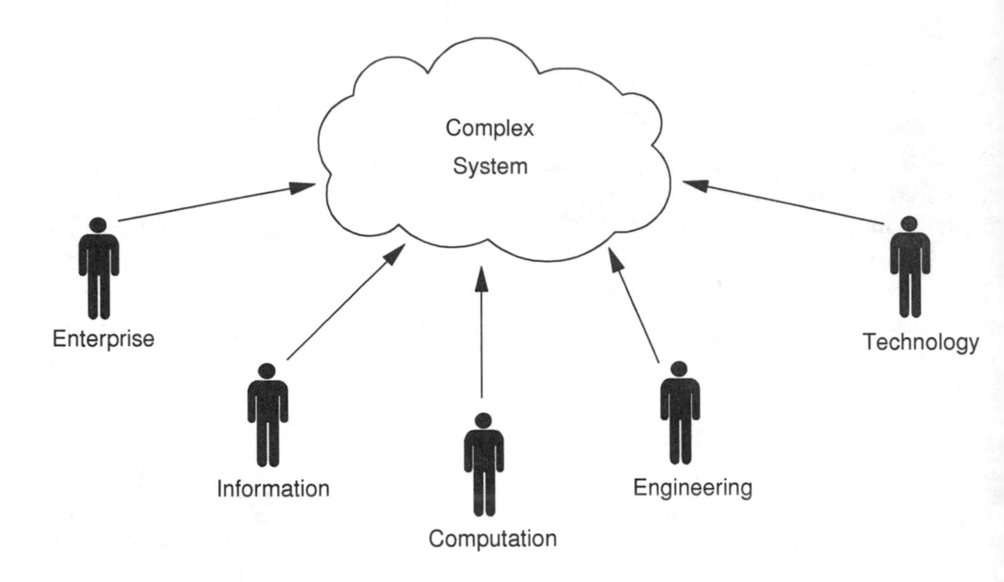

Figure 2.1 ISO ODP 5 architecture projections.

Additionally, the nature of information flows within the system needs to be considered. An important example is the information passed across a mobile data interface. Capacity is limited here and data transfer is relatively expensive. The nature and extent of these internal information transfers is closely linked with the computation and engineering projections.

Computation: This is the top-level software design, breaking down the software into manageable modules. It is an essential tool for the software designer. A very important element is to design the partitioning of computing power and databases within the system. How much should be in the vehicle and how much in the infrastructure? The answer clearly has an impact on the nature of information that must be passed to and from the vehicle (information model), and will have an impact on the overall system costs (enterprise projection).

Engineering: The split of the processing load carried out in the vehicle and in the infrastructure is affected by the processing power available, the data stored at each point, and the ability to transfer the required data between the vehicle and infrastructure processors in a timely way. This projection concentrates on system performance, interworking, protocols, and operating systems. The specification and performance of open interfaces are highly relevant, whereas the comparative performance of different implementations is a technology issue.

Technology: This describes the implementation of the other projections, taking account of particular geographical factors, availability of communications bearers, choice of specific host systems, and so on. Clearly, the cost of the particular implementations will have an impact on the enterprise model, and the performance of the technology used will need to be considered in the engineering projection. Whereas the engineering projection considers the specification of systems and protocols and their theoretical performance, the technology projection relates to practical, realizable implementations of the systems and protocols specified.

These five projections will each describe the same system using specialist language. The different projections will be used by different groups of experts. As the individual projections develop, there will need to be an overall ''system architect'' role to ensure that the individual projections remain in alignment. It is this level of coordination that gives the architectural approach its big advantage: making an initial implementation future-proof so as to accommodate new services that become available, and to allow existing services to continue to be operated with new technologies.

2.2.6 Alternative Architectural Representations

It must be stated that the five-projection approach to architecture has not been universally adopted, and there are many variations on the theme, many produced as extensions of *computer-aided software engineering* (CASE) tools, to extend these to introduce formal methods to the wider subject of computer-aided system engineering. One alternative approach is to adopt a four-viewpoint architectural description. This has enterprise, functional, information systems, and information technology, which can be seen to follow the general approach defined in ISO ODP. This leads to a sequential analysis:

- Enterprise: first identify the business need, then generate:
- Functional architecture: a functional specification that will define the data architecture (including data dictionary), leading to:
- Technical architecture: the system design, from which develops:
- Information technology: the physical implementation of the required system.

Within the DRIVE program [4], a version of *structured analysis and design technique* (SADT) [5,6] has been widely adopted. This is also a nested analysis approach supported by CASE tools. SADT uses a formal diagrammatic notation system to represent the linkages of modules to form complex structures (Figure 2.2). A complex system is represented by a series of decompositions, typically starting with a top-level view of all major elements in that system, then identifying a particular subsystem, then each element within that, and finally an analysis of each specific transaction. Components include databases, processes (or activities), interfaces, sources, and sinks. The activity module produces output (always on the right-hand side) by applying mechanisms (from the bottom) and controls (from the top) to inputs (from the left). The input may be changed or simply transferred by this process, but the controls and mechanisms are not affected by the process. In practice, controls and inputs are likely to be derived from the outputs of other

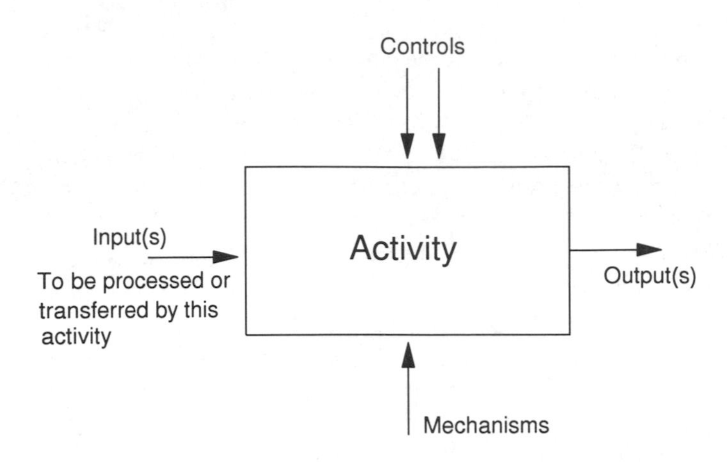

Figure 2.2 SADT diagrammatic notation.

activity modules. The spatial separation of the various controls, inputs, and outputs allows the functionality to be understood relatively quickly. This approach effectively starts with the informational projection (sources and sinks) and uses the decomposition of this to create the computational (processes), engineering (interfaces), and technological analyses. Ultimately it may not matter which techniques are used, as long as these techniques ensure that all the factors needed to design these complex systems have been understood and taken into account. The main objective is that these analyses produce common data dictionary definitions, database structures, and communication interfaces. Practical application of system architecture to RTI in considered in Section 2.4.

2.3 COMMUNICATION SYSTEMS

Communication systems are primarily of interest to the engineering and technology projections of the architecture. Additionally, the cost of communications and transmission delays have an impact on the enterprise projection, and the performance and capacity of the system have an impact on the split between the in-vehicle and infrastructure-based processing. The design of the communication system needs to consider the output from the Information model, which determines the characteristics and quantity of information that must be transferred via the communication system. The communications industry was one of the first to recognize the need for open architectures and has invested heavily in the concept of OSI.

2.3.1 OSI Reference Model

The term OSI implies the use of communication protocols that comply with the OSI reference model, shown in Figure 2.3. The ISO and *Consultative Committee in Interna-*

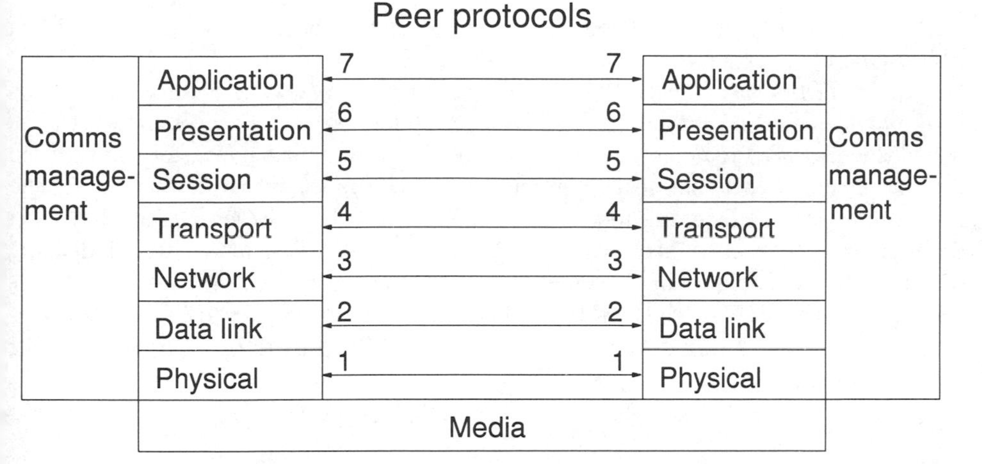

Figure 2.3 ISO OSI seven-layer model.

tional Telegraphy and Telephony (CCITT) have also defined a significant number of specific protocols that fit within the layers of the OSI model. The range of protocols defined to date are not all encompassing, and there is scope to define new protocols that fit within the OSI framework. It is, however, important to note that there are also protocols (e.g., the Internet suite—TCP/IP) that, while being "open," do not comply with the OSI framework and do not conform to OSI. The standards documents (X.200 series issued by the CCITT, plus many ISO documents) that describe the OSI reference model are lengthy and very complicated: many books (e.g., [7]) have been written about OSI, and the following text is intended only as an introduction to enable the relevance of OSI to RTI to be understood.

The OSI reference model is often described as the *OSI seven-layer model*. In practice, many of the layers are divided into sublayers. Additionally, there are elements of a communication system that perform important functions, such as communication management, which do actually process the data being transferred. The model was developed to allow the interconnectability between different computer hardware platforms using different software packages over a variety of networks. However, for dedicated communications, where an application always uses a particular communication network, the use of OSI may be thought unnecessary and found to increase costs and processing delays. Use of the OSI principles for communications to and from vehicles is essential if we are to achieve the vision of integrating many applications and allowing vehicles to operate outside their own countries using different communication systems.

The lower four layers provide a data transfer capability of the appropriate quality and are considered by the engineering and technology architectures. The upper three layers relate to the computation projection and ensure that data transfers are controlled and that data can be unambiguously coded and interpreted.

The functionality of each layer is defined in terms of services and protocols. Each layer provides a set of services to the next layer up and receives services from the layer below (Figure 2.4). Protocols determine the negotiation and dialogue performed between the peer layers at each end of the communication system (or intermediate node for the lowest three layers). Defining functionality in this way identifies what each layer must do in order to connect to other layers locally and to distant systems, without indicating how the system should be implemented. Note that there is not just one set of protocols and services defined for each layer. In practice, there will be several possible implementations of each layer. The exact choice of protocol profile needs to be clearly defined for two systems to interwork.

Application Layer—Layer 7

Layer 7 is the top layer, which has the primary task of using protocols to negotiate between the vehicle's processing equipment and the distant processor that is providing the RTI service, to ensure that the processor is capable of providing the RTI services the vehicle wants. Each application service is designed to support specific types of application processes. To ensure that the correct application has been accessed, each application process should have a unique address (note that this is completely independent of the network address described below).

Presentation Layer—Layer 6

The formal language *Abstract Syntax Notation.1* (ASN.1) has been developed to define the format of the data being passed so that there is no ambiguity about its meaning. In

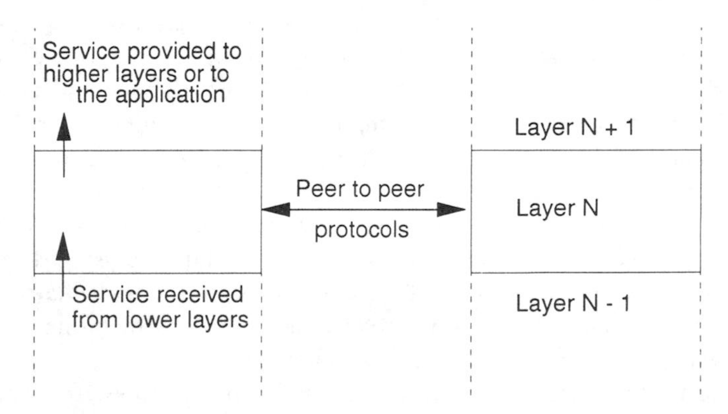

Figure 2.4 OSI services and protocols.

general, this layer is unlikely to be used for RTI applications, since the format and meaning of the data will be standardized for a particular application.

Session Layer—Layer 5

This layer regulates the flow of data to ensure that the transfer occurs in an orderly way. Typically, it might ensure that a request for action has been responded to before allowing further requests. It interprets the application's needs to call for a communication link when this is needed and to hold it open or clear the link down as appropriate. It also has a synchronization capability that allows a partial reset over the communication system, so that both the vehicle's and host processors may regain synchronization if the two processors lose synchronization momentarily.

Transport Layer—Layer 4

The transport layer ensures that the quality of service required by the application is achieved. From a "knowledge" of the performance of the underlying network, it can determine whether any further error protection is needed and perform this in addition to any protection provided in the data link and physical layers in order to provide a reliable connection. The transport layer can also assemble and disassemble data into packets of suitable size to be passed over the communications channel. The transport layer can handle connection-oriented or connectionless data transfer and can convert from the underlying network service to either mode of transfer. It provides *transport service access points* (TSAP), which are interfaces that enable selection of the appropriate application, where several applications are supported at a particular network address.

Network Layer—Layer 3

The network layer takes the network address information and translates this into a real route through the network. The network layer handles routing between connected subnetworks. It is the highest layer that should be implemented at a subnetwork intermediate node. It is at this layer that different subnetworks can be adapted to provide a normalized network service and global addressing schemes.

Data Link Layer—Layer 2

This layer provides a subnetwork physical address. It can also provide methods of protecting data and ensuring that lost or corrupted data are retransmitted. Adaptations of *high-level data link control* (HDLC) are often used: these employ *automatic retransmission request* (ARQ) (when errors are detected) to recover from errors. In mobile systems, this layer also implements the radio resource management, routing calls to terminals via the most appropriate base stations and radio channels.

Physical Layer—Layer 1

This layer provides the modulation/demodulation process: it may include *forward error correction* (FEC) as part of modulation or coding schemes. It includes the physical presentation (e.g., 25-way D-connector for V24) and various modem standards, together with voltages, power, modulation method, and channel bandwidth.

Media

This vital element is the actual physical connection between the vehicle and processor. This could be copper wire, optical fiber, or free space for radio and infrared systems. The performance of this medium, together with factors such as variation in attenuation, delay, phase change, multipath distortion, intermodulation distortion, and various kinds of interference is crucial to the success of the communication system. The primary task of layers 1 and 2 is to tame this intrinsically unreliable medium. The medium itself is not considered to be one of the OSI layers.

Communications Management

No data flow to or through the communications management subsystem; however, this is required to ensure that the communication system's condition is known and that corrective action is taken to avoid any problems, hopefully without the knowledge or intervention of the user in the vehicle or host system. Network and systems management are needed for all large communication systems in order to be able to identify and rectify problems quickly, possibly by reconfiguring the network in a controlled way and advising the maintenance technician of the nature and location of a fault. The requirements for network and systems management must be considered at the outset.

2.3.2 Mobile Data Transfer Modes

There are several mobile data networks available, but all use one or more of three data transfer modes: circuit-switched, connection mode packet, and connectionless packet. See Table 2.1.

Circuit-Switched Data

A circuit-switched data connection is operated in three phases: call establishment, data transfer, and call release, in the same way as conventional voice and modem calls. The

Table 2.1
Comparison of Data Transfer Modes

Transfer Type	*Relative Call Setup Delay*	*Relative Address Overhead*	*Mobility Management*	*Optimal Operation*	*Point to Multipoint*
Circuit-switched	Long	Part of call setup	Required	File transfer, voice, video	No
Connection mode	Short	Small	Required	Bursty transfer	No
Connectionless	None	Significant	Not required	Short messages	Yes

channel remains open for as long as the user requires and is normally allocated for that user's exclusive use until it is released. Consequently, system capacity is wasted if there are significant periods when no transfer takes place while the channel is open. Circuit-switched data introduces a number of problems in a mobile environment:

- There is a need to provide a comprehensive mobility management function with handover of the circuit as a mobile moves from the coverage range of one base station to another, without loss of data.
- The radio medium is prone to much larger error rates than are found on the fixed network. Error protection is applied using two techniques: FEC and ARQ offer quite different characteristics. Some mobile systems use both techniques to achieve the optimal solution.

Voice communications are provided via a circuit-switched connection using an FEC-protected digital channel.

Packet Data Modes

The data protection systems described above require the data to be packetized for processing purposes; however, the packets are concatenated and passed over a circuit. Having packetized the data, it is also possible to transmit each packet separately. In this way, packets from different users may be interspersed in a communications channel so that the channel is only assigned to each user when data are to be transferred. For bursty data flows, this can greatly increase the efficiency of channel utilization. Two packet transfer modes exist: connection mode and connectionless mode. Each mode suits different kinds of applications. For example, file transfer will require a connection mode system, while short messages such as location information contained within a single data packet would best suit a connectionless packet mode.

Connection Mode Packet Data. Connection mode transfer involves the same three call phases as used for circuit-switched connections. The call establishment phase allocates a route through the network for all the following data packets with a particular reference number. Each packet sent is routed individually over the same route, using lookup tables stored in the network. These tables are cleared when the call is released. The user sees a "virtual circuit," whereas in reality the channel may be shared by several users. For mobile communications, handover from one cell to another requires a mobility management function to update the call routing tables, even if no data is currently being sent.

Connectionless Packet Data. Connectionless packet transfer requires that each packet sent includes the full network destination and source addresses. Each packet (or datagram) is routed independently. Because packets follow different routes, they may arrive out of sequence: buffers and packet reassembly protocols are needed. Normally, the recipient returns an acknowledge datagram to confirm delivery and so achieve "reliable transfer." The dynamic routing of datagrams may be useful for the mobile environment because the packet can be sent to the most suitable base station as the need arises, without the overhead of maintaining a continuous connection using carefully managed handover between cells. Connectionless operation also lends itself to point-to-multipoint distribution of information (multicast), whereby a single message may be picked up by all mobiles in range. However, the return of many individual acknowledgments would be difficult to manage and they would normally be suppressed; hence, truly reliable multicast transfer would not be possible. With a unidirectional system, it is normal to include FEC with interleaving (to spread bursts of errors over several blocks of data and reduce the number of errors in each block). FEC allows a small number of errors in each block of data to be corrected. Messages could be repeated to further increase reliability.

2.4 APPLICATION OF THE ISO ODP MODEL TO RTI SYSTEMS

2.4.1 RTI Enterprise

Some key questions relating to the Enterprise model are:

- What new services will travelers want to buy?
- What will be the financial or other benefits to them?
- What will be the perceived value of these services?
- How much will users be prepared to pay for these services?
- What is the best (functionality and cost) service that can be offered?
- What performance will the user expect to receive and what will be the redress should this expectation not be achieved?
- What performance will actually be delivered both in the short term and as the number of users grows to a significant proportion of all vehicles?
- What commercial arrangements for partnerships will be needed?
- What role will regional and national governments take?
- What regulatory regime will apply?

Figure 2.5 shows some aspects that should be considered within the Enterprise projection. The end user needs to perceive that the service has a value to him or her that exceeds its

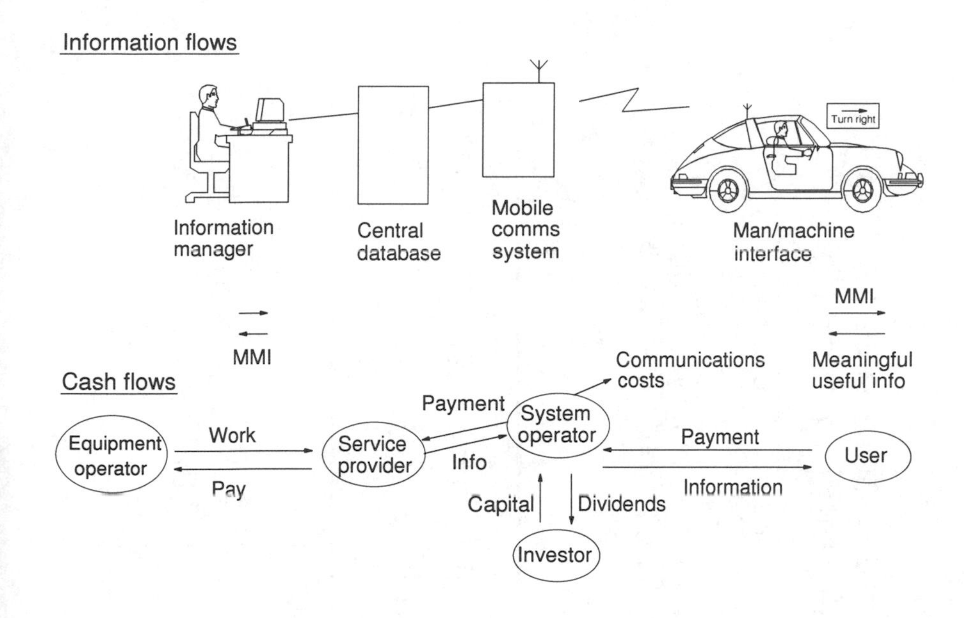

Figure 2.5 Simplified business elements of an RTI system.

cost. The perception of the service value will be greatly affected by the ease of use, as well as the accuracy of the information given. Employees of the service provider must find the work rewarding and be adequately paid. The initial investor will expect an adequate return on investment. Additionally, there are hidden beneficiaries: the road network owner should obtain better utilization of the road network, reducing the need to build new roads and having fewer accidents, less congestion, and pollution, which will benefit society as a whole. Will governments and authorities be prepared to contribute to commercial ventures to secure these benefits? Are these ventures viable without that contribution?

In practice, the Enterprise architecture is of crucial importance to the implementation. If a national road authority decides to pay for a route guidance system, it may want traffic information to be universally available, possibly through variable message signs or a local radio station. However, if the information is to be provided by a commercial venture, then it will be necessary to limit the availability of the information to only those who are subscribing to the service: information will then be presented to the driver in his or her vehicle via an encrypted data channel. The practical implementations would be quite different for these two cases.

Figure 2.6 shows the main components of an RTI system, including a vehicle with the ability to connect to one of several application hosts within the infrastructure. The vehicle subsystem may include an MMI, a processor, position sensors, and local databases,

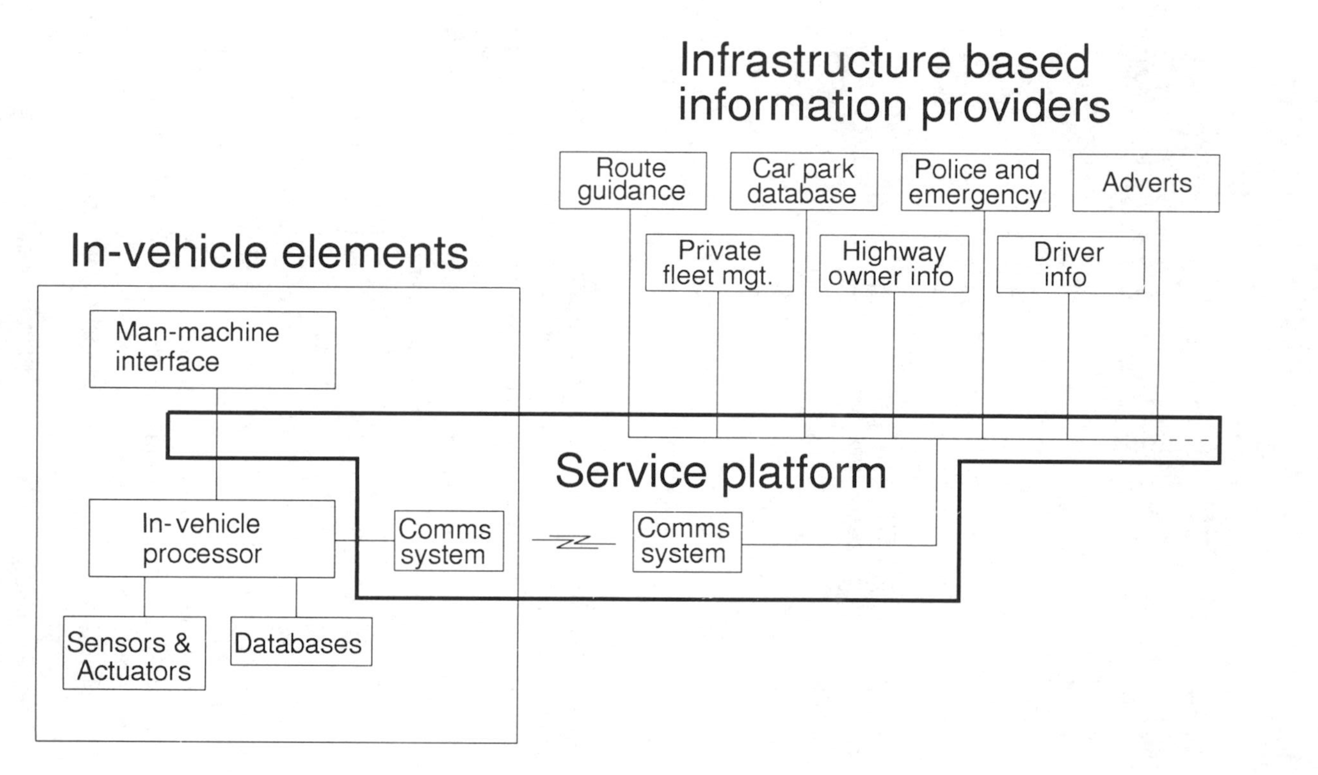

Figure 2.6 Main components of a vehicle-based RTI system.

connected to a mobile data communication system. Complex consortia will be established to implement practical systems, each partner bringing complementary skills:

- Vehicle manufacturers will want design authority for the MMI.
- Electronics systems manufacturers will produce the guidance computers and communications hardware.
- Component manufacturers will produce sensors.
- Road databases will be created by cartographers.
- Application software will be developed and operated by specialists.
- Communications will be provided and managed by communications operators.
- An overall system integrator will probably be needed.
- An organization will manage the service provided to the customers and manage their accounts.

An important issue is the impact on safety of these potentially intrusive systems. The MMIs will be optimized by each vehicle manufacturer, yet must provide a certain minimum set of services to support the full range of applications available from the infrastructure. Safe practice will need to be determined and guidelines or regulations issued to prevent any RTI systems diverting or confusing the driver and creating a safety hazard. Draft guidelines have been produced in the U.K. for the Department of Transport [8].

It is interesting to consider the possible introduction of "cooperative driving" systems (i.e., automated convoys of vehicles or "platooning"). While such systems will become feasible technically, their introduction may be prevented by legal considerations of responsibility should an accident occur following a system malfunction!

2.4.2 Information Architecture

From an Information viewpoint, it is necessary to use messages with meanings that are agreed upon and to implement open databases, so that once communications have been established with an information provider (possibly an alternative operator, when driving in a different country), the in-vehicle equipment is able to make sense of the information it receives. Some of the information being passed is of a statistical nature and can occasionally be lost without impact on the overall system performance. An example is the collection of "floating car" data: information transmitted by vehicles to report the time to travel across various links. This information is passed to the infrastructure processors, where it is analyzed statistically to determine the best interpretation of road conditions. Once a significant number of vehicles are equipped and statistically significant samples are returned, it would not matter if some of these uplink messages were lost. However, it must be emphasized that this tolerance to loss of data only occurs for certain applications. In normal data communications, achievement of reliable (guaranteed) transfer of data is essential. Typically, some data need to be sent to all valid users within a particular geographical area rather than sent to individual vehicles or to all users. Information of this type would include road status updates, and again some loss of data by individual vehicles could be tolerated.

2.4.3 RTI Technology Model

Figure 2.7 shows the diverse technologies that can be used to pass information (e.g.,, advice to turn left to avoid delays) from the infrastructure to the vehicle. The right-hand side shows some of the complex fixed-network infrastructure that will be needed to support these applications. This includes interconnected databases and control centers supported via a managed network, which may be implemented using *integrated services digital networks* (ISDN), *public switched packet data networks* (PSPDN), or private circuits.

Connection to the users may be via fixed-network-based terminals (e.g., for pretrip information) or over an untethered "mobile" link. This can use either true mobile communication systems (with wide-area, i.e., total, coverage) or short-range systems that only allow information to be transferred when in sight of the roadside node. The term *roadside node* is used to include nonelectronic communications between the vehicle and infrastructure—for example, traffic lights and variable message signs, which pass information direct to the driver, and surveillance systems, such as inductive loops and closed-circuit television, which can be used to detect vehicles. Electronic communications can be via infrared or microwave beacons. Beacon and mobile communication systems will be described later, together with their engineering aspects.

2.4.4 Dynamic Route Guidance Architecture

Dynamic route guidance is a system that provides the driver of a vehicle with specific recommendations based on data held in a central database, derived from a traffic monitoring, modeling, and predicting system. It is interesting to consider and compare a SOCRATES system (Chapter 6) and EURO-SCOUT system (Chapter 4). While the information drawn from the databases and that presented to the driver could be exactly the same in both systems, the information architecture within each system is radically different, because the Enterprise model for each system is radically different. SOCRATES relies on the provision of a powerful navigation system in each SOCRATES vehicle, whereas EURO-SCOUT has chosen to minimize the cost of the onboard equipment and rely on a comprehensive infrastructure of infrared beacons at most major intersections, which download a predetermined route to each vehicle according to its intended destination and the state of the roads at the time of calculating the route.

While some elements of the enterprise and information models are identical for the two systems, the computation, engineering, and technology models are different because different cost optimization assumptions have been made in the two Enterprise models. For EURO-SCOUT, the startup costs are very high, requiring the provision of an extensive dedicated communication system, but the cost of increasing the number of users is relatively

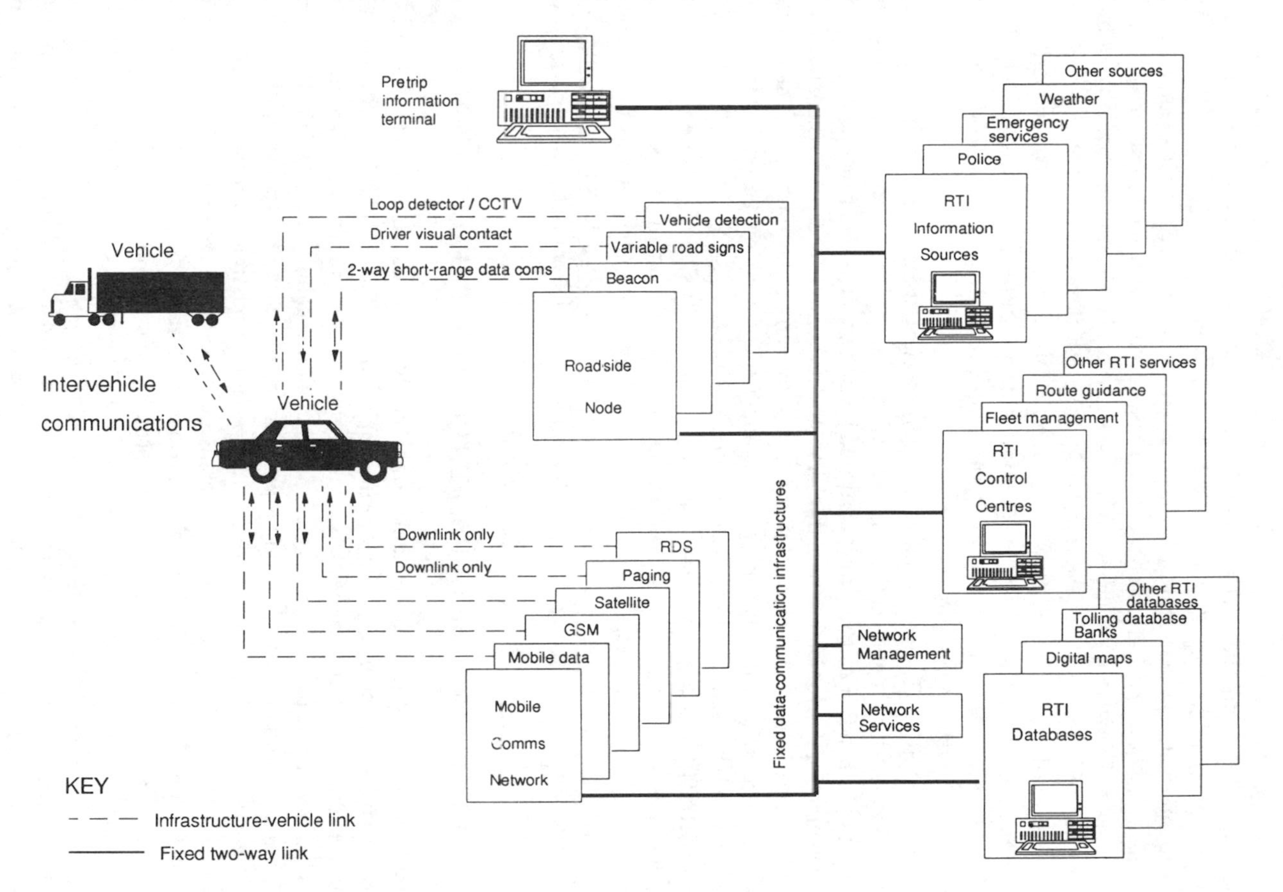

Figure 2.7 Technological implementation of an RTI system.

low, with low-cost in-vehicle equipment. Conversely, SOCRATES uses an existing shared mobile data network and has much lower startup costs, but the cost of equipping each vehicle is higher, so the cost of adding additional users is greater.

The informational requirement is that the vehicle communicates information about road transit times that have been encountered and receives either information on which specific route to follow (for a EURO-SCOUT system) or information on road travel times for a SOCRATES-type system. The internal information flow is quite different, because the computational approach is different. SOCRATES has a comprehensive onboard road database and is capable of planning the optimum route autonomously, whereas the EURO-SCOUT approach is to calculate the optimum routes centrally and download these into much simpler in-vehicle systems.

For EURO-SCOUT, recommended routes are calculated only from specific locations, and the recommended route is only transmitted while passing these locations. The communications can be handled by short-range infrared beacons, which also generate an accurate position datum for the vehicle's navigation system. The vehicle receives no guidance until it passes its first beacon. No change of advised route can be passed to the vehicle until it next passes a beacon, nor can information about road problems be reported as these are encountered, but only when the next beacon is passed.

SOCRATES relies on the vehicle having a comprehensive onboard database, and rather than receive specific recommended routes, the in-vehicle navigation system receives information on the transit times of the different road links and determines its own recommended route. SOCRATES uses a continuous-coverage mobile data communication system such that any change to the road link travel times can be notified immediately to or from vehicles.

2.5 COMMUNICATIONS REQUIREMENTS FOR RTI APPLICATIONS

RTI applications have been grouped under eight headings, and the communication requirements of each is reviewed below. The information is summarized in Table 2.2, which shows a matrix of these eight application sets against seven key communication requirements.

Emergency call requires universal coverage, high-reliability two-way data transfer. Privacy may be important, with accurate positioning and a rapid response desirable.

Automatic vehicle location and tracking would be possible as it passes electronic checkpoints built into beacons, but universal coverage for the immediate location is preferable. Protecting the privacy of the information is important.

Traffic and travel information would normally be broadcast to a closed user group (point to multipoint). The information would be frequently updated, and in general the loss of occasional packets of data would be acceptable.

In addition to the requirements for traffic information identified above, pretrip information could include data displayed at bus stops and train stations that could be freely available to encourage usage of public transport. However, some information will be packaged and passed to service subscribers.

Table 2.2
Importance of Communication Requirements for RTI Applications

	Broadcast Downlink	*Statistical Uplink*	*Two-Way Point-Point*	*Privacy*	*Positional Accuracy*	*Universal Coverage*	*Very Fast Response*
Emergency call	None	None	Very	Slight	Moderate	Essential	Slight
Vehicle tracking	None	None	Very	Very	None	Slight	None
Broadcast traffic information	Very	None	Slight	Slight	Nonc	Moderate	None
Pretrip information	Very	None	Slight	Slight	Slight	Moderate	None
Dynamic route guidance	Very	Very	Moderate	Moderate	Moderate	Moderate	None
Enquiry/reservations	None	None	Very	Very	None	Very	None
Automatic debiting	None	None	Moderate	Very	Essential	None	Moderate
Accident avoidance	None	None	None	None	None	None	Essential
Platooning	None	None	None	None	None	None	Essential

Regarding *dynamic route guidance*, the uplink requirement for both EURO-SCOUT and SOCRATES systems is very similar, each passing up information on the conditions encountered. SOCRATES offers scope for in-vehicle systems to reduce the amount of information that they contribute to the central database by preprocessing the information and only sending that which is significantly different from the value expected by onboard database. In both cases, the information is of a statistical nature and can tolerate some occasional loss. Although the data being sent need to be authenticated as coming from a valid source, it is likely that the users will not want to be identified (especially when speeding!). While it is desirable to transmit information about a problem as soon as it becomes apparent, the delay before the next beacon is passed is considered acceptable for the EURO-SCOUT system. The downlink requirements are radically different. EURO-SCOUT needs to receive a position update embedded in the transaction, which downloads specific recommended routes according to the required destination during a very short period while passing the beacon. The transaction is a point-to-point operation for each vehicle. SOCRATES relies on data about road conditions being received at the vehicle as changes are identified; therefore, constant coverage with a broadcast service should be acceptable.

Individual *enquiries* about the availability of services (e.g., hotel, restaurant, and car park *reservations*) will require a point-to-point communication and could be needed at vehicle location. Information is likely to be personal and may involve electronic funds transfer, and therefore needs to be secure.

Automatic debiting requires very precise knowledge of the movement of a vehicle so that only vehicles making use of a facility are charged and the correct vehicle is billed for the use of the resource.

Accident avoidance and platooning rely on very fast response systems. Typically, status messages will be transmitted continuously by equipped vehicles. Should any data become corrupted, it must be identified and discarded, with the system awaiting the next update rather than requesting a retransmission of the original data.

2.6 SUITABLE BEARER NETWORKS

The technology for providing reliable data transfer over fixed networks is well established for both packet transfer and circuit-switched data transfer. Fixed-network service can be provided by telecommunications operators, as a user of either a shared network such as ISDN (switched 64 kbps) or PSPDN, which may employ the well-established X.25 service or the expanding frame relay service. Alternatively, a dedicated private circuit may be leased from the telecommunications operator or purchased and installed exclusively for RTI applications. Fixed communication systems are well established and well understood and will not be explained in more detail here: attention will be focused on the important and more novel vehicle-to-infrastructure ''mobile'' data link. Use of a public communication system minimizes the capital investment of the service provider and eliminates the need for communication design specialists, installers, and maintainers. However, some service providers may want to have total control of their network irrespective of the startup costs. These are issues for the Enterprise model. Mobile communication systems may be grouped into four types:

- Two-way short-range beacons (infrared or microwave);
- One-way continuous coverage downlinks (RDS and paging);
- Two-way continuous coverage systems (Global System of Mobile Communication (GSM), IS54 (North American digital cellular telephony standard), North American cellular digital packet data (CDPD), European digital private mobile radio (PMR)—trans-European trunked radio (TETRA), proprietary mobile data networks, satellite, data over cellular, and third-generation mobile systems (TGMS);
- Vehicle-to-vehicle communications.

2.6.1 Beacons

Beacons have a very short range of operation. Consequently, periods of contact with the beacon are infrequent and, for moving vehicles, very short in duration. Spectrum for these systems has been allocated at 5.8 GHz in Europe, and infrared systems are also in service. The instantaneous bandwidth is much greater than that available over currently available mobile data networks, but the proportion of time that contact is available means that the average data rate is less. Furthermore, applications such as an emergency call service based on beacons are not feasible because of the low probability of being able to make an emergency call when this is required. Such systems may find favor for installations that already have a fixed-network infrastructure available, or that offer standalone applications, such as automatic debiting. If a dedicated fixed infrastructure has to be installed, the cost will exceed that of using a mobile data-based network.

The beacon has an interesting advantage: as well as providing communications it also gives an accurate identification of the vehicle's position, without any significant overhead. This benefit is not apparent when considering just the Engineering projection, but has an impact on the Information projection.

2.6.2 Downlink-Only Networks

Three candidates exist for carrying these data: band II (88 to 108 MHz) broadcast downlinks, terrestrial paging, and broadcast satellites. The DRIVE project RDS ALERT developed the ALERT protocol suite [9] to use the very small data broadcast capacity within the RDS service on band II broadcast FM radio. However, this protocol suite is now being adapted within the DRIVE II ATT-ALERT project to be used on other media, such as paging and the proposed *digital audio broadcasting* (DAB), and also two-way dynamic route guidance services on bearers such as those considered by SOCRATES.

Radio Data System

This system has found favor because it makes use of radio technology that is already found in all cars: FM radio. It uses a 57-kHz subcarrier intended primarily to provide station identification and indication of when traffic information is being broadcast, so that these may override any other sound source, such as a cassette. The total gross RDS capacity is 1,187.5 bps [10,11]. The part available to the traffic message channel is limited to about 30 bps.

Paging

Several paging systems exist in different countries [12]. A common *European radio messaging* standard, ERMES, has not yet been widely implemented, but should offer the advantage of being available throughout Europe. Capacity is 3,750 bps, which is shared with other messages, unless a dedicated channel is to be justified. Existing *Post Office Code for Standardization Advisory Group* (POCSAG) paging systems are widely used and offer a capacity of 1,200 bps. Paging has the advantage of allowing other non-RTI messages to be received and being designed expressly to give excellent coverage and exceptionally low power consumption—very important for portable terminals and even for in-vehicle units that need to remain active while the vehicle is not in use.

Satellite

Reception of satellite data on a downlink-only basis is well established with *global positioning system* (GPS) receivers now being produced with modest antennas. Television broadcasting satellites are already heavily used and could provide a medium to distribute RTI information. Satellites have the advantage of giving good coverage away from the major conurbations, where cellular radio and beacon systems may not have been installed. Ironically, satellite communication in builtup areas is notoriously difficult because of propagation shading by tall buildings and multipath interference due to reflections.

2.6.3 Mobile Data Systems

These systems include satellites, cellular telephony networks like GSM and IS54, proprietary dedicated mobile packet data networks (Mobitex (Ericsson), RD-LAP (Motorola), Paknet (U.K. Vodafone), Cognito (U.K.), CDPD, etc.) and the TETRA standard currently being developed by the *European Telecommunications Standards Institute* (ETSI).

Satellites

Bidirectional operation is now possible using Inmarsat C terminals, which were originally designed as compact terminals for maritime use, but are already finding application for long-distance heavy goods transportation. There are several other communication satellite ventures being discussed which plan to have a better distribution of satellite orbits which should overcome some of the propagation problems. However, satellites are expensive, and their transmissions cover relatively large areas of the Earth's surface and can serve only a small proportion of the potential users within that area (unlike cellular radio systems, where the range of transmission is limited to allow the spectrum to be reused within typically a few tens of kilometers).

Cellular Telephony

Using modems, mobile data communications have been available for some time as circuit-switched data over the analog cellular systems. Circuit-switched data systems are very suitable for point-to-point transfer of data, where a communication channel is reserved solely for the use of the connected parties for the duration of the call. The cost of the call depends on the duration rather than the amount of data sent. This becomes inefficient if the data flow is sporadic. Under such circumstances, it would be better to use a packet data access system. Mobile packet data systems also offer connectionless, multicast downlinks so that information can be passed to a closed user group.

Mobile packet data bearers are becoming available to proprietary designs and are being standardized in bodies such as the ETSI for implementation on the same timescales as the introduction of RTI services. Currently, packet data are a very significant part of the development of the TETRA system being developed within ETSI RES 6. GSM phase 1 includes a limited-capacity packet service: *short-message service* (SMS) [13], and the

ETSI SMG committees are now studying the requirements and feasibility of providing a *general packet radio service* (GPRS) as part of the next phase of the development of GSM. The *cellular digital packet data* (CDPD) system is being developed in North America by a group of leading companies. Work has already started on the definition of TGMS that will be implemented in the twenty-first century under the various guises of *future public land mobile telephony service* (FPLMTS) within CCIR and in Europe, as the *universal mobile telecommunications system* (UMTS) within ETSI SMG 5 supported by various RACE projects such as MONET, which are taking account of the needs of RTI services from the outset.

Intervehicle Systems

These systems are being developed specifically to support collision avoidance and ''platooning'' applications. However, it has been suggested that other applications could be supported by providing a connectionless link to systems in the fixed infrastructure by passing datagrams forwards and backwards between equipped vehicles until one is able to establish contact with the infrastructure, via either a beacon or cellular radio. This would only be feasible when a great many vehicles are equipped and could result in heavy and unnecessary loading of the fixed network if several vehicles were successful in passing the datagram to the infrastructure. See Table 2.3. CEPT has allocated spectrum at 63 to 64 GHz for this purpose. Use of spectrum in the 60-GHz oxygen absorption band will allow these systems to operate within a reasonable range of the equipped vehicle, with little risk of interference from distant vehicles.

Table 2.3
Ability of Communication Systems to Support Applications

	Wide-Area/ Cellular Radio	*One-Way Paging*	*Short-Range Beacon*	*Intervehicle Communications*
Emergency call	Ideal	Not supported	Possible	Just possible
Vehicle tracking	Supported	Not supported	Possible	Not supported
Broadcast traffic information	Supported	Ideal	Possible	Just possible
Pretrip information	Supported	Ideal	Possible	Not supported
Dynamic route guidance	Ideal	Supported	Supported	Just possible
Enquiry/reservations	Ideal	Not supported	Possible	Not supported
Automatic Debiting	Just possible	Not supported	Ideal	Not supported
Accident avoidance	Not supported	Not supported	Not supported	Ideal
Autopilot	Not supported	Not supported	Not supported	Ideal

2.7 CONVERGENCE OF COMMUNICATION SYSTEMS

Table 2.3 shows that the four different types of mobile communication systems identified in Section 2.6 each have advantages and disadvantages. There are several different implementations within each of the four classes, so there are many networks to choose from. There is currently no absolute "front runner" for a standard communication for RTI, although some will argue that as GSM is installed across Europe it will assume that mantle, for Europe at least. For the future, many hope that FPLMTS/TGMS will be able to support all the requirements identified.

One substitute for a standardized communication system for RTI is to define a standard for the network services that each of the communication systems should offer. This idea has not met with universal support, and the ideas presented here are subject to ongoing investigations within the second DRIVE program. Effectively, the interface is being standardized rather than the way that the service is provided. The ideas are being developed from the DRIVE normalized data transmission (DNT) concept from DRIVE project CIDER [14–16]. Essentially, a wide range of applications should be able to be supported over a variety of networks via a common interface (Figure 2.8).

Not all interfaces need to be standardized. Communications within the vehicle may use a form of vehicle area network. This should be standardized where there are to be multiple sources of the various components. Similarly, communications over the mobile data network should be open, as should any communications between operators. However, communications within an operator's own fixed network do not need to be open, since this does not have an impact on interconnectivity with other service providers.

The common interface may be implemented at both the application layer and at the network-to-transport interface. Standardizing the application layer was suggested by several DRIVE projects, including STRADA, which identified five types of application service needing to be standardized. This should simplify the task of developing and implementing new RTI applications, since they should be supportable by one of the application protocols that would be available on the communication system.

Standardizing the network layer service is also important to provide a "plug-and-go" capability such that if a vehicle were driven to a country or state that did not support its normal communication system, the driver could rent whatever communication system was available in that country and simply connect it to his or her RTI system, which would automatically adapt to the new communication system and discover how to connect to the appropriate applications in that country.

The normalized network layer can be implemented by adapting and enhancing the services normally provided by the subnetwork being used. The OSI network layer can be divided into three sublayers as described below. These nested layers can be used to bring the network service provided by the different networks to align with a normalized service. Work is progressing within the DRIVE program to identify the requirements for this normalized network service. Issues to be resolved include:

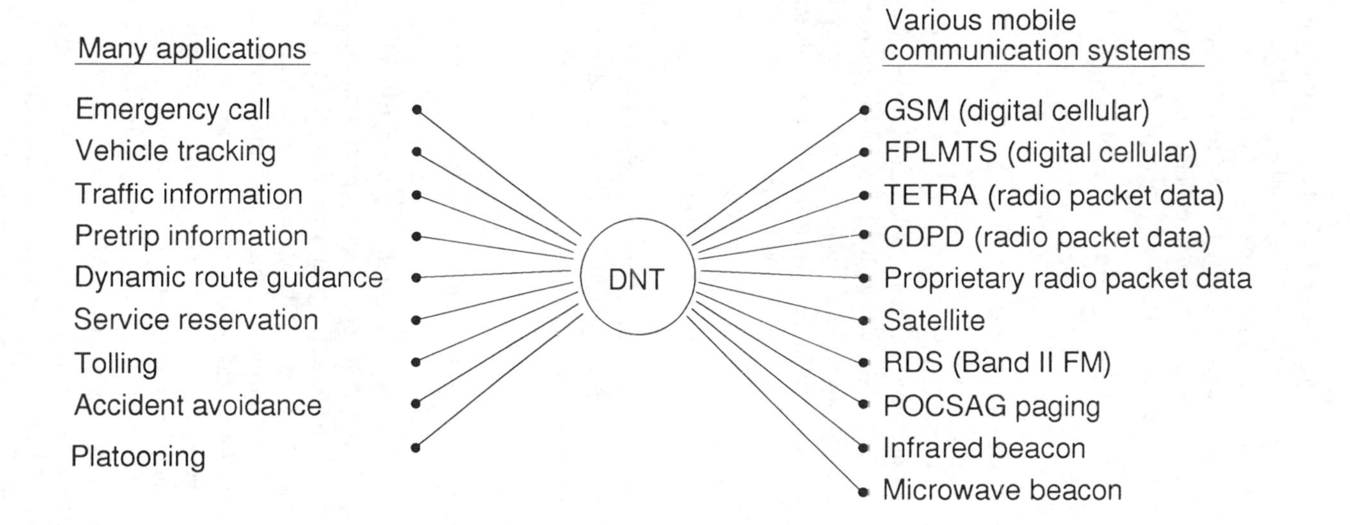

Figure 2.8 Many applications supported over various bearers. DNT is a common service interface that allows each network to offer communication services in the same way.

- Agreement on a global addressing scheme for RTI applications and users. This may include a geographical addressing capability to address all members of a closed user group within a certain geographical area.
- The provision of methods for address translation, so that an application or vehicle with a global address can be accessed unambiguously via the chosen mobile data network (which usually has a very limited address capacity).

The structure and function of the sublayers that will be used to achieve this normalized network service are identified below.

Subnetwork Access Facility (Subnetwork 3a)

This subnetwork sits immediately above the data link layer. Different subnetworks adopt different addressing schemes and present their services in different ways. The address range for X.25 packet data systems is defined within E.164 and is not directly compatible with the X.121 addressing scheme used for telephony. Mobile data systems have been designed for efficient support of a limited number of mobile terminals and have adopted very limited address fields.

Subnetwork-Dependent Convergence Facility (Sublayer 3b)

This sublayer converts the subnetwork-specific services and addressing scheme to align with the standardized services offered by the subnetwork-independent convergence function. This may involve conversion from connection mode to connectionless service and address translation.

Subnetwork-Independent Convergence Facility (Sublayer 3c)

This sublayer determines the services to be offered by the network and can be used to enhance the services of the subnetwork to meet a common set of services and the adoption of a global addressing scheme. The most likely service to be adopted for standardization is ISO 8473, which provides a connectionless data transfer system with a global addressing capability. The addressing scheme will need enhancement to allow broadcasts of data to specific geographical areas and multicast to closed user groups.

The DNT concept is based on creating an open interface at layers 4 and 3c in the OSI model. The underlying network provides the lower layers (1 and 2) and usually part of the network layer (3a), while the transport layer (layer 4) provides a means to ensure that any inadequacies in the underlying network's performance are managed so as to provide an adequate quality of service as perceived by the application.

Figure 2.9 shows the OSI seven-layer model as a "wine glass": the broad top and bottom indicating many different applications, each potentially connected to one of many

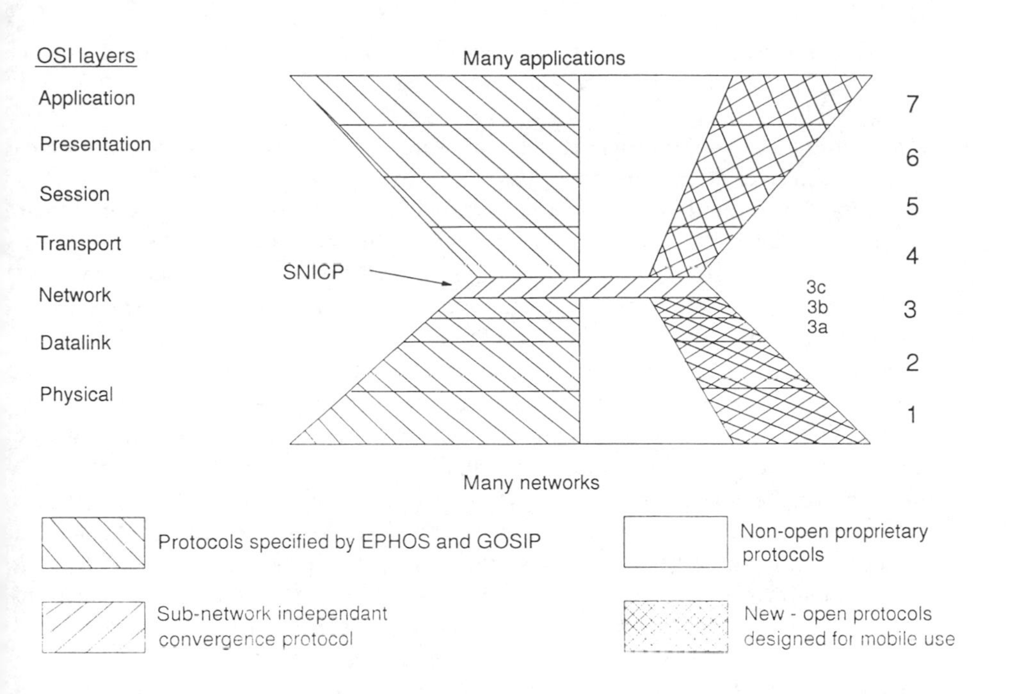

Figure 2.9 Use of a normalized network interface.

different networks, via a common interface at layers 4 and 3c. The OSI standard protocols are included in this diagram. These will be necessary where it is required to access an application in the fixed infrastructure, which is implemented using the OSI protocols. Some OSI application protocols may prove unacceptable in the mobile environment because of the enormous protocol overhead. A key point is that the subnetwork-dependent convergence function (layer 3b) can be implemented so that it provides address translation. In this way, only the subnetwork address need be passed over the network if both ends of the communication system know the translation to the global address. In principle, non-OSI protocols should also be able to run over this standardized network service, possibly by the addition of a suitable thin Transport layer. Such protocols may be required to improve the system efficiency at the expense of full openness.

The use of the seven-layer OSI reference model for communication systems is well established and heavily supported by the U.S. Government through the *Government OSI Profile* (GOSIP) and the by the European Commission through the *European Procurement Handbook for Open Systems* (EPHOS) [10]. However, the OSI protocols currently available have a number of limitations when operating in a mobile data environment:

1. Mobile network capacity is limited and therefore expensive (infrared beacons are less limited by this). In consequence:

   a. Efficient protocols are needed that introduce minimum overhead. Currently available OSI protocols can introduce significant overheads needed to allow very flexible protocol negotiation and interworking.
   b. A true multipoint transmission service is necessary to ensure that a single transmission over the air interface is available to all authorized users.
2. Coverage is discontinuous. This is especially a problem for beacon systems, where the vehicle may have no means of accessing the infrastructure for considerable periods. This is also a problem for radio systems, where a moving vehicle or terminal will often travel through conditions that introduce short periods of data loss. Many of the currently defined OSI protocols are intolerant to this kind of data loss or the delays caused by retransmission of damaged packets.
3. At any one time, it is possible that the vehicles will have access to more than one network, each with a different operator. Access to these different networks and the choice between them may need to be managed.
4. There are the related interests of security and confidentiality. For the network operator it is important to prevent unauthorized access to the network (to prevent blocking of legitimate traffic and loss of revenue) and to the applications, to prevent corruption of data and stealing of information. The user of the system will want security of personal information about funds transfer or user's movement (and possibly excess speeding!). There is a potential conflict between this need for anonymity and the network and application operators' requirement for access to be positively authenticated.

The comments on the special needs of mobile data systems apply equally to OSI and the Internet suite of protocols—transmission control protocol/Internet protocol (TCP/IP). Although the Internet protocols were originally developed for the U.S. Department of Defense, the U.S. Government has made a commitment to the use of OSI in the future. The Internet protocols will remain in use for many years, but it is likely that they will not receive the same amount of onward development as OSI. Work is already in hand within ISO to define enhanced protocols and within the Internet community to seek convergence with OSI. Internet software is at present more readily and cheaply available, but interest in OSI is growing. Future developments will be required to create more efficient standardized upper layer protocols to meet the needs of mobile telematics applications. This profile of new protocols has been tentatively called *Mobile Open Systems Interconnection* (MOSI). The MOSI protocols would align with the OSI framework, but would have reduced flexibility and greater efficiency.

2.8 CONCLUSIONS

The adoption of open architectures for RTI products and services is key to the commercial success of the RTI market. Developers will need to pool their resources to achieve the common standards needed to facilitate creation of open architectures with agreed-upon data dictionaries, database structures, and communication protocols.

REFERENCES

[1] ''Object Orientated Techniques for ROSA,'' *RACE Open Services Architecture*, Project Deliverable No. 1, RACE project R1068 68/BTR/425/DS/B/001/b1.

[2] *ANSA Reference Manual Release 01.01*, Architecture Projects Management, Ltd., Poseidon House, Castle Park, Cambridge, CB3 0RD U.K.

[3] ISO/ODP, ''Reference Model of Open Distributed Processing,'' ODP, ISO/TEC JTEC1.

[4] Braam and Freij, ''A Common Method for Describing Functional System Architectures,'' release 2, DRIVE project CORD V2056.

[5] Marca and Clement, *SADT. Structured Analysis and Design Technique*, 1986.

[6] *Applications of SADT. Case Histories through 1978*, Softech, 1978.

[7] Tanenbaum, A. S., *Computer Networks*, 2d ed., Prentice Hall, 1989.

[8] ICE Ergonomics, Ltd., ''The Design of In-Vehicle Information Systems: Code of Practice and Design Guidelines,'' draft proposal, Department of Transport, April 1993.

[9] Davies, P., and G. Klein, ''RDS-Alert—Advice and Problem Location for European Road Traffic,'' *Proc. DRIVE Conf.*, Brussels, 4–6 Feb. 1991.

[10] Mothersole, P. L., and N. W. White, *Broadcast Data Systems, Teletext and RDS*,'' Butterworths.

[11] Ely, S. R., and D. J. Jeffery, ''Traffic Information Broadcasting and RDS,'' *Mobile Information Systems*,'' J. Walker, ed., Dedham, MA: Artech House.

[12] Tridgell, R. H., ''Radio Paging and Messaging,'' *Mobile Information Systems*, J. Walker, ed., Dedham, MA: Artech House.

[13] Mouly, M., and M.-B. Pautet, *The GSM System for Mobile Communications*.

[14] Perez Marco, M., ''DRIVE Normalised Interface to Communication Networks. The DRIVE Network Terminal,'' *Advanced Telematics in Road Transport, Proc. DRIVE Conf.*, Brussels, 4–6 Feb. 1991.

[15] Freij, G. J., C.-H. Rokitansky, N. D. C. Wall, and F. Zijderhand, ''Integrated Communications Architecture for Road Transport Informatics,'' *IVHS VNIS'91*, Michigan, 20–23 Oct. 1991.

[16] Wall, N. D. C., ''An Integrated Communications Architecture for RTI Systems,'' *Proc. 25th ISATA Conf.*, Florence, 1–5 June 1992.

Chapter 3
Traffic Control
Michael Bell

3.1 INTRODUCTION

The cost of road construction, the shortage of space (particularly in urban areas), and environmental constraints are focusing attention on the better use of existing road capacity. In addition to operational road capacity, there is increasing awareness of safety and the environment. This, coupled with emerging information and communication technologies offering potential solutions, provided the basis for the DRIVE and PROMETHEUS research and development programs.

This chapter concentrates on developments in traffic control. A distinction is made between urban traffic control (Section 3.2) and highway traffic control (Section 3.3), although the two are functionally (if not administratively) interrelated in urban areas. While hardware, and particularly software, advances can improve the efficiency of traffic control, it is becoming clear that traffic control alone cannot solve the problem of traffic congestion. Considerable attention is being given to demand management and technologies such as automatic debiting, which will enable its implementation. Besides this, there is increasing interest in the integration of other systems with traffic control, especially in-vehicle information systems and public transport.

In-vehicle information systems, and particularly dynamic route guidance (see Section 3.4), lead to better informed travelers who make more efficient decisions. Dynamic route guidance and traffic control systems both collect traffic data of mutual interest and interact strongly with each other through their effects on the traffic, so there is a strong case for integration.

Public transport is generally accepted as a more efficient mode of transport and therefore worthy of priority at signal-controlled junctions (see Section 3.5). Road-bound public transport systems often monitor automatically the locations of their vehicles, information that is useful for implementing priority in signal control. There is also a little-explored potential for data exchange to the benefit of both traffic control and public transport operation.

3.2 URBAN TRAFFIC CONTROL

Junctions may be controlled individually (as in the case of the MOVA and LHOVRA systems described later), but in dense urban networks, substantial benefits are to be obtained through some form of coordination.

Traffic-responsive signal control requires information on traffic flows, which is usually obtained through the use of inductive loop detectors, although microwave and infrared devices are also to be found. Inductive loop detectors have the advantage of being located beneath the road surface, as opposed to above the highway, but there is increasing concern about their reliability. In the U.K., there is renewed interest in microwave devices. In Japan, the predominant form of detector is ultrasonic, which may be used on roads built on steel structures.

Another important means of monitoring traffic is video surveillance. At present, video is primarily used manually by the operator in the control center to supplement data received automatically from the detectors. There is great interest in image processing as a further means of automatically collecting traffic data. Earlier approaches, as exemplified by the CCATS system of Devlonics [1], endeavored to emulate conventional detectors. Here video has the advantage of being able to monitor many lanes at a number of different locations simultaneously through one camera and one processing unit. An interesting example of this use of image processing is offered by the FAST-TRAC field trial in Oakland County, Detroit [2], where Autoscope sensors replace inductive loop detectors in the Sydney Coordinated Adaptive Traffic System (SCATS) urban traffic control system (an Australian signal control system; see [3]). Autoscope is used to detect and measure significantly large gaps between vehicles, so the problem of occlusion, which bedevils most machine vision systems, does not arise. Interest is increasingly shifting to the use of image processing to automatically collect qualitative information relating to the state of traffic in an area, such as the presence or absence of queues. This is the approach adopted in the IMPACTS system, which is currently under investigation on the M25 in the U.K., was the approach developed in the DRIVE project INVAID and is the approach embodied in the FAST-Q system developed at the University of Newcastle [4]. There is a good review of the field in Hoose [5].

Most traffic-responsive control systems to date are based on the control of *stages* rather than *signal groups*, although many modern microprocessor controllers, such as the Siemens M32 controller, have the ability to control groups individually (a stage is a period during which no signals are changing, and a group is a collection of signals that must be switched simultaneously). Stage-based control implies substantially fewer control variables than does group-based control, but restricts the ability to modify the interstage structures (the times at which individual signal groups are switched on or off in the transition from one stage to the next). In most systems, the number of control variables is further reduced by fixing stage sequences and restricting interest to stage durations, although some allow stages for which there is no demand to be dropped.

There are two forms of traffic-responsive control to be found in practice. The first is *plan selection*, or *plan modification*, as implemented by, for example, Siemens through their TASS module. In this case, the available data are used to diagnose the current traffic state, and then the appropriate signal plan is selected or modified. The second is *online optimization*, or *online modification*. In general, a rolling horizon is defined over which the vehicle arrivals at each controlled junction are estimated (*feedforward control*), sometimes accompanied by the recursive estimation of certain parameters, such as saturation flow or turning proportions. Feedforward control requires the location of the vehicle detectors some distance upstream of the stop line. Vehicle delay and stops arising from a particular signal plan are estimated deterministically, normally using a "vertical queuing" model (vehicles are assumed to travel to the stop line undelayed before stopping).

The alternative to feedforward control is *feedback control*, which does not require the rolling horizon. Signal timings respond to the current traffic situation as measured by vehicle detectors. In the case of feedback control in SCATS, detectors are located just before the stop line in order to measure the degree of saturation.

One can further distinguish between two approaches to optimization, described in the following sections.

3.2.1 Discrete Time Optimization

In the first approach, as exemplified by PRODYN [6] and UTOPIA [7], time is discretized and the allocation of green over the rolling horizon is optimized directly as an assignment problem (in the operations research sense). In PRODYN, a terminal cost function, which essentially penalizes queues at the end of the rolling horizon, is included to prevent a bias in favor of those signal plans that are good over the horizon but bad thereafter. An alternative way of viewing the discrete time approach to optimization is in terms of decision trees. An efficient method for determining the optimum sequence of decisions over the rolling horizon, taking into account the terminal costs, is through the use of a shortest path algorithm, such as Dijkstra's algorithm [8]. In the case of a substantial dispersion of platoons of traffic, allowance should be made for the random element of arrivals [9,10].

3.2.2 Trilevel Approach

In the second, as exemplified by the split, cycle, and offset optimization technique (SCOOT) [11] and Siemens systems running the VERON (offset optimizer) and SAEWA (split optimizer) modules, control relates to three types of variables: *cycle time* (the time taken for all stages to receive green at a junction), *offset* (the difference between the start of green at adjacent junctions for, say, a stream of traffic passing through both), and (*green*) *split* (the allocation of green to each stage within the cycle at a particular junction). In the case of SCOOT, signal timings are modified in a direction that will improve performance in terms of forecast delays and stops over the next cycle; the system therefore tracks the forecast optimum rather than optimizing completely.

3.2.3 Junction Control Systems

A review of some important junction control systems is presented in the following.

MOVA

MOVA [12] is a control strategy for the isolated intersection developed by the Transport Research Laboratory to overcome some of the limitations of preceding forms of vehicle actuation, which were based on the termination of green when a significantly large gap in the oncoming flow is detected. For low to medium flows, MOVA compares the costs and benefits of a change to the next stage, making the change when it is feasible and beneficial to do so. For high flows, capacity is maximized. MOVA was developed to link to standard U.K. signal controllers through the urban traffic control (UTC) interface. The system is now approved in the U.K. and is in operation at about 30 junctions.

LHOVRA

LHOVRA [13] is a control strategy for isolated intersections. Developed in Sweden, it is used in many intersections in the Nordic countries and is implemented in controllers from EB Traffic, Philips, and others. LHOVRA gives a high degree of flexibility, since it is group (and not stage) oriented. LHOVRA contains a number of new functions to get high traffic safety, low delays, and priority for public-transport vehicles and trucks. However, it does not contain an optimization routine.

3.2.4 Network Control Systems

Three different system architectures have emerged for network control. There is the *centralized architecture* (see Figure 3.1), as exemplified by SCOOT, where the essential control decisions are taken centrally in the traffic computer. The roadside station implements decisions passed down and passes back data relating to detector and signal status. There is the *distributed architecture* (see Figure 3.2), as exemplified by Siemens systems, where some decisions are taken centrally (perhaps regarding cycle time and offsets) and some locally (perhaps green splits). Finally, there is the *decentralized architecture* (see

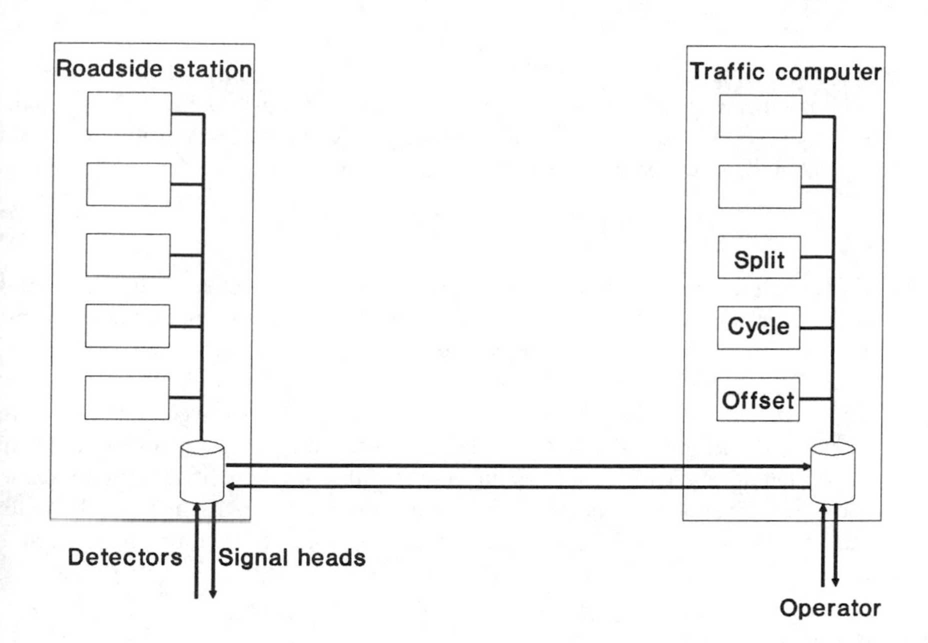

Figure 3.1 Centralized architecture as exemplified by SCOOT.

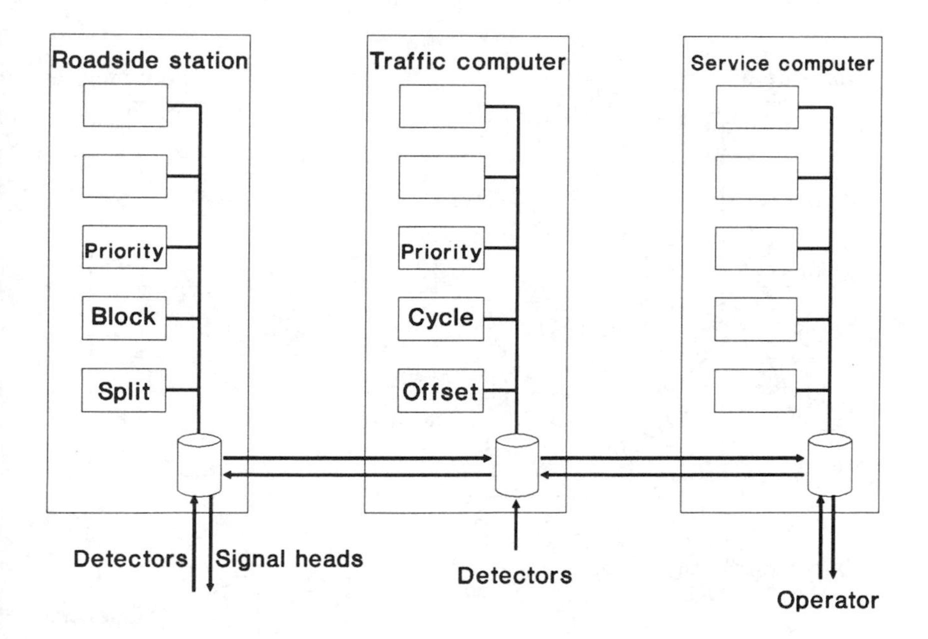

Figure 3.2 Distributed architecture as exemplified by Siemens systems.

Figure 3.3), as exemplified by the PRODYN and UTOPIA systems, where decisions are taken and implemented locally. Coordination, when required, can be achieved by including in the optimization the costs incurred at neighboring junctions. A description of some important network control systems follows.

SCOOT

SCOOT [11] is a network control strategy now implemented at around 40 sites, mainly in the U.K. It seeks to minimize delay and stops by making small modifications to split, offset, and cycle time (frequently when required). Delay and stops are evaluated over the next cycle using a traffic model similar to the model contained in the well-known TRANSYT program [14]. This assumes "vertical queuing" (cars travel undelayed to the stop line and queues form at the stop line, taking up no space). This assumption has the effect of concentrating the delay at the stop line, leading to an equality between modeled queue and delay. The optimizer determines in which direction to make changes. Detectors are located on the entrances to each link to provide as much forewarning as possible of demand.

Siemens Systems

Siemens [15] provides flexible, modular, hierarchical systems based around a versatile programmable microprocessor controller which can be programmed to respond in various

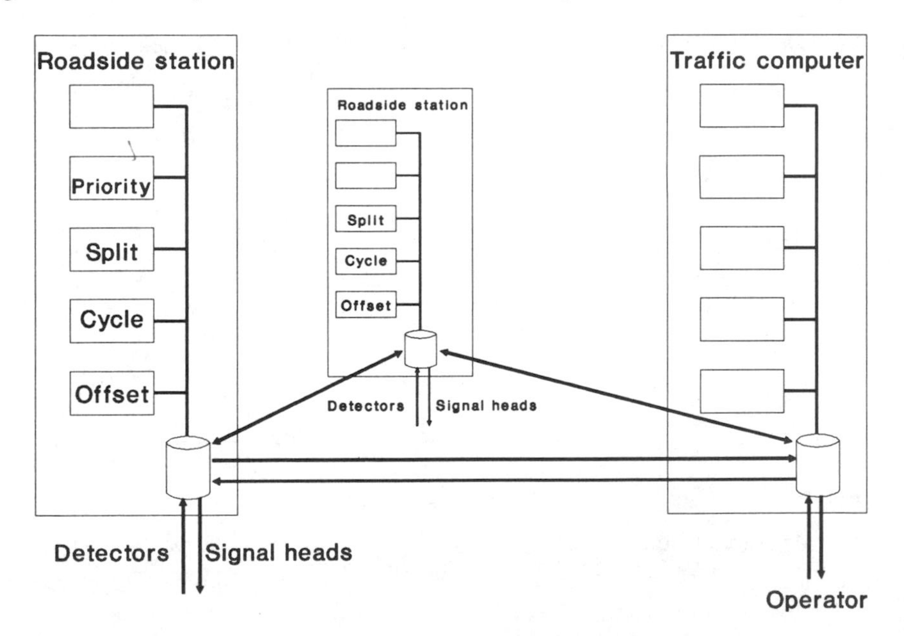

Figure 3.3 Decentralized architecture as exemplified by the PRODYN and UTOPIA systems.

ways, a traffic computer, a communications infrastructure to link the controllers and the traffic computer, and software modules, which may be implemented either in the controller or the traffic computer as appropriate. Modules include SAEWA to optimize green splits locally, VERON to optimize offsets centrally, and STAUKO to modify offsets locally to prevent queues blocking upstream junctions.

PRODYN and UTOPIA

These systems (see [6] on PRODYN and [7] on UTOPIA) optimize decentrally using the discrete time, rolling horizon approach. This requires intelligent local controllers, known as SPOT controllers in the case of UTOPIA. The approach potentially offers more flexibility by allowing group-based optimization without constraints on cycle time, stage sequence, or even stage or interstage structures. In practice, this leads to too many decision variables, so both PRODYN and UTOPIA have worked with stages rather than groups. UTOPIA enforces a fixed stage sequence, reducing the number of the decision variables still further. In the decentralized mode, coordination is achieved through information exchange between adjacent junctions. Public transport priority is an important part of UTOPIA.

3.3 HIGHWAY CONTROL

This refers to traffic control on highways and tunnels, both within and outside urban areas, and includes features such as incident detection, congestion monitoring, ramp metering, and collective route guidance. Variable-message signs (VMS) may be used for speed and lane use control (as in the Dutch Motorway Control and Signaling System (MCSS)) for forewarning drivers of conditions ahead or for giving route recommendations (as in the Rhein/Main highway network). It is useful to distinguish between *access control* (essentially ramp metering) and *line control* (essentially speed and lane use control). Extensive attention has been given to the use of ramp metering for access control. Algorithms have been developed for the control of isolated ramps or for a number of ramps jointly. The latter requires up-to-date information on the origin-destination (OD) flows and their assignment to the network dynamically (i.e., taking into account time lags; see, for example, [16]). The DRIVE project CHRISTIANE has been developing a feedback control algorithm, while the DRIVE project ODIN has been developing appropriate OD flow estimation techniques for use on highways. However, in densely populated urban areas there is often not the capacity on the onramps for storing vehicles at times of congestion on the highway. This raises the need for gating before the ramp by urban traffic control.

3.3.1 Incident Detection and Congestion Monitoring

Automatic incident detection and congestion monitoring are important functions of both urban and interurban traffic control. Incident detection is particularly important in tunnels and at other locations of high risk. The nature of the incident detection system required depends on the definition of the incident and the level of traffic flow.

Automatic incident detection algorithms have generally been based on point speed and occupancy measurements, usually obtained from inductive loops. Early algorithms, such as the California algorithm, endeavored to detect the shock waves emanating from incidents by looking for spatial and temporal discontinuities in flow and occupancy (the proportion of time that a loop is occupied, sometimes regarded as a proxy for density). Thresholds may be determined in various ways, such as by Bayesian estimation [17]. Algorithms of this type generally have the structure of a decision tree culminating in the classification of the traffic state [18].

A simple but effective algorithm of this type is HIOCC, developed by TRL [19], which uses thresholds to detect unusually high occupancy at the detection site; there is no pooling of information between adjacent sites. HIOCC has been used in the DRIVE project MONICA. While early algorithms applied simple thresholds to detect spatial discontinuity, later algorithms used time series statistical procedures to take into account the variation in measurements under nonincident conditions [20]. Kalman filtering techniques applied to macroscopic traffic flow parameters (flow, density, and speed) have also been used for incident detection [21].

Experience has shown that of the parameters measurable by inductive loop (occupancy, flow, and speed), speed is the one that allows the best discrimination of incidents. Because of the cost of false alarms in terms of lost capacity and system credibility, accurate diagnosis of incidents is important.

The algorithms so far described are suitable for medium to heavy traffic flows. For low traffic flows, aggregate parameters (occupancy, flow, or speed per unit time) are not useful. Experiments have been performed using fully disaggregated measurements (the times at which vehicles pass detection points) to perform a form of vehicle accounting, where the vehicles are counted in and out of sections of the road [22]. The objective is to identify vehicles that enter but do not leave a section of road within a reasonable period. Algorithms of this type are particularly dependent on detector accuracy.

There are limitations to incident detection using point measurements that cannot be overcome by improved algorithms. Until an incident produces a measurable effect at a detector, it will go undetected. This will generally slow the response time and correspondingly raise the risks of secondary incidents occurring before action can be taken. There is therefore interest in area detection. While experiments have been performed with long inductive loops [23], the most promising technology here appears to be image processing.

Automatic video analysis allows an area of road to be monitored for stationary or slow moving vehicles. The DRIVE project INVAID is examining this approach to incident detection. The FAST-Q system from the University of Newcastle detects queues of vehicles [4]. In general, however, video is used manually to complement other forms of incident detection.

3.3.2 Ramp Metering

The application of ramp-metering strategies are now widespread, with examples in the U.K., Japan, the U.S., the Netherlands, and France. In a recent review, Hadj-Salem et al. [24] distinguish between *local* and *coordinated* ramp-metering strategies, to which can be added *sequential* ramp metering (see below). A further distinction can be made between *feedforward* approaches, where demand is measured and compared with the available capacity at the merge site, and *feedback* approaches, where traffic characteristics at the merge site are measured and an appropriate metering strategy is chosen.

An example of feedforward local ramp metering is to be found at one junction on the M6 Motorway in the U.K. [25]. The access control system establishes the likely highway capacity in advance of it being exceeded through an automatic capacity estimation procedure. The technique relies on data obtained from automatic speed/flow measuring equipment in the critical section of the highway. To decide whether metering should take place, an up-to-date indication of traffic demand has to be compared with the current desirable maximum flow. If demand on the critical link would exceed this, the ramp signals will show red. The success of the metering is checked by monitoring the speed of traffic in the fast lane in the critical area downstream. If the speed falls below a limit, the algorithm will request a red signal to be shown on the onramp, thereby adding a feedback loop to what is otherwise feedforward control.

A local feedback control law, known as ALINEA, has been derived as part of DRIVE project CHRISTIANE [26]. Since the main aim of ramp metering is to maintain capacity flow downstream of the merge area, control could be based entirely on downstream measurements, if the response is not significantly lagged. Feedback control reacts to actual traffic conditions in order to avoid or eliminate congestion. The ALINEA strategy requires only one detector station, which measures the occupancy downstream of the merge area. When the occupancy rate is found to be higher than desired, the onramp flow is decreased, and vice versa. A cycle time of 40 seconds can be used for the ramp signals.

Sequential ramp metering has been implemented on the Hanshin Expressway in Japan with the aim of dissolving congestion as quickly as possible [27]. The strategy involves the closure of onramps successively away from the point of congestion in an upstream direction. Criteria to decide when and how many ramps should be closed or limited are derived from offline analyses and simulations. According to the criteria derived, the traffic control system indicates where and when sequential ramp closure should start.

Coordinated feedback control on the basis of linear quadratic (LQ) optimization theory underlies the METALINE strategies being developed by the CHRISTIANE project [24]. One strategy, the LQ regulator, is a generalization of the ALINEA strategy. The second strategy, the LQI regulator, seeks to eliminate the deviation of selected bottleneck densities from their desired values by modifying the onramp flows. Both approaches lead to similar results in the simulation tests, although the LQI regulator is judged to be more applicable in the case of the Boulevard Peripherique (the Paris ring road).

The SIRTAKI coordinated feedforward control strategy, also being developed in the CHRISTIANE project, is built around the SIMAUT simulation model [28]. Control in the event of an unexpected incident is aided by the model's ability to reconstruct in real time the current traffic situation. A form of coordinated feedforward control is also operated on the Hanshin Expressway in Japan. A linear programming solution to the control problem is sought in which the flow of traffic at every onramp of the expressway is controlled in order to maximize the total number of incoming cars without causing any congestion on any section of the expressway [29].

Key to the satisfactory functioning of the feedback regulators as developed by the CHRISTIANE project is the determination of the optimal densities. These may be specified as the solution to an optimization problem. The optimal densities will depend on the demand at the onramps, the OD composition of the demand, any blockages, and any VMS indications. Hence, a *trilevel control strategy* could be adopted whereby demand, its OD composition, and any reductions in network capacity are estimated (the *adaptation layer*), optimum densities are recalculated when traffic conditions have changed sufficiently (the *optimization layer*), and finally the ramp signals are controlled to keep measured densities close to their optimal values (the *direct control layer*). This configuration is shown in Figure 3.4.

While local ramp metering systems have been used very successfully, attention is now focused on coordinated ramp metering. System designers will therefore have to consider the estimation of OD flows (*OD estimation*) and their assignment to the network (*dynamic assignment*). A major issue is the degree of controllability that can be achieved where the highway entrances and exits are not directly meterable.

A problem with the implementation of ramp metering is the absence in many cases of sufficient onramp capacity to store traffic during periods of peak demand. To prevent blocking back (the blocking of junctions on the approach to the onramp), override strategies can be implemented, which generally involve releasing excess traffic onto the already congested highway. A more satisfactory approach is to limit access to the ramp through urban traffic signal control. The excess demand is thereby distributed across the network, avoiding blocking back.

3.3.3 Variable-Message Signs

VMSs can give the motorist information, advice, or instructions. Given an incident, there are differing philosophies as to what should be conveyed to the driver. It could be argued that explanation through pictograms aids system credibility. On the other hand, advice rather than explanation may reduce the variation of driver response. It is thought that variation in speed among vehicles is an important risk factor. In addition to inducing appropriate driver behavior under different circumstances (incident, fog, ice, congestion, etc.), VMSs may also be used to limit access to lanes through the use of arrows and crosses. Gantry-mounted signs may therefore be used in tidal flow systems. Highway

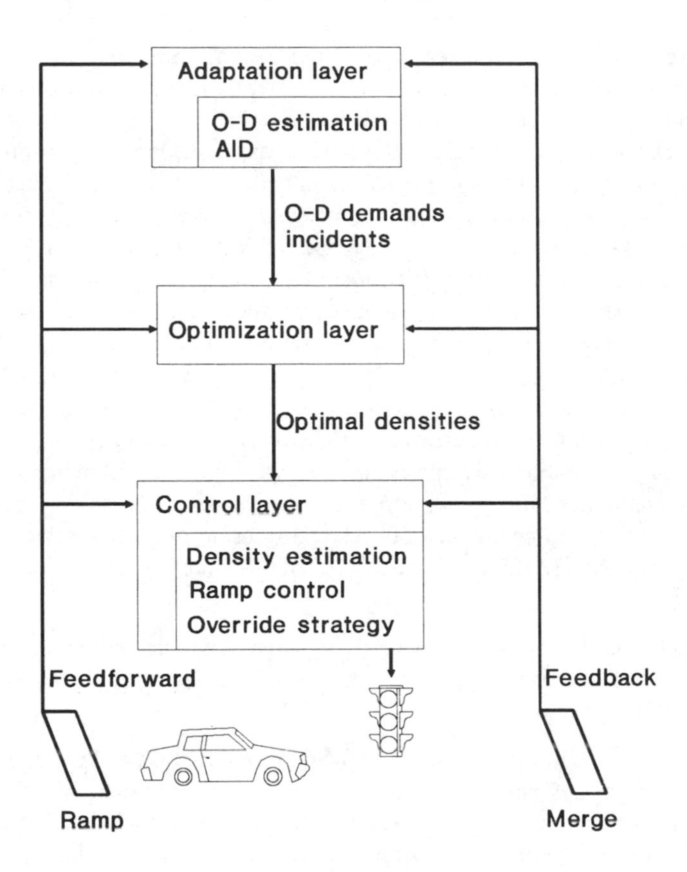

Figure 3.4 The trilevel control strategy.

control and signaling systems are increasingly being found on heavily trafficked urban highways. This involves the installation of gantry-mounted signs as well as vehicle detectors in each lane at regular intervals along the highway. Usually, as in the case of the MCSS, an incident detection algorithm is implemented, either locally in roadside stations or centrally in a traffic computer, or both.

3.4 INTEGRATION WITH DYNAMIC ROUTE GUIDANCE

Another way to improve traffic efficiency is to supply the driver with better information about the state of traffic. Of particular interest here is dynamic route guidance. One of the first systems of this kind, the ALI-SCOUT system of Siemens (the latest version is referred to as EURO-SCOUT and is described in detail in Chapter 4), has been the subject of a pilot project in Berlin. Communication with guided vehicles occurs via beacons located next to the signal heads and a two-way infrared link. Guided vehicles measure link travel times, which are returned to the central computer via the beacons in a so-called *vehicle telegram*. In this way, a centrally maintained database of link travel times at different times of the day and on different days is continually updated.

In EURO-SCOUT, the functions of database management and optimal route computation are performed centrally. At present, decentralized systems are also under investigation. Each junction controller can, in principle, monitor the link travel times on the adjoining links, either directly through the vehicle telegrams or indirectly through the vehicle detector data and the traffic model used in signal optimization. Through dialogue between adjacent junction controllers, news about congestion in the network may be disseminated, leading to modifications to route recommendations.

The DRIVE project CAR-GOES (also discussed in Chapter 4) investigated the integration of dynamic route guidance with network control, the data requirements of which overlap substantially. Moreover, the two systems interact. Route recommendations can influence the optimal signal plans, while the implemented signal plans can influence the route recommendations. Therefore, an integration of the two systems is desirable to pool observations, to counteract any instability or any negative effects of feedback, and to improve overall performance. In CAR-GOES, three levels of integration have been identified:

- Exchange of observations leading to improved state estimation;
- The feedback of the outputs of one system as inputs to the other, and vice versa;
- Complete integration.

The possible integration of the EURO-SCOUT dynamic route guidance system from Siemens with a Siemens form of network control is discussed in more detail in Bell et al. [30]. For each link in a guidance network, a guided vehicle can in principle determine the position and time of the first stop as well as the duration of the stop. With knowledge of the stage times, it is possible to derive estimates of the average arrival rate and the average saturation flow (or, more precisely, the cumulative arrivals and departures; see Figure 3.5) on the assumption that the first stop is to join a queue caused by the traffic signals. These parameters are of use for network control. In the other direction, the network control system can estimate average waiting times on particular links and, therefore, through knowledge of average free flow speeds and link lengths, estimate average travel times. Link travel times are of course required by dynamic route guidance. By combining the observations in this way, it is possible to improve the quality of state estimation for both systems, where the state variables are queue lengths, arrival rates, service rates, and travel times.

A complete integration requires the prediction of total travel demand, its distribution between origins and destinations, and its assignment to the road (and nonroad) networks. The assignment must be dynamic, in that the time dependency of link travel time is considered, and must distinguish between guided and unguided vehicles. A complete integration probably requires some form of rolling horizon approach. Figure 3.6 indicates the nature of the information flows under high-level integration. There are two databases—

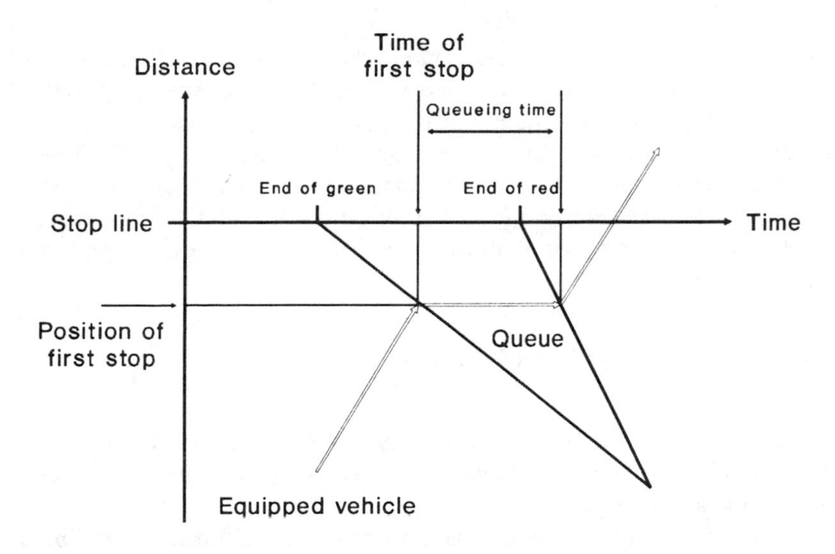

Figure 3.5 Cumulative arrivals and departures.

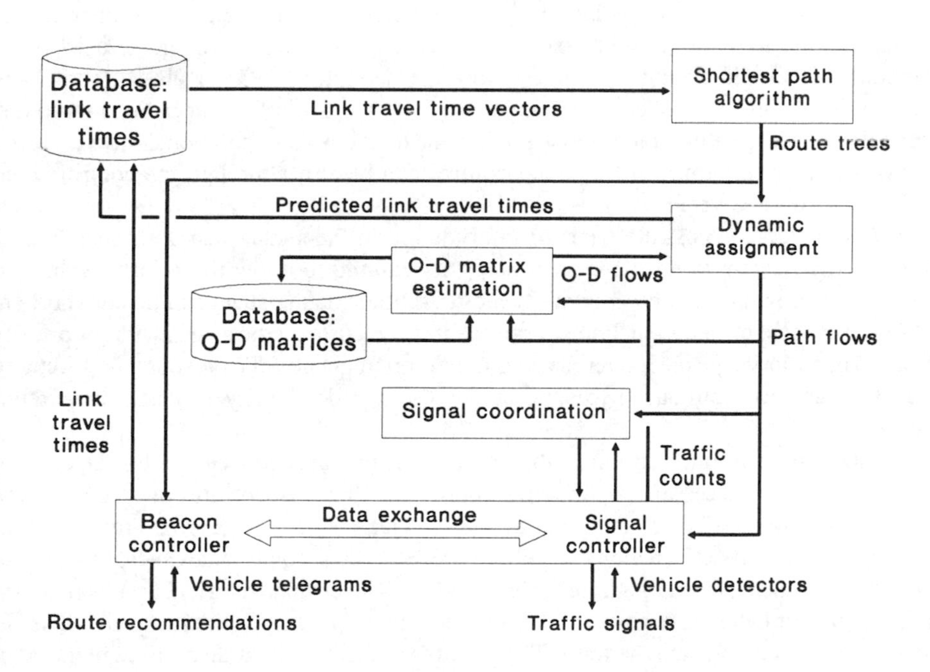

Figure 3.6 Information flows under high-level integration.

link travel times and origin-destination demands—that are updated on the basis of information received from the vehicle telegrams and vehicle detectors. Analogous to the Frank-Wolfe algorithm for finding an equilibrium assignment, the fastest path trees built for route guidance define the *direction* in which traffic will reassign itself. The extent to which unguided vehicles move to the fastest routes will depend on the speed with which information is disseminated, which in turn can be represented as a *learning curve*; guided drivers will know the fastest path at all times (at least in principle).

3.5 INTEGRATION WITH PUBLIC TRANSPORT

Increasingly in the U.K. and elsewhere, priority is required for public transport within signal control. This needs either selective detection or a monitoring system incorporating automatic vehicle locationing (AVL).

Selective detection occurs when a bus or a tram reaches the detector. The detector must lie sufficiently upstream to allow an effective intervention in the signal plan, but not so far upstream that a reliable estimate of the arrival time of the bus or tram at the stop line is no longer possible. Passenger stops near the stop line lead to particular difficulties. In the case of AVL, the vehicle determines its own location either through the measurement of wheel revolutions (the odometer) with the help of the opening and closing of the doors or location devices (short-range beacons or interactive loops) to counteract the accumulation of errors or through satellites (GPS) or else through radio beacons. The vehicle is polled on a regular basis by the control center using a radio data channel, providing information about its current location and operational status. Access to this locational information for signal control can be either through the control center or directly from the vehicle.

In practice, the possible types of intervention in the signal plan are rather limited. When a small extension of the current stage is required to allow the priority vehicle to pass the junction, this can be granted. If required, the existing stage can be cut short and the relevant stage recalled. Such interventions impose costs on the stages without priority, which may be unacceptable if interventions occur too frequently. To prevent this, additional rules are generally introduced to suppress or downgrade priority in particular circumstances.

Since frequent intervention in the signal plan probably reduces performance more than is absolutely necessary, optimizing approaches that respect priorities are of great interest. The first system of this kind is the UTOPIA system in Turin. From the tram monitoring system, each junction controller receives, 120 seconds in advance, information about the imminent arrival of a tram at the stop line. The estimated arrival time is regularly updated up until the tram has actually passed the stop line. Optimal signal plans are calculated to accommodate the tram. The result is control without disruptive intervention and with less cost imposed on the stages without priority.

3.6 CONCLUSIONS

The trend to more decentralized traffic control systems will continue, increasing the degree of parallelism in the processing and reducing the susceptibility to catastrophic failure. The discrete time, rolling horizon approach to signal control allows great flexibility regarding system architecture and priority to public transport. However, this approach to signal control is unlikely to prevail in the short to medium term.

While enhancements to traffic signal control techniques should increase system flexibility and performance, it is becoming clear that traffic control alone cannot solve congestion problems. Through technological developments, integrated solutions are becoming increasingly attractive.

One way to improve traffic efficiency is through the provision of better information to trip makers, particularly route recommendations through collective and individual route guidance. An integration of dynamic route guidance and traffic control can improve the reliability and performance of both. Through appropriate traffic signal timings, the negative side effects of dynamic route guidance can to some extent be reduced without departing from the principle of user optimization. However, with higher levels of integration in congested networks, some form of dynamic-assignment model is required in order to spread traffic across multiple routes.

Another way to improve traffic efficiency is through priority to public transport. The advent of AVL systems for buses and trams not only enables more effective priority to be given in traffic signal control, but also offers the same sort of potential for data exchange as is offered by dynamic route guidance. The potential benefit for traffic control offered by buses acting as moving observers of traffic conditions is currently under investigation by the author.

REFERENCES

[1] Versavel, J., F. Lemaire, and D. van der Stede, ''Camera and Computer Aided Traffic Sensor,'' *Proc. IEE 2nd Int. Conf. on Road Traffic Monitoring*, London, 1989.

[2] Michalopoulos, P. G., R. D. Jacobson, C. A. Anderson, and J. C. Barbaresso, ''Field Deployment of Autoscope in the FAST-TRAC ATMS/ATIS Programme,'' *Traffic Engineering & Control*, Vol. 33, 1992, pp. 475–483.

[3] Lowrie, P. R., ''The Sydney Coordinated Adaptive Traffic System—Principles, Methodology, Algorithms,'' *Proc. 1st Int. Conf. on Road Traffic Control*, London, 1982, pp. 67–70.

[4] Rourke, A., and M. G. H. Bell, ''Queue Detection and Congestion Monitoring Using Image Processing,'' *Traffic Engineering and Control*, Vol. 32, No. 9, 1991, pp. 412–421.

[5] Hoose, N., *Computer Image Processing in Traffic Engineering*, Research Studies Press Series in Traffic Engineering, Taunton, Somerset, 1991.

[6] Henry, J. J., J. L. Farges, J. Tuffal, ''The PRODYN Real Time Traffic Algorithm,'' *4th IFAC-IFIP-IFORS Conf. on Control in Transportation System*, Baden-Baden, 1983.

[7] Mauro, V., C. Di Taranto, ''UTOPIA,'' *6th IFAC-IFIP-IFORS Conf. on Control, Computers, Communications in Transport*, Paris, 1989.

[8] Bell, M. G. H., ''Vehicle Responsive Traffic Signal Control,'' *Mathematics in Transport Planning and Control*, J. D. Griffiths, ed., Oxford: Oxford University Press, 1992.

[9] Bell, M. G. H., "A Probabilistic Approach to Optimisation of Traffic Signal Settings in Discrete Time," *Proc. 11th Int. Symp. on Transportation and Traffic Theory*, Yokohama, 1990.

[10] Brookes, D., and M. G. H. Bell, "Expected Delay and Stop Calculation for Discrete Time Adaptive Traffic Signal Control," *Highway Capacity and Level of Service*, U. Brannolte, ed., Rotterdam: Balkema, 1991.

[11] Hunt, P. B., D. I. Robertson, R. D. Bretherton, and R. J. Winton, "SCOOT—A Traffic Responsive Method of Coordinating Signals," TRRL Laboratory Report LR 1014, 1981.

[12] Vincent, R. A., and J. R. Peirce, "MOVA: Traffic Responsive, Self-Optimising Control for Isolated Intersections," TRRL Research Report LR 170, 1988.

[13] Peterson, A., T. Bergh, and K. Steen, "LHOVRA—A New Traffic Signal Control Strategy for Isolated Junctions," *Proc. 2nd Int. Conf. on Road Traffic Control*, London, 1986, pp. 98–101.

[14] Robertson, D. I., "TRANSYT—A Traffic Network Study Tool," TRRL Laboratory Report LR 253, 1969.

[15] Böttger, R., "Moderne Steuerungsverfahren mit Dezentraler Wirkungsweise," *Grünlicht*, Ausgabe 27, 1989, pp. 5–11.

[16] Papageorgiou, M., "A Hierarchical Control System for Freeway Traffic," *Transportation Research*, Vol. 17B, 1983, pp. 251–261.

[17] Levin, M., and M. Krause, "A Probabilistic Approach to Incident Detection on Freeways," *Traffic Engineering & Control*, Vol. 20, 1979, pp. 107–109.

[18] Payne, H. J., and H. C. Tignor, "Freeway Incident Detection Algorithms Based on Decision Trees With States," *Transportation Research Record*, Vol. 682, 1978, 30–37.

[19] Collins, J. F., "Automatic Incident Detection—Experience With TRRL Algorithm HIOCC," TRRL Supplementary Report 775, 1983.

[20] Ahmed, S. A., and A. R. Cook, "Point Process Models for Freeway Incident Detection," *Proc. 8th Int. Symp. on Transportation and Traffic Theory*, Toronto, 20–30 June 1981.

[21] Busch, F., and M. Fellendorf, "Automatic Incident Detection on Highways," *Traffic Engineering & Control*, April 1990, pp. 221–227.

[22] Dudek, C. L., G. D. Weaver, G. P. Ritch, and C. J. Messer, "Detecting Freeway Incidents Under Low Volume Conditions," *Transportation Research Record*, Vol. 533, 1975, pp. 34–47.

[23] Bang, K. L., "Incident Detection in Europe," *Proc. Int. Symp. on Traffic Control Systems*, Berkeley, 1979.

[24] Hadj-Salem, H., A. Graham, and F. Middelham, "Field Trials Results of Ramp Metering Strategies," *Advanced Telematics in Road Transport*, Brussels: CEC, 1991, pp. 543–560.

[25] Keen, K. G., M. J. Schofield, and G. C. Hay, "Ramp Metering Access Control on M6 Motorway, *Proc. 2nd Int. Conf. on Road Traffic Control, Inst. of Electrical Engineers*, April 1986, pp. 39–42.

[26] Hadj-Salem, H., J. M. Blosseville, and M. Papageorgiou, "ALINEA: A Local Feedback Law for On-Ramp Metering; a Real-Life Study," *Proc. 3rd Int. Conf. on Road Traffic Control, Inst. of Electrical Engineers*, May 1990, pp. 194–198.

[27] Hasegawa, T., "Traffic Control Systems in Japan," *Research and Directions in Computer Control of Urban Traffic Systems*, American Society of Civil Engineers, 1979.

[28] Morin, J. M., M. Papageorgiou, H. Hadj-Salem, J. C. Pierrelee, and J. F. Gabard, "Validation Results of Traffic Flow Modelling on Linear Highways," *Advanced Telematics in Road Transport*, Brussels: CEC, 1991, pp. 981–1006.

[29] Sasaki, T., and S. Myojin, "Theory of Inflow on an Urban Expressway System, *Trans. Japanese Society of Civil Engineers*, Vol. 160, Dec. 1968.

[30] Bell, M. G. H., F. Busch, and G. Heymann, "Strategies for Integrating Dynamic Route Guidance and Traffic Control Systems," *Proc. 24th ISATA Int. Symp. on RTI/IVHS*, Florence, 1991, pp. 343–350.

Chapter 4
Cooperative Transport Management with EURO-SCOUT

Heinz Sodeikat

This chapter describes a new way to improve traffic conditions by introducing interactive dynamic route guidance (DRG) and driver information (DI). A DRG system guides every road user to his or her destination over the best route, taking the current traffic situation into account. See Figure 4.1(a,b).

4.1 DYNAMIC GUIDANCE BY INDIVIDUAL INFORMATION AND LINKAGE WITH OTHER SERVICES

4.1.1 Dynamic Route Guidance Over Time-Optimized Routes

DRG has had a successful three-year field trial in West Berlin. The vehicle has a navigation system on board consisting of a magnetic field sensor for the direction, a wheel sensor for the covered distance, and a navigation computer. It therefore always knows where it is and in which direction it is pointing. The only requirement of drivers is to enter their personal destination and to push the START button. They then receive visual and audible guidance recommendations that are clear and unequivocal and do not distract drivers from the task of driving. On the contrary, they help drivers concentrate better on the traffic because it is left to the system to select the route.

Principle of Operation

The vehicle receives the guidance recommendations in the form of a data package every time it passes a roadside infrared transceiver (i.e., an infrared beacon). The beacons receive

Figure 4.1(a) Interactive dynamic traffic management

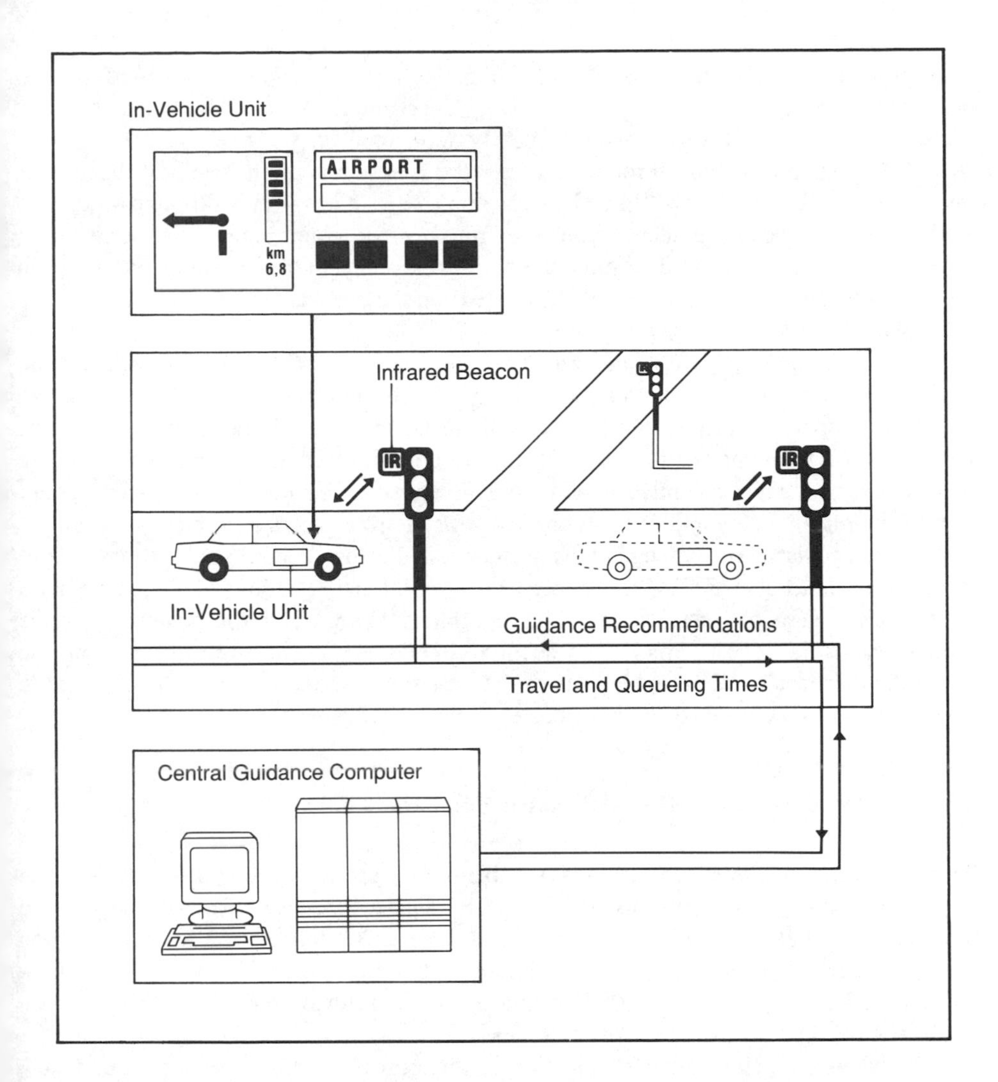

Figure 4.1(b) Interactive dynamic traffic management.

the data to be transmitted from a central guidance computer to which they are connected via cable. The vehicle is "forwarded" from beacon to beacon until the last one before its destination, where it selects only guidance information up to a "departure point"—the end of guidance mode. From here on, the vehicle navigates autonomously (i.e., in a compass mode). A simple arrow on the display indicates the direction of the destination. This autonomous mode is also used when starting a journey (i.e., before the first beacon contact has taken place). If several vehicles with different destinations now pass a beacon, all of them receive the same data package. Each vehicle then filters out the data relevant to its programed destination. The remaining data are rejected. Thus, it is ensured that the destination entered at the start of the journey does not leave the vehicle and that the guidance procedure will take place completely anonymously.

The basic recommended route is always the fastest. Variations can be "the correct one" (e.g., for heavy trucks), "the cheapest one" (e.g., during vacation), and so on. To achieve this, the central guidance computer must perform substantial computing work. Every five minutes it has to determine the shortest distance in time between every origin (beacon) and every destination (destination area) on the basis of arriving real-time traffic data. See Figure 4.2.

The real-time traffic data consist of journey and congestion times for each route section that the vehicles transmit to the central guidance computer via the infrared beacons. This is also done completely anonymously. Transfer of the guidance information to the vehicles and transmission of journey and congestion times back to the control center take place completely independently of each other. Even if a destination is not entered, every vehicle supplies journey and congestion times for the route sections it passes through.

Since guidance recommendations are generated in one central guidance computer, direct interventions in traffic occurrences are possible. By guiding equipped vehicles appropriately, parts of traffic flows can be distributed, shifted, and, for example, diverted around residential zones, schools, and hospitals. Thus, the public authorities responsible for traffic management are provided with an outstanding resource for asserting their traffic policies without the need for prohibitions and unpopular restrictions.

4.1.2 Dynamic Alternative (Modal Split): P&R and Public Transport

Nevertheless, how should drivers, arriving from the outside, reach a destination in the city if all access routes are congested or no parking places are available in the destination area, or the city had to be closed to traffic due to smog? In this case, it is only common sense that the destination can best be reached if drivers are guided to a favorable park and ride (P&R) location, where they change to public railway transport. Such a system is already planned in several European cities.

However, which of the P&R locations is the best one, which line should be taken, at what intervals do trains leave, and how long will the journey take when using public transport? The system provides the answer to all these questions and offers it to the driver as an *alternative* in the event that the programed destination cannot be reached by car within a reasonable time or if additional problems, such as a lack of parking spaces, have cropped up. This public transport or modal split alternative is generated as a function of the destination by referring to the electronic timetable file provided by the public transport companies.

If the alternative is accepted by the driver, the originally programed destination will be substituted by the most favorable P&R location (i.e., drivers will dynamically be guided to it). On the basis of the displayed public transport information, the journey can then be

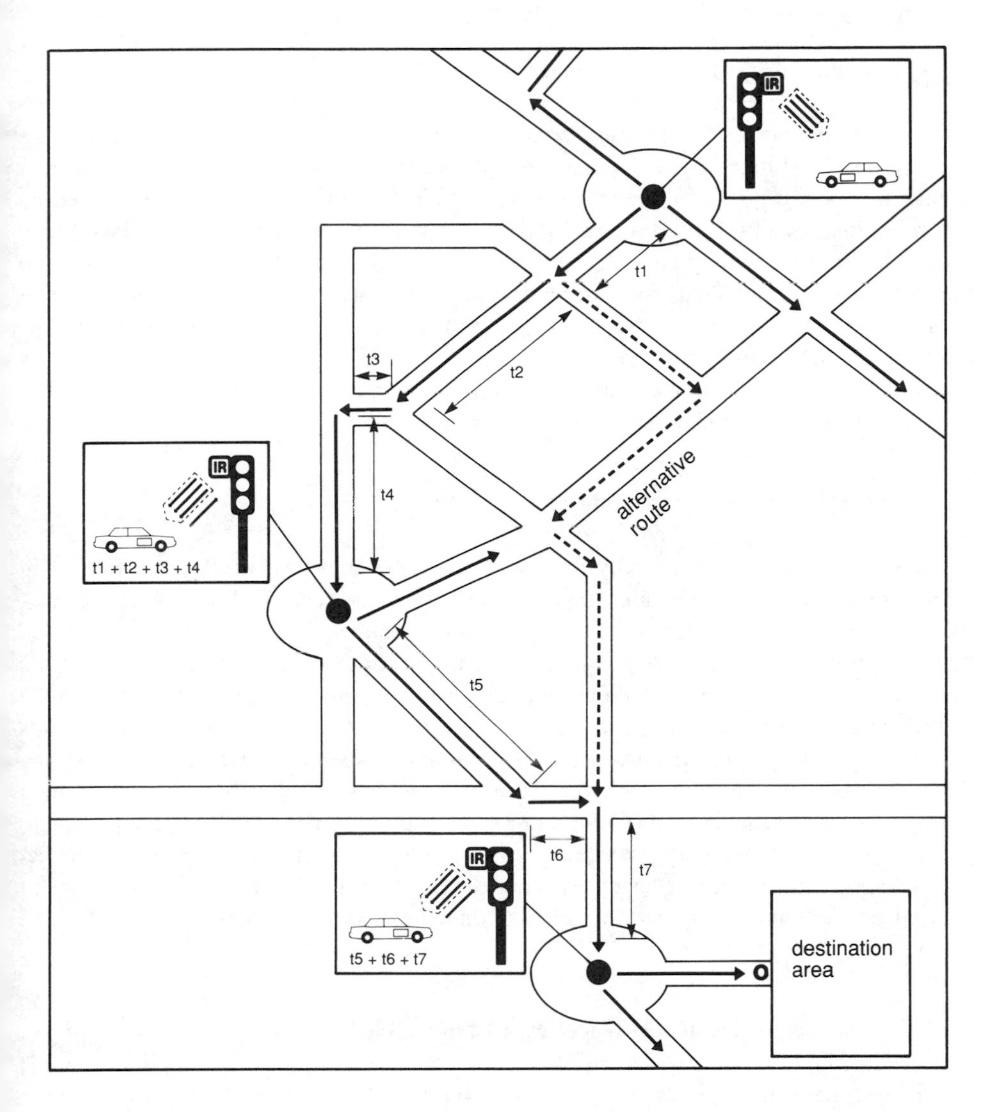

Figure 4.2 Dynamic route guidance—principle of operation (vectors show shortest route in time at a given moment. Travel times $t_1 \ldots t_7$ are sent back as "traffic probe data").

continued easily. The in-vehicle-unit (not bigger than a spectacle case) can be removed from the vehicle and taken along. It serves as an electronic memory for all steps to be performed (e.g., changes). This alternative is particularly interesting with regard to outer and innercity traffic in European cities with centers that have grown historically. Individually tailored guidance recommendations will hopefully induce more drivers to leave their vehicles outside the city and make use of public transport.

4.1.3 Trip Planning—Future Service

The central guidance computer can elaborate time-optimized guidance recommendations because historical data concerning standard journey times (patterns) exist for each five-minute time slot per section of a route. This historical knowledge is either confirmed by incoming journey times or corrected by them for the next two hours. By accessing this traffic database (e.g., through interactive videotex), it is not only possible to determine the most expedient moments for starting a journey (i.e., when the total journey time is at its minimum), but time comparisons with other means of transport can also be made, thus enabling the selection of the most expedient one before beginning the journey. Such a method of trip planning allows temporal distribution of traffic, the third method of distribution after spatial and modal distribution.

4.1.4 Dynamic Parking Management

Many car parks nowadays already monitor their occupancy and display the figures in various locations within a city area (e.g., car park 5, free spaces: 27). If the data pertaining to all car parks within a guidance area are now combined in a car park database and historical occupancy patterns established (i.e., the occupancy of each car park per time interval), parking spaces can be allocated to destination areas dynamically by coupling the central guidance and the central parking management computers. Anticipated occupancies derived from the parking patterns will allow optimum use of available parking space. Dynamic route guidance and dynamic parking management services can be performed through the same beacons or different ones. In the case of dynamic parking management, public authorities have again excellent means of displacing traffic flows. For instance, car parks located in areas of lower traffic density can be allocated during peak hours to prevent traffic approaching car parks worsening the situation in particularly congested arterials.

4.1.5 Urban Goods Transport (Fleet Management)

Nowadays, many haulage companies have computers to optimize their delivery tours. Particular significance is attached to optimum sequence of cargos. That is to say, for a tour to A, B, C, D, and E, the cargo must be loaded in the sequence E, D, B, C, A. Up to now, the tour including the unloading points A, B, C, D, and E has always been combined according to the shortest routes from A to B, B to C, and so on, which need not necessarily signify a route that is optimal in relation to time. By coupling the central guidance computer to the delivery tour computer, haulage contractors are able to select the most favorable time for each section of a route—a kind of trip planning. That is to say, the tour can be optimized in relation to a minimum overall journey time and other obstacles, such as prohibited stopping at certain times of day. This might lead to a completely different delivery sequence (e.g., A, E, C, B, D). By exploiting this process, haulage contractors will save time. Moreover, the traffic is relieved because goods delivery traffic, indispensable to a city, is distributed in such a way that it causes the least possible additional congestion.

4.1.6 Hazard Reports

As soon as roads are equipped with sensors (e.g., for black ice, fog, or rain), the resulting signals can be collected in a hazard reporting database and, by coupling with the central guidance computer, can be transmitted together with the guidance recommendations to vehicles approaching the danger zone. This would be an automatic warning service. Warnings through other vehicles are also possible. For example, if oncoming drivers have seen an accident, they can report it to the next beacon along with their current position by pressing the accident key. All vehicles approaching the accident site then receive the appropriate warning. Whether hazard reports are only transmitted together with guidance data through the route guidance beacons or are also transmitted through special hazard-reporting beacons (such as those situated at the highway emergency call points) is a question for the organization or system design. Both solutions are possible from the technical point of view.

4.1.7 Tourist Information

This may include diverse information concerning, for example, hotels, restaurants, places of interest, the police, hospitals, and pharmacies. The corresponding data packages are transmitted at the entries to towns or at important intersections, but are only displayed on request.

4.2 COLLECTIVE INFORMATION

4.2.1 Variable-Message Signs

The advantage of VMSs placed above roadways is that their information is seen by all road users. They represent collective dynamic traffic control. However, collectivity also involves a disadvantage, particularly when dealing with variable routing information. Many drivers think that such signs "only apply to others." Furthermore, the information content of VMSs is very limited, owing to the short viewing time involved. VMSs are controlled by stationary sensors (e.g., induction loops fitted in the road surface, the installation of which is generally rather costly). However, they must also receive information from areas into which the traffic flows. VMSs can only be supplied with this necessary traffic data *at reasonable cost* by using real-time data from the central guidance computer.

On the other hand, data obtained from induction loops can also be used for individual guidance of vehicles. This is particularly useful at the beginning, when vehicles equipped with in-vehicle units still account for less than 1% of the total and, therefore, only restricted dynamic guidance is possible. For instance, in the three-year large-scale LISB trial in Berlin, measurements from double induction loops on the urban highway were converted to journey times and evaluated as such.

4.2.2 Traffic-Signal Installations

Traffic-signal installations also perform collective traffic control. Stationary sensors and controllers already control green stages at important intersections. Such installations are called urban traffic control in Europe and advanced traffic management systems in the United States.

The journey and congestion times transmitted to the central guidance computer will be very helpful in optimizing traffic control. This was one of the largest work areas within DRIVE: V1011—CAR-GOES, "Integration of traffic control and traffic guidance."

Traffic control systems are already well established throughout the European Community. Taking current knowledge and experience from the ALI-SCOUT system in Berlin (LISB)—the only active DRG system in Europe—into account, V1011 has provided the necessary analysis of users' requirements and focused on strategies of integration in order to maximize the benefits through both UTC and DRG. But there are problems that have to be treated when integrating these two systems:

- Guidance and control strategies have to be balanced continuously against each other to ensure a proper, noncontradictive behavior of the integrated system.
- As different measurement methods are used by each system, differences and overlapping data will exist. Whereas the standard measurement equipment of traffic control systems is the inductive loop (or a comparable method), the DRG system uses the cars themselves as sensors (floating car measurement). UTC is based on data complete over the vehicle population, but not over space (only at specific parts of the network), DRG systems are based on data complete over space, but not over the vehicle population (only a proportion of all vehicles in the system are using DRG equipment). It is therefore important to combine these two kinds of data and to ensure their consistency.
- The penetration rate (percentage of vehicles with DRG equipment) induces some other problems: When deciding about the next control steps, the control strategy has to take into account the percentage of traffic volume reacting to guidance recommendations. The stablility of overall system control is therefore strongly related to the penetration rate.
- A good representation of the current as well as the expected traffic situation is extremly important for the proper action of the integrated guidance and control strategy. The reaction of drivers to traffic signals is assumed to be known exactly,

whereas the acceptance of route guidance recommendations in a specific situation will vary. This individual driver behavior induces some additional uncertainty in the database. The traffic models and forecasting algorithms used within the control algorithm have to take this uncertainty into account.

- Since it is not possible to store all traffic and control data in one central database—for practical reasons related to different system architectures and piecemeal system introduction—it is important to find effective solutions for data handling in distributed systems. The main part of this task is the definition of common data structures and access modes for the integrated traffic management system.

The research and development work was accompanied by an investigation of the behavioral and ergonomic aspects of route guidance, leading to clearer understanding of user requirements. The performance of different levels of integration has been studied, principally by simulation, for various types of DRG, ranging from centralized to distributed, and UTC, ranging from fixed-time to traffic-responsive. Some attention has been given to multirouting, which would be required with increasing rates of market penetration. The prediction of link travel times was looked at, as was the need for dynamic assignment and the estimation of OD flows required by high levels of market penetration. This work has resulted in a coherent set of recommendations for system design.

4.2.3 Methods, Advantages, and Problems of Integration

As there are many different traffic control policies and philosophies, the number of existing control systems is high. It will therefore not be possible to develop a unique management system integrating all control measures. Specific forms of an integrated system will be necessary that take into account the management philosophy followed by local authorities. In general, it is possible to distinguish between three levels of integration (see Figure 4.3). The improvements to traffic control, which are made possible by the additional use of DRG information and by linking the two systems together, are to be seen in different areas. Generally, the main advantage is the replacement of estimates by real measurements; the unknown, or at least very roughly estimated, OD behavior.

4.3 AREAS OF COOPERATION

4.3.1 Database Integration

The previous sections have already shown the advantages to be had by sharing data between different databases. The central database in Figure 4.4 is a computer network in which large quantities of data specific to individual services are exchanged between computers. Each of these computers, some of which already exist and others of which still have to be installed, retain their independent nature. This is the only practical solution from the point of view of legal responsibilities and divisional interests. Figure 4.4 schemati-

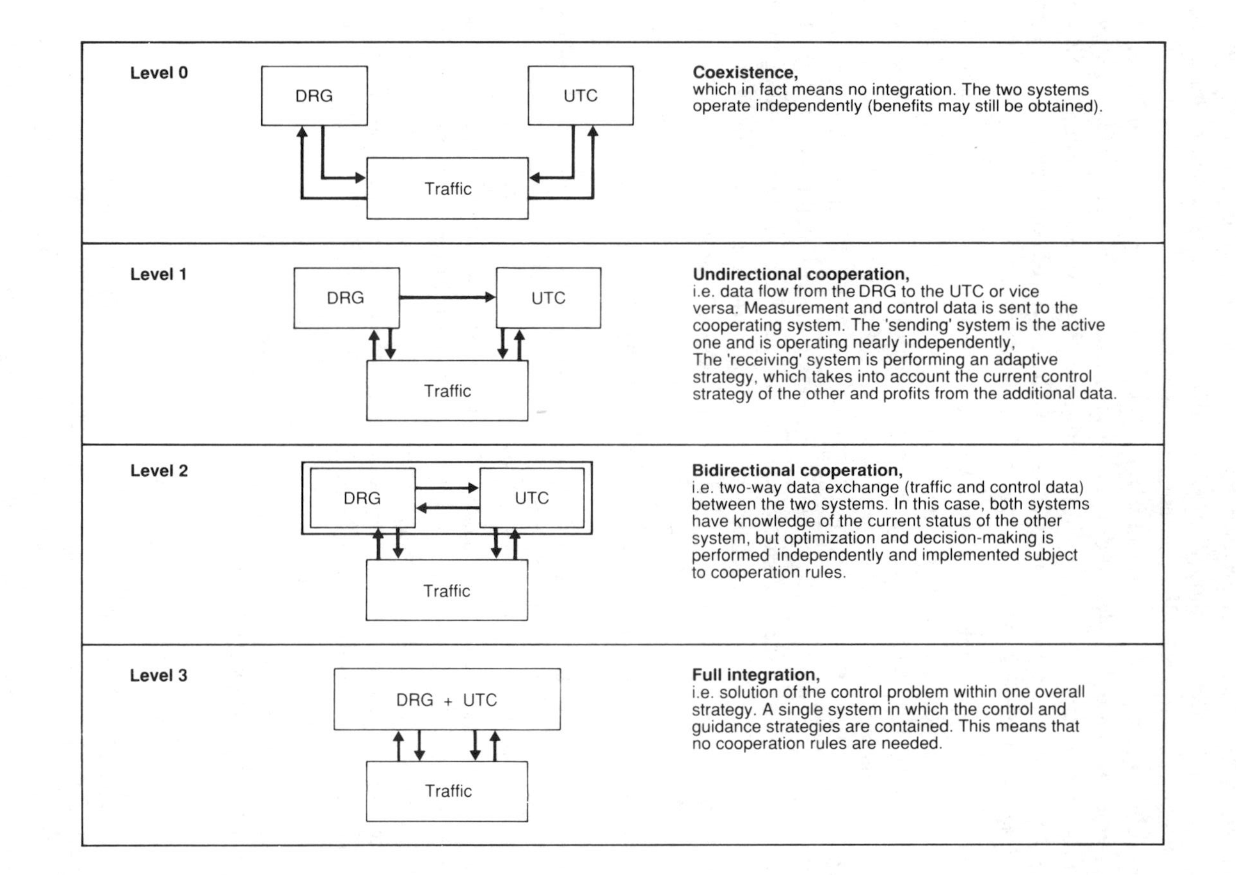

Figure 4.3 Integration levels of dynamic route guidance and urban traffic control.

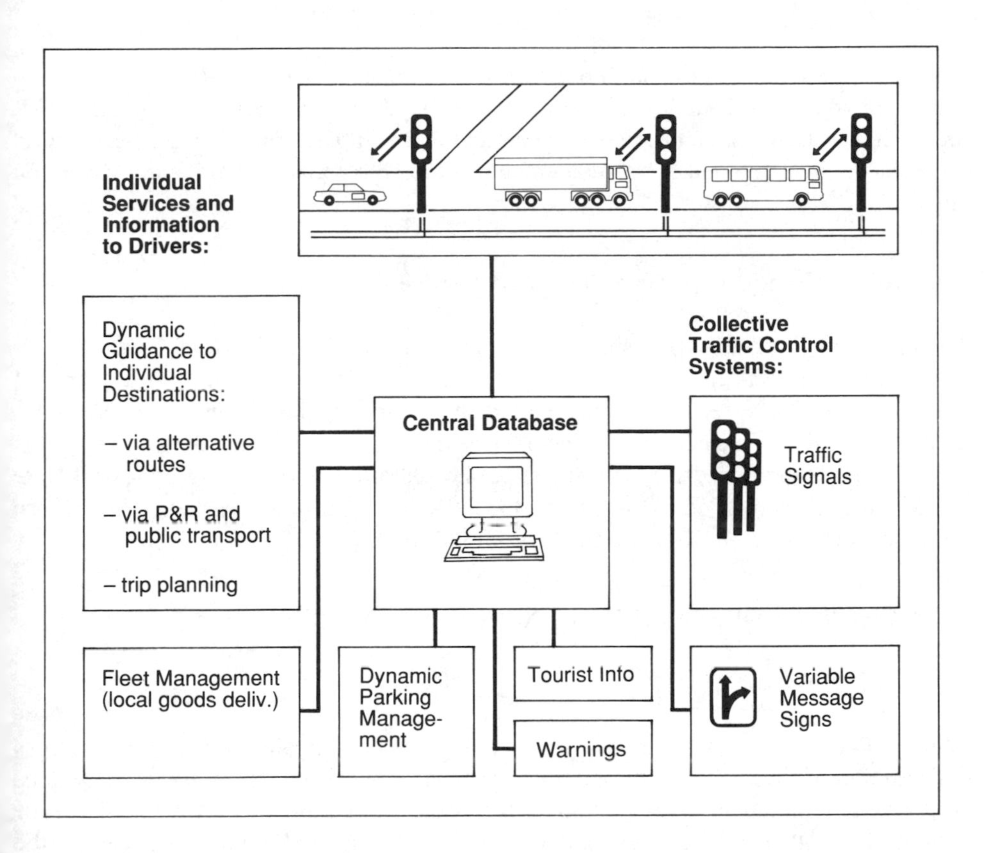

Figure 4.4 Integration of services and systems.

cally depicts how all relevant guidance computers and databases are coupled to each other.

4.3.2 Extraurban and Urban Traffic

Data coordination between the traffic situations inside the city and on the approach roads is essential. This exchange of data is not only a technical problem, it is also an administrative coordination problem. Traffic does not respect city, municipality, or national borders. Unfortunately, public authorities do. Therefore, they must cooperate in order to enable large-area system planning and its realization. Every attempt to go one's own way reduces some of the system's overall advantages.

4.3.3 Road Traffic and Public Transport

The dynamic alternative of P&R and public transport has been described. This cooperation between road traffic and public transport does not pose any real technical problems.

However, traffic authorities and public transport companies must collaborate closely and ensure that the crucial linking element between both, namely adequately situated P&R areas, are created and administered. Cooperation between road traffic and public transport represents a great challenge, but also embodies great potential for improving the traffic situation.

4.3.4 Regional and Local Authorities and Service Companies

The previous discussions have shown that there is a need for multilateral cooperation if we wish to be successful in the battle against total traffic breakdown. Coordinating all the different partners, such as regional and local authorities with extremely diverse tasks, as well as service companies and industrial enterprises, is a huge management task. This cannot be done successfully by any single public authority, institution, or company. Here we need the structure of an independent cooperative traffic management company, whose sole task is to create and manage such a complex system.

4.4 MUNICH COOPERATIVE TRANSPORT MANAGEMENT

4.4.1 POLIS Initiative

With DRIVE I, Europe has undertaken the attempt to perform joint traffic research across national borders. DRIVE II will put cities together with similar concepts for field trails. In the POLIS initiative, cities presented their concept of how they wish to solve their local traffic problems. Within the framework of this initiative, Munich has presented the concept depicted in Figure 4.5 and is currently cooperating with Amsterdam, Lyon, London, and Dublin, some of which having similar concepts.

4.4.2 Status of the Project

A feasibility study, ''Cooperative Transport Management for the City and Region of Munich,'' has been established. The whole project started in 1992. In a pilot area (north sector), existing technologies will first be linked together and new services will be experimented. ECC funds shall enhance R & D works. However, this pilot area is not only an experiment. It should already be the first step to an overall operational system.

4.4.3 Financing Model

Owing to the shortage of funds, realization of such a project may be very long and the imminent breakdown of traffic will have become reality. To avoid this, the model of mixed public/private financing appears to be expedient, in which case the following ideas

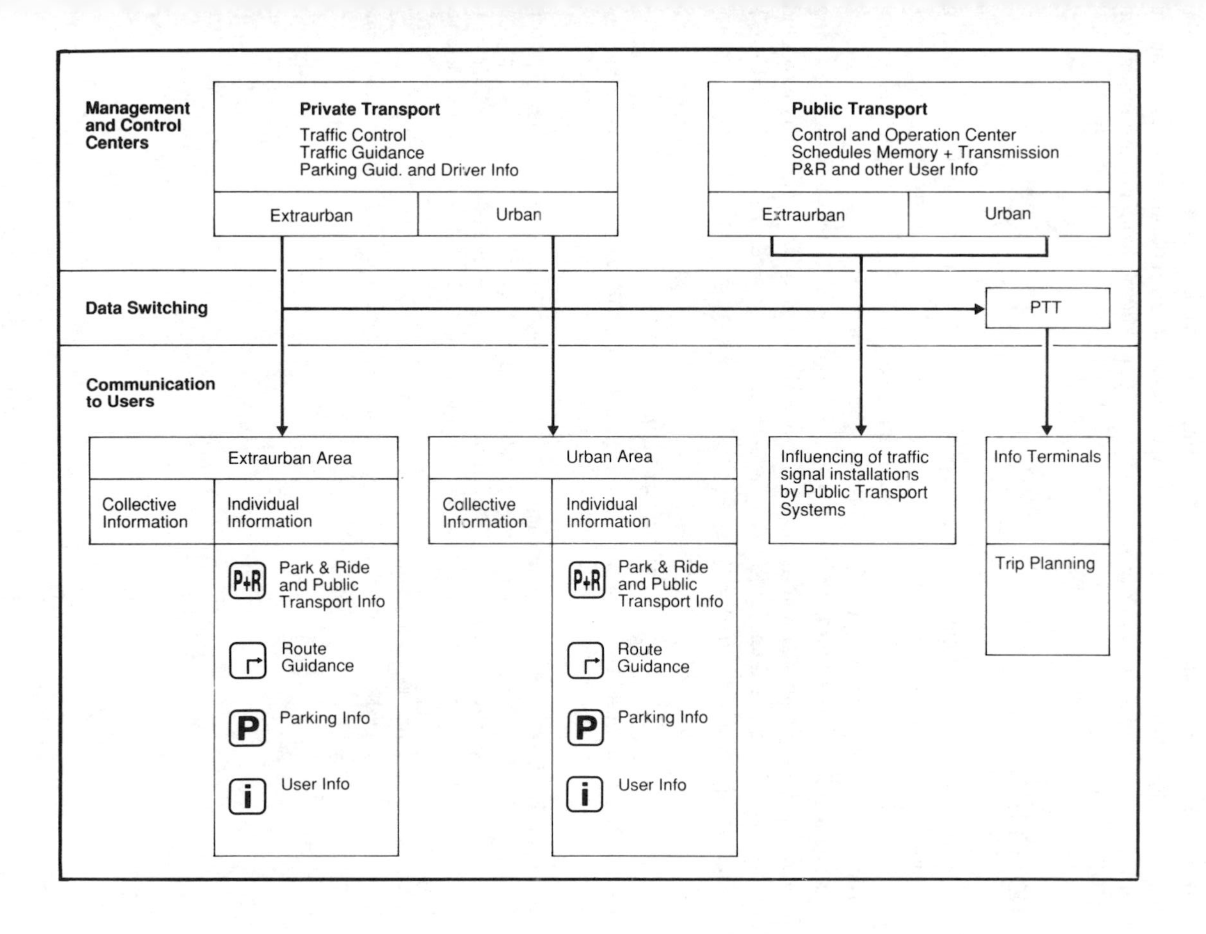

Figure 4.5 Cooperative transport management.

could be taken as a guideline. Infrastructure for collective control and information systems, as well as the central guidance computer for individual route guidance (owing to the possibility of intervention in the traffic situation) could come from public funds. Infrastructure for individual guidance and information systems could come from private funds (and be returned through user fees).

4.5 CONCLUSION

When looking all over Europe and even to the U.S. the idea of integrating existing technologies with new ones is prevailing everywhere, and dynamic route guidance as described above can be found in numerous city projects. It offers the indispensable new dimension for really improving traffic conditions.

It is anticipated here that by the mid 1990s not only R & D projects will be going on in major cities, but operational systems will see the light of day, and it is expected that Berlin will be the leader by starting a commerical service with EURO-SCOUT (successor of ALI-SCOUT) in 1996.

REFERENCES

[1] Sodeikat, H., "How Can the Dynamic Route Guidance System ALI-SCOUT help to Solve Traffic Problems and to Promote the Enforcement of Public Traffic Policy Measures?" *ISATA Conf. Proc.*, Florence, Italy, May 1990.

[2] von Tomkewitsch, R., "Dynamic Route Guidance and Interactive Transport Management with ALI-SCOUT," *IEEE Trans. on Vehicular Technology*, Vol. 40, Issue 1, 1991.

[3] Sodeikat, H., "Cooperative Transport Management. A New Way to Improve Traffic Conditions by Introducting Interactive Dynamic Route Guidance DRG and Driver Information DI," *ISATA Conf. Proc.*, Florence Italy, May 1991.

[4] LISB Schlußbericht (Final report), Berlin, July 1991.

[5] Sodeikat, H., "Dynamic Route Guidance and Traffic Management Operations," *IEE Sixth Int. Road Traffic Monitoring and Control Conf.* No. 355, London, April 1992.

Chapter 5
DRIVE and the ATT Program

*Willy Maes**

In Europe, the U.S., and Japan during recent years, a lot of research has been devoted to the development of a long list of ATT systems and applications that are supposed to reduce increasing road transport problems. A clear policy is needed now on how to introduce and implement the new systems in the years to come. This chapter is a brief overview of the actual situation in this respect in Europe and contains many results from several DRIVE I projects and committees, such as SECFO [1–3], SIRIUS [4], IMPACT [5], and DRIVE Strategic Consultative Committee [6]. It also aims at answering some questions that are often asked.

5.1 ATT IN EUROPE

5.1.1 What Conditions Have Stimulated ATT in Europe?

First of all, there is the pressing need to reduce considerably the huge problems created by road transport in Europe: around 55,000 people are killed and 1.7 million injured on the roads every year, and vehicle emissions contribute to an important extent towards environmental pollution and the greenhouse effect. And what is worse, a deterioration of the situation is still expected for the future. Indeed, car ownership has been increasing steadily in the last decade. In 1986, Western Europe had 350 cars per 1,000 inhabitants, a figure still much below the 560 cars per 1,000 inhabitants at the same time in the U.S. (It is thus expected that the demand for cars in Europe will grow further in the future: from 124.2 million cars in the European Community (EC) in 1990 to about 154 million cars in 2000, an increase of 24% in 10 years).

*The contents of this chapter reflect the view of the author, who is responsible for the facts and the accuracy of the data presented herein. The contents do not necessarily reflect the official views or policies of the Commission of the European Communities.

With the EC's aim of implementing the internal market by 1992 giving extra impetus to the forces creating demand, the intensification of diseconomies in transport arising from congestion has become even a more lively social, political, and economic issue. At the same time, the intended cohesion of the EC will be among others dependent on the efficient transport of passengers and goods. Other social factors also create extra requirements; for example, the fact that there are at least 12 sharply different languages in Western Europe alone places a premium on information systems using coded messages capable of automated presentation in oral or visual form in whatever language is desired.

The development of ATT will ride piggyback on efforts under way already in conventional automotive functions for cars and on the interdependent developments in component miniaturization, fixed-network telecommunications, and mobile telecommunication services, which are key enabling elements of ATT. Although additional roads are still needed to fill the missing links between the main capitals in Europe and to connect underdeveloped regions, there are strict limitations in the increase of traditional infrastructure due to scarcity of space and resources, as well as environmental constraints. Improvements in car performance for safety and emissions, while possible and necessary, cannot cope by themselves with the needs arising from the expected demand increase. As congestion is already a prevalent phenomenon in all transport modes, possible achievements from a simple redistribution of traffic between alternative modes are also limited. In this respect, it should, however, be emphasized that a given width of corridor can carry far more people in public service vehicles than in private cars.

5.1.2 What Conditions Have Deterred ATT in Europe?

The different countries have their own legal and administrative structure, which will not lead automatically to the harmonization of the technical features required for the interoperability of mobile equipment and for the efficient transmission of messages between information handling centers.

The diversity of applications that form the road transport environment and the diversity of systems that can support them complicate the implementation of new technologies. In addition to this, one can mention the considerable number of actors involved and their interdependence, which naturally leads to the inhibition of any tendency for action. Moreover, most of the ATT technologies are very new, they offer extended possibilities of new services, and most of the time they require new or retrained actors. This observation shows the great uncertainty that exists, in which one must find the optimal way to solve the actual road transport problems.

Other difficulties or constraints that exist concerning the steps for implementing ATT systems are mainly:

- The heavy cash resources required to finance the new infrastructure--the civil (costly) or electronic (less so);
- The reluctance of infrastructure providers to make long-lead-time investments before the new systems clearly indicate their benefits;

- The need to define a robust implementation strategy developed jointly and agreed on between users, infrastructure providers, and European industry;
- The differences in market demands, leading to a phasing-in timing of introduction according to local conditions;
- The differences in procedures of local and national budgetary authorities concerning investment in new infrastructure;
- Any requirement for competition in the selection of industrial partners when infrastructure owners are assembling consortia for carrying out projects;
- Commercial and intellectual property rights;
- The differences in the available infrastructure and informatics applications in the various countries of the EC;
- The absence of an overall view of infrastructure needs, particularly with regard to transport, at the level of the European continent.

5.1.3 Where Has the Initiative for ATT Come from in Europe?

The two major ATT initiatives in Europe are PROMETHEUS and DRIVE.

PROMETHEUS

PROMETHEUS is a EUREKA research and development (R&D) project involving the major indigenous European motor manufacturers in association with the relevant section of the electronics industry. EUREKA is a European governmentally funded R&D initiative, which provides a framework to encourage joint technological development of products, mainly between companies in the industrial sector, but often in partnership also with public research institutions. The main aim of PROMETHEUS is to increase the competitiveness of the European automobile industry in the world market in developing the "intelligent car" by cooperating in precompetitive R&D. The program started in 1986 with a one-year definition phase, followed by a R&D phase. During this second phase, prototype systems and components have been developed and partly evaluated with respect to their feasibility, functionality, and efficiency. In order to improve the connection between PROMETHEUS objectives at the societal level and the research projects developing techniques and components at the technology level, a series of ten Common European Demonstrators have been identified since 1989 in the fields of improved driver information, active driver support, cooperative maneuvering and traffic and fleet management. PROMETHEUS is described in more detail in Chapter 9.

DRIVE/ATT

The first DRIVE program was a three-year R&D program set up by the CEC in 1988. DRIVE II, or the ATT program [7], was launched in January 1992 as part of the new three-year R&D program of the CEC known as ''Telematic Systems in Areas of General Interest'' (Area 2: Transport). It is clear that both R&D programs, ATT and PROMETHEUS, are needed and are complementary. While PROMETHEUS emphasizes the intelligent vehicle, in the ATT program, more attention is given to the intelligent infrastructure, to the role of the public authorities, and to the EC issues (e.g., standardization issues and human behavioral aspects).

The ATT program aims particularly at reducing the present engineering and market uncertainty in the application of information and telecommunications technologies to road transport. To avoid premature adoption of techniques and standardization, which can discourage further R&D efforts, locking-in some system considerations and locking-out promising future applications, the ATT program is supporting precompetitive and cooperative R&D among alternative ATT systems, design, and technologies whose applications are likely to be characterized by network and functions integration benefits.

The orientation of the ATT program is focused on preparing for implementation of ATT systems expected to lead towards the IRTE. This represents a progression from the orientation of DRIVE on exploring options and broadens the range of participants to include a significant number of city and regional authorities who are including, as an important element of their own current and future programs, the European validation of earlier R&D within the transport telematics frame of DRIVE.

The principal DRIVE objectives of safety, efficiency, and environmental improvement continue in the ATT program. The projects of the program are concentrated around seven areas of major operational interest (Figure 5.1). Within each of the areas, the themes of systems engineering and implementation strategies (part I of the ATT program workplan), ATT systems and techniques (part II), and validation through pilot projects (Part III) are taken up. The ATT program is not only concerned with the drivers but also investigates the safety problem of the most vulnerable road users—pedestrians and cyclists—as well as the improvement of public transport as a means to reduce traffic congestion.

5.2 IMPORTANCE OF PUBLIC-PRIVATE INTERPLAY FOR THE IMPLEMENTATION OF ATT SYSTEMS

Planning and development of infrastructures and services have, for historical reasons of competence, traditionally been tackled on a national or regional basis. This has resulted in a fragmentation of networks if they are considered from an EC viewpoint. The new dimensions of the internal market make it essential to consider networks in the much wider context of the EC and, beyond that, the European continent as a whole [8]. This vital integration of infrastructures into that new context demands that each decision-making level (local, regional, national, EC) take account of the other levels, when this is justified by the nature of the project. This must lead to greater consultation between decision-makers at various political levels. Suitable form must be sought for optimizing such consultation and making it as operational as possible.

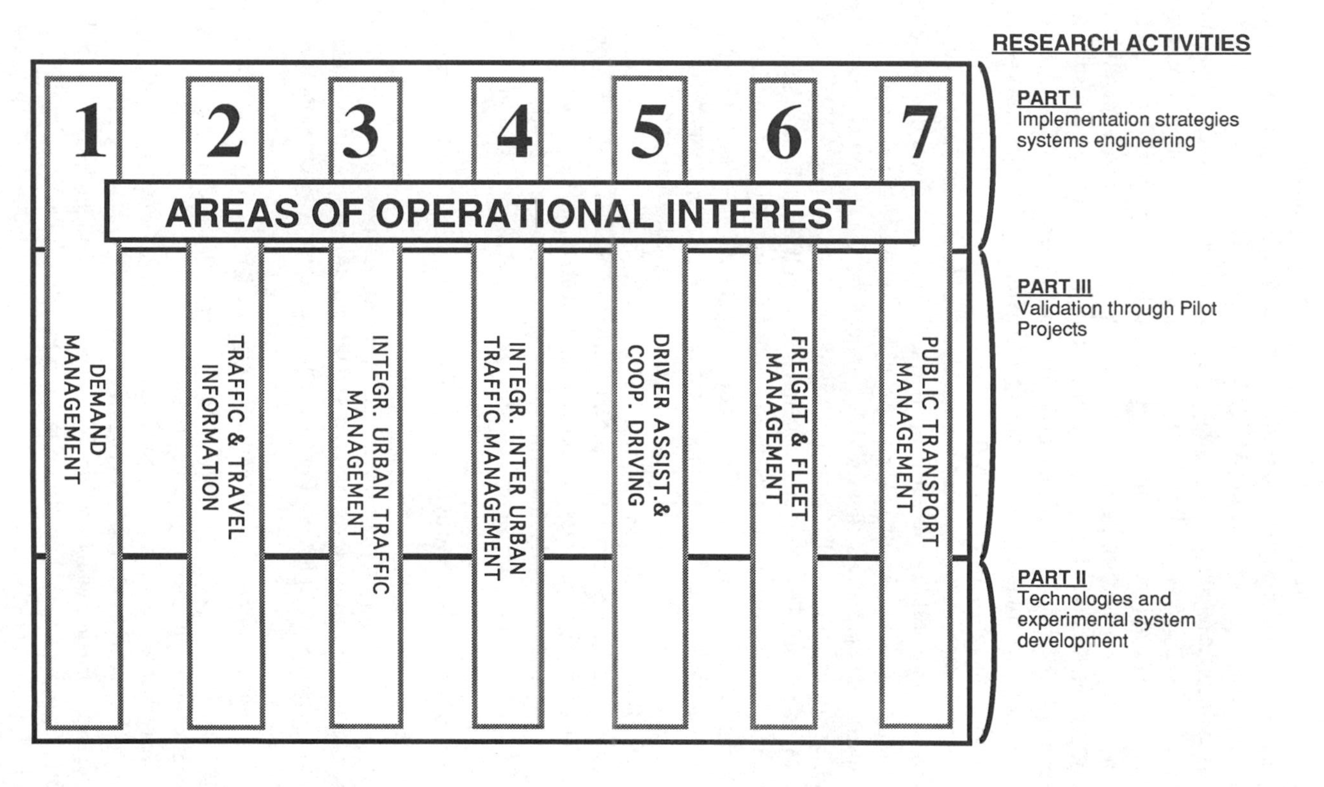

Figure 5.1 The ATT program—relationship between areas of major operational interest and research activities.

While public authorities play a major role in generating and in creating networks, particularly in the areas of transport and training, the importance of commercial operators in launching and executing infrastructure projects is growing. The increasing diversification of supply as a result of technological development is causing commercial operators to show more interest. However, this interest is closely linked to the development of corresponding markets and therefore implies greater user involvement. The development of the notion of service (user) charges, according to which users are prepared to pay for the quality of service they receive, should further strengthen this trend by facilitating the private financing of networks. In other words, the emergence of ATT systems depends as much on private sector initiatives as on action by the public authorities. This is frequently reflected in a partnership between the two.

ATT opens a completely new field for which neither a coherent policy nor the legal and institutional framework has so far been defined. But this knowledge is needed for system developers and for future system operators. As such, the need for consensus between industry and authorities is certainly stronger here than in other sectors because of the possibility of national and EC laws and regulations to influence ATT developments, and because it is the public sector that will have to install or at least regulate a major part of the roadside and central infrastructure in the final implementation phase.

All the analyses show that the logic underlying trans-European ATT systems and networks is that of the market and of better conditions for increased competitiveness: the fact that a project offers a satisfactory rate of return undoubtedly makes it easier to attract private finance. But profitability should not be understood in a strictly financial sense. Consideration should also be given to external factors, such as a project's more general positive repercussions for the areas concerned (reduction of isolation, decongestion of existing infrastructures, economic development of certain regions, location of economic activities). This will be all the more effective if the project is viewed in its entirety and particularly in its overall EC context.

This approach must not, however, lead to the conclusion that no financing problems exist. This is because:

- The risks are still high for the private sector (long-term commitment, difficulty of evaluating the potential return, the cost and the duration of construction, macroeconomic parameters, complexity of the legal and administrative environment, political uncertainties);
- The financial networks are not always structured in such a way as to be able to cope easily with trans-European projects, particularly since they are generally segmented on a national or regional basis;
- The emergence of projects is often delayed by the absence of feasibility studies owing to a lack of funds for this type of study;
- Private sector finance cannot be obtained in all cases, and public finance is therefore needed (combined with a contribution from private capital):
  - Where projects do not offer a sufficient rate of financial return, even though their socioeconomic profitability is established; this might be the case anywhere

in the EC, but it occurs more often in the peripheral regions, where the population is less dense and the distance from the EC's main economic centers constitutes a severe handicap.

- Where it is impossible to make the user pay for the corresponding service (e.g., difficulty of introducing tolls on some of the most heavily trafficked roads of the EC).

he financing of early ATT developments is often a problem for industries, especially 'hen a market does not yet exist and when the risks of nonimplementation are high. overnments can help to solve this problem and have a leading role to play in:

- Specifying their present and future needs towards industries;
- Setting up the rules in order to reduce the actual uncertainty that private investors have to face; defining the possible roles of the public and private sectors, including cooperation between them, as regulators, investors, managers, and operators of ATT services;
- Implementing the required equipment on the infrastructure side for supporting ATT systems;
- Subsidizing useful developments;
- Preparing the conditions for operating ATT services in the future: development of education and adapting regulations;
- Investing, but increasingly more in association with the private sector: creation of traffic control and information centers, enhancement of data collection systems, creation of data exchange networks, and so on. In that respect it cannot be stressed enough that the use of the road infrastructure could be optimized if no more than 2% of the initial budget for road construction could be allocated to ATT systems.

he recent launching in Europe of the European Road Transport Telematics Implementa- on Coordination Organization—*Société Coopérative* (ERTICO SC), in which members all interested groups, public and private, will participate, is an important step in nproving transport conditions in Europe. The objective of ERTICO is to identify and omote an effective implementation strategy for the development of ATT in road transport frastructures, exploring the results achieved by the EC, EUREKA, and national R&D ograms, thus ensuring smooth transition from precompetitive R&D to the market-driven vestment of sector actors.

3 WHAT ARE THE MOST USEFUL STEPS TO DERIVE SOCIAL BENEFIT FROM ATT IN EUROPE?

the next sections, a possible plan is outlined for the implementation of ATT systems Europe.

5.3.1 Validation of R&D Results Through Pilot Projects

Objectives

Some ATT technologies are reaching the stage where their technical feasibility is not in serious doubt, and in some cases have been the subject of demonstrations. The time has come to make a concerted effort to combine the emerging ATT technologies through well-structured pilot projects integrating different applications in order to enable assessment of ATT technologies in real-world situations and in combination with existing systems and infrastructure. Thus, public authorities and private companies will assess their potential. The pilot projects are the core of the ATT program (Figure 5.2) and incorporate the output of current work in DRIVE and other European activities (particularly PROMETHEUS Common European Demonstrators) (Figure 5.3). Pilot projects will almost always include feedback from real-world users.

Pilot projects will seek to achieve the following objectives, which are not easily realized on a small scale or in laboratory tests:

- To assess ATT technologies in public service so as to reduce the risks and uncertainties associated with general introduction;

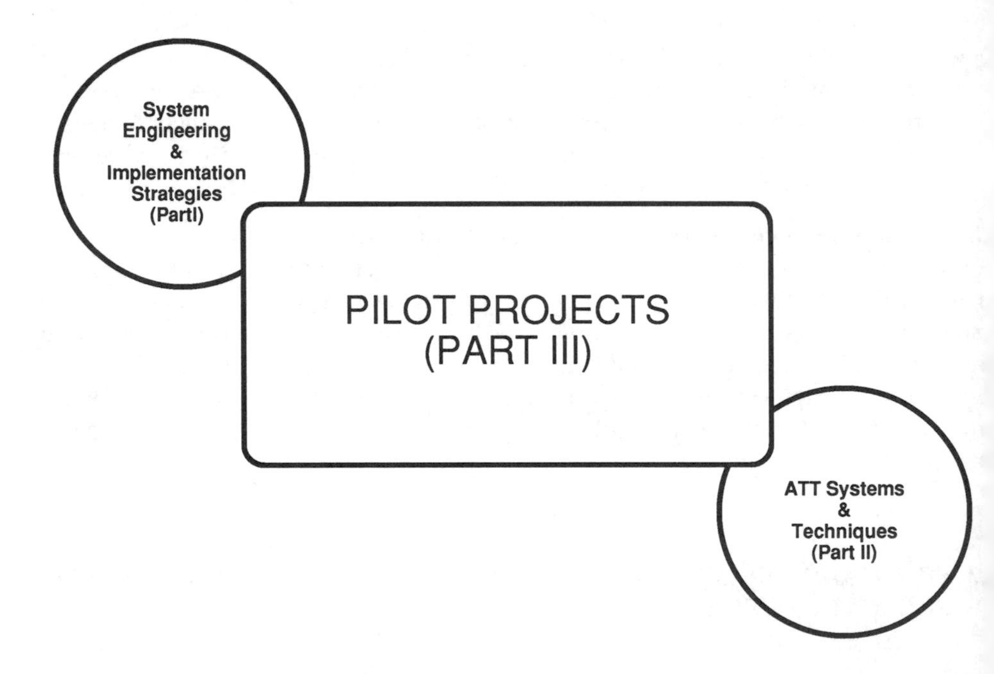

Figure 5.2 Interrelated activities of the ATT program.

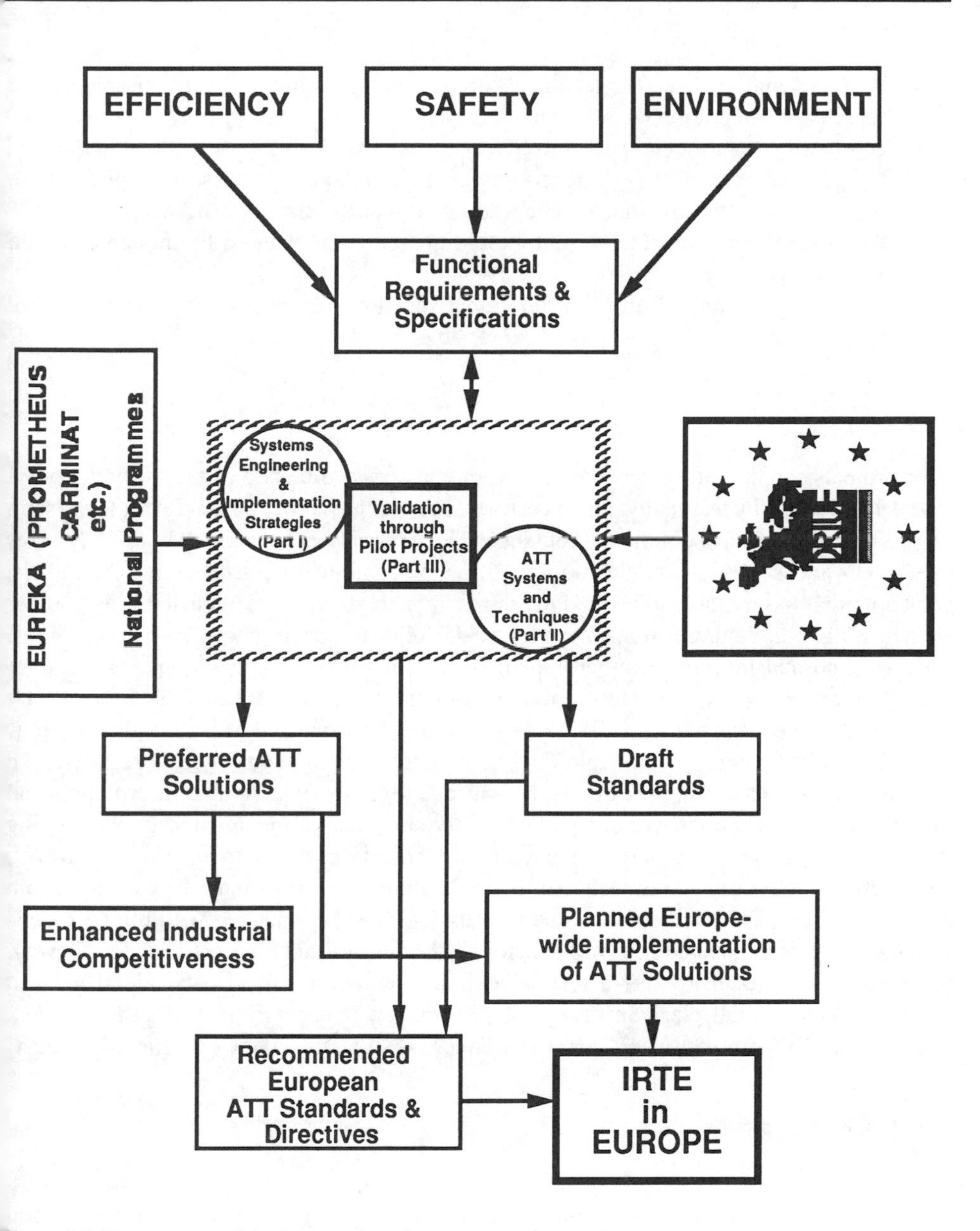

'igure 5.3 Progress toward the integrated road transport environment.

- To assess and evaluate the technical, operational, and administrative problems and benefits of integration of ATT technologies;
- To investigate the social acceptability and economic viability of ATT technologies;
- To gain acceptance of ATT technologies and methods as necessary tools, able to provide improvements in efficiency and safety in the transport network;
- To provide guidelines that would enable proven techniques to be implemented all over Europe;
- To develop common European functional specifications as a basis of formal European standards.

Scope

Pilot projects can help to reduce the uncertainty and risks attached to the introduction of new ATT systems by testing technical performance and providing a framework for system validation, evaluation, and public acceptance. The pilot projects are aimed at ATT systems integration and compatibility, including testing of combined control strategies. In this, great attention has not only to be paid to the technical performance, but also to many other elements, including administrative, managerial, political, social, and financial questions.

In a normal investment environment, there are various stages of investment over time (Figure 5.4). First, the telecommunications infrastructure is installed, followed by investment in the infrastructure of ATT systems (e.g., beacons and traffic control computers). The industry will also start producing in-vehicle equipment when it sees that the infrastructure exists to support uptake by various services (e.g., traffic information and freight services). Then the various parties (individuals and companies) will start buying the various items of equipment and paying for the services offered to them. However, the investment environment is such that the realization of these various stages is uncertain until the various parties are aware of the returns. This can be achieved with pilot projects, which, if well designed and run, will accelerate the decision-making process. In this way, other missing prerequisites for a real-scale implementation will also be identified and included in the overall plan. Several pilot projects are under way in the ATT program. They are briefly described here, classified under the areas of major operational interest.

Demand Management

ADEPT:	Four separate pilot projects (Gothenburg, Lisbon, Thessaloniki, and Trondheim) in the field of automatic debiting.
GAUDI:	Five major European cities (Barcelona, Bologne, Dublin, Marseille, Trondheim, and Rome) experimenting with multiservice urban debiting applications: road pricing, public transport ticketing, parking debiting, and zone access systems.

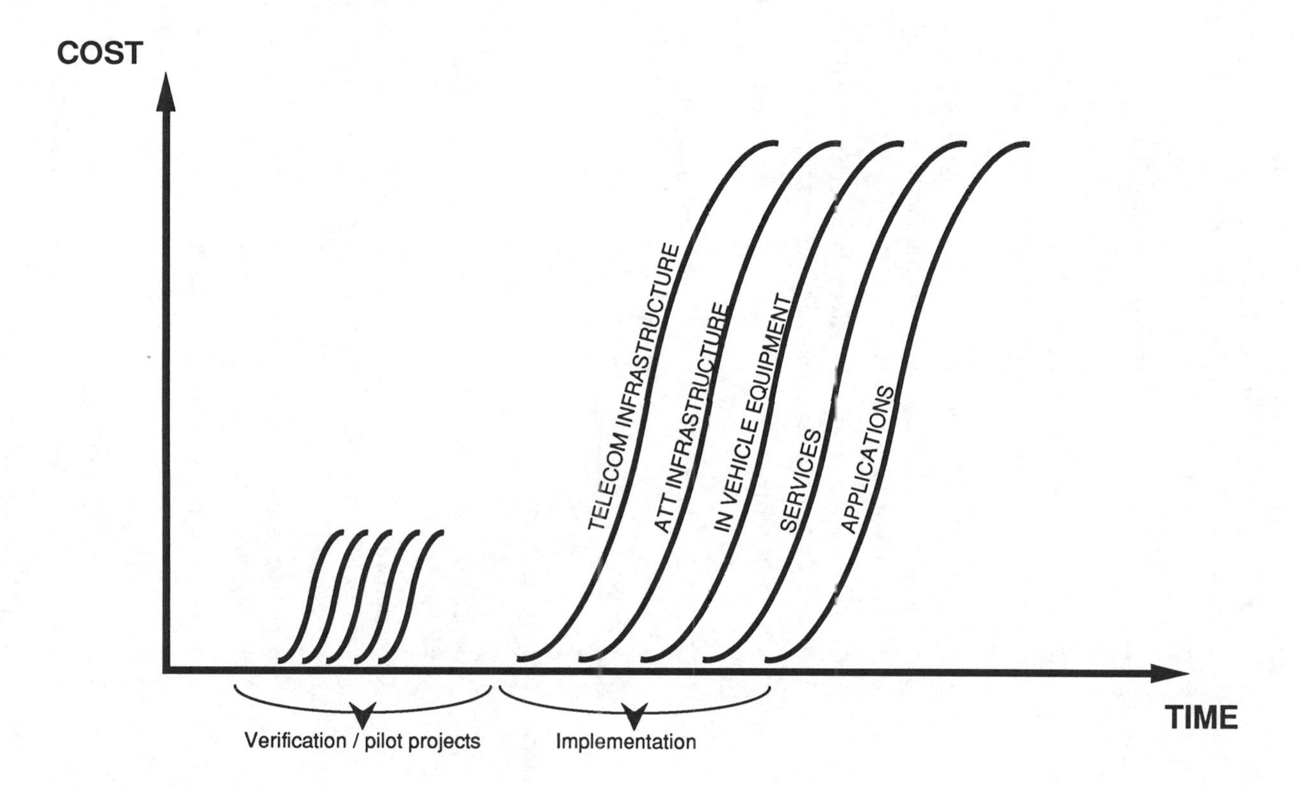

Figure 5.4 Investment stimulation through pilot projects.

ADS: Multilane nonstop payment and multimodal information exchange for advance booking, the topics of two field trials in Italy near the Mont Blanc tunnel and the harbor of Brindisi.

Travel and Traffic Information

INTERCHANGE: Will establish a European traveler information network for real-time exchange of ATT data between national traffic/travel information centers.

LLAMD: Cooperative pilot project between five cities (London, Lyon, Amsterdam, Munich, and Dublin) on the general theme of advanced travel and traffic information systems.

GEMINI: Will demonstrate an integrated information system based on RDS-TMC and VMS through trial sites in Italy and the U.K.

ACCEPT: Pilot projects for the testing of RDS-TMC in the Netherlands, Germany, and Paris, Ile de France.

CITIES: Deals with distribution and broadcasting of transport-related information, route guidance, traffic control, and demand management through pilot projects in Paris, Brussels, and Gothenburg.

Integrated Urban Traffic Management

VRU-TOO: Advanced detector systems to improve conditions for pedestrians at signalized junctions and crossings; tested in several European cities.

PRIMAVERA: Integrated strategies for managing queues while at the same time giving priorities to public transport in a calmed environment; tested in Leeds and Turin.

EUROCOR: Flexible corridor modeling and control applied to two test sites—both integrated urban networks and highways.

QUARTET: Pilot project to verify the benefit of integration and coordination of related ATT services in cities (Athens, Birmingham, Stuttgart, and Turin).

KITS: Testing of knowledge-based traffic control systems in urban and interurban sites (Cologne, Trondheim, Genova, and Madrid).

SCOPE: Testing of several ATT systems in Southampton, Cologne, and Piraeus.

Integrated Interurban Traffic Management

PORTICO: Several ATT systems for traffic management tested on two main interurban roads of the Portuguese highway network.

MELYSSA: A multitude of ATT applications to be tested on a highway corridor between Stuttgart and Lyon, with an extension to Spain.

QUO VADIS: Pilot projects in Scotland and Denmark dealing with traffic modeling approaches and VMS control strategies.

ARTIS: Several ATT applications to be tested on the Junquera-Sevilla corridor in Spain.

GERDIEN: A coherent network for road traffic data collection and exchange to be demonstrated on a highway in the Netherlands.

ROSES: Pilot tests in the Netherlands and Wales on road condition and weather monitoring and control systems.

PLEIADES: Integrated driver information and network management pilot project in the Paris-London corridor.

RHAPIT: Test in the Rhein/Main area of a dynamic route guidance system based on the SOCRATES concept.

Freight and Fleet Management

COMBICOM: Test of a road-rail informatics system on the link Munich-Kufstein-Brussels-Verona.

FRAME: Freight management pilot experiments to be performed on the channel crossings, the Welsh corridor, and the crossing to Ireland. Tests also included on remote terminal operation between the Netherlands and Greece (perishable goods monitoring).

CITRA: International alpine pilot project through Germany, Austria, and Italy, which proposes the realization of an integrated monitoring and control system to optimize hazardous goods transport.

METAFORA: Eleven pilot tests on several alternative routes between northwest Europe and Greece in the field of road freight operation (mobile data communications and electronic data transfer).

IFMS: An open system architecture for computer-aided and integrated transport to be validated within pilot projects in the areas of controlled logistics on a pan-European scale, including urban, interurban, and combined transport operations.

Public Transport Management

PHOEBUS:	Several different ATT systems for public transport optimization to be tested in Madrid, Brussels, and Ghent.
EUROBUS:	Will experiment on a set of advanced computer aids for passenger information.
PROMPT:	Pilot projects in London, Turin, and Gothenburg to test methods of giving active priority to buses, trams, and emergency vehicles in urban traffic control systems.

5.3.2 Preparation of the Infrastructure

First of all, a consensus of member states is required for a European implementation plan. It must include the choice of a European network (arteries and cities)—of course, under the auspices of national or regional authorities—where the first available ATT services must be implemented. It will also integrate a specific plan for education in ATT. In addition to this, the incorporation of ATT issues in future transport policy is a prerequisite for a successful implementation of some ATT technologies.

Since it is not easy to achieve a European consensus in one step, due to differences in the roles played by the different organizations in each country, a first stage could be a clarification of the national situations:

- Role of the public authorities according to the different types of traffic and travel information;
- Role of the private sector habits, legal framework such as licensing rules, and liability according to the different kinds of information.

This clarification is now being undertaken by the European Conference of Ministers of Transport (ECMT), who launched a survey; its report drew attention to present inadequacies and the need to establish regulations. As a result, a supportive resolution has been adopted by the Ministers in November 1991.

Traffic control centers and traffic information centers should be created in conformity with the situation in each country within the legal framework mentioned above. If it is clear that traffic control centers will remain under the responsibility of road operators (public or under concession), traffic information centers can be established in some countries on an independent basis. The crucial point is that these traffic information centers must operate in a clear legal framework for the following reasons:

- Traffic information influences the strategies in traffic control, and this influence will increase with ATT.
- The exchange of information among different operators must be organized to ensure a continuity of service to the drivers all over Europe.

Pilot projects are required to validate the first basic elements in this domain in order to establish a definitive structure before the target date of 1995. By then, the following specific tools must be implemented on the infrastructure side to support ATT systems operation:

- Dense data collection on the network identified in the European plan: This must include traffic data sensors, emergency telephones, video monitoring (computer-aided), weather monitoring, automatic incident detection based on loop sensors or on video, and, obviously, the related communication equipment. Most of these elements will also require standardization, or at least implementation of adequate interfaces in order to facilitate import and export of data. The first formal standards concerning road and traffic data can be expected by 1995, once the initial proposals have been validated through pilot projects.
- Data interchange networks in operation: A first step could be based on the exchange of traffic messages developed for RDS-TMC application. A second step could be the generalization of the results of some DRIVE I projects validated through pilot projects. A particularly important issue in this respect is the choice of a common location referencing system.
- Improvement of current technologies: Though the main objective is the development of new technologies in transport, penetration will be progressive. The use of current techniques will persist for a long time, although the above-mentioned tools will improve them. In some cases, it can also lead to specific actions in order to ensure a coherent approach with ATT (e.g., use of variable message signs).

5.3.3 Common Key Actions

Many of the actions proposed above are common to several application areas and systems and can surely be undertaken together. This underlines again the importance of a coordination body at the European level in order to minimize the necessary resources, obtain a synergistic effect, and ensure coherence in actions. For this purpose, ERTICO is expected to also undertake the following actions.

- Follow up pilot projects;
- Organize information dissemination;
- Carry out economic and market studies;
- Build consensus and promote common specifications.

In the following, we have checked what common actions have been identified in the implementation plan and how they can be fulfilled.

Economic Approach, Decision-Taking Process, and Financing

Most of the systems and techniques in DRIVE and PROMETHEUS have been investigated only from the technical point of view. Some attempt at evaluation has been made, but only in a very limited area, particularly due to the fact that little data are yet available. It is now time to undertake serious economic evaluation to determine the efficacy of the proposed ATT systems regarding the targeted objectives: safety, efficiency, and environment. These evaluations are needed by European and national authorities in order to facilitate the decision-taking process:

- ATT implementation for traffic information requires changes or adaptation in legislation: these changes will be taken into consideration only if the efficiency of such systems is proved.
- Many ATT systems are supposed to provide great benefits for the community, but will particularly, even totally, require public investment. Knowing the trends in public investment in the domain of transport in Europe, benefits will have to be clearly demonstrated to convince public authorities.

These evaluations are also obviously necessary to attract potential investors. Taking into account the complexity of some ATT systems, with a high degree of risk (new services, new technologies, new legal framework, etc.), it must be necessary to adopt a very progressive approach and to try to demonstrate the viability of limited subsystems first. It is worthwhile noting that, in many cases, private initiative will require assistance from the public authorities: authorization, licensing, information provision, and so on. It seems that giving a financial interest to the public sector will help to solve the problems: "In mixed systems where public authorities have a stake in the development, they have an interest in resolving questions of regulations more quickly and ensuring an adequate market for the technology by enforcing compatibilities" [4]. These evaluations and the corresponding market studies fall clearly within the role of a European coordination organization. Last but not the least, a coherent European transport policy is indispensable for the successful implementation of most ATT technologies.

Organizational Problems and Legal Framework

Implementing and operating ATT requires new relationships between actors, particularly due to the introduction of information technologies and new services. This cooperation requires setting up contracts between these different actors in order to share clearly their responsibilities and economic interests. In some cases, it is evident that new services and technologies will demand changes in organizations; this point is often sensitive because of long habits in some sectors and the consequential impact on employment and status. Lastly, the success of ATT services and product development is somewhat precarious because of the uncertainty of many factors. A first action should be to clarify the legal framework and fix the roles: this is in the hands of public authorities and it must be tackled urgently. Due to the limited resources in the public domain, a general solution certainly cannot be found. Ingenuity and imagination will be needed in order to best combine public and private resources within the context of the differing national, regional, and local policies and constraints.

Individual and Social Acceptance

Introduction of ATT requires a thorough evaluation of many factors, particularly sociopolitical ones. This issue has been addressed within the SIRIUS project [4], which emphasized the following points.

- The acceptance of a technology usually takes a long time and is part of a process in which many things can happen to prevent the technology from being accepted and thus from being implemented.
- Linking the introduction of a new technology for one purpose to other partly or fully controversial policies definitely decreases the chance of acceptance.
- The commercial marketing of technologies before high levels of reliability are achieved can adversely affect the development of the market.
- The discretionary adoption of onboard technologies is regarded as an important factor facilitating implementation. Providing choice is seen by ATT suppliers as an appropriate mechanism for minimizing resistance to the installation of ATT technologies. Suppliers' strategies thus require two prongs: first, they must persuade the relevant authorities to adopt the central facilities necessary for the provision of the service to the individual driver, and second, they must persuade the individual drivers that such facilities are useful to them.
- Work force resistance or other corporatist attitude (e.g., from trade unions) to the introduction of ATT technologies in the public transport area is an important element for consideration in any implementation strategy.
- Problems of acceptance (social, political, and technological) militate against the radical and immediate implementation of available technologies.
- Privacy is an important element in ATT acceptance. The introduction of ATT technologies without taking the protection of privacy explicitly into account may lead to a rejection of the technology. Privacy is not an obstacle to the implementation process when ATT applications can guarantee anonymous or voluntary use of the new technology.
- No single actor can be considered responsible for the implementation of ATT technologies in the European arena. ATT implementation can occur as a consequence of the involvement of many actors. This means that great effort must be devoted to reaching a mechanism of cooperation between all industries active in this field.
- It is widely recognized that the requirements of an implementation strategy are greater than the political acceptance or the efficient technical functioning of the system. The development of education, training, and marketing campaigns to educate public opinion is crucial to acceptance of the technologies.
- In order to minimize resistance, complementary measures are necessary when demand management measures are taken (road pricing, parking, and route restrictions). Examples of such measures are the improvement of the public transport system, P&R facilities, some financial compensation for low-income groups, and decrease in the fixed road tax.

- ATT implementations should be pioneered in situations where minimum legislative or regulatory changes are required to host its development.
- Sites where there is a strong desire to protect the architectural, cultural, or historical environment are more likely to be amenable to the acceptance and utilization of ATT.
- In view of the current environment or anticongestion culture, ATT applications requiring political commitment in order to be implemented should not create the impression of promoting car use; otherwise, political rejection is likely.
- Promotional activities of ATT towards potential buyers and users, such as political actors on the various levels (European, national, regional and local), companies in the public transport and freight sector, and private car users, are essential in order to stimulate its diffusion. A high-profile public relations strategy is required.
- An open systems architecture should be adopted, but with a well-developed evolution plan for the initial years of implementation.

Standardization of ATT Systems

A basic aim must be to create the pan-European compatibility of vehicle and infrastructure functions. That is, the functions installed in a vehicle should be able to serve the driver in a similar way throughout Europe, wherever the infrastructure exists to support these functions. Compatibility between equipment and system components allowing a modular structure is another important objective.

A primary issue will be the definition of interfaces wherever compatibility is affected. Standards in themselves are means, not ends. However, formal standards have a high degree of acceptance and a good record of effectiveness, especially in industry.

Terminology is one standardization task that could start immediately (e.g., to give names to and define basic functions in a way that is understandable to users). Basic performance requirements and criteria of the functions defined should then be standardized. This will facilitate the mutual understanding between equipment vendors and buyers, users, and drivers, and between users and infrastructure and service providers.

All characteristics of interfaces concerned with compatibility issues should be common, and they therefore need to be standardized. The elements between these interfaces and especially algorithms and other knowledge-based applications should be looked at as black boxes, and market mechanisms may be left free to operate in their development.

Some functions will have a significant influence on road safety, and performance requirements for these must be very strict and to the point. Safe design practices will probably be needed, especially for certification procedures regarding conformance to standards, quality assurance, and reliability. The same applies also to the security of economic operations and maybe to personal integrity (anonymity) matters.

In order not to block future developments, standards should be modular in design, allowing new modules or new solutions to be added as development continues. A special problem in relation to modularity is the compatibility over time that will be needed to allow a true add-on equipment facility. Although the information technology industry now understands the value of multivendor situations, some argument may still be expected concerning far-reaching modularization of systems, no matter whether hardware or software. Common, or possibly standardized, conceptual data models and data dictionaries may prove valuable tools in subdividing tasks between different suppliers.

Liability

Extensive legislation exists both at EC and at national levels on the subject of liability. There would be great difficulty in securing harmonized changes to these provisions in response solely to the needs identified in the context of ATT systems, but administrative provisions may require careful attention and consultation at the European level if the development of the market is not to be inhibited.

The following problems have to be recognized in this context.

- The economic benefits to be derived from the introduction of ATT systems will be put at risk if there is evidence of successful claims leading to high awards of compensation. If such claims are justified, corresponding improvements to the systems will have to be made. If, however, awards are made on the apparent basis that someone has suffered severe loss, and that the deepest available pocket in which to find compensation seems to be that of the ATT service provider or equipment manufacturer, this would be an unreasonable situation demanding whatever counteraction may be possible.
- Public authorities are particularly sensitive to incurring new sources of potential liability. Companies have to take some calculated risks (including that of the cost of insurance) if they are to maintain or expand their business. Authorities have, however, the option generally to do nothing if the risks appear to them large in relation to the scale of the benefits they can identify and for which they would be able to claim credit. They will look very hard at their position in this respect.
- The development of experience and of a history of judgments forming legal precedents is a slow process. It will be particularly slow if cases are few--a desirable situation; but if this is the result of caution in venturing into new markets, then a vicious circle may result. It is essential that the best professional assessments should be made and kept up to date by experts in both the legal and technical fields. In the latter case, it is necessary to be realistic, not merely about the risk of dangerous defects, but also about the prospective legal consequences: whether potential claims will be successfully resisted and whether, on the other hand, claims will succeed where the ATT element is not the root cause of the injury sustained.

ACKNOWLEDGMENTS

I wish to thank my director-general, Mr. M. Carpentier, for his comments and his agreement to publish this chapter, all my colleagues in DRIVE Central Office, especially Fotis

Karamitsos, Peter O'Neill, and Gitte Vogelbein, for their help in preparing and reviewing this paper, and the partners in the DRIVE projects SECFO, SIRIUS, and IMPACT for the use that has been made of their reports as an input for this chapter.

REFERENCES

[1] "IRTE Implementation Draft Plan," DRIVE project SECFO, July 1991.

[2] "Preliminary RTI Standardization Requirements," DRIVE project SECFO, June 1991.

[3] "Tentative Key Policies for the Implementation of RTI in Europe," DRIVE project SECFO, Feb. 1991.

[4] "Main Empirical Findings out of the SIRIUS Project on Sociopolitical Aspects of RTI Implementation," DRIVE project SIRIUS, June/July 1991.

[5] "Survey of Legal Problems Relevant to RTI Systems," DRIVE project IMPACT, September 1990.

[6] "The Challenge of Advanced Transport Telematics," First Report, DRIVE Consultative Committee, Commission of the European Communities, June 1990.

[7] "R&D in Advanced Road Transport Telematics in Europe," *Workplan '91*, Commission of the European Communities, Dec. 1990.

[8] "Towards Trans-European Networks for a Community Action Programme," Commission of the European Communities, Dec. 1990, Communication from the Commission to the Council and the European Parliament (ref. no. COM (90) 585).

Chapter 6
SOCRATES
Ian Catling

6.1 INTRODUCTION

SOCRATES (System of Cellular RAdio for Traffic Efficiency and Safety) is a concept, developed so far largely within the DRIVE program (see Chapter 5), that is intended to form the basis of the IRTE. SOCRATES uses cellular radio to provide two-way communication between information centers and computers onboard equipped vehicles. This chapter describes the basic SOCRATES principles and applications (Section 6.2), the original SOCRATES project (Section 6.3), the four projects taking SOCRATES forward during the DRIVE II ATT program (Section 6.4), some of the major areas of technical development (Section 6.5), and the commercial activities it is hoped will lead to the early implementation of viable SOCRATES services on a wide scale (Section 6.6). This chapter outlines the SOCRATES concept and introduces the four projects (collectively known as SOCRATES 2) connected with the DRIVE II program, which are actively implementing the results of the DRIVE I SOCRATES project (sometimes referred to as SOCRATES 1). This project demonstrated that the concepts for a SOCRATES system were soundly based and that there were no technical obstacles in the path of full SOCRATES implementation.

Pilot projects are being implemented in London, Gothenburg, and the Rhine-Main area in the southern part of the Hessen region in Germany. The SOCRATES Kernel project provides a center of excellence and expertise in which SOCRATES problems can be discussed and resolved, and is the focus for the coordination of continued SOCRATES developments. The main objective of each of the SOCRATES pilot projects is to speed up the process towards widespread commercial implementation of SOCRATES systems throughout Europe.

During the DRIVE I program (1989 to 1991), SOCRATES developed concepts for linking cellular telecommunications to the emerging in-vehicle intelligent computers. The result will be cars able to guide their drivers on the best available route, avoiding the worst congestion spots, and which can act as mobile communication stations for a range of applications of ATT. SOCRATES uses cellular radio in an efficient way to broadcast detailed digital information on traffic conditions to vehicles as they travel. This is linked to data stored in the vehicle's navigation computer, which combines these sources to calculate the best route for the driver. For some time now, route guidance equipment for cars has been under development. Taking input from an electronic compass, wheel sensors, and a map stored in its memory, a system like CARIN or Travelpilot will find the shortest route to a given destination. By speaking directly to the driver and backing this up with a simple display, these systems give easy-to-follow directions. The use of SOCRATES communications allows the onboard unit to receive detailed traffic updates and automatically to adapt itself to the traffic conditions (e.g., to avoid congestion). When the system transmits the updates, the onboard unit will find the quickest or cheapest route instead of the shortest one. It will continue to provide up-to-the-minute information as the control center continuously monitors the network.

6.2 BASIC SOCRATES PRINCIPLES AND APPLICATIONS

SOCRATES is developing techniques for using cellular radio as the basic communication medium of the IRTE. Many applications will depend on the widespread availability of two-way communication between vehicles and control centers; cellular radio offers a potential pan-European infrastructure which should provide an economically efficient basis for the IRTE and should provide for most of the ATT applications within it. The main applications considered within SOCRATES and which it will support are listed below.

Dynamic Route Guidance. This is the major ATT application, giving in-vehicle routing recommendations to drivers based on detailed knowledge not only of the road network, but also of the current and forecast traffic conditions. Early estimates [1] by the TRRL (now TRL) of the benefits of dynamic route guidance show that savings of time and vehicle operating costs will be substantial; for example, savings of at least £100 million per annum were expected to follow from a dynamic route guidance system installed in London.

Advanced Traffic Control. The improved traffic monitoring that will follow from the installation of SOCRATES systems, together with the ability to influence overall traffic routing patterns, will allow traffic managers and automatic traffic control systems to control traffic flows in order to optimize the efficiency of operation of the road network.

Fleet Management. The IRTE will provide the facilities for fleet operators to monitor the location and status of their vehicles and to carry out efficient scheduling and control.

Parking Management and Information Systems. Linking information from parking facilities will improve parking management, allowing drivers to locate the most convenient car park spaces at the end of their journeys and ultimately to reserve and even pay for their spaces in advance.

Public Transport Management and Information Systems. Dynamic vehicle scheduling, passenger information services, and public transport fleet management will be included in the IRTE.

Hazard and Local Warnings. Onboard communications will provide for drivers to be warned of hazards such as accidents, fog, and ice.

Emergency Call. The SOCRATES system will provide an emergency call facility, activated either by the driver in an emergency or by automatic crash sensors.

Emergency Paging. The system will allow individuals to be paged over the communications infrastructure for emergency purposes.

Automatic Debiting. The ability to charge drivers for toll collection, for road pricing, or for the provision of services will be an important part of the IRTE. Chapter 7 deals with automatic debiting systems; to date, SOCRATES has not concentrated on this major application area, although a short-range SOCRATES-compatible beacon was demonstrated during the SOCRATES 1 project.

Driver Information. The link to the vehicle will provide for general information to be given to the driver on traffic conditions and specific problem spots. It has been an important part of the SOCRATES development that compatibility has been maintained with the development of the RDS-TMC.

Tourist Information. Information of specific interest to tourists will be provided, covering the availability of specific services such as hotels and fuel stations, and perhaps including options such as choosing scenic routes and details of special events.

Data for Traffic Management and Traffic Planning. The improved traffic monitoring of the IRTE will provide an important source of traffic data, producing significant savings in conventional traffic surveys.

Trip Planning. The linking of dynamic route guidance with public transport information will allow pretrip planning services to be offered, so that travelers can plan not only the time but also the modes of their journey.

At the center of the ATT applications considered in the IRTE is the concept of a traffic information and control center. The SOCRATES control center is more sophisticated than the conventional traffic control center of today, because it uses the communication facilities of the IRTE to monitor traffic flows and speeds in real time with an accuracy not possible with current systems. It uses this information, for example, to generate information for traffic managers, but it will also carry out short-term traffic forecasting using predictive models. The results of the models will be used for generating route guidance information.

SOCRATES makes use of a cellular radio infrastructure in order to achieve two-way communication between vehicles and control centers, but with an important difference from conventional telephony. Telephone calls are made on a one-to-one, or point-to-point, basis. SOCRATES uses only a limited amount of the scarce communication bandwidth resource in each cell of the cellular radio system. This is because instead of setting up one-to-one links with equipped vehicles, the data to be sent to each vehicle in a cell are *broadcast* to as many SOCRATES vehicles as happen to be in the cell at the time. Thus, the bandwidth used is independent of the number of vehicles using the system.

For the uplink, or communication link back from the equipped vehicles to the control center, a multiple-access protocol is used that makes the most efficient use of a limited capacity. The main data transmitted back by the vehicles are the *floating car* data (i.e., journey times measured directly by the computers on board the equipped vehicles). When there are many equipped vehicles in a particular geographic area, only a sample of this data will be needed; by controlling the frequency of attempted transmission using broadcast parameters, an optimum amount of data can be received without exceeding a fixed channel capacity for any cell in the network.

Cells in a cellular radio system are typically between 2 and 35 km across. The SOCRATES control centers will generate messages to be transmitted in particular geographic areas, which will be translated to messages for appropriate base stations in the relevant regions; in turn, the base stations will receive data transmitted by vehicles in each cell and forward these data to the SOCRATES control center.

The basic principles of the SOCRATES system are illustrated in Figure 6.1.

Dynamic route guidance is the primary application considered within SOCRATES and within the IRTE as a whole. Autonomous systems are able to give navigation advice to the driver based on a knowledge of the vehicle's position and of the road network. Both Travelpilot and CARIN rely on a combination of dead reckoning and map matching in order to maintain the vehicle's position; both systems use compact disc to store the digital map representation of the road network on board the vehicle. Philips and Bosch have joined forces in several projects (most recently EDRM2 in DRIVE II) to produce the *Geographic Data Format* (GDF), a common European data exchange standard for the digital map base on which both systems depend.

Given a suitable up-to-date map, both CARIN and the latest versions of Travelpilot are able to give routing advice based on static information about the links in the stored network. However, without access to up-to-the-minute traffic information, a fully autonomous system cannot give the driver the best route at the time it is required under the traffic conditions being experienced. The work at TRL [1] and elsewhere estimated that the benefits of a route guidance system would double by changing from a purely autonomous, or static, route calculation to one which fully took account of existing and predicted traffic conditions—a dynamic route guidance system. This would need some form of communication between the vehicle and an information center monitoring the traffic over the complete area of relevance.

The CARMINAT project [3] investigated the use of RDS-TMC to provide dynamic traffic information to vehicles equipped with CARIN. This will certainly improve the quality of information available to the driver. However, RDS has only a limited data

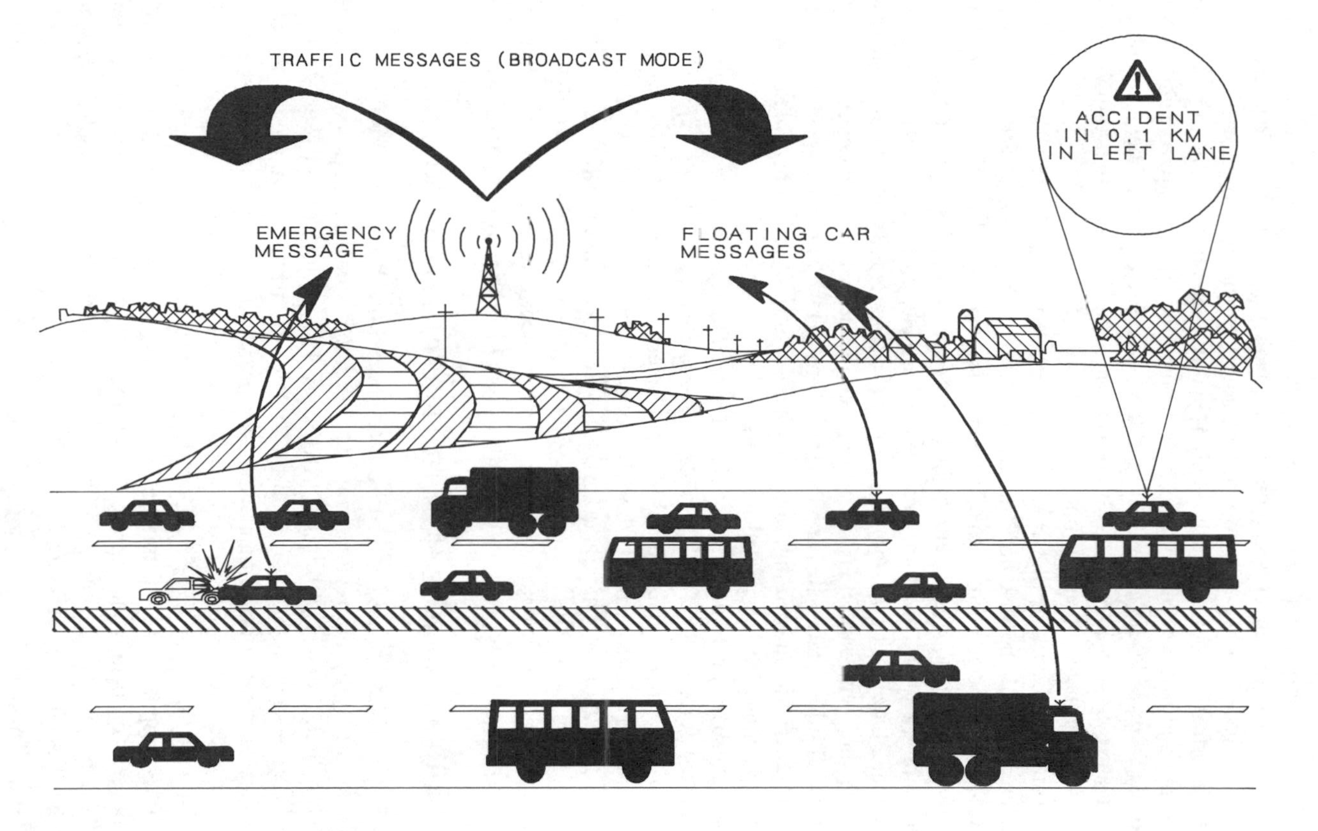

Figure 6.1 The basic SOCRATES concept (from [2]).

capacity; it is also only a one-way communication medium, and its use leaves the actual monitoring of traffic to conventional techniques, which have many inadequacies.

A system based on two-way communication provides not only the means of giving the driver information, but also a new high-quality method of collecting traffic data, both real-time and historic. Messages can be transmitted from equipped vehicles totally anonymously to provide the equivalent of a large number of simultaneous, continuous, floating car surveys—these are the costly conventional methods by which highway authorities collect data on network travel times.

By using cellular radio, SOCRATES is investigating the use of a communications infrastructure that will be installed for the whole of Europe—the GSM cellular radio system. GSM was designed to be the first pan-European digital mobile radio system. It is quickly becoming a global standard. Over 18 European countries signed a Memorandum of Understanding (MoU), providing for service introduction by late 1991, and there are now more than 30 network operators. This figure is rising steadily. GSM has the following benefits compared with earlier analog systems: common frequency allocation throughout Europe, a broad suite of integrated services, solutions to many problems peculiar to analog cellular, and international roaming, through which a subscriber is reachable anywhere in Europe via the subscriber's personal number.

The fact that only a limited amount of the bandwidth available in each communication cell is required for the SOCRATES system means that SOCRATES can coexist with telephony and that the service offered will not deteriorate as more and more users join it. Over the SOCRATES channel, the system will transmit current and predicted link travel time information to vehicles equipped with otherwise autonomous systems such as CARIN and Travelpilot. The navigation system will then be able to calculate the best route for the driver, taking into account his or her precise requirements and having the detailed real-time data necessary to take full account of the prevailing traffic conditions.

6.3 THE SOCRATES PROJECT IN THE FIRST DRIVE PROGRAM

The first SOCRATES project evolved from research work being done by Philips, which was inspired largely by the recognition that the autonomous navigation systems being developed by both Philips and Bosch (CARIN and Travelpilot, respectively) would need methods for providing up-to-the-minute information on traffic conditions. The concept of an ATT system based on cellular radio was proposed and a consortium was formed to submit the SOCRATES project for consideration within DRIVE at the end of 1988. It was the largest project in the first DRIVE program, and it cost a total of nearly 6 million ECUs (approximately 6 million U.S. dollars). The consortium consisted of the organizations listed below and represented all the key sectors necessary for developing SOCRATES systems and for setting up a SOCRATES service operation. The partners in the first SOCRATES project were:

Ian Catling Consultancy, acting jointly with Tate Associates, U.K., prime contractor
British Telecom, U.K.

Philips Research Laboratories, U.K.
Philips Project Centre, the Netherlands
SEMA Group, France
Bundesanstalt für Strassenwesen (BASt), Germany
Siemens, Germany
Robert Bosch, Germany
Volvo, Sweden
Saab-Scania, Sweden
Universitat Politecnica de Catalunya, Spain.

The objectives of the project were to:

- Demonstrate the feasibility of dynamic route guidance systems based on cellular radio;
- Show how the proposed communication link can also support other applications, such as hazard warning, emergency calls, automatic vehicle location, road pricing, and hotel/parking status;
- Quantify the capacity of the system in terms of numbers of users;
- Show how the technology developed for cellular radio can be used in simplified equipment for DRIVE users;
- Provide computer simulations of the data processing, the information flows to and from the vehicles, and the navigation system;
- Equip a test site and use laboratory models and prototypes to verify and validate the theoretical predictions; and
- Make preliminary recommendations for a coherent system with route guidance and other applications supported by cellular radio.

The project began on January 1, 1989 and was completed successfully at the end of 1991 with a functioning demonstration site in Gothenburg, which was a substantial part of the West Sweden RTI field trial coordinated by the Swedish National Road Administration (SNRA). The project was organized into five tasks, or groups of work packages, outlined below.

6.3.1 Traffic Modeling and Traffic Management

This task developed models to run in the control center in order to build the traffic messages to be transmitted to equipped vehicles. These messages contain current and predicted link travel times, or *impedances*. An important element of the work in this task dealt with development of equilibrium assignment techniques capable of running in near-real-time in order to update current and predicted link flows and travel times. This work continues in SOCRATES 2.

The task included the investigation of the different objectives of the traffic management authorities and those of the individual driver. There is a well-known difference between optimizing routing patterns for individuals and for various community objectives. One aspect still under investigation is the potential for weighting link impedances to modify slightly the otherwise individual optima in order to move closer towards the community optimum. This is sometimes put forward as a major difference between SOCRATES and the alternative EURO-SCOUT approach described in Chapter 4, but provisional results in SOCRATES have indicated that the differences may not be so great in terms of what is realistically achievable. Figure 6.2 shows the structure of the data collection and processing within the SOCRATES control center. Data are collected from a number of sources—conventional sources and the new floating car data source—and processed through the modeling procedures to produce the data transmitted to vehicles.

6.3.2 Communications

This task included the development of protocols suitable for transmitting traffic messages via SOCRATES, both for the common downlink and the multiple-access uplink. It involved close liaison with the ETSI GSM committees in order to feed the requirements of SOCRATES to the process of fully specifying the GSM system. Links were also established with the RACE UMTS (universal mobile telephone system) project, which is looking further ahead than GSM, to the next pan-European cellular radio system. Included in this task was the development of short-range beacons able to provide accurate positioning data to vehicles and to transmit local information.

6.3.3 System Design

This task was concerned with the overall design of the SOCRATES system, whose specification was the main output from the first SOCRATES project. It included the consideration of all the ATT applications discussed in Section 6.2, some of which are represented in Figure 6.3. This task included the development of an initial demonstration site at the Philips Project Centre in Geldrop, which included the transmission of data and messages to a vehicle equipped with a CARIN unit and a short-range beacon.

6.3.4 In-Vehicle Equipment

This task included the development of existing or new onboard systems able to make use of the data transmitted via SOCRATES. An initial work package investigated the requirements of the driver. Work continued on the definition of onboard data structures and the development of equipment able to combine the existing autonomous systems with real-time data from SOCRATES.

6.3.5 Test Site

A main objective of the project was to be able to demonstrate the concepts in a major test site. The city of Gothenburg was chosen during 1989, and the concept of the Test

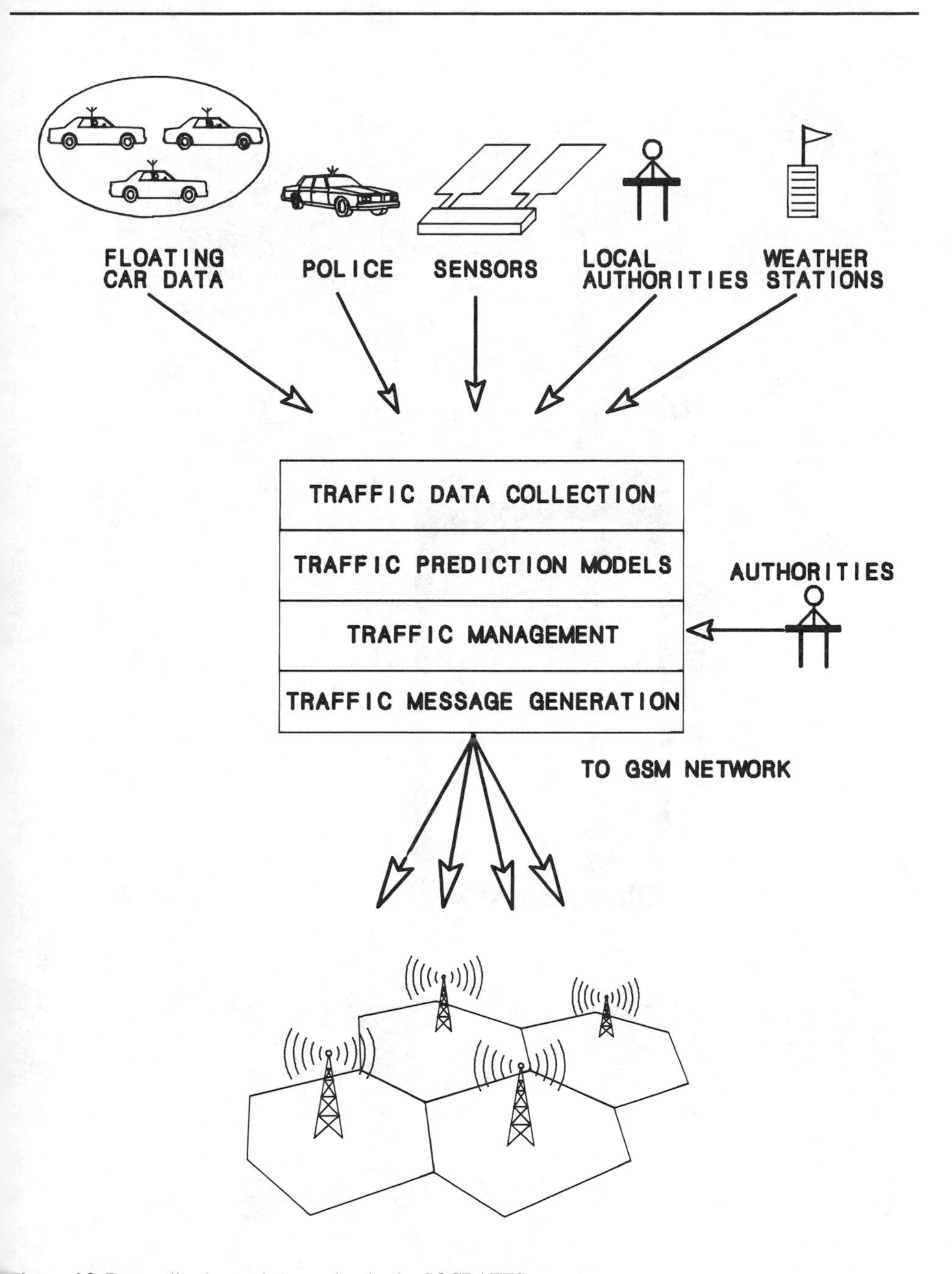

Figure 6.2 Data collection and processing in the SOCRATES system.

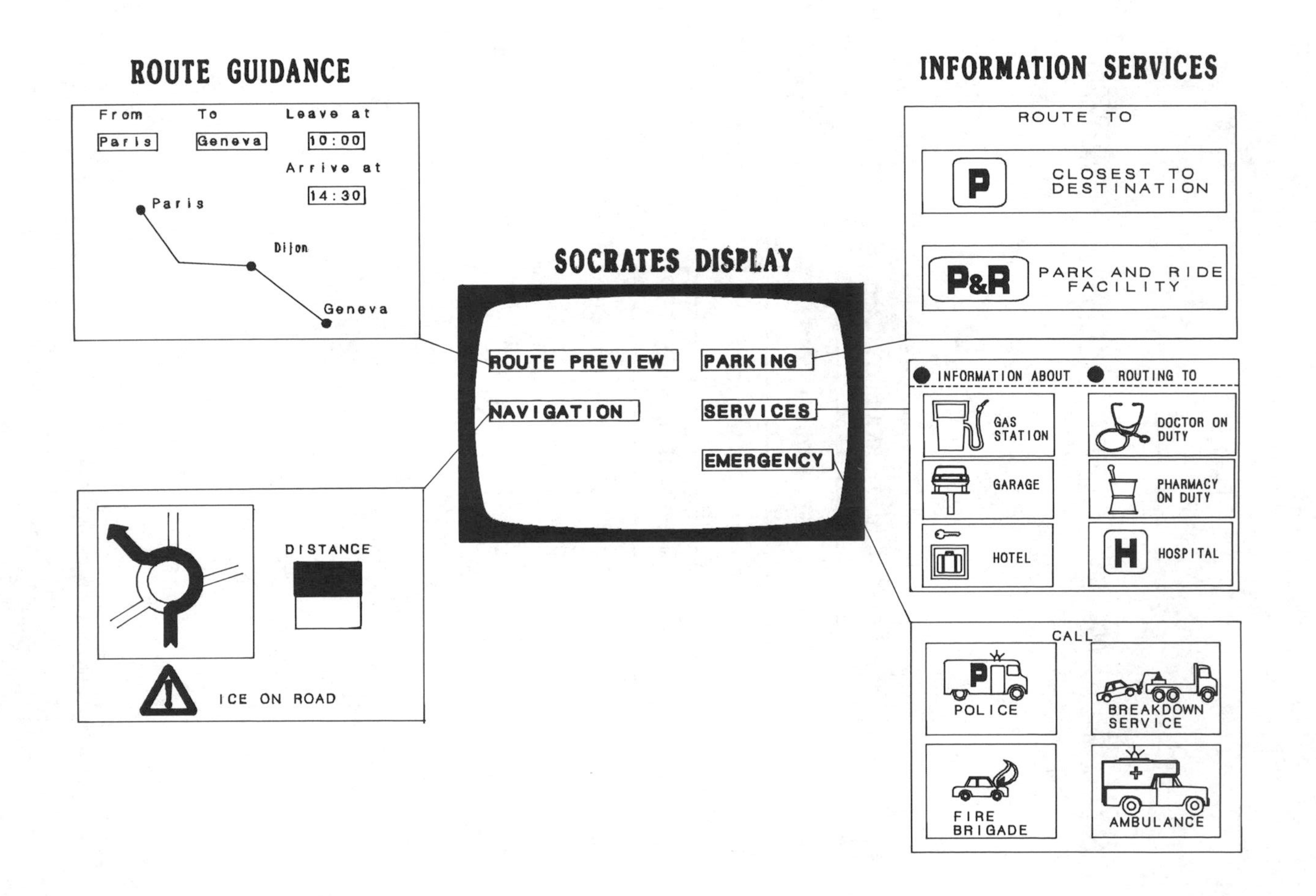

Figure 6.3 SOCRATES applications in the vehicle.

Site West Sweden, now known as ARENA, emerged from this decision. The test site became operational during the second half of 1991, and in November 1991 the results of the project [4] were presented during a conference and exhibition in Gothenburg, during which delegates were able to see SOCRATES working in six demonstration vehicles. True dynamic guidance was demonstrated using four base stations and direct connections with the traffic control center in which the SOCRATES information center was installed.

6.4 THE FOUR SOCRATES PROJECTS IN THE DRIVE II PROGRAM

This section outlines the four projects connected with the DRIVE II program, which are actively implementing the results of the DRIVE I SOCRATES project. The original SOCRATES project demonstrated that the concepts were soundly based and that there were no technical obstacles in the path of full implementation.

6.4.1 SOCRATES Kernel Project

During the concluding stages of the SOCRATES 1 project, the partners realized that there was a continuing need for the overall coordination of SOCRATES developments. Plans were being made for the implementation of SOCRATES pilot projects, and the concept emerged of a *Kernel* project, which would perform this function of overall coordination. The overall objectives of the SOCRATES Kernel project are therefore to coordinate the continued development of SOCRATES concepts in a number of specific pilot projects and services in order to make further progress towards an IRTE and to validate the results of the SOCRATES DRIVE I project. While the SOCRATES pilot projects are the center of a few specific developments, the Kernel serves as a central focus for contacts with standardization bodies for the development of certain central tasks such as traffic modeling, for investigating common aspects of the implementation of SOCRATES systems, and for the further development of SOCRATES concepts for a common system architecture for ATT systems. Specific objectives of the Kernel are:

- Liaison with pilot projects and overall coordination of SOCRATES developments;
- Continued liaison with ETSI-GSM and other standardization bodies (e.g., RES6, CEN) in order to contribute to the process of standardization;
- Research topics central to SOCRATES which were not answered in DRIVE I, such as developing and testing a basic MMI (hardware and dialog rules) for the core SOCRATES applications of dynamic route guidance and presentation of traffic information (RDS-TMC definitions), which can use head-up and/or head-down display technology and can also be developed in the future to support other applications;
- Further limited monitoring of traffic management strategy developments and database requirements for general use in SOCRATES control centers;

- Establishment of internal SOCRATES in-vehicle standards for equipment, especially those relating to equipment interfacing (these ''internal'' standards/views can then be presented to external standardization activities);
- Limited liaison with relevant organizations necessary to establish the commercial framework for SOCRATES services;
- Progress towards the establishment of the general SOCRATES system architecture common to all the SOCRATES pilots; and
- Representation of SOCRATES in Brussels.

The ultimate objective of the complete set of SOCRATES projects during the ATT program is to have moved SOCRATES closer to the point where commercial implementation is realistic in the immediate future.

6.4.2 SOCRATES Pilot Projects

The overall concept of SOCRATES is based on the collection, storage, and processing of road traffic information within traffic control centers and on the two-way information flow between vehicles and roadside infrastructure. One of the important outcomes of the original SOCRATES project, based on work carried out in conjunction with the other DRIVE I projects CIDER (V1043) and SECFO (V1056), was the development of concepts for a standardized (open) systems architecture for the IRTE, incorporating standardized communication protocols as far as possible. This would promote the interoperability of systems in different countries and the compatibility of in-vehicle equipment for different systems and services (see Chapter 2).

The next stage of SOCRATES development was seen as the validation of existing results in a few coordinated pilot projects and the preparation for commercial implementation of SOCRATES in Europe during the 1990s based on the establishment of standards, common communication protocols, and common systems architectures. There are three pilot projects that, in conjunction with the Kernel, are carrying out development work on specific aspects of SOCRATES implementations. These are taking place in Rhine-Main in Hessen, London, and Gothenburg and are described briefly in the next subsections.

Hessen—DRIVE II Project RHAPIT (V2055)

RHAPIT is the Rhein-Main Area Project for Integrated Traffic management. Its objective is to improve the powerful traffic management system in the Rhine-Main area by integrating with a SOCRATES dynamic route guidance system, and to interface highway control with public transport in the urban area of Frankfurt. RHAPIT is a corridor project that will use ''live'' GSM fixed and mobile equipment for the first time, with the cooperation and participation of the main German telecommunications operator and equipment manufacturers.

London—DRIVE II Project LLAMD/APPLE (V2033) and the TIGER Project

LLAMD is a major DRIVE II urban pilot project linking ATT developments in five European cities—London, Lyon, Amsterdam, Munich, and Dublin, together with the MARGOT subproject on modeling and assessment of route guidance (see Chapter 8).

In London, the APPLE (Advanced Pilot Project for London and Europe) subproject is linked to the planned implementation of a SOCRATES system of dynamic route guidance. APPLE includes the development of links between route guidance and traffic control, particular concentration on the development of a common system architecture for ATIS, and specific tasks relating to data collection for navigation systems.

In turn, APPLE is linked to the independently funded TIGER (Travel Information and Guidance for European Roads) project, which will provide for the actual SOCRATES system implementation.

Initial work focused on the existing analog TACS (Total Access Communication System) cellular radio system, but SOCRATES is planned to be based on GSM in the U.K. in the near future.

Gothenburg—DRIVE Project CITIES/TANGO (V2054)

The CITIES (Cooperation for Integrated Traffic Management and Information Exchange Systems) project links trial systems in Paris, Brussels, and Gothenburg to solve traffic problems using ATT technologies, including in-car information systems, paratransit systems, advanced traffic control, multimodal multimedia broadcast information, and advances in databases.

The TANGO (Traffic information And Navigation for GOthenburg) subproject is implementing the SOCRATES pilot project in Gothenburg using the commercially available Mobitex mobile packet data service.

6.4.3 Partners in the SOCRATES Projects

There are 37 organizations involved directly in the four SOCRATES projects in DRIVE II. Together, the total investment in SOCRATES committed to date by these organizations amounts to around 200 man-years. Table 6.1 lists the partners in each of the four SOCRATES DRIVE II projects.

6.4.4 Applications in the Pilot Projects

SOCRATES provides a range of ATT applications, as described in Section 6.2. In the future, this will lead to a range of products and services, providing customers with a choice of applications and levels of service. The first customer choice will involve the

Table 6.1
Partners in Each of the SOCRATES Projects

	SOCRATES Kernel	*RHAPIT (Hessen)*	*APPLE (London)*	*TANGO (Gothenburg)*
Coordinating partner	Ian Catling Consultancy	Hessisches Landesamt für Strassenbau	Ian Catling Consultancy	Test Site West Sweden
Main partners	Philips GEC Traffic BT Robert Bosch SEMA Group SAAB Automobile Daimler Benz Advanced Research Partners Swedish National Road Administration Universitat Politecnica de Catalunya	Philips Heusch Boesefeldt City of Frankfurt Robert Bosch Technische Universität München Daimler Benz Ford Motor Co. Flughafen Frankfurt Main Technische Universität Hamburg-Harburg Detecon Adam Opel BMW European Geographic Technologies Messegesellschaft Frankfurt	Philips GEC Traffic BT London Transport RAC Enterprises Lockheed IMS Corporation of London Ford Motor Co.	Philips Nobeltech Systems Traffic Research Institute Robert Bosch SEMA Group SAAB Automobile Swedish Telecom Radio Volvo Swedish Institute of Computer Science
Associated partners	Swedish Institute of Computer Science Sowerby Research Centre Rover Group Laboratoire d'Electronique Philips			

hardware to support the SOCRATES services, to be chosen typically from the following products:

- MMI computer;
- Navigation computer:
  - CARIN;
  - Travelpilot;
  - Others (e.g., Motorola or Sumitomo; see Chapters 11 and 15).
- Optional location improvement device (e.g., GPS receiver)
- Communication method:
  - RDS-TMC;
  - GSM;
- Others (e.g., Mobitex, as in TANGO).

The second selection will involve the choice of services to which to subscribe. Currently, the following SOCRATES applications are envisaged:

- Dynamic route guidance;
- Driver information;
- Fleet management;
- Tourist information;
- Traffic management;
- Emergency call;
- P&R/public transport information.

All seven applications are being tested in the three SOCRATES pilot projects in identical ways in each project. The level of service will, however, be less than envisaged for the future SOCRATES commercial introduction. An important task of the pilot projects is to provide feedback from the public and authorities about interests and requirements for these applications.

6.5 SOME MAJOR AREAS OF SOCRATES TECHNICAL DEVELOPMENT

Although the three pilot projects are using different radio bearer services, there is emphasis within the Kernel on the development of SOCRATES services based on GSM, which will be the first true pan-European communication system. This section describes each of the main activities in the Kernel project, which are concerned mainly with horizontal tasks.

6.5.1 Communications Protocols

In order for the three SOCRATES pilot projects to produce systems with equivalent core components and a convergent evolution path, it is essential to specify a common interface to communications functions. The decision has been taken in the SOCRATES pilots to use the Internet protocol standards as the basis for this common interface. Significant progress has been made in developing a proposal to use User Datagram Protocol (UDP) with Internetwork Protocol (IP). There are many advantages to UDP/IP, and this common approach is being adopted in each of the SOCRATES projects. In the longer term, the evolution to protocols supported by the ISO is being investigated. This path is also being taken by the Internet Activities Board, which is responsible for maintaining and developing the Internet suite of protocols.

6.5.2 Application Centers

At the heart of any SOCRATES system will be the application and information center. This work is coordinating the development of such centers. It includes the functional specifications of the SOCRATES road network and traffic databases, the applications within the information center, the interfaces between the traffic database and the applications, and the link with the communication network.

Agreement has been reached on the adoption of GDF as the common data standard for the three pilot projects, and the Kernel will review the implications of this decision. This work area also deals with the system engineering of the SOCRATES application center. It is concerned with the hardware and software platform of the centers, as well as implementational aspects of the various applications.

6.5.3 Communication System Modeling

This work concerns modeling the fixed and mobile communications used in the pilots, formulation of an interfacing profile, and liaison with bodies working on future mobile systems (to avoid the problems of retrospective standardization such as are necessary with GSM). The modeling work is common to all the pilots and deals with the performance of typical commercial SOCRATES systems which will follow the pilots.

6.5.4 Application Coding

The Kernel is coordinating work to produce a common set of standards for application data coding, both to and from equipped vehicles. This work is coordinated with other relevant projects, particularly ATT-ALERT (V2028) and PROMISE (V2012), through the TRACE (TRansport Application Coding for Europe) working group. SOCRATES is developing common data coding protocols for use in all the pilots for the main SOCRATES applications: dynamic route guidance, emergency call, and AVL/fleet management. SOCRATES coding for other applications will use structures developed in the other TRACE projects. In particular, the SOCRATES 1 project ensured compatibility between SOCRATES driver information messages and RDS-TMC; this compatibility is being actively maintained.

6.5.5 Location Coding

SOCRATES is actively contributing to the requirement for an internationally agreed-upon location coding standard that is suitable for the detailed nature of SOCRATES applications. This involves linking the SOCRATES requirements, from both the pilot projects and from later full-scale implementations, with both the RDS-TMC coding methodology and the future codes being developed within ATT-ALERT and other projects. This work is being carried out in the context of the adoption of GDF as the data exchange format for the SOCRATES projects.

6.5.6 Dynamic Route Planning

The Kernel is developing advanced techniques for in-vehicle route calculation. The work is targeted partly towards possible use in the pilots, but mainly towards future SOCRATES implementations. The work encompasses developments in both in-vehicle and control center systems in order to improve the quality of dynamic route planning while optimizing the use of the SOCRATES communication link. These developments include aspects of traffic prediction modeling, the parameterization of link travel times, hierarchical road network representations, and improved route planning algorithms.

6.5.7 Man-Machine Interface (MMI)

A common approach to MMI is being taken throughout the SOCRATES pilots under the overall coordination of the Kernel. The aim of kernel activities is not to develop specific dialogues for route guidance systems, but to consider the basic elements of the dynamic route guidance role from a user's perspective in terms of the user's behavioral and perceptual requirements rather than relating to an applications or facilities list.

There are two paths for kernel activity: one that concentrates on defining the technology availability and limitations in terms of size of display, resolution, brightness, contrast achievable, and so on, and one which concentrates on the user's access to applications. The latter uses the same display as for the route guidance messages, and other information sources (e.g., RDS-TMC), but will also allow the driver to access different facilities (e.g., P&R, emergency call, yellow pages, and so on). This means that although the display may be simple at any one time, the nested information within the system will need to be recalled by the user, meaning that the user will need to know the route through the system.

6.5.8 DRIVE Normalized Transmission (DNT)

The Kernel is making a significant contribution to the development of the DNT bearer-independent protocols for use with many ATT applications. This builds upon the work in the DRIVE I projects CIDER and SOCRATES 1 (see Chapter 2).

6.5.9 SOCRATES Proposal for a GSM General Packet Radio Service

SOCRATES combines advances in in-vehicle computers with the next generation of cellular telecommunications. For SOCRATES to achieve its goal of being a pan-European system for traffic efficiency and safety, it requires a pan-European telecommunications system. Optimally, the cellular network will provide common frequency allocation throughout Europe, high availability and quality based on an existing infrastructure, bidirectional digital communications, suitable addressing options, and sufficient data transfer capability. Currently, only GSM can meet these general requirements. SOCRATES communication requirements are summarized as follows.

Downlink

- Information needs to be broadcast (essential for dynamic route guidance, public information, P&R services), multicast (essential for corporate-based services, such as fleet management), and single-cast (for messages sent to a unique subscriber).
- The bulk of information is broadcast (over one or more cells).
- Data rate ranges from zero (in rural areas during the night) to about 8 kbps (in areas with very heavy traffic).
- Typical packet size is 150 to 1000 bits.

Uplink

- Information needs to be forwarded to a traffic center, an emergency center, a fleet owner, and so on.
- The bulk of the data will be floating car data.
- Data rate ranges from zero (in rural areas during the night) to a maximum of 8 packets per second per cell (in areas with heavy traffic).
- Typical packet size is 150 to 300 bits.

A number of further requirements have been specified [5]. The current phase of GSM goes some way to being able to meet SOCRATES communications requirements. Cell broadcast has been specified and is already appearing in networks. However, in order to provide SOCRATES with more suitable features and a more efficient data transmission capability, GSM's data services have to be extended. This extension has been called a *general packet radio service* (GPRS). Close liaison has been maintained between the SOCRATES projects and the GSM MoU group, and the proposal for the GPRS has been adopted as an important extension to be included in GSM. At the time of publication, work is already under way on the implementation of the GPRS, which is expected to become available within the same timetable as the commercial availability of SOCRATES services (i.e., during the mid 1990s).

6.5.10 Assessment of the Pilot Projects

A critical task for the Kernel is to coordinate as far as is possible the approach to be adopted towards assessment in each of the SOCRATES pilot projects. A specific work package was established in the Kernel to do this. The objectives of the evaluation work have been agreed upon: as far as possible a common approach to evaluation should be taken in the three SOCRATES pilot projects, with the Kernel performing the role of promoting this common approach. It should include common terminology that has been agreed on, shared approaches to questionnaire and experiment design, and common analysis of data collected in the pilots.

APPLE is part of the LLAMD Euro-Project, within which a similar approach is being taken towards a common assessment framework, but which includes EURO-SCOUT as well as SOCRATES systems. The SOCRATES projects have agreed to cooperate as far as possible with the LLAMD approach, which is partly based on the EVA (DRIVE I project V1036) recommendations, taking into account the field trials project (DRIVE I project V1049) results. A common set of experimental specifications is to be adopted by each of the pilots (although each pilot might not implement it in its entirety).

6.6 SOCRATES COMMERCIAL ACTIVITIES

SOCRATES 1 demonstrated the technical feasibility of the SOCRATES concept for ATT applications within the IRTE. Although the four DRIVE II SOCRATES projects are making technical progress towards a pan-European system, the main objective is to bring closer the commercial framework in which SOCRATES systems and services can be implemented.

The main aim is to compile a comprehensive business case that identifies the commercial exploitation value to be derived from SOCRATES services. Secondary aims include:

- Providing a SOCRATES-wide forum for debate on commercial issues;
- Acting as a dissemination center for the exchange of relevant information;
- Supporting the pilots in international promotional campaigns;
- Ensuring that relevant market data on ATT are passed on to the pilot projects.

The commercial task is divided into a number of activities encompassing both implementation and operational aspects and the definition of suitable operating structures for SOCRATES. The latter includes the determination of a generic service architecture applicable to the different circumstances in different regions, taking into account billing and subscription issues and information flows throughout the system. SOCRATES is now moving beyond research and development and into a more commercial atmosphere. Consequently, new obligations are appearing.

The engagement of different partners on different levels is necessary to provide confidence that SOCRATES partners are willing to set up and operate a business. Groups who require this confidence include traffic authorities and managers, political institutions, standards bodies, license-granting authorities, and future business partners, so a SOCRATES MoU has been proposed and is currently being considered by the organizations actively involved in SOCRATES.

The responsibilities of a SOCRATES MoU would include the following:

- To argue for SOCRATES on behalf of all partners on a political level;
- To represent the interests of SOCRATES within standardization bodies;
- To coordinate SOCRATES's industrial base;
- To ensure the technical standardization of basic services;

- To coordinate marketing activities on behalf of SOCRATES;
- For partners to find their role within a SOCRATES MoU.

By definition, a SOCRATES MoU means that signatories agree upon a set of obligations. Such a set of obligations would include the type of service each signatory would provide and when it would be provided. An intermediate body, perhaps within the Kernel, has been proposed to prepare the ground for an MoU group to take forward the implementation of SOCRATES into the next stage beyond the current pilot projects.

REFERENCES

[1] Jeffery, D. J., K. Russam, and D. I. Robertson, ''Electronic Route Guidance by Autoguide: the Research Background,'' *Traffic Engineering and Control*, London, England, Oct. 1987.

[2] Weling, F., B. Jønsson, and D. Demery, ''The Use of Cellular Mobile Radio for Traffic Responsive Navigation,'' *Telecom 91: 6th World Telecommunication Exhibition and Forum*, Palexpo, Geneva, Oct. 1991.

[3] Challe, P., 1990, ''CARMINAT,'' *Proc. Workshop on Navigation and Planning*, Nasslingen, Sweden.

[4] DRIVE: SOCRATES 1 Final Report, 1992.

[5] Zijderhand, F., ''SOCRATES Overview,'' internal document, Dec. 1992.

Chapter 7

Automatic Toll Collection for Pricing the Use of Road Space—Using Microwave Communications Technology

Peter Hills and Philip Blythe

7.1 INTRODUCTION AND BACKGROUND

7.1.1 Overview

The trend in transport policy in Europe is increasingly towards the recovery of construction and maintenance costs of new roads and car parks by the use of tolls. This "user pays" trend and the re-emergence on the political agenda of some form of variable road-use pricing to manage traffic demand means that an automatic variable for enabling a financial transaction between equipment mounted in a vehicle and the roadside will soon be needed. Automatic debiting of this kind, without the necessity of stopping the vehicle or for any action by the driver, has long been recognized as the only efficient way of achieving this. So far, most automatic nonstop debiting systems have been developed for the conventional toll-road market. Consequently, a profusion of these systems now exist across Europe and elsewhere. However, most of these current systems of automatic revenue collection have a limited functionality and cannot support all the requirements necessary for a pan-European debiting system, which would be capable of such diverse applications as nonstop tolling, car park information and management, and, ultimately, variable road-use pricing.

This chapter will describe the ongoing research being performed to develop an acceptable pan-European system for automatic debiting in a transport environment by the EC DRIVE. In DRIVE I (1989 to 1991), the PAMELA (*Pricing and Monitoring Electronically of Automobiles*) project has been responsible for the design and development of standard equipment for the nonstop automatic debiting of vehicles and related applica-tions requiring communications between a roadside beacon and a transponder in a vehicle Furthermore, the results of the recent small-scale evaluation trials performed with th system for three different automatic debiting applications will be described. Finally, th continuing development and the most recent test installations of the PAMELA technolog will be described in the context of the DRIVE II/ATT project ADEPT (1992 to 1994) which is described in Section 7.5.

The PAMELA consortium was headed jointly by the University of Newcastle Upo Tyne and Newcastle Upon Tyne Polytechnic (U.K.). Other partners in the consortiun were Philips Research Laboratories (U.K.) Saab-Scania Automation (Sweden), Compagni de Signaux et d'Equipments Electroniques (CSEE) (France), Philips Components Applica-tion Laboratory (Germany), and Empresa de Investigacao e Disenvolvimento de Electron-ica (EID) (Portugal).

7.1.2 The Automation of Toll Collection

As the use of tolls becomes more widely accepted, the drawbacks of conventional tol collection methods will be accentuated. The disruption of traffic flow due to the need t stop at toll sites will become acute as the predicted increases in road traffic materializ (in the U.K., for example, traffic demand has risen by 40% in the past decade, whil main road capacity has increased by only 5%). It is generally accepted that, for each lan of a highway, three conventional toll lanes are necessary to process the traffic at "stop and-pay" tolls, whereas a nonstop toll collection system would increase the vehicle processing capability of a single toll lane (up to threefold). The reduced congestion a the site would, in turn, reduce journey times. Financial benefits for the operator will als include a steady reduction in staff costs as the number of automated lanes is increase and the physical area necessary for each toll site is reduced. The scope for debt, frauc and evasion should be substantially reduced as well, since less cash is handled.

The first notable experiments in the use of nonstop tolling were performed by th Port Authority of New York and New Jersey in the late 1970s [1]. By the use of a automatic vehicle identification (AVI) system, toll payments could be charged to th user's credit account with the toll company. However, the first large-scale demonstratio scheme of AVI was the Hong Kong ERP experiment, which used inductive loop technolog to facilitate communications between a vehicle and an automatic tolling station at th roadside.

Although the technology was shown to be highly successful, the ERP system wa severely limited in its scope due to the low rate of data transfer that can be achieved wit inductive loop communications. This, together with the size of the vehicle unit and th cost of installation and maintenance of the buried loops, makes the use of inductive loo communications unattractive for future AVI and tolling applications.

Despite the growing number of experimental systems, the world's first automati tolling system was installed for commercial use at the Ålesund tunnel in Norway at th end of 1987. The system, called PREMID, had been developed by Philips A/B in Sweden, but the rights to PREMID were bought by Saab-Scania Combitech, who replaced Philips as a member of the PAMELA consortium at that time. The PREMID device uses a transponder, which is about the size of a cigarette packet, mounted in the side window of each vehicle. As in the Hong Kong experiment, the transponder contains coded information relating to the identity of the vehicle, and when passing the toll site, the incident microwave signal from the roadside interrogator is reflected back from the transponder. The successful operation of the PREMID installation and other technology-based tolling systems (such as TELEPASS, KøFRI, and AMTECH, to name but a few) suggest that such systems will find increasing markets worldwide. At present, however, the AVI systems only convey a limited amount of information to and from the vehicle to the roadside computer. It is clear that if a large-scale road-use pricing scheme is to be successfully introduced, it will need to use some form of automatic system for revenue collection. However, even the high-technology equipment described above may not have sufficient functionality to meet the requirements of high speed, reliability, and, above all, anonymity for the users. It is likely that the vehicle-roadside communications system for future tolling applications will be based on either microwave or infrared communications, but the trend is towards microwave due to its relative immunity to environmental disturbances over short ranges (less than 50m) and to the high data rates that can potentially be supported (several hundred kbps). The following section describes a new generation of system of a sufficiently advanced modular design to meet the requirements of any road-revenue collection system or road-use pricing system.

7.2 THE PAMELA PROJECT

7.2.1 Objectives of the PAMELA Project

The objectives of the project were to specify, design, develop, and demonstrate equipment to facilitate two-way data communications between a moving vehicle and a fixed roadside station for nonstop automatic debiting applications such as road tolling, road-use pricing, and car parking. The heart of the system is a high-capacity, short-range microwave communications link. Above all, the link must be reliable and have the ability to allow communications between roadside beacons and vehicles' transponders at high speed (up to 160 km/h) in both single-lane and unrestricted multilane environments.

The onboard unit consists of a small transponder mounted in the windscreen of a vehicle, which will contain the necessary communications circuits and a dedicated microprocessor, as well as the ability to interface to other peripheral equipment in the vehicle (e.g., smart-card reader, display, keyboard, CPU, and sensors). Hence, the transponder may be standalone, or it may ultimately be interfaced to other in-vehicle equipment to support any number of other RTI applications.

Alongside the technical R&D work, substantial resources are also employed in the specification and design of field trials, so that the feasibility of this new communications link and the full systems can be tested. Two important areas of application have been chosen for the demonstration tests: namely, automatic tolling and parking control and pricing. These probably represent the most immediate and promising areas of Europewide application using this technology. However, future applications of the technology such as cordon-based road-use pricing (whereby a watertight cordon of road pricing points are used to define a ''prices'' area) and congestion monitoring and pricing have also been catered to in the design, although field trials of these applications were not scheduled before the end of the PAMELA contract under the DRIVE I program. Finally, the results of monitoring each of these field tests will be evaluated to establish, in broad social cost-benefit terms, the likely returns from large-scale investment in this new technology to tackle RTI problems.

7.2.2 Automatic Charging

The use of cashless payment systems to collect road tolls or car parking charges is not a recent innovation. Indeed, a number of systems have been demonstrated over the past two decades. Most of these cashless systems still require drivers to stop and pay using some kind of card or token. However, nonstop electronic payment systems are now in use in toll collection [2]. The first-generation electronic systems have all relied on some means to identify the vehicle (AVI), and a charge is levied accordingly (off line) from an account held at the roadside. Second-generation systems generally offer some read-write capability on the transponder, though with a limited functionality. Such systems have taken their place in single-lane toll sites at bridges and tunnels, but a system that can support a number of different applications (potentially on a large scale) must have a higher level of performance and greater functionality built into it. The PAMELA system, therefore, leads the third generation of such systems. In principle, there are four possible ways of implementing automatic toll collection based on transactions between a roadside charge station and an automatic debiting system (ADS) device fitted to a vehicle, as follows.

Simple AVI/Postpayment

Currently the most widespread method of nonstop toll payment, simple AVI requires the least complex equipment. Simple AVI merely records the unique identity of each vehicle and the time of day that the vehicle passed through the toll site, whose location is known. The validation of the identity code is carried out on line, but, in most cases, the collection of the toll revenue is a subsequent offline process, either by deducting the fee from an account held with the toll authority or by billing the vehicle owner at a later date, as was the case with the Hong Kong ERP scheme. Fears of an individual's privacy being invaded may arise due to the necessity of having a central computer record of the information regarding each vehicle's movement and identity collected and stored at the toll site. It is also a clumsy and bureaucratic way of collecting fees.

Secure AVI/EFTPOS

Secure AVI is the method of toll payment favored in a number of proposed automatic tolling schemes. An encrypted code relating to each vehicle's identity is transmitted to the roadside tolling station. Once the identification has been validated, the financial transaction may be performed by means of electronic funds transfer at point-of-sale (EFTPOS), which can guaranty the "external" security of the information. Once the transaction has been completed, the information gathered can then be destroyed. In practice, however, the vehicle owner may wish to have access to a record of recent transactions carried out with his or her debiting device in case it is necessary to contest the validity of the transactions.

Crucial to the success of this method is the built-in security of the data and of the funds-transfer mechanism and the need to perform the transaction in real time. This may not be a problem where only a small number of subscribers are involved, but where a large scheme is to be implemented (e.g., the road pricing scheme that was proposed for the Netherlands) millions of vehicles may be involved. This begs the question as to what access time is required if a computer must search though a vast number of information files in a database (even at a local or regional level, let alone nationally) prior to finding each user's correct account. The problem would be multiplied enormously if the ADS system were to be part of a comprehensive pan-European road tolling or pricing system.

Subscription and Pre- or Postpayment

Using a tag as a subscription record offers the possibility of operating either with identification or with anonymity. Identification of the user or subscription profile enables the details of the subscription, such as the number of passages allowed ("carnet") or period of subscription (week, month), to be stored in a roadside database. Each recorded passage of a tag results in a deduction from the subscriber's account. Anonymous subscription may be realized by storing the pertinent information concerning the terms or contract for the subscription directly in the tag's memory (or on a separate smart card).

ADS Prepayment

There are bound to be problems with any system that needs vehicle owners to subscribe to an account operated by the toll authority, and that is debited each time a subscriber's vehicle passes through a toll site. A system giving more intelligence to the transponder unit on the vehicle should overcome these problems. A "smartcard" device, similar to that of a phone card, but rechargeable, would enable credit units to be deducted without the need to identify either the vehicle or its owner. The credit units can be electronically stored on the transponder card in a *secure* area of a microprocessor's memory, along with other relevant information, such as the class of vehicle. In this way, a tariff with differential charges for vehicles of different size or weight can be operated automatically.

These credit units could then be recharged, using the portable smartcard concept, in an online debiting facility linked directly to the vehicle owner's bank account; alternatively, credit units could be bought and stored on the card using cash or a normal credit card. Again, the need for a personal record, stored on the transponder, containing information regarding the more recent transactions is necessary to give the user a comprehensive record of the transactions and to check for any erroneous debiting of the device [3].

Initially, the PAMELA consortium considered the concept of prepayment using a single integrated device, which contains the credit units and all the necessary logic and microwave communications circuits. However, as the project developed, it became clear that although this approach would satisfy many existing user organizations, a *separate* (portable) smartcard interfaced to the transponder would also be desirable for other debiting applications. This led the consortium to define a number of different versions of the transponder, each with essentially the same core of equipment, but with different levels of functionality. This is discussed in more detail later.

7.2.3 Anonymity of the Transaction

The introduction of automatic debiting technology is bound to raise a number of contentious social and political issues. At present, nonstop tolling systems require that each vehicle is uniquely identified using AVI, and the appropriate charge is either deducted directly from the user's account or sent as a bill for using the facility to the vehicle owner at a later date. Both methods necessitate that information about each vehicle's movements are recorded by a central computer. This may well be unacceptable to vehicle users, even if the responsibility for the protection of the data is clearly defined and legislated for. Indeed, the Hong Kong ERP experiment was canceled, not because of any problems with the technology, but, in part, because of social and political objections of this kind, mainly the perceived threat to individual's freedom of movement which postpayment methods of pricing imply.

The use of a prepayment method for revenue collection overcomes a number of the publicly expressed reservations concerning the system's operation, particularly the anonymity of users and the security of information. However, crucial to the success of any automatic system of revenue collection will be the voluntary acceptance by vehicle users who, by direct example, come to appreciate the advantages to them and to their business of the more efficient automatic option. This has been proved time and again. For example, the installation of the PREMID toll collection system in Ålesund has shown that potential subscribers can be induced to participate in the new automatic system as the benefits become apparent. After only one year of operation, over 60% of the frequent users of the Ålesund Tunnel had opted for the automatic toll as opposed to the conventional payment of tolls using manual cash or card machines. Now, more than 85% have done so. As with the Hong Kong experience, the compulsory imposition of an unknown system, to which everyone must subscribe, is unlikely to be accepted politically.

7.3 AN OUTLINE OF THE PAMELA SYSTEM

7.3.1 System Requirements

The fruits of the PAMELA research program will be a third-generation automatic debiting system, which will be able to support a number of different applications such as road tolling, road-use pricing, and car parking debiting. The functionality of the equipment has been defined in close cooperation with a number of leading European user groups, both within and outside the DRIVE program. The automatic road-tolling systems have been defined to meet the requirements of the VITA group [4], which consists of the highway toll associations of France (ASFA), Spain (ASETA), and Italy (AISCAT). For road-use pricing, the functional requirements have been defined, to a large extent, to meet the requirements of the Rijkswaterstaat project *Rekening Rijden* in the Netherlands [5], and the requirements for onstreet car parking have been produced in cooperation with the Camara Municipal of Lisboa. The functional and technical requirements for a generic high-performance automatic debiting system have been further analyzed in the DRIVE II/ATT project CASH, which aims to develop a common functional specification for such equipment and systems that will be input to European standardization activities. The PAMELA (and subsequent ADEPT) project plans to have open system architectures, which will be readily adaptable to such specifications if and when they become available.

7.3.2 Description of the System

7.3.2.1 Modules of the System

The system consists of three distinct modules: (1) a physical communications link between the roadside and in-vehicle transponder equipment (using microwave technology), (2) transponder logic circuits and other in-vehicle equipment, (3) a roadside charging station (RCS) and central control interface.

7.3.2.2 The Physical (Vehicle-to-Roadside) Communications Link

The roadside beacon in the PAMELA system will be mounted either on a gantry above the roadway or on a post at the side of the road, and the transponder, being of small size, will be mounted unobtrusively in the windscreen of each vehicle. Online enforcement of noncompliant vehicles will be a key requirement from the user organizations. This has led to the two-way communications range of the microwave link being limited to about 40m. The constraint on the range of the system has permitted the PAMELA consortium to adopt the semipassive approach to transponder design, whereby the transponder receives modulated data from the roadside beacon when in a ''listening'' mode, and an unmodulated carrier signal from the roadside beacon when in the ''talking'' mode. The transponder then modulates the received carrier signal and ''reflects'' this signal back to the roadside. The unmodulated incident signal and the reflected data signal can be separated either by modulation or by polarization. This technique is a cost-effective solution to the problem, since no frequency generation source is required on the transponder, and the frequency stability of the system is governed solely by the roadside equipment. Other advantages of this approach are:

- The transponders may be made at a relatively low cost;
- Frequency stability is looked after by the interrogator;
- The communication volume is better defined;
- There is no radiation interference from one vehicle to another;
- The transponder has a low battery power requirement; and
- Frequency reuse and multifrequency transmissions from adjacent roadside beacons are governed solely by the roadside equipment.

Current prototypes use an array of microstrip antennas at the roadside and two single microstrip antenna patches on the transponder. Initial prototypes developed in 1990 operated at a frequency of 2.45 GHz. The 2.45-GHz microwave communications link was evaluated on a completed but unopened stretch of the Newcastle Western Bypass. High-speed and multivehicle tests were undertaken and the performance of the link was comprehensively evaluated with promising results, which are reported in [6]. However, to comply with a decision of the CEPT to allocate a higher frequency band for short-range road-to-vehicle communication links, a second version was developed at 5.8 GHz in early 1991. This new link was used for all the field trial evaluations described in this chapter. The basic parameters of current link prototypes are shown in Table 7.1.

7.3.2.3 In-Vehicle Equipment

Transponder

The vehicle-mounted transponder must be capable of supporting all the necessary functions to perform and validate the debiting transaction. All the payment options described previously are provided for in the design, since some users may require only an AVI system rather than the more complex prepayment automatic debiting. Three versions of the transponder have been defined and are shown in Figure 7.1. The core of the transponder is identical in all three versions and contains a microprocessor, memory, microwave

Table 7.1
The Basic Parameters of Current Link Prototypes

Prototype	*Parameter*
Transceiver:	
Transmitted (Tx) power	500 mW EIRP
Frequency range (Norm)	5.795–5.805 GHz
Frequency range (Multilane)	5.795–5.815 GHz
Tx antenna gain (16-patch array)	16.5 dB
Receive (Rx) antenna gain (16-patch array)	16.5 dB
Tx and Rx antenna beamwidth	±5°
Polarization (downlink)	LH circular
Polarization (uplink)	RH circular
Transponder:	
Tx and Rx antenna gain	4 dB
Tx and Rx antenna beamwidth	±45°
Gain on reflected sideband	>5dB
Bit rate and modulation:	
Bit rate (downlink)	187.5 kbps
Bit rate (uplink)	250.0 kbps
Modulation (downlink)	FM-0, ASK
Modulation (uplink)	NRZ-I, FSK (subcarrier) ASK (double sideband)
Shift frequencies	750 kHz and 1,000 kHz
Data protocol	HDLC modified
Effective range:*	
Downlink	>40m
Uplink	>30m

Note: LH = left-hand; RH = right-hand; FM = frequency modulations; ASK = amplitude shift key; FSK = frequency shift key; NRZI = non–return to zero (inverted).
*Given good onsite environmental conditions

interface, transaction register, data encryption, and a transaction indicator. However, the interfaces to the driver and other in-vehicle equipment vary in complexity between the versions. The transaction register is a section of the E^2PROM memory used to store information regarding a number of the most recent transactions (between 100 and 200); the information can only be accessed by the registered user via a personal identification number (PIN). The information stored could, for example, be used to contest a transaction if a user feels a mistake has arisen. It also enables the user to monitor the amount of credit remaining on the transponder. Using a secret key, sensitive data messages are encrypted to protect the data and check the authenticity of the transponder. Figure 7.2 is a photograph of the internal components of the prototype transponder including the microstrip communications board.

Versions 1 and 2 of the equipment are integrated devices that perform all of the necessary automatic debiting functions and facilitate communications to the RCS, while

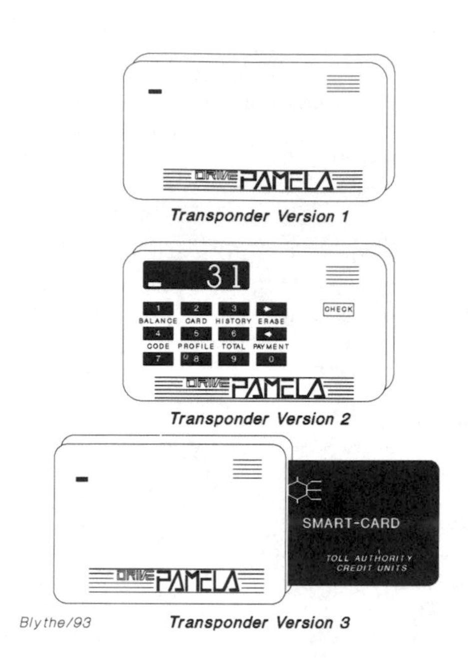

Figure 7.1 Transponder.

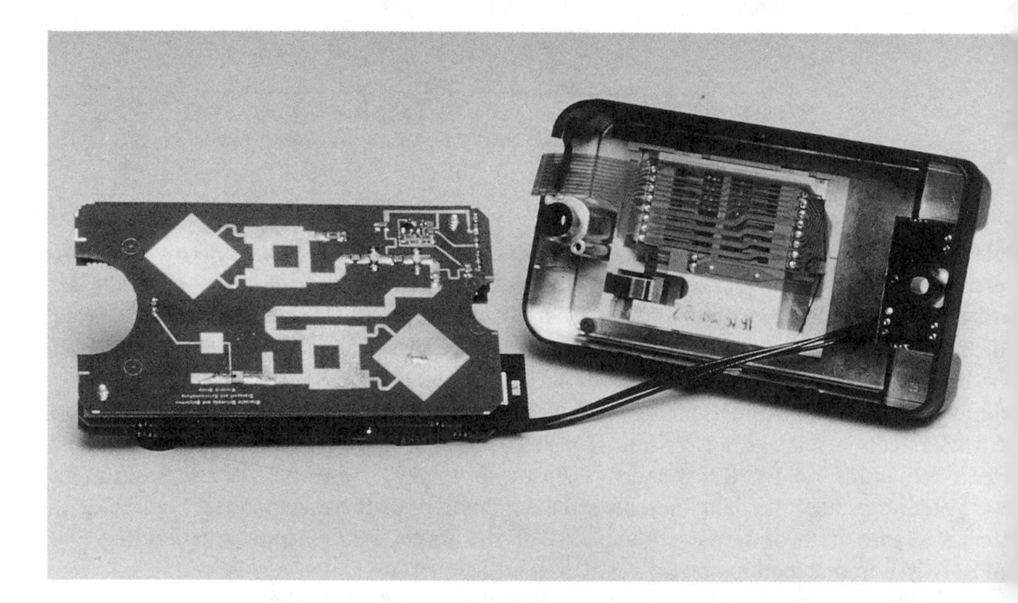

Figure 7.2 Internal components of the prototype transponder, including the microstip communications board.

version 3 contains a separate credit-carrying smartcard. All three versions consist of the same basic core, and each version provides a general purpose interface bus for connection to other external in-vehicle peripherals. The interface could be used to support such in-vehicle devices as a dashboard display and keyboard. This demonstrates the potential for using the road-vehicle communications system for other functions besides just automatic debiting (such as in-vehicle driver information and guidance). A more detailed description of the PAMELA system is given by [7].

Onboard Unit

The PAMELA onboard unit (OBU) links the two-way communications with a roadside unit using a microwave data link to other equipment modules covering the whole range of different RTI applications. In field trials to date, it has primarily been used for automatic debiting applications such as car parking, road-use tolling, and road-use pricing. The OBU itself is an intelligent device, which can handle real-time, high-speed data communications and processing for each desired application. For nondebiting applications (such as driver information and route guidance), the OBU is effectively transparent to data and passes the data directly to and from other dashboard or in-vehicle equipment, using an I^2C or CAN interface bus, which has already been tested successfully in the road-vehicle environment.

Modularity of Design

The design of the OBU electronics is essentially modular, allowing different components such as the peripheral devices (display, keyboard, buzzer, LED, etc.), analog circuits, microwave circuits, and smartcard reader to be connected to the OBU's digital core by serial data links. In turn, this allows a high degree of flexibility in the production of variants of the design and peripheral devices, to be integrated with them into the OBU or in the vehicle dashboard or even as a separate peripheral device. See Figure 7.3.

Use of Smartcards

The separate portable smartcard, interfaced to the in-vehicle transponder, is an option that is being considered by both Rijkswaterstaat and the VITA group. This option would enable a multimodal smartcard to be carried by an individual to pay for different services (including automatic debiting) when the transponder in the vehicle is equipped with a smartcard reader. This is catered to in version 3 of the equipment.

In-Vehicle Data Bus

To facilitate a modular structure to the transponder, an in-vehicle data-bus using the I^2C interface is provided for in the OBU design. We are investigating whether a different

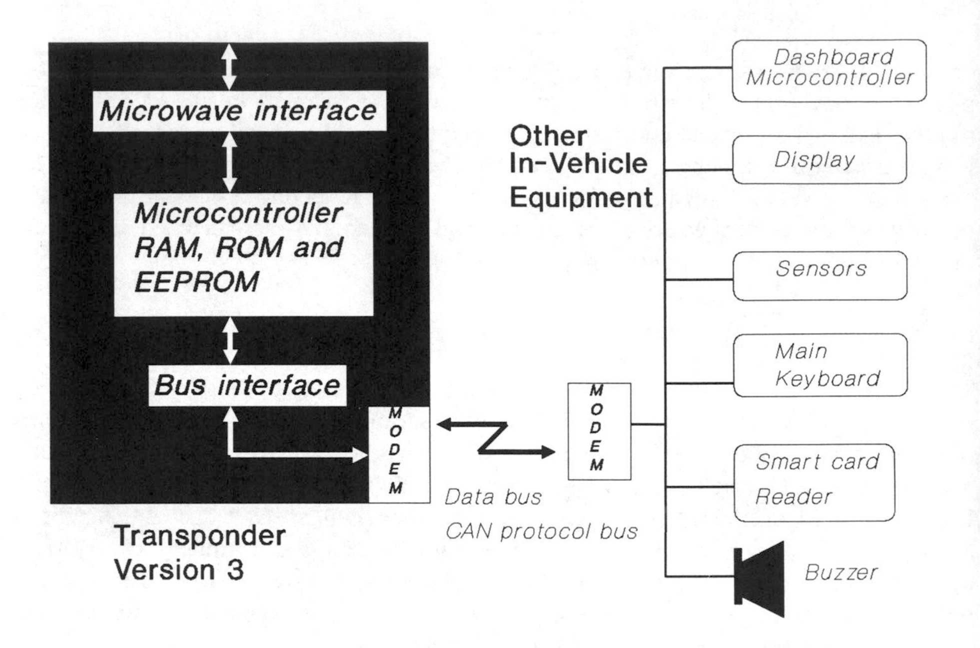

Figure 7.3 Flexibility in the production of variants of the design and the peripheral devices.

standard bus should be implemented for automotive applications; the controller area network (CAN) is currently the most favored alternative. All in-vehicle peripherals would then be connected to this data bus (display, keyboard, sensors, smartcard reader, vehicle, CPU). The peripherals may thus be integrated with the OBU (in the case of the smart card reader in some versions of the equipment) or located elsewhere in the vehicle, as illustrated in Figure 7.4. This flexibility enables the transponder-based system to be expanded to support other RTI applications when the need arises.

7.3.2.4 Roadside Charging Station

The RCS may be considered as a number of interconnected subsystems. The system may stand alone if the charging operation is only for a single pricing site, such as an open-tolled road, bridge, or tunnel site. However, in most cases the toll site will be part of a closed-toll, cordon pricing, or an onstreet parking network. If this is the case, the RCS will require a communications link to a central control unit, where information on subscribers' bank accounts would be held. (The networking to a central computer may not be necessary where prepaid credit units are to be deducted. However, this facility should be an available option.) There are three main subsystems of the RCS.

1. Roadside transceiver is the communications equipment necessary for microwave communications with the vehicle transponder.

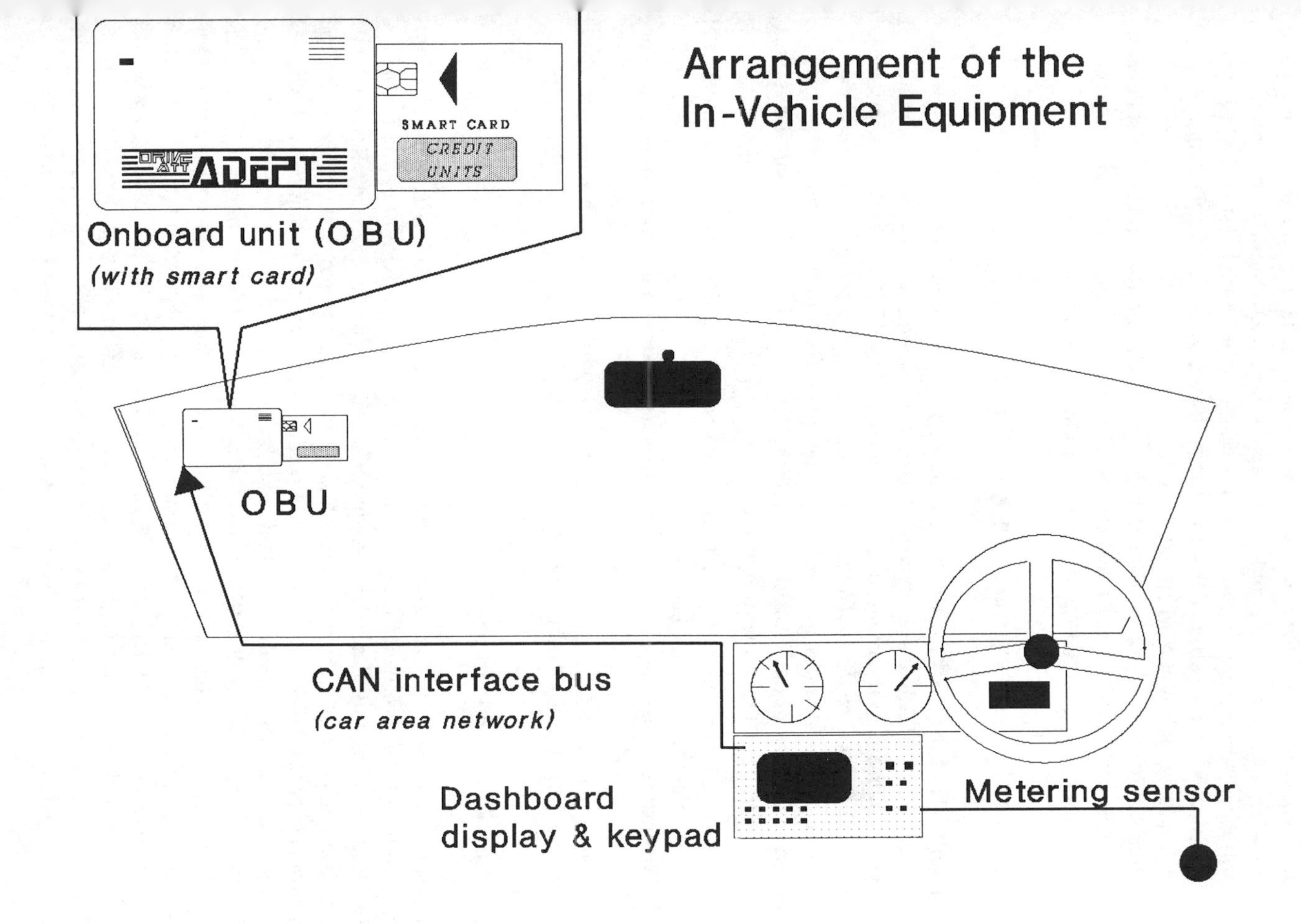

Figure 7.4 Peripherals located elsewhere in the vehicle.

2. Roadside lane and link controllers handle the real-time communications and application processing within the roadside system. This includes the communications protocol handling, transaction, and other application and multilane communications software. Furthermore, it provides connections to the central system and peripheral roadside devices, such as detection loops, lights, variable-message signs (VMS), and barriers (when and where appropriate).
3. Roadside central control is for batch processing, subscription, and blacklist handling routines developed for the PAMELA system. These routines would be integrated into an existing central control system in most applications.

7.4 FIELD TRIALS OF THE PAMELA SYSTEM

The field trials of the PAMELA system were carried out during the last six months of 1991. Since the PAMELA system is still under development, only small numbers of prototype equipment were produced for these initial trials 25 OBUs (two with integrated displays), 20 TB100 smartcards, 6 roadside transceivers, 4 communications boards (PC-based lane controllers), and 1 multilane link controller. Each of these field trials used the same core equipment of the PAMELA system, which was adapted to support the applications to be demonstrated at the different pilot sites. The trials undertaken were:

1. High-speed, nonstop automatic tolling by prepayment, demonstrated on the SAPN (Paris-Normandie) autoroute in France;
2. An onstreet car parking debiting and management experiment, carried out in Lisbon, Portugal; and
3. Multivehicle, multilane communications for road-use pricing in free-flow, high-speed traffic, performed in Sweden.

7.4.1 Paris-Normandie Autoroute

The operators of the Paris-Normandie toll highway kindly allowed CSEE to install equipment on two of their toll lanes (one in each direction) for test purposes. The PAMELA lane controller was linked to the conventional toll equipment so that tests could be carried out with or without barriers, vehicle detectors, and enforcement. Furthermore, the performance of the PAMELA system could be directly compared to that of the PREMID tag equipment, which was also installed (and operated commercially) on the toll lanes. The toll site layout for the Paris-Normandie autoroute field trial is shown in Figure 7.5.

The evaluation of the system was carried out on three days (in separate weeks) in September 1991. During this time, 490 separate passages by vehicles fitted with PAMELA OBUs were carried out. An automatic transaction was performed and recorded by the tag for each run. OBUs were placed in the vehicles' windscreen and were found not to be at all sensitive to the mounting location or angle. Tests were performed in accordance with the VITA test specification [4]. Vehicle speeds were limited in the tests to 70 km/h.

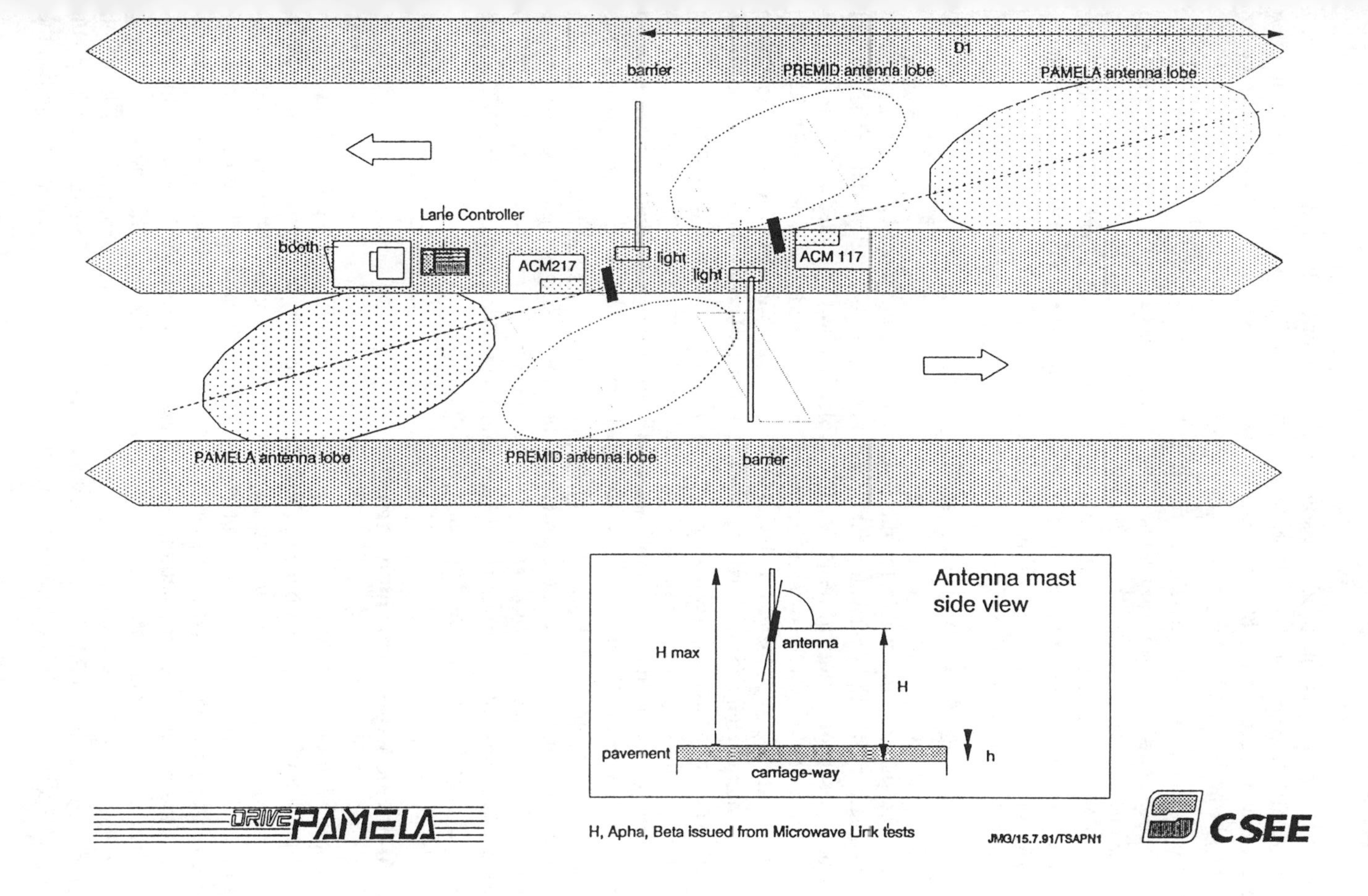

Figure 7.5 Toll site layout for the Paris-Normandie autoroute field trial: monolane field tests.

However, this restriction of speed was solely a function of the test site geometry and not of the PAMELA system itself. Indeed, tests were carried out successfully on the open road at vehicle speeds up to 180 km/h. During the 490 passages, four different categories of test were performed:

- Regular transit of single vehicles fitted with OBUs;
- Regular transit with several vehicles fitted with OBUs following each other through the site at close spacing (1m or 2m separation);
- Transit tests including mixed traffic (i.e., some vehicles with OBUs and some without) to test the performance of the detection and enforcement systems; and
- Transit with a vehicle being driven backwards.

7.4.2 Car Parking Management and Debiting in Lisbon

EID was the partner responsible for the integration of the PAMELA system with the existing onstreet car parking management system in Lisbon, operated by Camara Municipal de Lisboa (a subcontractor in the PAMELA project). It was planned that two onstreet parking zones would be defined using three PAMELA roadside transceivers. The roadside network would monitor vehicles fitted with OBUs passing through the network and charge the driver automatically for the time the vehicle spent parked in one of these controlled zones, thus providing dynamic parking occupancy information for real-time traffic information purposes. Initially, these tests were planned to start in November 1991. However, problems with some of the communications software in the lane controller has delayed the main tests until 1993. Nevertheless, some early tests have been performed with the system to demonstrate the in-vehicle parking information functions. A larger demonstration of the car parking management and control (including prebooking and guidance to available spaces) will be set up in Lisbon as part of the DRIVE II project ADEPT. Figure 7.6 shows a photograph of the prototype display and keypad connected to the OBU (using the I^2C bus) for the car parking demonstration equipment.

7.4.3 Multilane Experiments in Sweden

A demonstration of the multi-lane communications capabilities of the PAMELA system was made by Saab-Scania Combitech in Enjöping, Sweden, during the autumn of 1991. For the multilane communications, the slotted ALOHA communications protocol was used to handle a whole set of transponders simultaneously within range of the roadside transceivers. This approach is described in [8]. In the experiment, three roadside transceivers were used which were mounted on an overhead gantry to provide a communications zone covering the whole road (approximately 2½ lane widths). The transceivers were linked together using one link controller. In the experiment, a number of vehicles fitted with between one and six PAMELA OBUs were driven under the gantry at speeds between 10 and 160 km/h in order to simulate a multilane environment. Figure 7.7 shows the

Figure 7.6 Prototype display and keypad.

Figure 7.7 Arrangement of the test site at Enjöping.

arrangement of the test site at Enjöping. A summary of the dynamic tests carried out in this first multilane demonstration are:

- High speed. Ten passages with two cars (driving side by side) with two transponders in each car at a speed of 120 km/h;
- Worst case. Ten passages with one car fitted with six transponders at a speed of 120 km/h (as shown in Figure 7.8);
- Congestion. Ten passages with six vehicles (in two parallel lanes) with two transponders in each vehicle at speeds less than 10 km/h;
- Maximal flow. Ten passages with six vehicles, each fitted with two transponders (in two lanes) with a mean headway of 20m; and
- Occlusion. Ten passages with a car fitted with an OBU driving closely behind and obscured by a vehicle with a high rear of at least 4.5m (a bus and trucks were used for these tests) at various passing speeds.

In all of the multilane tests, error-free communications were achieved with the data correctly passed and recorded at both the roadside and in the OBU. Only one transponder was found to operate differently from the others, in that it seemed to be more sensitive. This ''rogue'' transponder tended to begin a dialogue with the roadside approximately 10m before the others, right on the very edge of the communications zone. This caused

Figure 7.8 One car fitted with *six* transponders at a speed of 120 km/h.

it to switch into a long ALOHA delay, and hence, in a number of passages, this transponder failed to complete its communications dialogue with the roadside. All other transponders operated correctly on every occasion in the course of testing.

7.5 FUTURE OF THE PAMELA SYSTEM: THE ADEPT PROJECT

The results of the first round of various field trials using the 5.8-GHz PAMELA system have, therefore, been extremely encouraging. Each of the experiments demonstrates the high performance and flexibility of its modular design. We now plan to develop the prototypes further and to extend the range of applications and the scope and size of the field trials in a followup project ADEPT, which has been sponsored under the new DRIVE II/ATT research program, which started in January 1992.

7.5.1 Objectives of the ADEPT Project

The ADEPT project will use the results of the DRIVE I program to further the concept of an intelligent transponder and smart card for a multitude of automatic debiting, electronic payment, and other complementary RTI applications. Furthermore, the core technology will be developed to meet the requirements of different applications and the needs of the operators. Individual pilot projects will be incorporated in the system's modular design. Finally, the equipment will be installed in a number European cites for the purpose of full-scale evaluation and cross-comparison.

7.5.2 Technical Approach of the ADEPT Project

The ADEPT consortium has a core group of seven partners drawn from two DRIVE I projects (PAMELA and SMART), with one or two specialist companies added. This core, with its powerful and wide-ranging expertise, will provide the main technological input to four separate but coordinated field trials. Each site will have its own group of partners (totaling nine in all) responsible for the management and implementation of field trials locally, but able to call upon the technical backup of the core group. The participants in ADEPT are given in Table 7.2.

Within ADEPT, four separate pilot sites for field trials of the PAMELA system are planned; each will demonstrate at least one payment application (road-use pricing, mono-lane and multilane tolling, car parking, congestion pricing, integrated payment) and other short-range RTI applications. Although the basic technology for the field trials will be the same (the 5.8-GHz PAMELA microwave system integrated with the latest smartcard technology), the range of applications will be different in each case. Thus, for example, parking management, debiting, and booking will be developed in Lisbon; nonstop tolling, multilane road-use pricing, and other transponder-based applications in Trondheim and

Table 7.2
Participants in ADEPT

	Member	*Country*
Prime contractor	University of Newcastle upon Tyne	U.K.
Core partners	Newcastle Upon Tyne Polytechnic	U.K.
	CSEE	France
	Saab-Scania Combitech	Sweden
	TFK & VTI Transportforchung	Denmark
	Microdesign A/S	Norway
	Rijkswaterstaat	Netherlands
Site partners	University of Thessaloniki (TRUTh)	Greece
	TRADEMCO	Greece
	National Fund for Highways	Greece
	Transport Research Institute (TFK)	Sweden
	Camara Municipal de Lisboa	Portugal
	EID	Portugal
	National Technical University of Athens	Greece
	INTRACOM	Greece
	Norwegian Public Roads Administration	Norway

West Sweden; and monolane and multilane tolling and enforcement in Thessaloniki. Also, a prototype add-on module for congestion metering and pricing will be developed and demonstrated in the city of Cambridge. This will enable the ADEPT consortium as a whole to develop application-specific systems, yet, at the same time, pursue the possibilities of integrating them all within a single system architecture.

If this R&D program is successful, the ideal of a single multipurpose chip card providing for all the payment needs on all forms of transport by electronic means will be within our grasp. The benefits of this for users are self-evident, but the spin-off benefits, in terms of information and demand monitoring, security and protection against fraud will be of great value too.

The groundwork for this R&D has been done within DRIVE I, with the emergence of microwave as the best medium of communication and with the successful testing of components and prototype devices. The need now is to concentrate on system development and integration within an agreed set of European standards in cooperation with other relevant ADS projects and CASH. The core technology serving a whole series of related field trials is a cost-effective way of achieving this. Because ADEPT has been planned as a coordinated pan-European program, it reflects the structure and orientation of DRIVE II itself. Thus, although the proposal is centered on automatic debiting, it has wide implications for RTI generally. The modular design of the in-vehicle unit and the high-capacity secure communications link to the roadside opens the way to all kinds of information services for drivers on the one hand, and much more effective forms of traffic control on the other.

7.5.3 Issues

Several key issues to be addressed by the ADEPT project include:

- The demonstration of a multipurpose short-range two-way communications link between the roadside and vehicle for automatic debiting and other RTI applications;
- Demonstration of high-level automatic debiting systems;
- Real-time parking guidance, booking, and debiting (both open and closed parking garages);
- Demonstration of the *congestion metering* concept;
- Multilane communications and the associated enforcement technologies;
- The definition of a common communications architecture and protocol;
- The use of a single smart card for ADS and other electronic payments;
- The development of a central system architecture that links integrated RTI services and payment services;
- Common experimental design; and
- Multisite validation.

7.5.4 Different Approaches to Demand Management Through Pricing

A number of different approaches to managing traffic demand through automatic pricing are to be evaluated in the ADEPT project. Each will use the same basic core architecture of the PAMELA debiting system, but the approach and application of the system differ. There are four different approaches to road-use pricing that are to be undertaken in major European cities in the ADEPT project.

Managing Traffic Demand Through Onstreet Car Parking Management and Automatic Debiting

Based on the strategies for predicting parking space availability developed by the PARC-MAN consortium during the DRIVE I program, an enhanced field trial of the PAMELA system will be set up in Lisbon; however, unlike the DRIVE I experiment, the experiment will be confined to open and closed parking garages rather than onstreet parking facilities.

The inadequacies of current predictive algorithms used to inform drivers and traffic controllers that a parking facility is full, part-full, or empty are notoriously inaccurate when applied to onstreet parking. Typically, this results in a flow of traffic to a car parking area that may or may not have spaces vacant. In many cities, up to 10% of vehicles on the move at any given time are actually searching for a parking space and hence are unnecessarily adding to the congestion and pollution problems in the city.

It is clear that more reliable, dynamic information is required. The PARCMAN II strategies incorporate the use of dynamic information on vehicles parked, those wishing to park, and those predicted as likely to have vacated the parking spaces. This information can be collected and conveyed by the PAMELA transponder system.

Apart from automatic payment for parking, the PAMELA system could be used by the driver to indicate to the roadside that he or she wishes to have a parking space reserved in a certain parking zone. A booked car then receives some in-vehicle guidance to the parking space, thus reducing the time each vehicle spends searching for a space. Figure 7.6 illustrates the first prototype of the transponder and in-vehicle equipment to be used in the trials. If the parking reservation and space availability information can be made sufficiently timely and accurate, then the uncertainty and subsequent congestion caused by cars searching for parking spaces can be reduced [9].

Variable Cordon Pricing

The city of Trondheim in Norway has recently installed a simple AVI tag (KøFRI) for automated payment of a fixed toll for entering a cordon around the city. Studies of the users' perceptions and acceptance of this approach to pricing were recently carried out in Norway [10].

Within the ADEPT project, there is a plan to install a variable pricing system on the main arterial roads leading to the city of Trondheim. This system will be a variant of the PAMELA system and will incorporate payment through a multiservice smartcard interfaced to the transponder. The criteria for setting the charge have not yet been selected. However, a decision is expected soon. The main interest in the Norwegian experiment is that extensive surveys (using stated preference) have already been carried out both before and after the installation and operation of the Trondheim AVI-based toll ring. Hence, the change in attitudes by people to the more advanced, variable forms of pricing will be of great value to research.

Within the DRIVE II/ATT program, Trondheim is the host city for a number of different automatic debiting technologies; the cross-evaluation of different approaches and technologies will be invaluable in determining the relative merits of the various types of equipment of different functionality.

Multilane Debiting and Other RTI Services

The experiments in the Test Site West Sweden (near Göteborg) will encompass a number of different RTI applications. The ADEPT project will provide a full multilane debiting system for a three-lane highway, with vehicle speeds of up to 180 km/h in an unrestricted multilane environment. The communications and enforcement problems associated with such an installation make this experiment of great interest to many European operators, since no successful system has yet been demonstrated that overcomes all these problems. Sweden will also be demonstrating other applications of the PAMELA transponder such as driver information, traffic monitoring, and preinformation for use in (so-called intelligent cruise control. Multilane and single-lane nonstop tolling will also be demonstrated by ADEPT on a toll highway near Thessaloniki in Greece.

Congestion Pricing

So far the concept of road-use pricing has only been extended to collecting a variable toll automatically from a vehicle at a specific pricing point. This may be a simple road toll or a more demand-responsive charge at a cordon of points around a city or other urban area. There are still some fundamental inequity problems that exist with such a system: (1) primarily the fact that the charge is simply an entry fee when crossing a cordon, but also (2) the fact that the charge does not take into account trip length once the vehicle is inside the cordon, and finally, (3) the fact that the charge is unrelated to the actual level of congestion existing on the roads inside the cordon at a given time of day.

To overcome these inequities, a new approach to road-use pricing is being actively considered, that of *congestion pricing.* The objective is to improve the existing system of road-use charges to reflect more accurately the marginal total cost of travel in the overall price paid by individual vehicle users. Users are therefore charged for the delay and other marginal costs that they impose on fellow road users under congested conditions. By the addition to an ADS system (including a communications link to the roadside) of some in-vehicle sensors (which measure appropriate parameters experienced by the vehicle), congestion may be monitored continuously. A charge is then made automatically as and when congestion is actually encountered. By using the microwave link to switch on and off the device when the vehicle passes a cordon of beacons around a "priced area," the system will measure *and* price congestion only within the predefined area and only when congestion is encountered.

It is expected that the city of Cambridge will be the first to implement a pilot experiment of this novel approach to pricing. ADEPT will provide one or two roadside beacons and a small amount of prototype in-vehicle equipment to demonstrate the congestion metering principle (based on the core PAMELA technology with external interfaces to vehicle sensors and other in-vehicle peripherals).

7.6 INTEGRATION WITH OTHER RTI APPLICATIONS

To date, the microwave-based communications system developed by the PAMELA consortium has been demonstrated for automatic debiting applications in a number of small-scale field trials. The stringent performance and security requirements that have been imposed on the system by the operators of toll roads and national roads has led to a highly specified and reliable communications system being developed. The open architecture of PAMELA and the modularity of the design readily allow other RTI services to share the

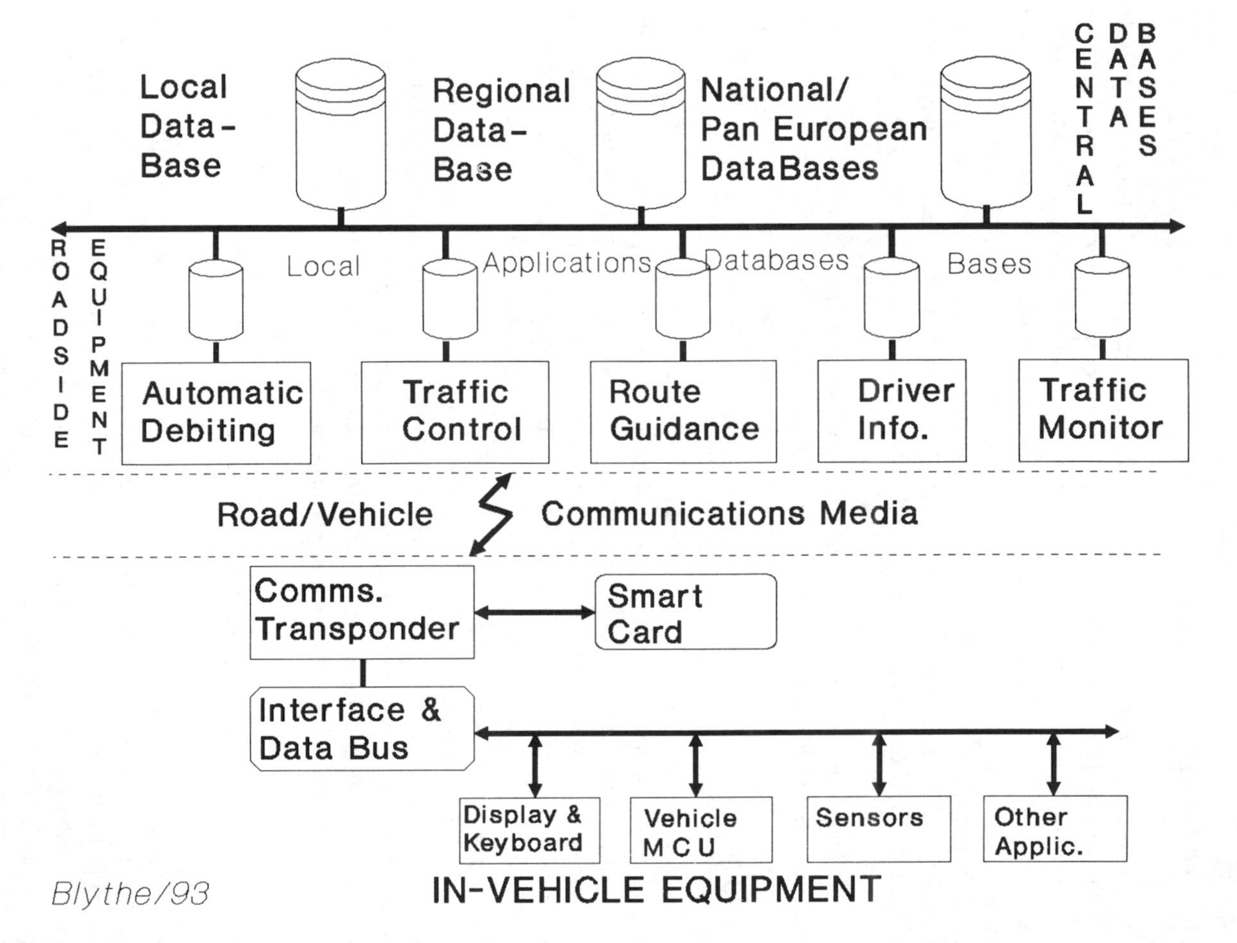

Figure 7.9 Integrated traffic management and control functions.

same communications link and in-vehicle equipment. This will be an important marketing consideration in the next few years.

It is intended that within ADEPT and in other European demonstrations, the PAMELA system will be demonstrated as a multiservice link which can support many different applications. The potential for a single communications link between the roadside and fast-moving vehicles for integrated traffic management and control functions is being actively studied in Europe, as illustrated in Figure 7.9. If an agreed-on specification for such a link can be achieved between the different agencies and industries with an interest in this field, then it could be commercially available well before the end of the century.

7.7 CONCLUSIONS

The recent advances in RTI offer, for the first time, the opportunity for traffic engineers and transport economists to begin contemplating the actual implementation and validation of their various models and strategies for demand management through variable pricing of road use. The demonstration of many RTI applications using a single communications media and an *open* system architecture will offer both operators and users the opportunity to gauge the benefits of such a system concept. The cross-validation of the site experiments will provide a valuable source of results for the analysis of the benefits of a systems approach such as ADEPT. Since this will be one of the first implementations of such an integrated transponder architecture for ADS and other RTI applications, the results will also provide background information for the standardization process across the whole of Europe. This opens the prospect of substantial markets for ADS equipment in the closing years of this decade.

ACKNOWLEDGMENTS

The authors wish to acknowledge that the work described in this chapter is that of the PAMELA and ADEPT consortia of different partners and persons, too many to mention individually. Nevertheless, we thank them all for their support as well as for their continuing enthusiasm and vision. Figures 7.2, 7.7, and 7.8 are reproduced by courtesy of Saab-Scania Combitech A/B. Figure 7.5 is by courtesy of CSEE, and Figure 7.6 is by courtesy of EID.

REFERENCES

[1] Foote, R. S., "Prospects for Non-Stop Toll Collection Using Automatic Vehicle Identification," *Traffic Quarterly,* No. 35, 1981.

[2] Blythe, P. T., "The State of the Art of Current Automatic Debiting System Technology and Applications," Commission of the European Communities DRIVE project V1030, contract report ME2, Brussels, 1989.

[3] Hills, P. J., and P. T. Blythe, "A System for the Non-Stop Automatic Debiting of Vehicles," *Proc. 23rd ISATA Conf. on RTI/IVHS,* Florence, Italy, May 1990.

[4] VITA, ''VITA: Vehicle Information and Transaction Aid,'' reference document, March 1990.

[5] Stoelhorst, H. J., and A. J. Zandbergen, ''The Development of a Road-Pricing System in the Netherlands,'' *Traffic Engineering and Control,* Vol. 31, No. 2, Feb. 1990, pp. 66–71.

[6] Blythe, P. T., E. Korolkiewicz, A. F. Dadds, et al., (1991) ''A Short-Range Road to Vehicle Microwave Communications Link for Automatic Debiting and Other RTI Services,'' *Proc. 1st Int. DRIVE Conf. on Advanced Telematics in Road Transport,* Elsevier/Commission of the European Communities, Bruxelles, Belgium, Feb. 1991, pp. 248–268.

[7] Hills, P. J., and P. T. Blythe, ''Road-Pricing—Solving the Technical Issues,'' *J. Economic Affairs,* Vol. 10, No. 5, June/July 1990, pp. 8–10.

[8] Egnell, L., ''Performance of Vehicle-to-Roadside Communication for Tolling in a Free Traffic Flow on Multi-Lane Roads,'' *Proc. 24th ISATA Conf. on RTI/IVHS,* Florence, Italy, May 1991.

[9] Stathopoulos, A., N. Papachristou, and D. Nunes, ''Developing New Tools for Parking Control: PARCMAN II,'' *Proc. 25th ISATA Conf. on RTI/IVHS,* Florence, Italy, June 1992 (to be published).

[10] Hills, P. J. and N. Thorpe, ''Public Attitudes to Road-Use Pricing: A Report of a Norwegian Case Study,'' Commission of the European Communities DRIVE project V1030, contract report ME15, Brussels, 1992.

Chapter 8
Major DRIVE/ATT Pilot Projects
Hartmut Keller

8.1 INTRODUCTION

Pilot projects in ATT are central elements of the EC DG XIII R&D program DRIVE/ATT. The objective for these projects is to carry out field trials of ATT applications in real-world environments based on achievements of the DRIVE (1989 to 1991) program. As described in Chapter 5, the main areas of operational interest of this program are: demand management, travel and traffic information, integrated urban traffic management, driver assistance and cooperative driving, and freight and fleet transport; Public transport.

8.2 STRUCTURE OF ATT PILOT PROJECTS

The projects, such as vehicle detection, intelligent driver support, or traffic management applying ATT, are grouped in Table 8.1 into different levels of application. The first level refers basically to individual man-machine interactions. The second level includes individual systems, strategies, or techniques, such as public transport or variable-message signs. Both levels include so-called supporting projects (SP) and pilot projects (PP). The third level encompasses basic information (digital road map), communication (RDS-TMC, SOCRATES), and transaction (automated debiting systems) techniques for ATT. The importance of this level for DRIVE/ATT is shown by the majority of so-called kernel projects (KP). The next level summarizes the pilot projects and feasibility studies (FS) for integrated urban and interurban transport management. These are here considered to be the major pilot projects, some of which are to be described in detail in Sections 8.3 and 8.4. The last level includes the horizontal tasks of behavioral modeling and safety and the program management (PM) project CORD.

Table 8.1
Structure of DRIVE/ATT Projects

Project	*Type*	*Name*	*Description*
Level 1			
Detection/	PP	INVAID II	Computer vision
communication	SP	COMIS	Microwave circuit
Collision	SP	ARIADNE	Internal driver support
avoidance	SP	TESCO	Internal cruise control
Man-machine-	SP	EMMIS	On-board information
interface	FS	HARDIE	On-road, in-vehicle information
	SP	DETER	Tutoring for error reduction
Level 2			
Multimodal	KP	PROMISE	Mobile multimodal information
information	FS	ASTRA	Travel information and service
	PP	COMBICOM	Road and rail information and architecture
Control strategies	PP	EUROCOR	Urban corridor on-line strategies
	SP	HERMES	Control strategies: O-D, AID
Public transport	SP	PHOEBUS	Vehicle scheduling and control
I and M	SP	EUROBUS	Database and information desks
Real-time control	SP	KITS	Knowledge-based real-time control
	SP	DYNA	Dynamic real-time traffic models
Public transport priority	SP	PRIMAVERA	Public transportation priority and environmental protection
	SP	PROMPT	Public transportation priority strategies
Data collection	KP	INTERCHANGE	Travel data and information network
and exchange	PP	GERDIEN	Interurban traffic data collection and exchange
Vulnerable users	SP	TELAID	Disability needs
	SP	EDDIT	Elderly driver needs
	SP	VRU-TOO	Pedestrian detection and control
Variable message	PP	QUO VADIS	Implementation of VMS systems
signs	PP	GEMINI	RDS and VMS information
	KP	EAVES	Assessment of VMS
Freight	PP	METAFORA	Road freight operations
	PP	IMFS	Freight logistics and management
	PP	FRAME	Management communication infrastructure
Level 3			
Monetics	SP	ADEPT	Microwave automatic debiting
	SP	ADS	Enhance and assess ADS
	KP	CASH	Coordination of ADS
Radio data	KP	ATT-ALERT	ALERT protocol
system-TMC	PP	ACCEPT	Enhance and coordinate RDS-TMC
GSM	KP	SOCRATES	Coordination and technology
	SP	ICAR	GSM for tunnels
Digital road map	KP	EDRM2	Geographic data file
Level 4			
Integrated regional and urban transport management	PP	QUARTET	Integration, architectures, environmental control, dynamic route guidance, public transportation management (in Athens, Birmingham, Stuttgart, and Turin)

Project	Type	Name	Description
Level 4 (cont.)	PP	LLAMD	Pre- and on-trip information, dynamic route guidance, VMS systems, public transportation information and priority, freight management modeling, route guidance (MARGOT) (in London, Lyon, Amsterdam, Munich, and Dublin)
	PP	CITIES	In-car information systems, paratransit systems, UTC/VMS control, multimodal broadcasting, databases (Paris, Brussels, and Gothenburg)
	PP	GAUDI	Integrated urban debiting, public and private transport, parking, access control (Barcelona, Bologna, Dublin, Marseilles, and Trondheim)
	PP	SCOPE	Integrated urban traffic management, travel and traffic information, strategic information system (Southampton, Cologne, and Piraeus)
	FS	LIAISON	Public-transportation and commercial-vehicle priority, electronic vehicle identification, tagging systems (Berlin)
Integrated interurban transport management	PP	MELYSSA	Linking control centers, pre- and on-trip information, dual-mode route guidance, freight management (Stuttgart and Lyon to Spain)
	PP	CITRA	Hazardous-goods transport control, communication infrastructure, strategies for emergency services (Munich, Brenner, and Modena)
	PP	PLEIADES	Travel and traffic information, interurban traffic management, RDS, VMS, paging (Paris, the Eurotunnel, and London)
	PP	PORTICO	Surveillance of hazardous goods, automatic detection, integrated automatic debiting (Lisboa and Porto)
	PP	RHAPIT	Transport-management system, public-transportation management, DRG, SOCRATES applications (Rhine/Main and Frankfurt)
	PP	ARTIS	Travel and traffic information, KB-based UTC, ADT, VMS via RDS-TMC, dangerous-goods control (Junquera and Seville)
	FS	EURO-TRIANGLE	Linking control centers, image processing, incident detection and handling (Flanders, Wallonia, and NR Westphalia)
Level 5			
Behavior	KP	BATT	Behavior and ATT
	SP	MARTA	Attitudes versus automation
Safety	KP	HOPES	Safety evaluation
	PP	ROSES	Weather, winter, and safety
	FS	SAMOVAR	On-vehicle monitoring
Level 6			
Program management	PM	CORD	Coordination of research and development

Note: PP = pilot projects; SP= supporting projects; FS = feasibilty study; and KP = Kernal projects.

8.3 REGIONAL AND URBAN PROJECTS

There are five pilot projects on integrated regional and urban transport management.

- QUARTET: Quadrilateral Advanced Research on Telematics for Environment and Transport, emphasizing integrated transport environment.
- LLAMD: London, Lyon, Amsterdam, Munich, Dublin, emphasizing advanced traveler information systems in integrated metropolitan environments.
- CITIES: Cooperation for Integrated Traffic Management and Information Exchange Systems, emphasizing urban/regional traffic control.
- SCOPE: Southampton, Cologne, Piraeus, emphasizing integrated urban traffic management, harbor information systems.
- GAUDI: Generalized and Advanced Urban Debiting Innovation.

All five projects emerged from the activities of the POLIS initiative. Two of the projects are described here in detail to show the structure of the projects, the approach to field trials, and the different application areas.

8.3.1 LLAMD Euro-Project

The LLAMD Euro-Project is a single project in the DRIVE/ATT program involving five cities (London, Lyon, Amsterdam, Munich, and Dublin), encompassing linked field trials in advanced transport telematics in a coordinated program of R&D. The goal of the project is to develop and demonstrate aspects of the integration of ATT systems within an integrated road transport environment based on linked field trials. LLAMD is a three-year project which started in 1992 with the major project stages of systems design, field trials, impact analysis, and assessment.

The common theme of LLAMD is ATIS. Each of the cities includes the development of one or more aspects of ATIS in its site mode activities. A second major theme and for some cities the major orientation is the development and implementation of systems for public transport, parking, and P&R services. Other key elements of the project include advanced traffic control, both urban and regional, commercial fleet management, trip planning, and road safety aspects. The focus of the many ATT applications within the LLAMD group is the work on integration of applications into a single environment. The five cities encompass some differences in approach, but the common activities seek to identify areas of potential compatibility and to exploit this potential to the maximum in order to progress towards a single pan-European integrated transport environment.

LLAMD Project Structure

The LLAMD project is organized into eight work areas.

1. Common tasks: between the six subprojects, mainly referring to the design of the ATT systems and the assessments of the field trials.

2–6. Field trials of pilot projects: APPLE, LEADER, WEGWIJS, COMFORT, and DUBSAFE, with emphasis on traveler information systems in the five participating cities.
7. MARGOT (Modeling and Assessing Route Guidance of Traffic): a subproject with emphasis on development and application of design and modeling techniques for integrated urban signal control and dynamic route guidance systems.
8. Project management, system coordination: via steering and technical committees.

Table 8.2 shows this structure of the LLAMD project, in which there are 50 full and associate partners (effectively equal partners under a collaborative agreement established for the project).

Common Tasks

The common tasks organized in work packages provide interlinking between the cities' pilot projects and the guaranty of the European dimension of the joint approach. Normally,

Table 8.2
LLAMD Project Committees and Partners

Project/Committee	*Make-up*	*Number*
Steering committee	Chairman	1
	Member	1–2*
Project Administration	Full partner	1
Technical committee	Chairman (project manager)	1
	Joint system coordinators	2
	Member	1†
Common workpackage leaders	Member or leader of a common work package	1
City Subprojects:	Partners	8
APPLE (London)	Full partner	1
	Associate partners	8
LEADER (Lyon)	Full partner	1
	Associate partners	11
	Subcontractors	2
WEGWIJS (Amsterdam)	Full partner	1
	Associate partners	4
	Subcontractor	1
COMFORT (Munich)	Full partners	2
	Associate partners	9
	Subcontractor	1
DUBSAFE (Dublin)	Full partner	1
MARGOT	Full partner	1
	Associate partners	9

Note: Associate partners are effectively equivalent to full partners under the terms of the project-collaboration agreement, although only full partners sign the EC contract.
*Per city. †Per subproject.

partners of two or more of the cities are involved in these work packages. They encompass the common methodological approach, common technological approaches, and interlinking with other projects (see Table 8.3).

City Subprojects—Field Trials of Pilot Projects

The five subprojects that encompass the field trials of the pilot projects in the cities are explained below.

The *London* APPLE project is directly linked to the separate implementation of a major route guidance pilot system. This is the TIGER (Travel Information and Guidance for European Roads) project, which is independently funded. APPLE is specifically concerned with the development of a common systems architecture for ATIS, the development of an integrated traffic control center, and the integration of dynamic route guidance with urban traffic control.

The *Lyon LEADER* project is sited in the urban area of Lyon. Its main aim is to assess the implementation, promotion, operation, and validation of a coordinated strategy for traffic and transport management, incorporating ATT systems for both public and private transport based on a centralized real-time information system. LEADER includes the following specific subprojects: Traffic Control Strategy and Service Center, and Public Transport Priority.

Amsterdam WEGWIJS is the assessment of a possible dynamic route guidance system based on a beacon-based concept, but extended to incorporate P&R, parking, and public transport information.

The *Munich-COMFORT* (Cooperative Management for Urban and Regional Transport) project covers the following application areas within the overall concept of a compre-

Table 8.3
Structure of Common Work Packages in LLAMD

Work Package	*Administrator/Subproject*
Project administration	Project coordinators
System coordination	Joint system coordinators
Assessment and evaluation	COMFORT
External liaison, topic groups	WEGWIJS
Systems approach	LEADER
In-vehicle equipment	COMFORT
Trip planning	LEADER
Public transport, P and R information	COMFORT
Traffic management	LEADER
Navigation database	APPLE
Commercial-fleet management	APPLE
Accident analysis	DUBSAFE

hensive transport management system: transport control strategy and service center, public transport information and management, P&R services, advanced urban traffic control, advanced regional traffic control, advanced traveler information system, commercial fleet management, and safety aspects. Field trials will be carried out for the new transport control policies, strategies, and technologies in a test site in Munich.

Dublin's DUBSAFE is concerned with accident data recording and identifying engineering solutions to improve safety. It specifically deals with the use of ATT technology to help improve the quality of accident data.

The *MARGOT* (Modeling and Assessing Route Guidance of Traffic) subproject will develop strategies, methodologies, models, algorithms, and assessment techniques specifically concerned with dynamic route guidance systems. The results of the research work within MARGOT will be directly used in some of the cities' field trials, particularly those relating to the integration of dynamic route guidance with urban traffic control.

The key issues addressed by LLAMD are:

- The development of a common system architecture for ATT systems in a metropolitan transport environment;
- The comparative assessment of different methodological and technical approaches in the five cities to advanced traveler information systems;
- The integration of ATT systems in a comprehensive urban and regional development framework

Each of the five linked field trials is intended to provide the basis for a subsequent full implementation of the ATT systems developed and tested during the project.

Methodological Approaches and Technical Systems in LLAMD

The pilot projects in the five cities represent integral parts of future integrated transport environments. The field trials to be carried out in the context of the DRIVE/ATT program constitute a step in the direction of a large-scale ATT implementation. For this purpose, the cities provide their infrastructures and test beds. At the same time, it is the cities' expectation that the efforts of cooperation with other European cities as part of the DRIVE/ATT R&D program will facilitate future system introduction due to common approaches to traffic information and control systems at a pan-European level.

The city projects are highly interrelated with respect to the political, methodological, and technical aspects. It is common to all cities that transport telematics systems are considered as a means to serve in the fulfillment of urban and regional requirements to solve transport problems. This stresses the importance that the ATT systems have to be instrumental to influence modal choice for more use of public transport systems, besides the more efficient use of the transport network and the expected effects on improved safety and environment.

Table 8.4 provides the contents of the methodological approaches and technical systems studied in LLAMD. Common to all subprojects is the methodological approach

Table 8.4
Methodological Approaches and Technical Systems Studied in LLAMD Cities

	Effort Level				
Approach	*London*	*Lyon*	*Amsterdam*	*Munich*	*Dublin*
1. Coordination					
1.1 Project coordination					
1.2 System coordination—common methodological approaches and interlinking					
1.3 Common methodological aspects					
1.4 DRIVE topic group participation					
2. Basic technical common tasks					
3. Urban and regional policies					
4. Technical systems LLAMD					
4.1 Integrated control strategy and service center	High	High	High	High	Low
4.2 Public transport information and management	——	High	Low	High	——
4.3 P and R guidance and management	——	——	Medium	Low	——
4.4 Advanced UTC including public transportation priority at intersections	Medium	Medium	——	Medium	——
4.5 Advanced regional transport control	——	——	——	Medium	——
4.6 Advanced Traveler Information systems	High	——	High	High	——
4.7 Trip planning	——	——	——	Medium	——
4.8 Commercial-fleet management	Medium	——	——	Medium	——
5. Safety	——	——	——	Medium	High
6. MARGOT: DRG modeling and assessment					

of system development, emphasizing the experimental design for the field trials and their assessment. This is reflected in the detailed work plan structure for these work packages (items 1.3 and 1.4) and in the anticipated cooperation of the cities in the basic technical common tasks (item 2). The analysis and formulation of *urban and regional policies* (item 3) are considered to be an important work area for the Munich COMFORT and the Amsterdam WEGWIJS projects. This refers in particular to the definition of objectives for traffic control strategies to be applied for the ATT systems based on the urban and regional requirements. The aspects of administration, organization, and financing of metropolitan transport systems are also part of this approach. The core of the technical systems (item 4) is the development and design of integrated control strategy and service centers for all city subprojects. Traffic safety aspects (item 5) are of particular concern in the Dublin DUBSAFE project, while at the same time the analysis of traffic safety aspects is a common task of LLAMD. DUBSAFE will carry out field trials on ATT systems for accident recording and analysis systems. Links to the horizontal safety project HOPES are established by joint partnerships. The leading motive of the technical approach for the MARGOT subproject of LLAMD (item 6) is the development of a common awareness and understanding of how the scenario of full integration between traffic control system and dynamic route guidance will evolve and what the key implications are in terms of key research issues. MARGOT will provide support to field trials in the areas of strategies and simulation considering the pilot projects, particularly in LLAMD cities. Its main technical areas are improved journey time prediction, route guidance integration for management of local traffic problems, network control: dynamic route guidance integrated with traffic control systems for real-time traffic management, advanced route guidance, and stability analysis and behavioral aspects.

Summary

The structure of the DRIVE/ATT LLAMD Euro-Project has evolved from the concepts developed in the POLIS Initiative. LLAMD addresses the key issues: integration of ATT systems in a comprehensive metropolitan transport environment, including public transport, development of a common systems architecture for ATT systems, and a comparative assessment of different approaches to ATIS. LLAMD builds directly upon results from a large number of DRIVE I projects and related programs such as PROMETHEUS. Specific elements of LLAMD incorporate results from the following: EVA, field trials, CAR-GOES, SOCRATES, TARDIS, ODIN, and VAMOS. Each of the five linked city field trials is intended to provide a basis for subsequent full implementation of ATT systems developed and tested during this project.

8.3.2 QUARTET Project

QUARTET is a single project of DRIVE/ATT. It involves four cities: Athens, Birmingham, Stuttgart, and Turin. It is the prime objective of all cities in this project to trial ATT from the perspective of an overall IRTE system. Thus, while the cities are undertaking trials of specific ATT functions and technologies, a prime objective is to assess the added value that can be achieved through system integration.

There are five major work modules, for each of which one city is site mode; that is, it provides the test bed for the field trials and coordinates the activities between the cities in this application area. Figure 8.1 shows the general structure of the project with the work modules and the cities in charge. These activities supported by the DRIVE/ATT program constitute, however, only one part of the four cities' very comprehensive projects to implement ATT systems.

The Turin T5 project is the test site for the Target IRTE Architectures, thus the design of efficient architecture for the overall system. The key objective of the IRTE architecture is to improve the exchange of information and the cooperation in short- and long-term decisions between all participating partners. This will provide for increased efficiency in online management and control of private traffic and public transport, as

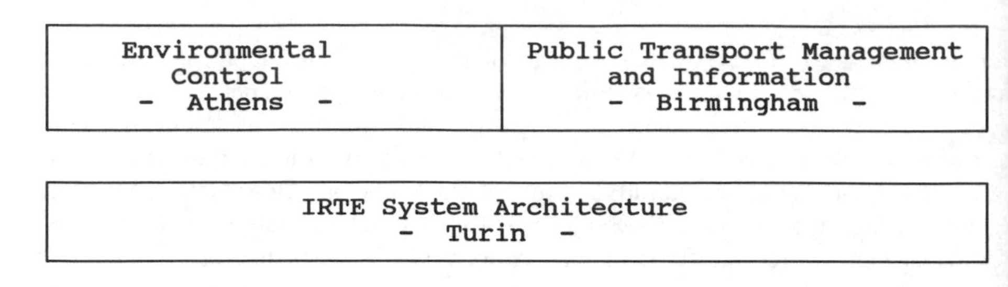

Figure 8.1 QUARTET project work module structure.

well as in long-term planning. Finally, complete, reliable, and up-to-date information wil be available for travelers. A wide spectrum of architectures will be explored, rangin from mostly centralized (as in Stuttgart), to distributed (as in Birmingham and Athens) to a distributed and hierarchical approach (as in Torino). Particular attention will be give to the definition of tests and assessments of comprehensive control strategies for th transport and traffic management. The Birmingham BLUEPRINT project leads the wor module Public Transport Management and Information. For the development of high quality passenger information systems, the following work is considered to be required developing integrated technologies (public transport (PT) with linkages to other RTIs) adapting systems to deal with a deregulated environment, and defining and respondin to user's needs.

These areas will be studied for *bus priority* within a UTC system, which is SCOO in Birmingham, and for a public transport passenger information system (PTPIS), includin at-home, in-street, and at-stop systems, as well as for an automatic vehicle location system covering both buses and trains. The aim will be to develop an integrated system linke where necessary to other components of the IRTE.

The Athens project leads the Environmental Control module. Due to the significar environmental problems because of the climatic and topographical conditions, Athen provides an interesting test site for the control of car pollution. The environment-oriente control strategies of the PREDICT model suite will be studied, including monitorin environmental conditions, determining when control measures are needed, indicating wha control strategy should be implemented, and providing the technology to implement th strategies.

The Stuttgart STORM project coordinates the work on dual-mode route guidanc (DMRG) and in-vehicle emergency call systems. In cooperation with T5 and BLUEPRINT a DMRG system will be tested in Stuttgart. The experience with the RDS systems c Birmingham will be taken into account, and the beacon-based system of Turin as part c a DMRG designed for Stuttgart will be considered with respect to a future standardization of beacon supported systems. The common task concentrates on the field trial and on the exchange of experience between the cities, the definition of requirements for data collection and provided information, and the development and rerouting strategies.

A common specification and development of an *emergency call system* is planned for Stuttgart as lead city and Birmingham as follower city. The basic concept of the emergency call system is to raise an alarm by means of an emergency car phone in the event of an accident. The system of locating the accident vehicle functions on the basis of position locating signals by the GSM telephone network. The call system is triggered either automatically via a crash sensor or manually. It is the objective of this activity to perform a field trial with a fleet of equipped vehicles to be able to assess its operations.

The four QUARTET cities concur in their key objectives: the implementation of integrated transport systems to cater to the growing demand for mobility, the achievement of a modal shift in favor of public transport, to improve traffic flow and benefit safety and the environment, and the implementation of new telematics technologies.

8.4 CORRIDOR (INTERURBAN) PROJECTS

Table 8.1 list seven major integrated interurban projects that are planned for European corridors between England and France, France and Germany, and Germany, Austria, and Italy. Three national corridors are designed in Germany, Portugal, and Spain. The MELYSSA and the CITRA projects are described as examples in more detail.

8.4.1 CITRA

The CITRA (Corridor Initiative for Transit Route Through the Alps) project has its main emphasis in the control of dangerous goods transport in the international alpine corridor of Munich-Brenner-Modena. The Brenner pass is one of the few alpine road crossings of the alps. It operates at a high degree of saturation with congestions and risks of accident, particularly during the European holiday season. The aim of the project is to increase safety with dedicated traffic surveillance and management, with particular concern for the environmental aspects. Three major areas of hazardous goods control are covered.

- Legal aspects (common base of reference);
- Methodological aspects (surveillance strategies, emergency service coordination);
- Technical aspects (linking control centers, STRADA nodes, X.25 network).

In all three countries (Austria, Germany, and Italy), traffic of the Brenner corridor is controlled by regional control centers. It is one objective of CITRA to link these centers and to design a coordinated control strategy for hazardous or dangerous goods transport. The following project phases are planned.

- System integration on a national level and design of a control system based on existing installations;

- Design of a common system architecture on a national level;
- Preparation and production of field trials as the designed systems architecture and surveillance and control strategies on an international level.

The anticipated test site runs along the highway from Munich, via Innsbruck, Brenner, Bolzano, Verona, to Modena. The major technical systems and test installation to be studied along the CITRA corridor are:

- Integrated traffic and environmental monitoring and control. **I**: Val d'Isario; **D**: A93–A8–Munich.
- Control of hazardous or dangerous goods transport. **I**: Val d'Adige (Verona, Trento, Brenner); **A**: A10 Tauern–A12 Inntal–A13 Brenner Autobahn; **D**: A93 Kiefersfelden–A8 Munich (truck fleet).
- Noncontacting toll collection and border control. **D**: Munich; Kiefersfelden.
- International traffic radio system. **D**: Munich–A8–A93 (truck fleet).
- Bidirectional data exchange. **D**: München–A8–A93 (truck fleet).
- National and international integration of control systems. **I**: Trento; **A**: A12 Inntal Autobahn–B13 Brenner–B171 Tiroler–B183 Brenner Bundesstraße; **D**: A93 Kiefersfelden–A8 Munich.

After completion of a feasibility study, an experimental system will be installed for a critical assessment of the proposed methodology on hazardous goods transport control. The system designed could form a common approach for European highway dangerous goods control. There are high expectations that this common approach to system architectures and control strategies will increase the reliability of the traffic management and environmental control for the Brenner corridor.

8.4.2 MELYSSA

The objective of MELYSSA (Mediterranean-Lyon-Stuttgart Site for ATT) is to improve road transport efficiency, safety, and environment by enhancing traffic information to all road users. The test site for MELYSSA is the highway (and, possibly, the railway) corridor between Stuttgart (the German test site) and Lyon (the French test site), with its extension to Spain. The technical approach of MELYSSA can be summarized by the following.

- Provide a safe and incident-free traffic flow on a European transport corridor by extending existing control systems (e.g., variable-message signs);
- Increase efficiency and safety for freight transport between Lyon and Stuttgart by applying fleet management and emergency call systems;
- Test advanced information and control technologies on highways for common European standardization;
- Provide test installations for a border crossing traffic data exchange and a dynamic transport management to assess the potentials of traffic control systems on an international level.

The individual work areas with the institutions in charge of them are shown in Table 8.5. The MELYSSA corridor encompasses basically the highway network between Stuttgart (A5, A8, A6, A81) and Lyon (A36, A6, A7, A40/1/2/3/4/9), with the French-German border crossing at Neuenburg-Mulhouse. A feasibility study will be produced in the first phase of the project that will analyze future implementation potentials of the defined systems.

8.5 COORDINATION AND EXPECTATIONS

Besides these pilot projects of integrated transport management, which comply with several application areas in different geographical areas, there are further pilot projects (which are not described here) and supporting projects in the DRIVE/ATT program that address mainly single control systems. An important role is given to the kernel projects ERDM2: digital road map, ATT-ALERT: RDS, SOCRATES, INTERCHANGE, CASH, BATT, and HOPES, which will be instrumental in assisting CORD, the program management project of ATT, to monitor the activities in all ATT projects.

Table 8.5
MELYSSA Project

Work Module	*Cite Mode*
1. General management	CETE-Lyon
2. Integrated interurban management	CETE-Lyon
2.1 Integrated and interurban information exchange	
2.2 Interurban and urban information exchange	
2.3 Automated incident detection techniques	
2.4 Weather-related traffic management	
2.5 Control strategies for traffic management	
3. Travel and traffic information	
• Pretrip and at-stop information	ISIS
3.1 Info terminals	
3.2 Videotext	
3.3 Audiotext	R. Bosch-ANT
• On-trip information and control	
3.4 Travel services and booking system	
3.5 Variable message signs	
3.6 On-board information systems	
3.7 Dual-mode route guidance	
4. Freight and fleet management	DB DA DO
5. Common tasks	CETE L'Est
5.1 General evaluation	
5.2 Traffic safety	

Note: CETE = Centre d'Études Techniques de L'Equipment; ISIS = Ingenierie de Systèmes d'Information et de Securité; DB DA DO = Daimler-Benz DASA Dornier; Bosch-ANT = Bosch-Anlagen Nachrichten Technik.

The projects are coordinated via so-called *areas of major operational interest* and *topic groups*, to which all project consortia send a partner as a member. The areas provide platforms for reporting the project achievements for an exchange of experience. The topic groups aim at consensus formation at a European level for specific issues.

The pilot projects with their ATT field trials in real-world traffic environments provide the basis for the last phase of system development, the *implementation* of ATT systems across Europe. An important link to this implementation of ATT can be provided by the *client networks* of the POLIS initiative for urban projects and of the CORRIDOR initiative for interurban projects, which represent the interests and requirements of the infrastructure owners for future transport operations in the cities and the corridors.

SELECT BIBLIOGRAPHY

EC-DG XIII program DRIVE/ATT: LLAMD, QUARTET, MELYSSA, CITRA Project Profiles, 1992.
EC-DG XIII program DRIVE/ATT: Workplan, Brussels, 1991.

Chapter 9

PROMETHEUS

Hans-Georg Zimmer, M. J. Andrews, A. Kemeny, and P. Häußermann

9.1 OVERVIEW*

9.1.1 Introduction and Project Summary

Since 1986, the European automotive industry has been cooperating in PROMETHEUS (Program for a European Traffic With Highest Efficiency and Unprecedented Safety). An interim demonstration of the achievements of the program was given to the policy makers of European research, transport, and industry in Torino in September 1991. In the following, this event is referred to as Board Member Meeting '91 (BMM'91) [1]. The features of the program were summarized there as follows.

- Precompetitive research for common specifications of transport informatics components in vehicles and infrastructure.
- Initiated by European automotive companies and established as EUREKA project EU-45 in 1986.
- Definition phase 1987 provided topics of research as basis for cooperation with 56 electronics and supplier companies and 115 basic research institutes.
- Launching phase 1988 established European cooperation with first demonstrations at Board Member Meeting in January 1989.
- Research phase since 1989. Annual budget about 90 MECU; two-thirds provided by industry, one-third by national ministries of research, technology, and industry.
- Cooperation with the road transport-related EC programs DRIVE, ATT, and other European programs; open for information exchange with IVHS of America.

*This section was written by Hans-Georg Zimmer.

The program aims to improve the European transport system as a whole because traffic problems neither disappear at borders nor are they limited to road transport. PROMETHEUS promotes the development of a transport system exploiting the full potential of information and telecommunication technologies to improve efficiency and safety in traffic. The remainder of Section 9.1 describes the policy framework.

With the PROMETHEUS program, the automotive industry expands its topics of research from vehicles-only to a transportation system with vehicles as key elements. Therefore, the integration of vehicle and traffic control becomes the essential means to improve efficiency and safety in road traffic. This will be done on three levels of control.

- *Safe Driving*: Autonomous vehicle control for safer driving with less mental load on the driver. This is described by M. Andrews in Section 9.2.
- *Traffic Flow Harmonization*: The cooperation within local groups of drivers for safer and smoother traffic flow. This topic is addressed by A. Kemeny in Section 9.3, ‘‘Cooperative Driving.’’
- *Travel and Transport Management*: Trip planning and reaction to actual traffic situations for better use of the available infrastructure. This is addressed by P. Häußermann and H.-G. Zimmer in Section 9.4 with emphasis on dual-mode route guidance, a combination of static route guidance and dynamic traffic information. Additional information on commercial fleet management and travel information service is given in Section 9.1.4.

9.1.2 Road Transport in Europe—Situation and Projections

During the last three decades, a tremendous demand for transport has grown parallel with the European economy. In fact, the increased transport capacity made available constituted a key factor for economic growth. However, in road transport, the expansion of the network and its related infrastructure has not kept pace with the increase in the number of vehicles. This discrepancy leads to more congestion, accidents, pollution of the environment, noise, stress, and other discomforts.

A complete description of the traffic situation would require a huge amount of data. The following text only deals with road traffic, which is responsible for almost 90% of the energy consumption in transportation, and specifically with passenger cars, which make up almost 90% of all motorized vehicles. To keep matters more transparent, freight transport is not addressed here, despite its importance for traffic and PROMETHEUS. As a basis for statistics and forecasts, France, Great Britain, Italy, the Netherlands, Spain, Sweden, and the former West Germany were selected. In 1989, these countries combined had a fleet of 116 million passenger cars, compared with 141 million in the U.S. and 168 million in all of Europe. From 1970 to 1990, the passenger car park grew at an average of 3.8% per year. Forecasts until 2010 show an increase of 40%, with an average annual growth of 1.7%, which is less than half the previous rate. Partly duc to different transport policy objectives, the national forecasts show a large margin (e.g., a growth of 15% in

Sweden versus 80% in Spain). In any case, the implementation of the single market in Western Europe by 1993 and the changes in Eastern Europe are expected to generate a higher demand for transport. Another reason for the increased vehicle population is the advantage the automobile offers to individuals with respect to autonomy, flexibility, and support of a wide range of transportation tasks. All the discussions about alternative solutions have not produced a consistent system or policy yet. In the countries mentioned above, the total road network length remained nearly constant since 1970, while the network of highways has doubled. Mileage driven on these highways almost quadrupled, whereas total vehicle mileage only doubled. Almost no growth of the total network is expected up to the year 2010, but the share of highways will continue to increase: with the length of the highways in 1988 set at 100, the forecast growth is 167 for France, 167 for Great Britain, 150 for the Netherlands, and 179 for Spain. Of course, the continuing progress in road construction and maintenance will further improve the safety and quality of the network. But the gap between demand for road transport capacity for people and goods and the provision of an adequate infrastructure will widen and further deteriorate the service level of road transport, notably in urban areas.

The major problem for road transport efficiency is congestion. For urban traffic, there is some data available: A model for Paris/Ile de France measures congestion by queue length integrated over time, and finds congestion to grow five times faster than total vehicle mileage. For the Randstad area in the Netherlands, which is mainly urban with some intercity links, another model predicts the total time lost in queues to grow three times faster than total mileage. For three representative towns, traffic engineers of Centro Studi Sistemi di Trasporto, Torino, and Steierwald Schönharting und Partner, Stuttgart, have calculated the increase of total and average travel time:

- Town A: Italy, 35,000 inhabitants, 637 links, 133-km network;
- Town B: Italy, 250,000 inhabitants, 2,700 links, 454-km network;
- Town C: Germany, 1 million inhabitants, 712 zones, 276 nodes.

Based on the PROMETHEUS assumption of a 40% growth of vehicle mileage by 2010, they obtained the figures in Table 9.1.

Congestion has an adverse impact on fuel consumption. With the 40% growth of vehicle mileage by 2010, the average speed in cities is predicted to decrease by 52%. Fuel consumption in urban congestions—according to models tested in Torino and Stockholm—

Table 9.1
Increase in Travel Time Needed for a 40% Growth in Total Mileage

Town	*Total Travel Time*	*Average Travel Time*
A	+120%	+58%
B	+140%	+70%
C	+200%	+110%

will then rise by 76%. Corresponding data for highways and extra-urban traffic are not available yet.

Road traffic safety can be characterized by the number of accidents with injuries, which account for 15% to 20% of all accidents registered by police. In 1989, the countries selected above reported 1.1 million accidents with injuries. The statistics show that the absolute figures remained almost constant with a slight decrease during the past 20 years. Accordingly, the accident rate (i.e., the number of accidents with injuries per million vehicle-kilometers) has decreased. The PROMETHEUS experts for safety expect this trend to continue due to better training combined with improvements of vehicles and roads and despite the increasing workload for the driver. On highways, however, there could be a reversal of this trend. It is the general opinion that the toll of lives taken in road traffic is too high and, therefore, that specific efforts are needed to reduce it.

Traffic efficiency is not independent of traffic safety. In the Paris/Ile de France expressway network, one-third of the congestion (in queue length × time) is caused by accidents. There is general consensus that traffic safety must not be sacrificed to improve efficiency. PROMETHEUS treats both objectives without ranking them. Due to the close correlation between individual vehicle control and safe driving on the one hand and collective traffic control and transport efficiency on the other, self-sufficient equipment in vehicles will primarily affect safety, whereas cooperation with traffic control is the primary means to improve efficiency. The driver has to consider both these aspects simultaneously.

9.1.3 System Approach

Faced with the problems described above, the European automotive industry initiated the EUREKA program PROMETHEUS in 1986. Today, 15 European companies are participating: BMW, Daimler-Benz, Fiat, Ford, Jaguar, MAN, Matra, Opel, Peugeot, Porsche, Renault, Saab, Steyr-Daimler-Puch, Volkswagen, and Volvo. The basic questions addressed by PROMETHEUS are:

- How to balance supply and demand within the entire transport system;
- How to optimize road transport as an integrated component of that system.

With PROMETHEUS, the European automotive industry takes a step from considering vehicles as separate topics of research, to researching the total transportation system, with vehicles as key elements. The revolutionary new approach of PROMETHEUS is characterized by fully recognizing vehicles as actuators of the future road traffic control system and no longer as passive objects of traffic research. The integration of vehicle and traffic control is the essential means to improve safety and efficiency in road traffic. This approach requires a common model of traffic, common information on the traffic state, and mutual strategies for specific traffic situations.

The model adapted by PROMETHEUS may be called *cooperative equilibrium* and is depicted in Figure 9.1. It is a feedback control loop with roughly three time scales of

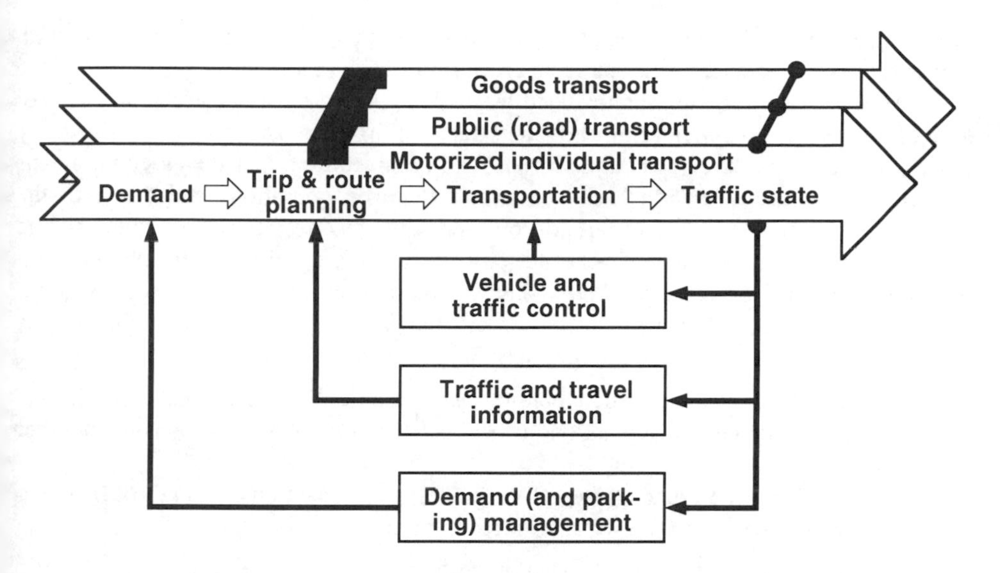

Figure 9.1 Feedback control loops for cooperative equilibrium in traffic.

feedback: fast, for vehicle and traffic control; average, for traffic and travel information; and slow, for demand control and network design. Governments and authorities are the main participants in the outer loop. They determine the service level of the equilibrium as a compromise between individual and social needs (e.g., the modal split) by establishing a framework for generalized transportation costs like expenses, time, and convenience. The inner loop—*cooperative control*—addresses the cooperation of vehicle control and traffic control by implementing real-time control on the basis of a common source of information.

At present, drivers can obtain a good picture of their immediate surroundings, but lack knowledge about the traffic state elsewhere. At some strategic points, traffic managers have good data acquisition of the network, but only indirect information of current traffic disturbances. Bidirectional data exchange between control centers and vehicles would allow *cooperative state estimation* as the basis for a cooperative control system, where vehicles are traffic sensors as well as actuators of traffic control. Modern information and communication technologies can support both functions. The main participants in the implementation of cooperative control are the automotive industry with their suppliers, as well as the electronics and communication industries in cooperation with traffic managers.

The model does not imply that every vehicle has to issue "requests for movement" or will be directed by the control center. On the contrary, it has to accommodate "unequipped" vehicles like today's cars with the driver as sensor and actuator. In their daily tasks, drivers acquire a reasonable "state estimation" and reasonable strategies to counter some disturbances just by learning. Therefore, they can participate in cooperative traffic, with a possible loss in efficiency and more stress during traffic disturbances.

All transport users, drivers included, will be supported by the intermediate control loop of Figure 9.1. This service of traffic and travel information is available to everybody (e.g., at home, in public information stations, or in the vehicle). It is the essential means to plan trips or transportation based on expected traffic conditions and costs. In the car, this service would improve transport efficiency by issuing information about public transport, hotels, vehicle maintenance, and so on. Participating actively in the implementation of such a service, the automotive industry promotes an integrated transport system.

In accordance with the model, PROMETHEUS addresses three subtopics of the cooperative equilibrium, which are described in Sections 9.2 to 9.4.

- Safe driving: Improved vehicle control by informing or supporting the driver;
- Cooperative driving: Cooperation of local groups of drivers for safer and smoother traffic flow;
- Travel and transport management: Trip planning and reaction to actual traffic situation for better use of the available infrastructure.

In short, PROMETHEUS aims at providing drivers with a driver assistant, a traffic organizer, and a transport manager.

9.1.4 PROMETHEUS Feasibility Studies

The implementation of a system for integrated vehicle and traffic control is a difficult process. As a minimum, it requires a demonstration of technical feasibility, an assessment of the impact on traffic, and a consensus on the functions of interfaces between different components. The *common European demonstrations* (CED) serve these purposes. These are not prototypes of future vehicles or devices. PROMETHEUS is a precompetitive research program, and when a consensus on functionalities has been reached, the partners will serve the market in competition. The precompetitive cooperation of several companies in one CED is an essential means to reach a consensus on the basis of common experience. In addition, the CEDs prepare field trials as the next step for a realistic evaluation. The impact on traffic and the acceptance by the users cannot be assessed reasonably on the basis of functional specifications alone. Safety experts and traffic engineers need information on technical realization for such assessments. A sound solution must address the aspects of technical feasibility—not a trivial task, since the vehicle represents a very demanding environment for microelectronics. The human-machine interaction is also very important, since the mental workload for the driver is already high nowadays.

Safe driving includes the following CEDs: vision enhancement, proper vehicle operation, and collision avoidance. The latter term has been used in several PROMETHEUS publications and is maintained here for consistency, although the project would be more accurately reflected by the term *collision risk determination*. The work on these three demonstrations is described in detail by M. Andrews in Section 9.2 of this chapter.

Cooperative driving includes the following CEDs: cooperative driving, autonomous intelligent cruise control, and emergency call. These are described in detail by A. Kemeny in Section 9.3.

Today, we have four transportation systems—road, rail, waterways, and air—each with its own characteristics. Customers and operators both lack vital information on the whole range of transportation and their actual or expected availability. The travel and transport management under development in PROMETHEUS tries to improve this situation by giving customers or operators the means to choose the best mode of transportation, type of vehicle, route, departure time, and so on. It primarily addresses the planning and administrative aspects of transportation and is complementary to the operational aspect of safe and cooperative driving.

In freight and fleet management today, insufficient information flow along the transport chain causes unnecessary trips, idle periods, empty hauls, and a fleet load factor below optimum (i.e., additional and inefficient transport). The CED *commercial fleet management* is a cooperation among the automotive companies Daimler-Benz, Fiat, MAN Nutzfahrzeuge, Renault, and Volvo, together with Dornier, MAN Technologie, and Thomson as partners [2]. It primarily aims at the development of an uninterrupted information flow along the transport chain, including the connection between vehicle and fleet management (Figure 9.2). The major tasks are the integration of different communication and

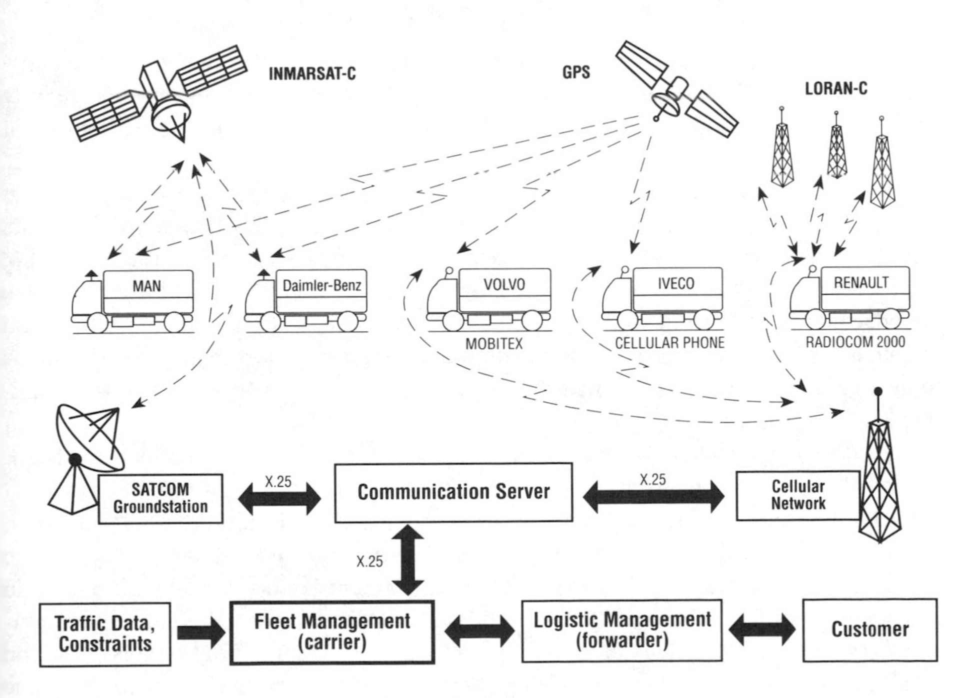

Figure 9.2 Communication network for commercial fleet management.

localization systems, the specification of standardized messages, and the implementation of the vehicular components at the driver's workplace.

At present, work concentrates on the following topics.

- Tests of mobile communication systems for fleet management: INMARSAT-C, PRODAT, and EUTELTRACS as examples of satellite communication; C-NET and D-NET mobile phones; RDS broadcasting, data packet switching by MOBITEX or MODACOM;
- Development of user-friendly input and output devices suited to operation in trucks en route;
- Test and integration of different localization systems: GPS, EUTELTRACS, INMARSAT-C (planned); GSM (perhaps in the D-NET); possibly EURO-SCOUT beacons;
- Classification, coding, and standardization of macro-encoded messages for the message exchange between all participants in freight and fleet management;
- Connection to an international electronic data interchange (EDI) network;
- Use of current traffic data for trip planning;
- Tracking of dangerous goods by automatic localization;
- Transfer of emergency calls to rescue service centers;
- Collection of vehicle and tour- and freight-specific data.

In September 1991, a first test was conducted with ten vehicles distributed across Europe and connected to different communication systems. The management center in the vicinity of Torino performed both the freight and fleet management and optimized the routing of vehicles using topical traffic information.

This CED is closely linked to the EC DRIVE program (i.e., the FLEET project V1044 in DRIVE I and the IFMS project V2051 in DRIVE II). By the end of 1992, the PROMETHEUS partners will have evaluated their systems and the information chain, and proposed a standard for messages to be exchanged. Further functional tests will then be conducted in cooperation with selected customers as preparation, implementation, and evaluation of a large-scale field test with integrated freight and fleet management systems and international transport chains including sectors such as intermodal operations, hazardous goods, or just-in-time delivery.

On dual-mode route guidance systems, see Section 9.4 by P. Häußermann and H.-G. Zimmer. Under most circumstances, individual motorized transport provides an excellent means for transportation, ensuring the highest flexibility and comfort for the traveler combined with immediate availability and broad coverage of the different transportation tasks. But when the road network is saturated, when there is no space to park the car at the destination, or when the driving conditions are bad, the car sometimes causes problems for society and the individuals in terms of increased congestion, harmful emissions, and accidents. Public transport does provide an alternative to the private car, at least for some transportation tasks. But due to unfamiliarity with public transport and lack of information on the actual availability of their services, it is difficult to make the habitual car driver consider other means of transportation.

The CED *travel information services* aims at integrating different transport modes by providing topical information about the current alternatives. In its final stage, it will support a well-balanced usage of all transport means by giving up-to-date and easy-to-use information and services to all travelers. In principle, the objective is complementary to commercial fleet management, where a complete information chain ensures highest efficiency and economy in goods transport. In fact, the travel information service is much more ambitious because:

- There are a large number of eligible services, such as:
  - Airline, rail, and bus timetables for, at a minimum, Europe;
  - Seat reservation and ticket sales for public transport;
  - Car rental, parking guidance, and booking;
  - Traffic messages, driving conditions, and weather forecast;
  - Hotel, maintenance, repair, and emergency;
  - Tourist, visitor, and business information.
- There is a variety of prospective users, all of which have specific needs (e.g., tourists, business people, residents, foreigners, the handicapped, and so on);
- There are considerable differences in the equipment required for use at home or in the office, in travel or in the car, at public places or in information centers.

Underneath the surface visible to the user there are:

- Several independent information providers with different architectures of their computer and information management systems for the retrieval and update services;
- A heterogeneous communication network between the information providers and different communication means connecting the network with the individual user (e.g., telephone, mobile phone, radio (RDS-TMC), and data packet switching networks).
- Administrative problems, such as addressing and accessing the desired source of information, or mechanisms to charge user fees and liability problems. For commercial or political reasons, difficulties have to be expected in getting access to data from different transportation operators. They may not like their data to be freely compared with other alternatives, a situation we experience in the airline industry today.

Considering that this service eventually will be available throughout Europe, it becomes obvious that the only solution is a distributed system with an open architecture to accommodate information sources with different geographical or topical context, a wide range of travel services, and the modes to access them. A good solution requires cooperation between basic research and applied technology. PROMETHEUS research in computer science and communication technology is devoted to the topics of data models, databases, communication in computer networks, and communication protocols. Telia AB in Sweden and IBM in Germany are competent R&D partners of the European automotive industry.

With regard to applications, one has to consider the travel information services that already exist in a fragmented form for specific transport offers, such as national trains or public transport in metropolitan areas. In a realistic approach, those pieces have to be taken as the basis for further development. In close cooperation with local authorities and service providers, PROMETHEUS partners are involved in ongoing field trials in Gothenburg, Hanover, Munich [3], Paris, Stuttgart [4], and Turin. Pooling of information, a basic principle of PROMETHEUS, gives all partners access to the know-how acquired at different sites by different approaches and fosters the development of a unified system for Europe and an agreement on standards.

Due to its complexity, a universal travel information service is a long-term project. Useful subsets can be implemented soon. The new DRIVE-project PROMISE aims at a multimodal travel information system with a portable terminal for the user. This could provide traffic information and hazard warnings, information about public transport, parking availability, parking reservations, and tourist and visitor information. It will use multiple communication bearers, such as RDS-TMC, GSM, and one-way and two-way paging and mobile data services. There is good reason to promote portable terminals: the travel information has to be readily available. The traveler will have no excuses for not checking all possible alternatives.

The PROMISE project relies on results of previous work in PROMETHEUS and DRIVE (RDS-ALERT, SOCRATES, CIDER) and exemplifies clearly how both programs cooperate with complementary emphasis and the same objectives, with different time horizons for the same traffic problems.

9.1.5 System Architecture and Introductory Strategy

Some problems of safe driving, cooperative driving, and travel and transport management could be solved or alleviated by dedicated components or subsystems now under development in industry. Simply bringing them together and adding their control devices to the dashboard will not provide the maximum effect; perhaps it will even overload or distract the driver. The whole system for information and control must have a coherent structure. This applies to the software (i.e., the decision and control strategies implemented in computer programs) as well as the hardware (i.e., the communication network within the vehicle, between the vehicle and its environment, and with the driver). Figure 9.3 symbolizes the proposed architecture of the system components in the vehicle. In general, every application program (in Figure 9.3 indicated by App. x) needs communication with the driver, with sensors and actuators in the vehicle, and with roadside equipment. For route guidance, for example, dead reckoning takes data from sensors, traffic messages from radio, or beacons and displays guidance information to the driver. At the same time, cruise control reads speed limits from the roadside, measures own speed and distance, controls throttle or brakes, and informs the driver if necessary.

The system has to meet two sometimes conflicting requirements. It should be open for new functionalities and services in order to leave room for improvements, and it

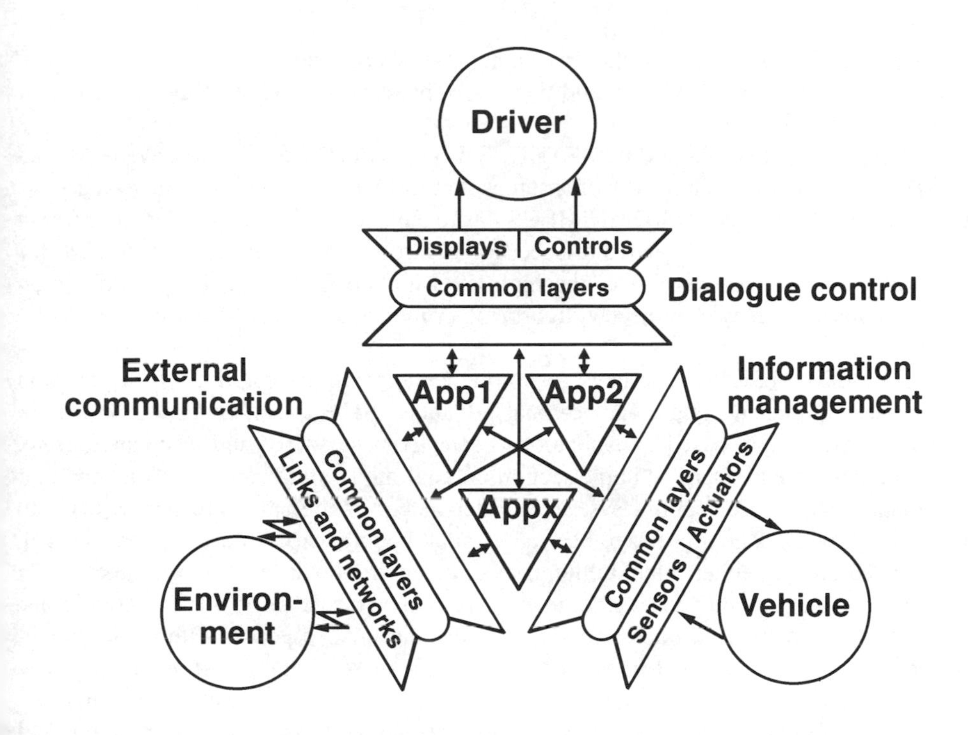

Figure 9.3 Proposed system architecture of the vehicular components for cooperative vehicle and traffic control.

should be standardized for compatibility of implementations by different suppliers, for uniform interaction with the user, and as incentive for higher market penetration.

Reasons for an open-system architecture are given in the descriptions of the feasibility studies. Dual-mode route guidance and especially travel information services show that this characteristic is not only required for vehicular components. The services by components in the infrastructure address different users and rely on different information providers, using different equipment for processing and dissemination. Architectural aspects for future freeway information and control systems have been described in [5].

At present, the system has not been defined yet. At the level of communication within the vehicle, the PROMETHEUS working group "Architectures" has elaborated proposals for bus structures and the associated communication protocols which enter the standardization procedure now. Computer scientists of the Basic Research Subgroup PRO-ART investigate the high-level architecture for onboard computer systems, which has to provide a common framework of access to the peripheral devices (i.e., the driver, the current traffic situation, and the vehicle state).

While driving, it is not acceptable that different modules of a complex control system try to "access" the driver independently of the others. A reasonable human-machine interaction has to be monitored by dialogue control based on models of the driver, the present traffic situation, and the driving capabilities in order to ensure consistency of distributed information, decisions, and controls. This aspect is relevant to the misuse of technology in driving as well.

The potential benefits of PROMETHEUS devices could be degraded or even reversed by risk compensation when the driver assumes that technology widens the safety margins. To counteract their misuse, PROMETHEUS has to embed the new devices into a coherent system where functions are related to specified control strategies and cannot be used for other than the intended purposes. The high-level architecture of vehicle control is an ongoing long-term research project with early experimental implementations in cooperative driving.

Basic PROMETHEUS strategy for implementation is an evolutionary introduction of optional equipment bought for personal advantage. The transition from optional to mandatory use must be based on evaluation of effectiveness, safety, and acceptance. Here, we face the dilemma described in the section on dual-mode route guidance: if a vehicular information, support, or control system is independent of infrastructure services, it can be introduced now. The user has to bear the cost and public expenditures are not needed. But such equipment either refers to the immediate environment (e.g., friction coefficient or distance to the preceding vehicle) or to average data on the network or traffic conditions. It thus has the potential to improve individual driving with respect to safety and convenience, but has a rather small impact on avoiding or dissolving congestion. These tasks require current traffic data for route selection or cruise control, which can only be provided by the infrastructure. Such services can be implemented only gradually. At first there will be equipped vehicles in an unequipped environment and vice versa. Both situations reduce the effect of cooperative control equipment and will extend the introductory phase.

With regard to the impending traffic problems, Europe needs short-term progress towards a universal solution. Monitoring the road and environment with sensors in the vehicle provides data with more actuality and relevance for the driving task at that very moment than collective data. Therefore, PROMETHEUS advocates concerted actions where infrastructure-independent devices pave the way for cooperative control. Collective data is more relevant for a preview, but imply the existence of a communication system. In the final system, both are required. The implementation process can actually start from either end as long as the automotive industry cooperates closely with the providers of the infrastructure services and the system design guaranties that both approaches come up with the same solution.

The CEDs described above and in more detail in the following sections of this chapter give an idea of the contributions to be expected from the automotive industry. It must be stated, however, that the decision on the implementation is at the discretion of the individual industrial company. The precompetitive research of PROMETHEUS ends when the technical feasibility, relevance for traffic, and the cost-benefit relation have been shown. The effectiveness of the industry's contributions to road transport informatics depends on a close collaboration between national, regional, and local government departments, infrastructure operators, and industry in developing a European strategy for introduction and implementation. A recommendation of joint actions was presented by the chairman of the European Automotive Manufacturers Association (ACEA), Mr. Levy, to the ECMT at their conference in Paris in November 1991. It covered the items listed below.

Traffic Information

1. Traffic data collection and processing facilities as a basis for traffic information are needed now on a national basis, and a European traffic data interchange is needed before 1995.
2. Location coding of traffic information supplied by ministers of transport should be harmonized within Europe.
3. A study addressing liability of traffic information is valuable and will be supported by PROMETHEUS experts.
4. ECMT should establish European rules for electronic display of road and traffic information, the ECMT Road Signs and Signals committee could start such work by using the current traffic message channel prestandard as a basis.
5. ECMT should enforce the interconnection of databases containing information on traffic, travel, and public transport.

RDS-TMC

6. ECMT should enforce this prestandard and support any national or European field test complying with this standard.
7. Since RDS-TMC protocols are already available for interurban application, ECMT should foster further R&D to obtain protocols compatible with urban traffic application.

Pan-European Cellular Digital Radio Telephone (GSM)

8. ECMT should ask the European Conference of Ministers of Post and Telecommunication (CEPT) to support the implementation of a traffic information service and a localization feature within GSM.

Pan-European Commercial Fleet Management System

9. ECMT should ask CEPT to support the implementation of a dedicated European mobile data communication service as they have done for GSM.

Autonomous Intelligent Cruise Control

10. ECMT should start discussion with the automotive industry on the current regulation constraints and should support field tests in this domain.

Short-Range Communication Between Road and Vehicle

11. ECMT should enforce European standards in this domain and oblige—via ad hoc regulation—suppliers, providers, licensees, and so on of any road or vehicle information service to comply with European standards at the time they will be available.

PROMETHEUS Counterpart in European Ministries of Transport

12. A more efficient cooperation between PROMETHEUS and ECMT requires the nomination of a PROMETHEUS counterpart or coordinator in each ministry of transport. In order to create active common working groups, ECMT should mandate a Transport, Computers, and Telecommunications Ad Hoc Group (TCT) as a counterpart to start the process.

Organization

13. ECMT should strongly support the definition and installation of a public or private organization for the implementation of road transport informatics, taking care of coordination, planning, and introduction.

This list of recommended joint actions was officially accepted by the ECMT. In January 1992, the Committee of Deputies instructed the TCT to examine the practical aspects of this matter and to find ways to cooperate with PROMETHEUS. Meanwhile, a link between TCT and the PROMETHEUS working group ''Infrastructure-Based Systems'' has been established and is operational now. As an example of item 13, Mr. Levy named ERTICO (European Road Transport Informatics Implementation Coordination Organization), established in Brussels in November 1991, with representatives of road users, communication and automotive industry, infrastructure operators, and administration on its supervisory board. ERTICO decided to have a permanent exchange of representatives with the ECMT. The European Commission is represented in ERTICO by DG VII and DG XIII. Some car manufacturers are already members of ERTICO, and the role of PROMETHEUS in ERTICO is under negotiation. The ERTICO work plan is still under development, but since its emphasis will be on system architecture evaluation, monitoring, coordination, and assessment of pilot projects, as well as promotion of the implementation, the collaboration with PROMETHEUS is essential and, in fact, has already begun.

ACKNOWLEDGMENTS

This section summarizes the continuous discussion among the PROMETHEUS partners and to give a picture of the dynamic progress. Therefore, it is a compilation of material coming from many sources, especially the PROMETHEUS handout [1]. I gratefully acknowledge the support of D. Augello (Renault), G. Brusaglino (Fiat), F. de Charentenay (Peugeot), and G. Rosengren (Volvo) for the task of giving a survey on this multifaceted program. I would like to express my sincere appreciation to Jan Hellåker (Volvo), E. Hipp (MAN), and V. Mauro (MIZAR), who in personal discussions provided technical details used in this chapter without explicit reference. I am also grateful to M. Andrews (Porsche), P. Häußermann (Daimler-Benz), and A. Kemeny (Renault) for their complementary sections in this book, and to my colleagues in PROMETHEUS Office for technical assistance.

9.2 THE INTELLIGENT VEHICLE—A MEANS OF SAFE DRIVING*

9.2.1 Introduction

Since its invention, the automobile has seen rapid development from its origins as a modified version of the horse-drawn carriage to the sophisticated vehicles on the road today. Industrial society has grown with it and has built large networks of infrastructure and services to develop, manufacture, and maintain it and, most important, to make use of it. Its ability to transport people and goods have made the automobile a fundamental part of daily life, giving individuals opportunities for easy and fast movement, and perhaps equally importantly, providing leisure enjoyment and a means of self-expression. Almost everything we do at some time relies on it for transportation. The automobile and associated industries provide employment for millions. Some people have described this relationship as a love affair, with the combination of the human and its machine creation being a mixture of science, art, technology, and philosophy. At the pragmatic level, too, we have to realize the ambiguity of motorized individual transport, ranging from the enjoyment of easy and fast movement to the impediment of mobility by congestion, from leisure driving to the transportation task.

The automobile is not, however, without its critics, who point to such drawbacks as its impact on the environment, both direct, such as exhaust emissions and noise, and indirect, such as the use of land for roads and the consumption of raw materials and their subsequent waste in both building and running vehicles. In addition, increasing traffic congestion and overcrowding of the road network is reducing somewhat the inherent mobility advantages that the automobile has brought. These problems are being addressed in many public discussions, but this chapter will concentrate on the safety, comfort, and

*This section was written by M. J. Andrews.

convenience aspects that the future intelligent vehicle could have as a result of current research in the PROMETHEUS program of cooperative research in Europe.

9.2.2 Goals and Potential Pitfalls

Safety is an obvious and most important goal, since deaths, injuries, and damage caused by automobile accidents, plus all the associated social and commercial costs, must still be regarded as unacceptable, despite having shown some reductions over recent years due to improved vehicle safety design. However, comfort and convenience must also be considered as safety-relevant, as more relaxed, less distracted drivers and passengers will also lead to fewer accidents.

The modern automobile has a host of safety-, comfort-, and convenience-related features the driver has come to expect. The safety features include seatbelts, passive restraints/airbags, laminated windscreens, protective bodyshells, dual-circuit/antilock brakes, and many warning systems, to name but a few, and the list of comfort and convenience features ranges from air-conditioning to illuminated vanity mirrors.

However, any superficial study of today's traffic conditions would indicate that there are still numerous accidents resulting in injuries and deaths. PROMETHEUS, with its integral goal of unprecedented safety, set out to analyze the fundamental problems encountered in accidents and to apply modern technology to solve or alleviate them.

It is important at this point to state that the raw use of technology in the modern vehicle has been tried in recent years with sometimes unexpected or even comic results, and unfortunately often with less-than-expected improvements in safety, comfort, and convenience. So the lesson has been learned that the appropriate technology and techniques must be used to solve the real problem, not to implement gimmicks. To understand why this is, one must realize what is perhaps obvious, but nevertheless will be stated here. The driving task involves the interaction of the driver with the vehicle and the environment, which is made up of other vehicles and drivers, the road, signs, weather conditions, all of which are changing temporally and spatially. The involvement of the human element makes the definition, modeling, simulation, and evaluation of the driving task extremely difficult. The infinite variety of human behavior, reactions, and attitudes in the driving task makes the successful application of technology an enormous task, one that the European automotive industry has decided to share in the cooperative PROMETHEUS program.

The intelligent vehicle of the future must help the driver in a manner that is natural and acceptable, meeting the driver's needs in a timely manner; otherwise, the system will fall into disrepute and be ignored or switched off, negating any possible benefits. Equally important, the driver must remain an integral part of the driving and vehicle control task, with any change in the division of competence being clearly understood by the driver.

In all this, the aspect of responsibility and liability is always in the mind of the automotive research engineer, besides which a reduction of the driver contribution to the driving task would make driving an automobile altogether less pleasurable and take away the pride that most people have about their driving. However, complex driving situations cannot be avoided. An alleviation of the associated burden on the driver is necessary to maintain the efficiency of individual transport.

Available Technology

Modern technology will enter vehicles to improve their functionality. Indeed, PROMETHEUS and other similar complementary RTI projects have come to a point where the necessary technologies and techniques can be provided for the intelligent vehicle. It is now becoming possible to produce the required hardware and software components at automotive prices with the appropriate quality, accuracy, and reliability.

Their availability is being fueled by the entry of what have been, up to the end of the 1980s, purely military- and defense-oriented industries, anxious to transfer their technologies and expertise to the automotive sector. Their increasing desire to make available previously secret know-how has been spurred on by the reduction in defense expenditure in most countries and the subsequent need to look for new commercial outlets. As will be shown, the technological gap between the aerospace and automotive industries is not as large as it was formerly. In many ways, the vehicle provides one of the greatest challenges to the successful introduction of intelligent systems and components, greater even perhaps than in aerospace.

Structuring the Approach

From the very beginning of PROMETHEUS, three main groupings were used in order to manage the program efficiently. These are based on the combinations of communication partners, namely, systems within the individual vehicle, groups of vehicles, and vehicles together with infrastructure. The last two involve communication with systems external to the individual vehicle: vehicle-with-vehicle and vehicle-with-infrastructure, described in Sections 9.3 and 9.4. Here, autonomous systems installed on individual vehicles are described (although reference is made wherever use of communication systems would be beneficial to the functionality of the autonomous system).

As has already been stated, the needs of the driver had to be identified. To do this, the traffic engineering research area of PROMETHEUS, called PRO-GEN, was called upon to provide the answers, principally through the analysis of accident data already available. In addition, researchers in industry identified 23 basic functions that could be feasibly implemented in the intelligent vehicle [6], although only the first nine were principally autonomous in nature. These, together with their subfunctions, are listed in Table 9.2. Both these inputs were brought together to identify the sort of situations in which accidents occur and the needs of the driver in such situations to prevent such accidents. Figure 9.4 shows the needs expressed as a percentage of injury-producing

Table 9.2 PROMETHEUS Basic Functions

Number and Title	*Description*	*Subfunction*
1. Obstacle detection	Detecting and evaluating objects as obstacles in time for collision avoidance, where objects are moving and stationary entities within possible trajectories of the vehicle and obstacles are objects with a potential for collision.	Trajectory prediction Maneuvring zone determination Object detection Object trajectory determination Collision probability determination
2. Monitoring environment and road	Acquiring information on the status and possible changes in the immediate external vehicle operating environment	Road geometry, regulations, surface, and markings; friction-related parameters; visibility
3. Monitoring driver	Observing the driver's operation of the vehicle and psychological condition of with respect to normal safe behavior.	Monitor driver activation of vehicle control and movement of vehicle Creation of current driver profile Identification of trends in profile
4. Monitoring vehicle	Acquiring and processing of data on vehicle dynamics and operational status to diagnose and prognose vehicle failures and to monitor and predict vehicle dynamic behavior.	Data acquisition of vehicle dynamics and operating status Modeling of vehicle behavior Identification of vehicle failures Interface with diagnostic system
5. Vision enhancement	Improving the visibility of the driving scene by autonomous and noncooperative means in subnormal visibility conditions by providing direct visual information to the driver	Active illumination of the scene Enhancement of the scene contrast Enhancement of the sensitivity and range of driver vision
6. Safety margin determination	Continuously determining the margin of dynamic vehicle performance that allows stable driving maneuvers, considering all relevant factors related to the vehicle and the environment, both in actual and predictive manner	Determination of maximum potential limits Determination of the actual and predicted position of the driving situation within the limits Determination of the safety margin
7. Critical course determination	Continuous determination of course related to road boundaries and stationary and moving objects related to trajectory to avoid potential conflicts	Determination of trajectory Identification of potential collisions Identification of a course which minimizes the risk of a collision
8. Dynamic vehicle control	Control of the lateral, longitudinal, and vertical dynamic behavior of the vehicle to influence the vehicle in order to stabilize driving according to the demand of the driver or higher level control system, with priority given to safety requirements	Evaluation of input values set by the driver or higher level system Selection of the appropriate control strategy and control of corresponding actuating system Control system activation/control
9. Supportive driver information	Information to driver to achieve the behavior appropriate the situation (by warnings, advice, or active support) to help make the driver more aware of vehicle reaction or required action	Identification of information priority and relevance to the driving situation Presentation of information to the driver using the correct method Monitoring of driver response

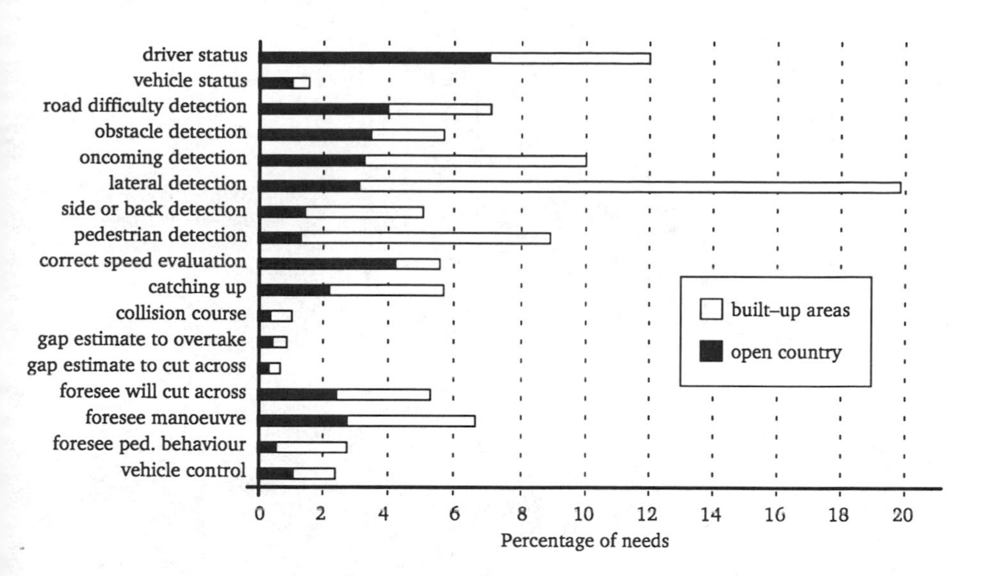

igure 9.4 Breakdown in 17 categories of four-wheeler needs (after [7]).

ccidents, divided into built-up areas or open country [7]. For each of the needs, further nalysis was made describing the maneuver or collision situation, the road geometry/ ayout at the point of collision, the environmental conditions (e.g., visibility and state of oad surface), time of day, driver type/condition, and vehicle-related factors such as oading, condition, and category.

The subsequent assessment of all these results and feasibility inputs led to the identification f three distinct topics of technical research oriented towards reducing these types of ccidents.

1. Vision enhancement: addressing accidents in reduced visibility conditions such as darkness, rain/spray, and fog;
2. Proper vehicle operation: addressing accidents caused by the loss of control of a vehicle;
3. Collision avoidance: addressing accidents caused by the nondetection or late detection of obstacles.

he relationship of these topics to the previously defined functions can be seen in Figure .5. These topics were opened to the primary research groups within PROMETHEUS: he automotive companies, electronics and supplier industries, and basic research institutes, who were invited to make contributions based on their specific areas of interest and research ctivities relevant to these topics. Many experts also contributed to the development of hese programs into CEDs, including the writing of mission statements, development of ork packages, and agreement on time plans and milestones. The concept of CEDs is escribed Section 9.1 above, but it suffices here to say that it allowed contributions to

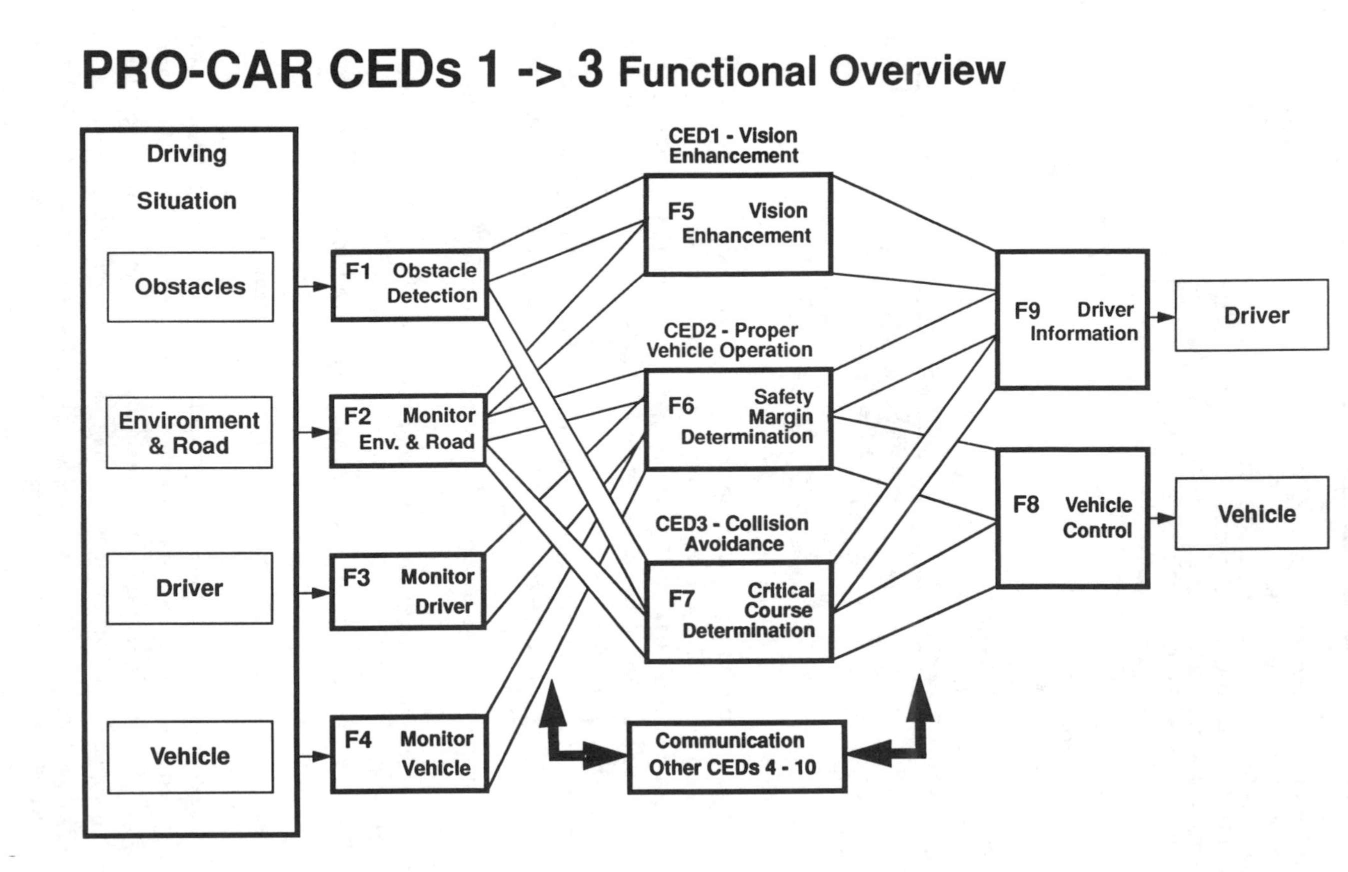

Figure 9.5 The implementation of functions in the three primarily autonomous CEDs.

be made at many levels from components (hardware or software) to subsystems to complete systems, promoting their integration both as an autonomous solution and their further integration into the overall PROMETHEUS systems engineering approach.

The following sections describe the three CEDs and include details of the sort of solutions being investigated and contributions being made by the various research groupings within PROMETHEUS, and highlight some of the questions yet to be answered.

9.2.3 Vision Enhancement

Analyzing the Problem and Setting the Goal

Sight is the primary sense used in the driving task: to see the road ahead of the vehicle, to detect the presence of obstacles, to observe surrounding traffic, and to read road signs. However, there are many conditions that impair the driver's vision and therefore reduce driving safety, including fog, heavy rain, spray from other vehicles, snow, darkness, or dazzle caused by the headlights of oncoming vehicles either in wet or night situations. Even if these conditions do not cause complete obstruction of vision, they reduce the range of vision and the ability to determine the range and relative velocity of vehicles and potential obstacles.

A detailed analysis revealed that the most publicized accidents caused by poor visibility (i.e., fog on highways) are only a small percentage of this type of accident. Collisions in curves with stationary or moving obstacles and head-on collisions on straight roads or while overtaking are much more common. Indeed, there are only small differences in these figures from passenger cars to trucks, showing that they are influenced little by either the viewing point or the skill and experience of the driver. The analysis also showed that these accidents are divided roughly equally between normal night-time conditions and those of poor visibility, either night or day, caused by adverse weather conditions, although it is often difficult to attribute a single cause to a particular accident.

Based on this initial problem evaluation and using the expertise of the contributing companies, the basic goals, means, and approach were defined and a work-breakdown structure was developed to cover all the activities required to ensure that all the tasks are identified and covered, including problem analysis, system specification/development, and evaluation/assessment.

Problem analysis ranges from the description of atmospheric and road conditions to the development of scenarios, defining a set of conditions serving as an aim, a set of functional requirements, and as the basis for common testing and evaluation of system performance. System specification covers the initial selection of sensing, processing, and driver interface technologies, leading to the first system design and eventually to component specifications. An overview of the possible vision enhancement system components is given as Figure 9.6. The system development area covers the tasks necessary to take initial systems and develop, test, and integrate them using the appropriate combination

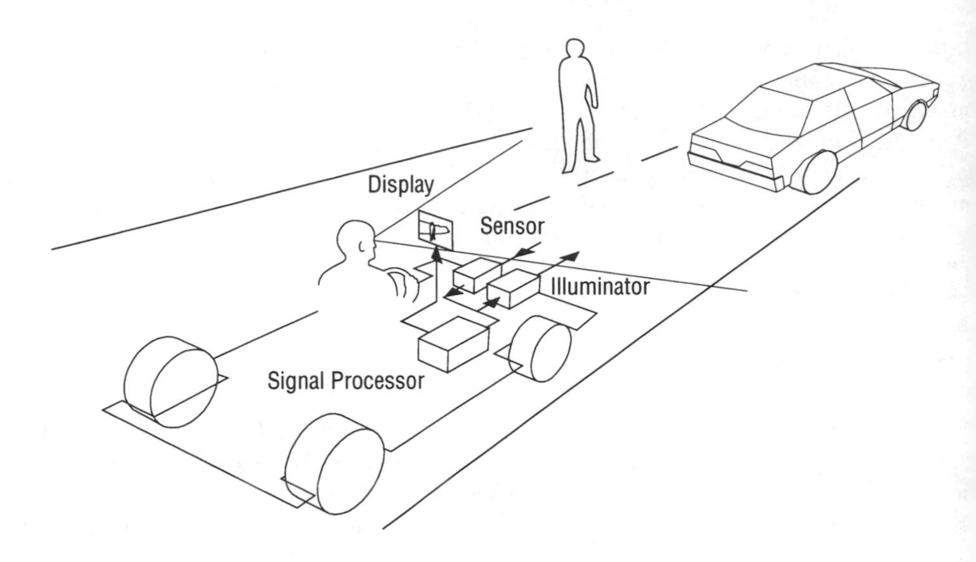

Figure 9.6 An overview of the possible vision enhancement system components.

of components. Evaluation/assessment takes into account the wider aspects of systen implementation, including driver acceptance, safety and reliability issues, and, mos importantly, recommendations for standardization where appropriate.

The aim of vision enhancement, therefore, is to improve driving safety in reduce visibility conditions by providing information to the driver on the road situation ahead The goal has been set to provide information on the traffic scene up to 200 meter ahead of the vehicle, approximately equivalent to the visibility range given by high-bean headlights in clear night conditions. However, the driver will remain responsible for th interpretation of the information provided, and no attempt is being made to intervene i the control of the vehicle. This area is researched in collision avoidance, described later

Principal Technologies

Ultraviolet Illumination. The first and perhaps the most promising technology for short term introduction is that of ultraviolet (UV) illumination based on the use of gas-discharg lamps. This type of lamp will soon be introduced into serial production as a complemen to conventional halogen headlamps, with power consumption combined with increase light output at shorter wavelengths (a ''whiter'' light), together with a longer lifetime. It requirements for a higher operating voltage and better headlamp design are currently nea a solution. There is, in addition, the ability to ''tune'' the lamp to give significant ultraviole energy output. By using filters to remove both the visible light, preventing dazzle, an the potentially harmful UVB radiation, and by designing the reflector to give a high-bea UVA light pattern, the visibility of objects can be improved using their inherent fluoresce characteristics. Many dyes or pigments present in both natural and manmade materials have this ability to absorb UVA radiation and re-emit visible light. This property is enhanced by the use of detergents, many of which contain "fluorescers" to enhance the appearance of whites and colors. As an interesting note, the coats of many animals are also fluorescent, including elk, which cause a large number of serious accidents in northern countries. The driver interface is obviously a completely natural one, requiring no additional display. The enhancement is visible directly through the windscreen. Work is currently ongoing to determine the integration of UV sources into the normal headlamp cluster of vehicles and the effects of UVA radiation on other traffic participants. Further benefits could be achieved by including fluorescent dyes and pigments in road markings, signs, and vehicles to enhance their visibility. The benefits of this system are primarily in night or low-light conditions.

Infrared. The infrared spectrum is also being investigated in two main areas. The first, called *near infrared* (NIR), is the wavelength band between 0.8 and 1.2 μm just above the visible band between 0.4 and 0.7 μm. Again, illumination of the driving scene with NIR light is possible using a filtered source with a high-beam spread pattern. However, the light is returned by straightforward reflection at the same wavelength and detected using a *charge-coupled device* (CCD) camera similar to those used in domestic video camcorders, which is sensitive to NIR radiation. The images obtained can be processed and combined with data from other sensors, such as range finders, and presented to the driver using a display, providing additional visual information on the scene ahead.

The second IR system uses the longer wavelengths, 8 to 12 μm, known as *far infrared* (FIR). At these wavelengths, even moderately warm objects (10° to 100°C) give off significant amounts of radiated energy, and therefore require no additional illumination from vehicle lamps. The cameras, again using CCD arrays, capture the FIR radiation from these objects, including human bodies and other vehicles, to form images based on differences in their temperatures. However, one drawback has been the need to cool the array to very low temperatures using liquified nitrogen refrigeration. Recently, devices requiring only moderate cooling, using pyroelectric technology, have become available, and these may be significantly cheaper in the future. These cameras can improve vision in all reduced visibility conditions, but require considerable development to reach automotive price levels, not to mention the ergonomics of their use by drivers.

The fourth system uses a gated intensified camera, synchronized with a light pulse generator, again working in the NIR part of the spectrum. These light pulses are reflected from objects in front of the vehicle and are captured by the camera, giving information both on the nature of the obstacle and its distance in front of the vehicle, the latter based on the time required for the light to travel to and back from the object. The image of intensification is based on conventional intensifier technology. This system works in night and fog conditions.

Driver Interface

Apart from the UV light system, all the camera-based sensors produce images that must be processed to enhance the picture, extract relevant information, and prepare it for presentation to the driver. Image enhancement is a well-proven technique, used in such areas as satellite photography; noise reduction methods, inversion, edge detection, and feature extraction can be used to provide an enhanced picture. Temporal matching techniques using a sequence of images can also provide three-dimensional data on detected objects, such as distance and direction, which could also be represented to the driver in some way.

The processing of the image produces enhanced information to be presented to the driver in a way that is easy to understand, natural, and acceptable, which is crucial to the success of the camera-based system. Image displays using many technologies (e.g., LCD, CRT, or electroluminescence) are available, but these force the driver to refocus away from the real scene outside of the windscreen, and require some measure of spatial interpretation to relate the image to the real scene. A great deal of work remains to be done to assess the appropriateness of this solution. A more natural solution may be a contact-analog virtual image head-up display, effectively making the enhanced image coincide with the real scene in front of the driver using holographic techniques. Simple head-up displays are already in use in some vehicles today, presenting information such as speed or fuel level. However, the device described above is very much more complex, similar to those used in military aircraft, and therefore requires considerable development before an economic and ergonomic solution is available.

When considering what information should be presented to the driver as well as how and where, there is the considerable problem of risk compensation if the driver is presented with such an enhanced view of the situation in front of the vehicle that the sense of danger is removed completely. Other traffic participants, vehicles, or pedestrians may not have such systems and rely on other vehicles driving slower. It could lead to higher speed differentials in poor visibility conditions or the belief by the driver that the systems make everything, including his or her own vehicle, more visible, which for some technologies may not necessarily be the case. One possibility is only to highlight some parts of the scene, such as objects in front of the vehicle, not road markings, and warn the driver of the potential hazard. The effects on driver behavior must be studied to ensure the risk compensation is minimized and safety is improved. The many solutions, the many unsolved problems, and long-term nature of some of the technologies makes vision enhancement an ideal PROMETHEUS research topic. The solutions are being investigated in parallel to identify the best ones. The problems are being addressed by combined contributions and the results are being shared to the benefit of all. UV illumination is a shorter term prospect, but the rapid advance in IR camera technology is making its introduction in the medium term a real possibility.

9.2.4 Proper Vehicle Operation

Driver-Vehicle Partnership

In the early stages of defining the problems to be solved by proper vehicle operation some statements were developed as a basis. First, most drivers are not aware of the general dynamic capabilities or, more importantly, limitations of their vehicles, even in normal, let alone adverse, driving conditions. Second, most drivers are not aware of the current dynamic status of their vehicles in these various conditions. Taken together, these two statements define a safety or stability margin. Most drivers, in some driving conditions, reduce the safety margin, sometimes resulting in loss of control with potentially disastrous consequences.

These statements were backed up again by the independent accident analysis work carried out by PRO-GEN, which identified specific needs. Again looking at Figure 9.4, they were driver status, vehicle status, detection of the road surface condition, evaluation of the correct speed, and vehicle control. With further analysis, these accidents were defined as those caused when an individual vehicle went out of control and highlighted the sort of contributory factors that later formed the basis of the three technical solutions currently being researched.

1. The determination of the current and predicted safety margin based on:
   a. The prevailing road surface friction limit and visibility conditions;
   b. The vehicle dynamic condition (essentially vehicle stability and friction demand);
   c. The condition of the vehicle systems themselves in terms of reduced performance or fault conditions;
   d. The status and behavior of the third component in the system, the driver. The final aim is to warn the driver that the safety margin is severely reduced and advise on possible corrective action.
2. Implementation of the driver's requested maneuver in the safest and most efficient manner using advanced control and actuation systems. It is essential here to remember that the driver is part of the vehicle control loop, together with the control and feedback elements that implement control actions. Much can still be done in adapting the characteristics and performance of these elements, depending on the current and predicted dynamic situation, to enhance the performance of this loop.
3. Support of the driver by reducing the workload by:
   a. Performing a certain subtask in a certain situation, such as lane keeping on highways;
   b. Intervening in critical situations, such as slowing the vehicle automatically before a bend if the driver fails to do this voluntarily. However, it should be pointed out here that automatic driving is not the aim of Proper Vehicle Operation and that the driver always remains responsible, able to override any intervention in the control of the vehicle. An overview of this approach is given in Figure 9.7.

Advice/Warning

In the category of advice/warning, several systems are being tested. The first system addresses the problem of vehicle condition monitoring, essential to the safety of any vehicle maneuver. The specific area is that of tire pressure, but this technique can be extended to other problems.

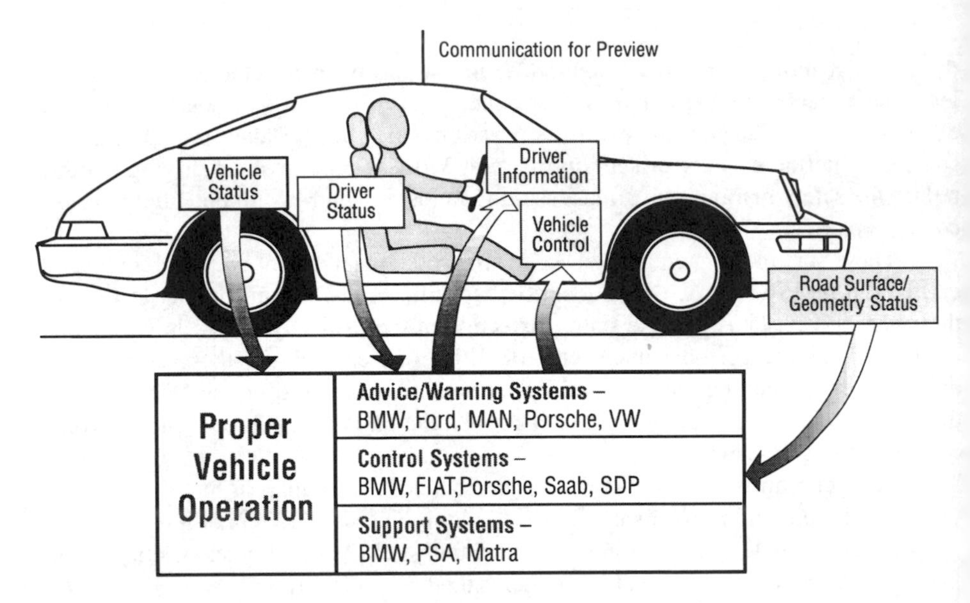

Figure 9.7 The three types of systems in the concept of proper vehicle operation.

A significant number of vehicles on the road today have incorrectly inflated tires which can adversely affect handling characteristics or even cause a catastrophic failur of the tires, particularly dangerous at high speeds. Tire pressure monitors already exist but are dependent on sensors inside the rotating tire-hub assembly and require sophisticate methods to transmit the data to the fixed receiver mounted on the suspension. A ne technique involves monitoring the response characteristic of the tire-wheel suspensio system to dynamic inputs from the road surface (e.g., road undulations or bumps) usin accelerometers mounted on the unsprung part of the suspension, one near each wheel o the vehicle. These are relatively cheap components and can be directly connected to th processing unit. Their outputs are processed to correlate the individual outputs with eac other and with the expected response. Any deviation due to either over- or underinflatio of the tire is detected and a warning is given to the driver. This technique may be extende to include the detection of other faulty or worn suspension components, such as shoc absorbers.

A system to detect visibility range is also being researched, but its goal is n improving the visibility range, which is part of the vision enhancement program discusse earlier. The system is based on the detection of backscattered light from an IR laser. Th is dependent on the density of the fog, or, more correctly, of the water droplets. This ca then be compared with a driver-perceived visibility range, with the ultimate goal o recommending a safe speed. The sensor can also be used as an object ranging device an could be incorporated as part of an "intelligent" cruise control system with distanc keeping capability (see Section 9.3).

Accidents caused by loss of control due to reduced road surface friction are being addressed by several PROMETHEUS car companies and basic research institutes. The ability to continually determine the friction potential of the tire-road interface has been described as a key task in the area of vehicle dynamics, being of use to braking and traction control systems and to suspension and steering systems. Two fundamental approaches are being used either separately or in combination. The first is to measure the effects of the forces at the tire-road interface (e.g., the slip generated at the driven wheels compared with the undriven wheels, or the movement of the vehicle relative to the road surface, or the forces generated in the suspension-steering systems, or the forces on the vehicle body itself). The second approach is to measure the factors that contribute to the friction potential, such as road surface texture and type, and the presence and depth of lubricants, principally water and ice. These parameters are then fed into an expert system to give the friction-slip curve associated with the conditions.

Both approaches have their advantages and disadvantages, and it is likely that the final implementation will be a combination of both. Much work remains to be done in the field of sensors, some of which use very expensive technologies or are optically based (and therefore prone to degradation due to dirt). Also, more testing is required to ensure a high level of confidence in the friction values obtained over the wide range of road surfaces and in the surface conditions encountered when driving. An additional step is to compare this potential friction value with the used friction value based on the vehicle longitudinal and lateral body movements to estimate a friction-based safety margin. However, whatever friction information is derived, the initial goal is to warn the driver of low-friction conditions or of a significantly reduced safety margin in such a way that the driver does not lose control of the vehicle, but also does not drive faster, feeling safe in the knowledge that the system will warn before the situation becomes critical.

The final system in this category aims to identify dangerous changes in vehicle stability related to the loading and current dynamic conditions, such as speed and vehicle maneuvers. This is especially relevant for heavy goods vehicles, where monitoring of vehicle stability and the estimation of braking potential by the driver are made more difficult by the decoupling of the driver from the vehicle by cab and seat suspension systems. Anticipatory estimation of a future driving condition and of vehicle stability is based on an observer model. The estimation uses a discretized filter containing a vehicle model that includes parameters for loading and road surface conditions. Inputs for the model include speed and driver-dependent actions, such as steering angle, braking effort, and drive torque. The outputs of the state estimation are compared with actual values from vehicle sensors, such as wheel speed; ground speed; yaw rate; longitudinal, lateral, and vertical acceleration; relative displacements of axles; and vehicle frame and air suspension pressure. Deviations between the two sets of values signify a change in the boundary parameters (e.g., road condition), and the driver can be warned if the stability, steerability, rollover resistance, or braking potential is seriously impaired. The question of how to give this warning to the driver remains unanswered, but could be some kind of kinesthetic transfer through the driver's seat. All the systems described in this category provide results on the immediate local situation. In order to provide a preview of the situation ahead of the vehicle, it will be necessary to implement the medium-range preinformation function described in Section 9.3.

Driver Status and Behavior

No subprogram with the aims and target problems as described in proper vehicle operation would be complete without the study of driver status and behavior. The driver will remain a fundamental partner in the driving task, a task so complicated that it requires almost all the human's mental capacity to perform it well and safely. All such studies must take into account the wide variations in "normal" behavior characteristics, attitudes, abilities, and reactions. However, looking at the number of accidents attributable to driver error, it is an area of research that cannot be ignored. Indeed, many of the systems being developed both in PROMETHEUS and elsewhere would be enhanced by an input relate to current driver status, particularly that indicating reduced driver vigilance due to tiredness alcohol, and so on. The task of assessing driver status would be much easier if every driver was prepared to become a laboratory experiment and could be monitored physiologi cally with body thermometers, skin resistance detectors, and brain-pattern scanners, bu this seems a little unlikely.

In PROMETHEUS, two approaches in detecting a drop in driver vigilance are bein investigated. The first uses the correlation between the driver's blink rate and his use o vehicle controls together with other related information obtainable unobtrusively. Th blink rate is a good indication of the driver's vigilance. A camera, coupled with an imag processing system, locates the head, eyes, and iris in the picture, providing outputs o the blink rate and the percentage of time the eye is open or closed. These primary dat and the other inputs are correlated using two neural networks, one to find correlation between input patterns and the other to identify principal components in the input data The second approach takes, as the primary indicator, the driver's lane-keeping performanc and is a by-product of one of the lane-keeping systems described below. The camera an image processing system this time is used to detect, in real time, the lane edges, th position of the vehicle in the lane, and the angle of the vehicle to the lane edges. A diagnostic tool takes this and other data on vehicle speed, the use of indicators, brakes and so on, and creates a driver profile that is monitored over time to detect any chang due to somnolence or a loss of vigilance.

Having obtained this information on the status of the driver, the question is wha to do with it to ensure the situation does not become dangerous. How could the vigilanc level be raised and the safety of the situation improved? It is unlikely that one specifi solution, such as warning the driver and advising the driver to stop, would be acceptabl or practical. More likely are such actions as changing the interior climate of the vehicl altering the dynamic characteristics of the vehicle, lowering the workload on the drive by reducing the secondary levels of information available, modifying the sensitivity o obstacle detection systems to provide longer warning times, and increasing the following distances of intelligent cruise control systems. If a copilot system is to be an acceptable part of the vehicle of the future, helping but not replacing the driver, it needs to know the status of the driver in order to improve the safety margin of the driving situation.

Adaptive Control

This category of control systems is aimed at intelligently adapting the response of the vehicle to the input actions, primarily from the driver, and providing improved feedback to the driver as part of the vehicle control loop. There has been much progress in the area of longitudinal control, notably with electronically controlled gearboxes, throttle, and traction control systems. PROMETHEUS research into advanced torque management is taking four-wheel drive systems a stage further. Using an electronically regulated viscous coupling with a variable torque transfer characteristic in the driveline to the rear wheels, not only can the vehicle's dynamic behavior in critical situations be improved, but, as a useful by-product, information can be given to the driver concerning the current safety reserve. The principal benefits include the reduced dependence of the vehicle's driving behavior on payload and/or friction change and the minimized feedback from the all-wheel drive transmission to the braking behavior.

Considerable PROMETHEUS research effort is being put into active steering. This is one of the longer term areas in regard to possible serial introduction, due to the considerable safety implications of a fully decoupled steering system (i.e., where there is no physical connection between the driver interface device, normally the steering wheel) and the steered wheels. From the block diagram of such a system given in Figure 9.8, it can be seen that there are four main elements. The first is the driver interface device, which is usually a steering wheel. However, one project involves the use of a joystick, and possible benefits such as better precision, a more ergonomic driving position, better utilization of the instrument panel, and improved safety in case of collision are being investigated. The second element is the feedback actuation unit. Without a direct coupling to the steered wheels and power assistance systems, the feedback to the driver must be artificially created by a combination of torque motor, springs, and dampers. However, this also gives the possibility of eliminating unwanted feedback and experimenting with variable inertia, hysteresis, centering torque, and so on to provide the best feedback to the driver in any given dynamic situation. The third element is the computer, which receives the steering input angle and generates required steered wheel angle and the driver feedback based on that input and others, such as vehicle movements, side wind, and data from "higher" level systems such as lane keeping or collision avoidance. The fourth element is the actuation system for the steered wheels, which is currently either an electric motor turning the lower end of the steering column or hydraulic servo-valves placed directly in the power assistance system. The primary benefits are improved compensation due to road surface irregularities and side winds, and improved vehicle lateral dynamics.

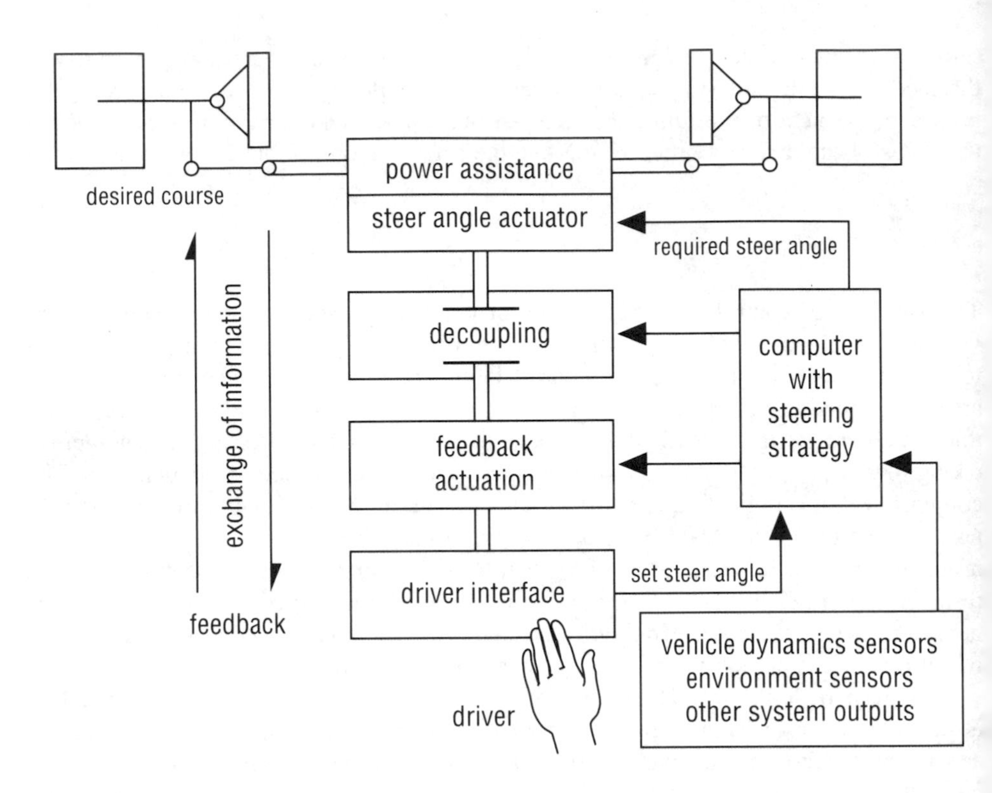

Figure 9.8 Overview of an intelligent steering system.

Even in the research phase, considerable emphasis is being placed on the fail-safety of the systems with fast acting clutches to recouple the two system halves, redundant sensors and control circuitry.

Finally in this area, there is a project looking at the active control of rear wheel camber angle to provide better controllability and stability in maneuvers and improved driver feedback near the vehicle limits. Much remains to be done to prove the functionality, safety, and cost benefit of such systems, but the work and risks can be shared in cooperative research like PROMETHEUS.

Driving Support

The last category of driving support can be divided into two areas, lane-keeping support and longitudinal support. Keeping the vehicle inside the lane is an onerous driving subtask and supporting the driver can both reduce the workload and warn or intervene in critical lane-leaving situations. Cameras and associated image processing are used to extract the lane edges and to determine the position of the vehicle in the lane. Many methods of supporting the driver to keep inside the lane are possible. One is to provide a small torque through the steering wheel if the vehicle drifts away from the set lane position, the torque increasing with the size of deviation. However, the torque is only intended to indicate which direction to steer in, and the driver must still react appropriately; there is no delegation of responsibility to an automatic driving system. A second method is to provide optical and/or acoustic warnings to the driver when leaving the lane without the signal, a reminder type of support. In fact, it is the latter system that incorporates the driver vigilance function discussed earlier in the chapter, since its support is primarily passive and does not significantly affect the normal driver lane-keeping performance.

Longitudinal support prompts the driver to maintain the proper speed profile in critical situations, such as on curves, approaching junctions in low-friction areas, or other speed-restricted areas. It first warns the driver of the hazard and advises a recommended speed profile. If it detects that the driver has not heeded the warning, the system automatically intervenes by closing the throttle and braking if necessary to enforce the required speed profile. Again, such intervention must be carefully handled if the driver is to react properly, and the system must not intervene unintentionally or fail to intervene when necessary; so reliability and redundancy are key areas to be researched.

Systems Integration

Systems integration, with many of the previously described systems linked together, can form a part of the foreseen copilot function, enabling a wide-ranging definition of the proper operation of the intelligent vehicle to be implemented. It provides the driver with a vehicle that gives necessary warning and advice to help maintain an adequate safety margin, which intelligently adapts its response to the driver's control inputs and which provides support in the performance of certain driving tasks, reducing the driving workload, only intervening should the situation become critical.

9.2.5 Collision Avoidance

The third CED contributing to the goal of the intelligent vehicle is collision avoidance. Looking again at Figure 9.4, we can see that collisions with obstacles are both significant in number and are avoidable by the implementation of PROMETHEUS functions. The primary cause of collisions is that the drivers involved fail to understand the driving situation, whether through lack of perception, recognition, or reaction. A Collision Avoidance system must first perceive the environment and traffic situations using multisensory techniques and sophisticated data processing; second, detect potentially hazardous objects or obstacles; and third, provide the necessary warnings or vehicle intervention in order to help the driver avoid a collision. An overview of the technical approach is given in Figure 9.9. These tasks would be sufficiently difficult given a comparatively well-structured and defined situation as found on highways, but much larger safety benefits are to be had

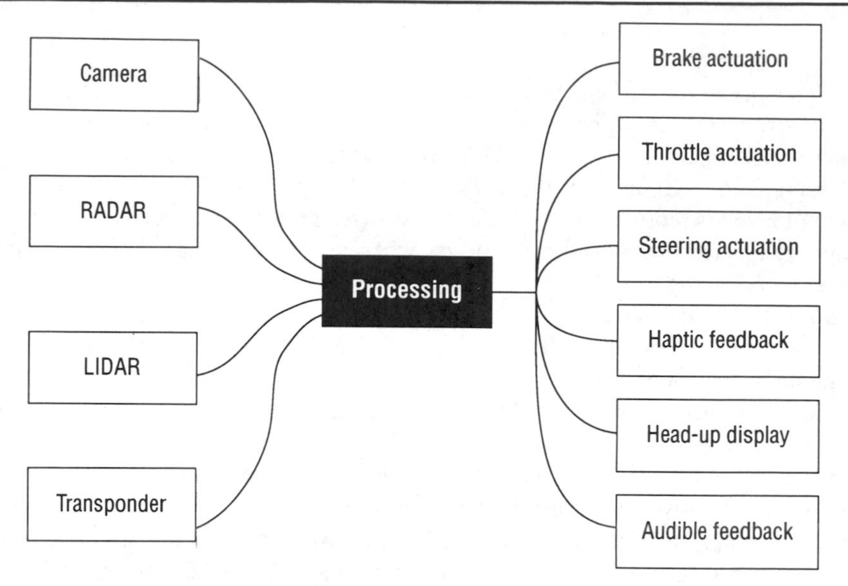

Figure 9.9 The technical approach to collision avoidance.

when the system can also function in the more complex driving situation found in urban areas. This makes the introduction of a collision avoidance system with full functionality a long-term prospect, but intermediate systems could be developed much earlier.

Any solution, however, is based on the perception of the environment and driving scene around and particularly ahead of the vehicle. This includes the detection of road and lane markings, objects such as cars and pedestrians, the spatial position relative to the vehicle, and the relative velocities where appropriate. Therefore, high-resolution sensors are required. The systems currently being researched include such sensors as cameras, high-performance radar, laser-based scanning detectors, and transponders. The latter, of course, are not essentially autonomous, but have distinct applications in this field if the appropriate standardization and legislative actions can be made, and shows that the final solution may well be a combination of these techniques. However, the main research task is processing the data to extract the required information, and again benefits from previous military research into tracking and missile guidance systems are helping this work progress rapidly.

The software development is being supported by research into high-performance processing systems and massively parallel architectures, including transputers. This is not only true at the lower levels of object extraction, but also at the higher levels, where the system must interpret the extracted scene and evaluate it, assessing and prioritizing the *threat potential* of objects. On yet another level is the planning of the required vehicle course and deciding on the appropriate action necessary from a response catalog, resulting in either information to the driver or intervention to control the vehicle. Obviously the latter response has significant implications for product liability and driver acceptance, but it should be pointed out here that the former response requires the system to detect the danger far sooner, placing greater demands on the sensors in terms of range and on the software in terms of perception and prediction. This is because the driver will require time to detect the warning, understand the advice given, and react accordingly. Any vehicle maneuver must, of course, also take into account information from the proper vehicle operation systems concerning vehicle status, friction conditions, and so on, showing the necessity for integration in order to provide the complete functionality necessary.

Like other CEDs, collision avoidance is using the scenario technique to test and compare various technologies and systems to provide milestones in the research work and to identify intermediate solutions that could be brought into production earlier. The first scenario is stopping at an obstacle that should enable the vehicle to detect that there is an obstacle in its path sufficiently far ahead for the vehicle to be brought to a halt in front of it. This could form the basis of a stop-go support system for urban traffic. By refining the ability to identify obstacles and adding road marking and lane-edge detection, a second scenario of distance supervision could be realized aimed at reducing the number of rear-end collisions. A third scenario is lane keeping, taking the support function implemented in proper vehicle operation a stage further by intervening and automatically steering the vehicle back onto a safe course. The next scenario is lane changing and/or overtaking to indicate that the driver wishes to change lanes and to advise whether it is safe to do so, bringing the possibility of blind-spot detection as an intermediate system. This could be coupled with obstacle detection to implement a lane change to avoid the obstacle if stopping before it is not possible. The final scenario is in-town collisions, particularly at junctions. This is certainly the most arduous because of the complexity of the scene, but it is already possible for the system to detect a side road ahead and slow the vehicle down before it crosses the junction.

The major topics still to be addressed in this area include an ongoing assessment of what can be achieved with the available technologies, the definition and understanding of appropriate system responses to various situations, including the determination of the safest course, and closely connected with this, the development of driver interaction together with the legal and liability implications raised by such systems. It is also clear that collision avoidance depends on systems being developed in proper vehicle operation to provide information on road, driver, and vehicle status, for example, and that proper vehicle operation control systems will need to react to commands from collision avoidance systems.

9.2.6 Common Research Areas

The interdependence of the various functional systems being developed within PROMETHEUS is the driving force behind the integration activities, which are concentrated into five working groups. They are responsible for thematic research into sensors and processing, actuation and vehicle operation, in-vehicle architecture, driver-vehicle interaction, and safety and dependability. These groups coordinate the requirements of the CED programs into common specifications, allowing the participating electronics and supply industries to develop the necessary hardware or software. In addition, as centers of expertise in these fields, they provide guidelines for the demonstration programs on how to solve specific problems. In cases where there is a more fundamental lack of knowledge or understanding, basic research organizations are supporting the work, with two groups particularly relevant to the intelligent vehicle area of PROMETHEUS. These are PRO-CHIP, working in the areas of custom hardware for the intelligent acquisition and processing of data, and PRO-ART, researching intelligent software and processing techniques. The expert groups and the regular workshops provide the necessary forum for meeting and exchanging ideas and information.

Sensors and Actuators

It is clear that nearly all systems require sensors for their primary data. Already we are seeing more sensors appearing on current vehicles, such as accelerometers and angle sensors. In the near future, yaw rate sensors will be introduced, along with advanced displacement or movement sensors. However, many sensors used in the research systems are either too expensive or use technologies unsuited to the automotive environment. For example, if thermal or optical cameras are to find a place in the intelligent vehicle, then common agreements on performance, packaging, and interfaces need to be reached to allow the necessary technological development and manufacturing investment for economies of scale, and this is common to many other kinds of sensors. In data processing, the use of hardware and software must be the most cost-effective solution. For example, in image processing, neural networks and parallel architectures must be dependable both functionally and from the standpoint of safety and reliability. Similarly, actuators are an increasingly important part of the intelligent vehicle; one only needs to count the number of electric motors and solenoids on today's cars. The trend is towards lower weight and size and higher performance and functionality. New materials are being developed, for example with magnetostrictive properties, that promise solutions for the control-by-wire systems of tomorrow, incorporating not only the actuation element itself, but also the control, monitoring, and diagnostic electronics, with a built-in intelligent interface to its master control unit via a data bus. All these elements must have the necessary safety, reliability, and redundancy for the particular application (e.g., intelligent steering).

In-Vehicle Architectures

The intelligent vehicle of the future must also remove the current bottleneck of component-systems interconnection and power distribution, both electrical and hydraulic. The wiring harness of a modern car could almost be used as a structural part of the vehicle, and there are already vehicles in production that use a data bus to link noncritical systems together to provide increased functionality and reduce harness size. Future systems will have many components and sensors in common, and will be very much more interdependent than today's systems, requiring considerable exchange of data to provide enhanced functional performance and redundancy. An open architecture is being developed that will allow the exchange of data between processing units and the sharing of information from and control of intelligent components on the network. Here, the experience of the computer industry is being applied in the areas of networking, real-time operating systems, multitasking executives, and the application of the OSI seven-layer model to define the necessary interfaces. This is further complicated by the multiple networks likely to be present in the intelligent car necessary to achieve the most cost-effective solution. These include a low-speed network (<900 kHz) for functions such as body systems, which is generally understood to include lighting, power windows, and central locking systems, and multiplexing, where the network components are simple, cheap, and can operate with minimal supervising intelligence. Medium-speed networks (100 kHz to 1 MHz) for communication between intelligent processing units in time- and safety-critical applications require high levels of reliability and data integrity with some degree of fault tolerance and redundancy. The latter attributes are well-known and understood in the aerospace industry, but require particularly careful consideration in the cost-conscious automotive field. To this end, more than one communication protocol, physical layer design, and silicon implementation are being developed to enable the required safety levels to be reached. High-speed networks or links (>1 MHz) are also being researched for use where large blocks of data must be communicated at high speed, between, for example, a camera and image processing systems or between a communication receiver and dependent data processing units (e.g., the availability of navigation or driver information system). Here, fiber optics may be the solution, given cheaper optical components.

Gateways between these different networks will be required, along with network supervision and monitoring, raising the possibility of distributed intelligence as opposed to master controllers, further enhancing the redundancy of the total vehicle network. Indeed, monitoring and diagnosis is one application certain to use these networks, since it will become increasingly necessary to determine the correct functioning of the complete network to identify any failures and locate the failed components, and to interface to driver-warning and off-vehicle diagnostic systems as required.

An additional and often overlooked aspect of in-vehicle architecture is that of electrical power generation, storage, and distribution, including hydraulic systems. The output of alternators stands now at well over 100A for luxury cars. The associated weight penalties, including the necessity for thick cabling, and the considerable problems of switching and controlling the high currents involved can be reduced if a multivoltage supply system is used, with the appropriate allocation of loads between the supplies and the application of new alternator and battery technologies. However, these systems have to be modeled and tested on vehicles to verify their performance and ensure that the correct architecture and voltage levels are chosen. The latter is particularly important for the switching component manufacturers to know in order to ensure that the control elements, particularly those that are semiconductor-based, are developed with the correct voltage specification, including transient protection. A similar argument applies to hydraulic architecture, where the commonizing of system components, operating pressures, and distribution network would ensure the most cost-effective solution. Work in all these architecture areas is aimed at producing components with which to build the PROMETHEUS systems and on which to base future standardization work.

Safety Aspects

Throughout this chapter, safety, reliability, redundancy, and fault tolerance have been mentioned several times in connection with particular functional systems or areas of research. To supply an overview of this activity and contribute original and specific input in this area, there is a PROMETHEUS group researching the subject of vehicle safety and dependability. When considering active safety systems, there are considerable liability implications if countermeasures are not taken against system failure. These failures include the noninitiation of a needed action, the unacceptably late initiation of an action, an incorrect action in response to a real input demand, or the initiation of an unnecessary action. There are two possible approaches: to identify safe states into which the system should go in case of failures and to reduce the likelihood of such a failure to an acceptably low level.

Three areas have been identified as focuses for such research: (1) systems dependability, where the aim is the development of assessment methods and safety and reliability checklists, (2) fault-tolerant systems, including a case study to be made of an active steering system, and (3) software dependability, since software is also safety-critical. Whatever concepts and recommendations emerge from this work will form the legal basis for the introduction of such safety-critical functions and systems, addressing the areas of reliability and fail-safe performance.

Driver Acceptance

Another important area being researched is driver acceptance. If systems of the future do not achieve this, the safety, comfort, or convenience benefits will be significantly reduced. The driver must perceive the benefit of the system, trust the system, and feel comfortable interacting with the system, whether it provides information, advice or warnings, helps the driver control the vehicle, or provides support by performing a part of the driving task. There are three main work areas: (1) fundamental research into MMI to produce guidelines, rules, and recommendations to support the applied research; (2) the development of prototype software and hardware components and subsystems needed to implement MMI designs; (3) the development of simulation and evaluation methods to assess driver reaction to the implemented MMI design. The driving task is complex, and the human processes required to carry it out are even more complex. The advanced systems in the intelligent car could constitute a so-called copilot. However, it would not be sensible to blindly apply aerospace industry techniques directly to the automobile given the major differences in the tasks being performed and the two user populations, one highly trained, the other not.

Many experts argue that the driver already receives too much information from the vehicle, and that to perform the driving task safely in some traffic situations requires nearly all the driver's mental capacity. Even though some systems will reduce this workload, only a very limited mental capacity will be available for the processing of additional system-derived information. Such effects as distraction or overload of the driver and risk compensation behavior are to be avoided by making the presented information clear and easily understood and making it evoke naturally the correct response. When systems intervene in the driving task, the process of delegation from the driver to the system should be clear and natural, and, equally important, so should the process of handing back control. Many channels of interaction, such as tactile feedback through vehicle control elements like the steering wheel or foot pedals, remain largely as in the earliest vehicles and provide possible MMI solutions to many systems being researched. Technologies such as speech recognition and head-up displays may prove the best interaction media for other systems. The aim, however, must be the best MMI design to achieve driver acceptance and safety, not the raw use of technology for its own sake. It is also realized that, although guidelines may be developed on general principles of MMI, the final solution must allow for the different philosophies of vehicle manufacturers.

9.2.7 Conclusion

The intelligent car of the future will have many more electronic systems capable of improving the safety, comfort, and convenience of the individual vehicle. It is also clear that considerable integration of these systems will be required to achieve their full functional and cost-benefit potential. This integration is to be achieved with common components, interfaces, and defined interactions to ensure compatibility, interconnectability, and the maximum possible economies of scale and flexibility in manufacture, installation, and maintenance.

Integration entails the adoption of systems engineering techniques, especially when considering the complete picture of the intelligent car as part of an intelligent group of vehicles, which in turn is a part of an intelligent traffic system linked by communication systems, benefiting the individual driver and the whole traffic and transport network.

Certainly, no individual automotive company is capable of researching, developing, and implementing all the systems described in this section. PROMETHEUS is enabling the distribution of the research tasks, the exchange of information and results, and the preparation of guidelines and recommendations to industry, traffic authorities, and regulatory bodies. These will form the basis of future standardization and possible legislation, allowing the many possible solutions to be researched and the best solution to be identified in the knowledge that the solution will form part of the integrated system implemented in the intelligent car of the future, which together with the driver will form a partnership of unprecedented safety, comfort, and convenience.

ACKNOWLEDGMENTS

I would like to express my appreciation for the considerable help I received from the many people who make up PROMETHEUS. These include my colleagues at the various research partners, in the automotive companies, in the electronics and supply industries, and at the university research departments and traffic research institutes. Many thanks are also due to the staff at PROMETHEUS Office, who assisted me greatly in the preparation of this chapter. Some of the source information used was originally published [1] at the BMM'91 event held near Turin, where many of the systems and concepts, described here briefly, were demonstrated to government representatives, company executives, and journalists. Copies of the literature from BMM'91 can be obtained by contacting PROMETHEUS Office, based at Daimler-Benz in Stuttgart.

9.3 COOPERATIVE DRIVING*

9.3.1 Objectives

Cooperative driving is a new RTI approach to integrate the vehicle in its surrounding environment. Information is exchanged between cooperating vehicles themselves and/or between these vehicles and the infrastructure. Safeguarding and optimizing driving in a file, lane changing, or intersection flow will improve traffic safety and efficiency. This cooperation allows the driver to enhance his or her perception level using information on the surrounding traffic situation and environment. Active driver support may also be defined for specific application cases. The Cooperative Control Task Force (CCTF) was created within PROMETHEUS in February 1990, and Cooperative Driving applications have been specified by the CCTF [8,9] in order to identify the corresponding concepts and technical solutions.

CEDs have also been defined to demonstrate the concepts and corresponding technology. The aim of the *CopDrive* demonstrator has been the validation of the Cooperative Driving concepts through simulation [10] and the definition of a communication technological platform for the evaluation of mobile radio networks. *Autonomous intelligent cruise control* (AICC) and *emergency warning* (EW) have been demonstrated through prototype systems and identified for short- or medium-term development.

A common European strategy has recently been defined for the introduction of cooperative systems on the market [11]. *Medium-range preinformation* (MRP) systems have been specified for medium-term implementation [12], and general purpose multiappli-

*This section was written by A. Kemeny.

cation systems may be based on existing and/or planned toll payment technology. Consequently, specific short-range communication (SRC) systems should be developed to introduce limited vehicle-to-vehicle transmission capabilities. In cooperation with the EC DRIVE II program in the TESCO project, field trials will be performed for endurance tests in a controlled environment starting in 1993.

9.3.2 Application Specifications

The CCTF specifications [9] include five application classes (see [13] and Figures 9.10 to 9.14).

Intelligent Cruise Control. Intelligent cruise control (ICC) supports cooperative longitudinal control between interdependent vehicles on single lanes for speed and distance harmonization and reacts to significant events ahead.

Intelligent Maneuvering and Control. Intelligent maneuvering and control (IMC) performs cooperative maneuvering in order to safeguard and optimize lane changes and overtakings.

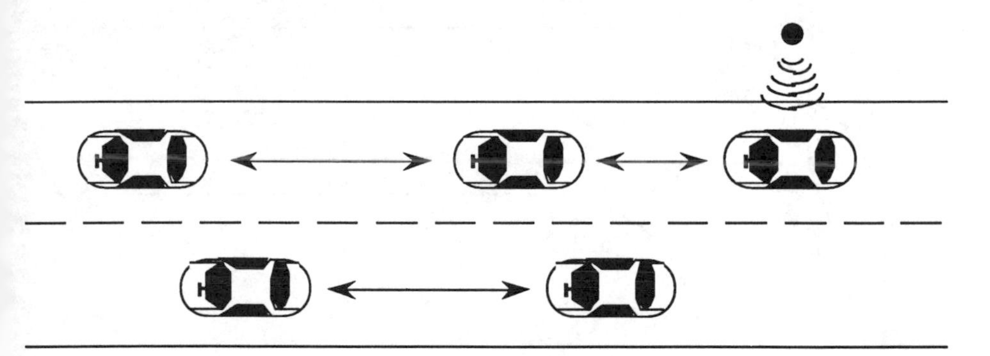

Figure 9.10 Intelligent cruise control.

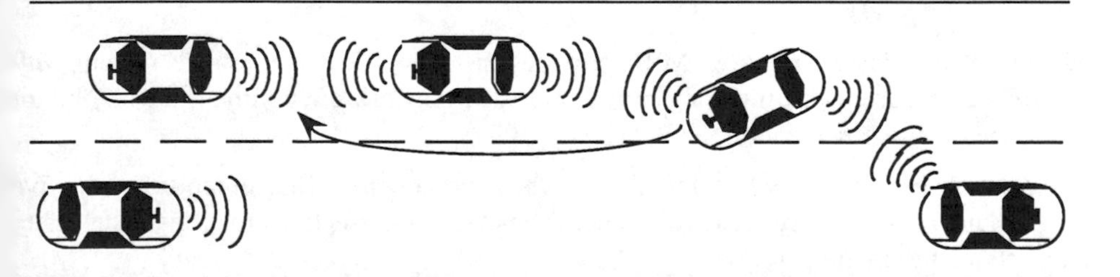

Figure 9.11 Intelligent maneuvering and control.

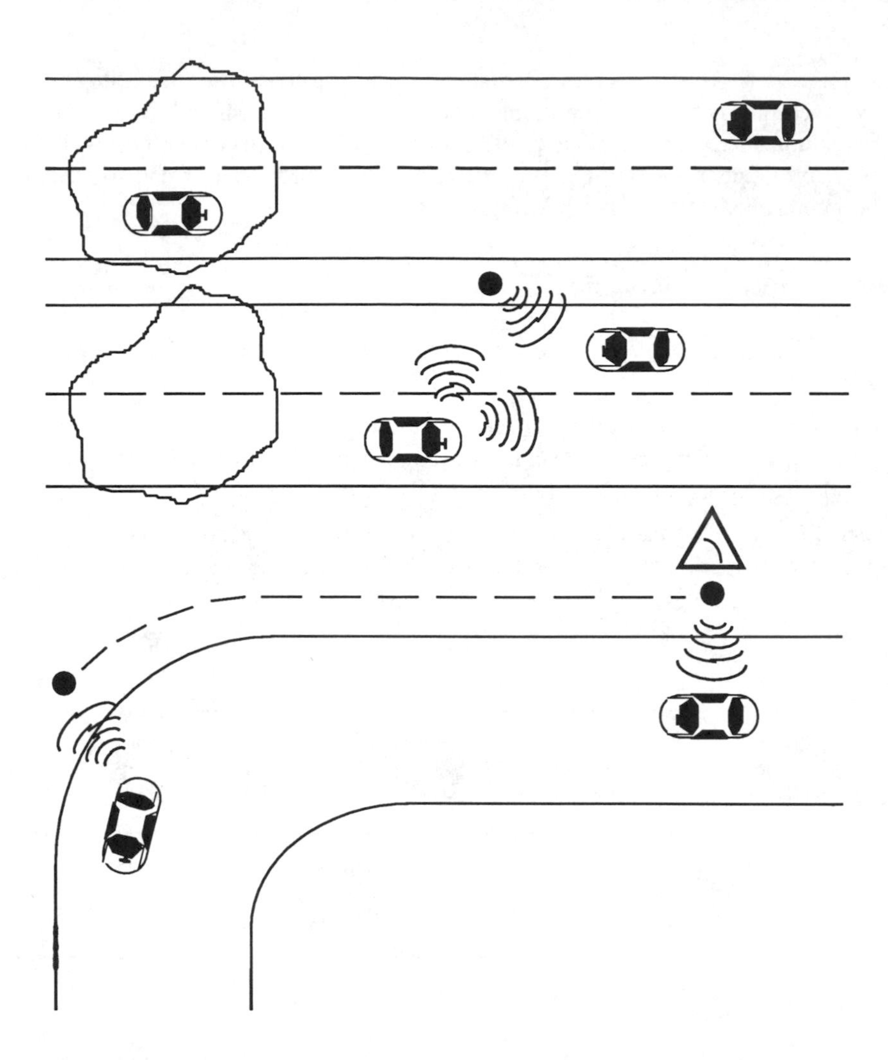

Figure 9.12 Medium-range preinformation.

Medium-Range Preinformation. MRP provides the driver and the vehicle system with information regarding surrounding traffic and road network environment beyond his or her range of direct perception.

Intelligent Intersection Control. Intelligent intersection control (IIC) supports cooperative longitudinal control between interdependent vehicles at intersections for enhancing safety and optimizing traffic flow.

Emergency Warning. EW informs the driver of emergencies in the vicinity of his or her location.

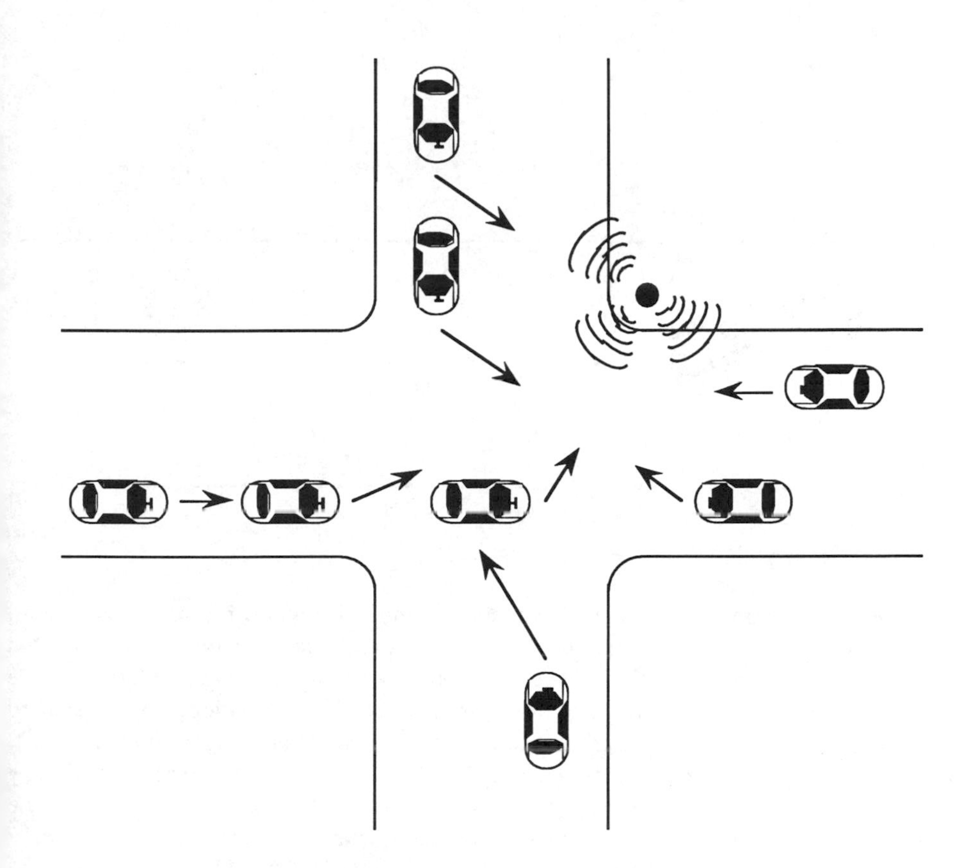

Figure 9.13 Intelligent intersection control.

Intervehicle communication range should be at about 500m maximum. Adaptable transmission range techniques may be implemented to adapt increasing message rates for dense traffic areas [14]. Roadside-to-vehicle transmission range may be more limited (about 10m). Interbeacon communication along the roadside extends the validity of messages coming from the vehicles. Intervehicle distance is computed for ICC, IMC, and IIC according to relative speed. During information mode, a warning message is displayed and may be associated with a beep. Semiautomatic or automatic mode, including steering, accelerator, and/or brake action, will be specified as a later phase.

A first, limited, version of ICC applications is the AICC system, which does not use intervehicle communication. Consequently, it can be introduced without infrastructure support and its efficiency does not require any equipment for other vehicles. Full ICC systems should be associated with an onboard radar system to detect nonequipped vehicles, or should use specially reserved lanes.

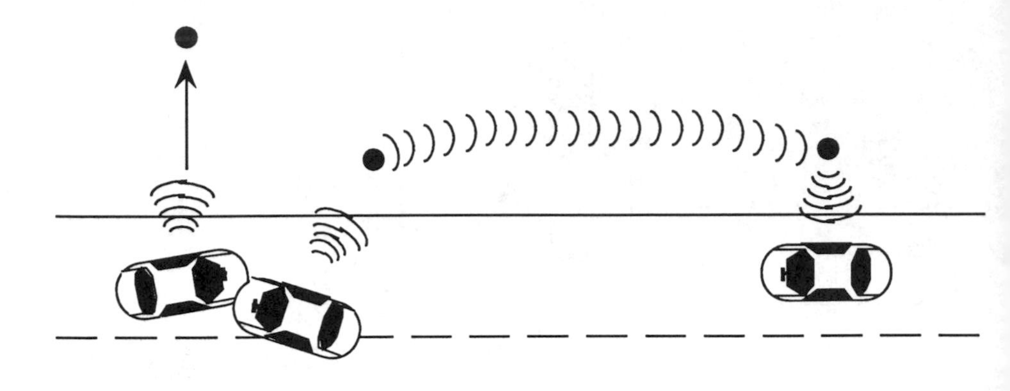

Figure 9.14 Emergency warning.

MRP applications (including EW) require communications with the infrastructure, but may be introduced on the market in the near future. The available communication technology for automatic debiting systems should be easily adaptable. Most of these applications rely on already existing RTI information (traffic information, road signs, road and climatic conditions). An overall assessment of the benefits in terms of safety (see [13] and Figure 9.15) was presented at PROMETHEUS BMM'91 in Turin. A first evaluation by simulation [15] gives an increasing highway capacity of 13% for ICC if 40% of the vehicles are equipped (on a two-lane highway and with a headway of 1 sec). Other Cooperative Driving applications are under evaluation by PROMETHEUS [16].

9.3.3 Common European Demonstrators

As in many European programs, demonstrators were defined in order to validate technical feasibility and to initiate efficient cooperation in the realization of prototypes.

Previous PROMETHEUS Demonstrators

In the early 1987-88 definition phase of the PROMETHEUS program, different demonstrators had already been defined in the field of the Cooperative Driving area (named at that time PRO-NET), and focused more on intervehicle communication than today. Among the different presentations concerning PRO-NET at the 1989 January BMM in Munich were company demonstrators (ICAD, ARTHUR, and HANDSHAKE), while the N89EX demonstrator, initiated by Daimler-Benz, was commonly implemented on BMW, Daimler-

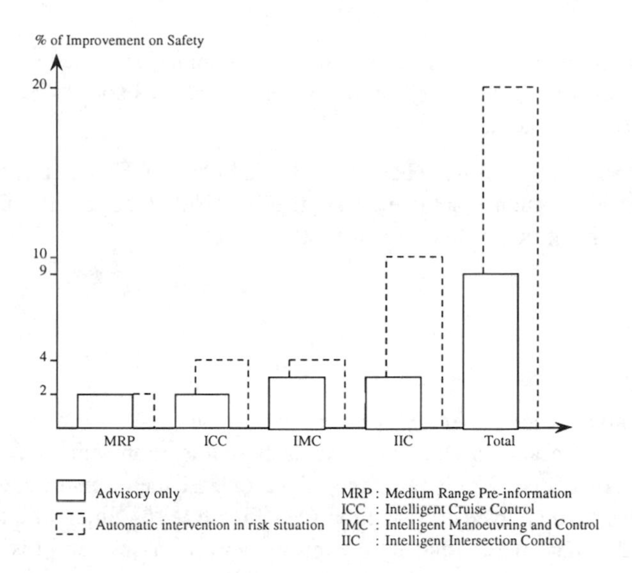

Figure 9.15 Safety Benefits.

Benz, MAN, Peugeot, Renault, Saab, and Volvo cars. These demonstrators were the following.

- ICAD (intelligent computer aided driving). Volkswagen's company demonstrator for longitudinal and lateral control for convoy driving has included IR laser ultrasonic, gyro-acceleration sensors and a VHF data communication system.
- ARTHUR (Automatic Radiocommunication system for Traffic emergency situations on Highways and Urban Roads). Daimler-Benz's company demonstrator, using the German C cellular radio network, warns road users in cases of accidents.
- HANDSHAKE. Fiat's company demonstrator with detection, processing, and VHF emitter/receiver transmits dynamic road and environment conditions (slowdowns, traffic jams, visibility (fog), and meteorological (precipitation) conditions). The principle of detection, data processing, and transmission strategy was integrated later into the MRP application specifications.
- N89EX. A common European Pro-Net demonstrator was initiated by Daimler-Benz and implemented on BMW, Daimler-Benz, MAN, Peugeot, Renault, Saab, and Volvo cars. It demonstrated both IIC and IMC scenarios using a Bosch VHF communication system.

CopDrive Demonstrator

Cooperative Driving applications are based on cooperative maneuvering (i.e., each vehicle exchanges information continuously with the infrastructure and with other vehicles). To achieve these applications, the following technological issues have to be addressed.

- Intervehicle and vehicle-infrastructure communication systems;
- High-precision relative positioning systems; Onboard software executing Cooperative Driving strategies.

Two different research tools have been introduced by the CCTF to study the corresponding system design and system characteristics: the SCANeR Cooperative Driving Simulator and the Communication Technological Platform.

SCANeR Simulator

SCANeR (Simulator of Cooperative Automotive Network) has been developed by Renault. It is a network of graphics workstations; each station represents a cooperative vehicle functioning in real time. The 3-D image of the overall scene, including the interactively driven vehicles, is displayed in real time (see Figure 9.16). Intervehicle communication is simulated through an Ethernet local-area network to assess and test the feasibility of cooperative driving concepts and strategies, MMI, and communication and positioning systems. Onboard strategies have been specified by the CCTF with Daimler-Benz, Fiat, Matra, Opel, Renault, and PSA as active members. The demonstrated strategies include:

- Driving-in-file: Safety-level information (ICC) is displayed, and a reference speed taking into account information transmitted by roadside beacons is also displayed.

Figure 9.16 SCANeR image.

- Lane changing, overtaking, highway entering/exiting: Safety level information is displayed (IMC).
- Providing drivers with information about situations beyond their range of direct perception through mailbox roadside beacons (MRP).
- Informing drivers of emergencies in the vicinity of their location (EW).

SCANeR was interfaced with BMW, Daimler-Benz, and Renault cars for the September 1991 Turin BMM demonstration. BMW has developed a specific vehicle dynamics model and Daimler-Benz a specific dashboard safety indicator MMI, which were integrated in SCANeR for the demonstration.

Communication Technological Platform

The communication technological platform has been defined by the CCTF to test communication systems dedicated to cooperative driving. In November 1990, the CCTF organized in Paris the first Cooperative Driving Workshop in order to identify electronics and supplier companies that have already developed intervehicle communication systems and to present cooperative driving applications and requirements to them. Bosch, Catella, Dassault, Marconi, Matra Communication, Telefunken, and Thomson gave presentations on their system developments. The CCTF has defined an evaluation procedure for testing available communication systems and to select candidates for Cooperative Driving demonstrations for the Turin BMM [17]. With an active engineering contribution from Opel, the Bosch intervehicle communication system was finally selected and presented. This presentation has allowed the testing of the feasibility of intervehicle and vehicle-infrastructure communication links and the study and qualifying of transmission interferences (e.g., obstacles).

AICC Demonstration

AICC is an onboard speed and distance control system which reacts to the vehicle ahead in the same lane. The aim of AICC is to enhance driver safety and comfort and decrease stress. When no vehicle is detected, the system behaves like a classic cruise control system. Distance control is activated if a vehicle is detected ahead. AICC can be deactivated at any moment by the driver by resuming or using acceleration or brake pedals. This application, which is one of the first cooperative driving applications to be introduced on the market, has some specific issues to be addressed.

- Sensors for intervehicle distance and speed measurement (on the same lane);
- Actuators for longitudinal speed control;
- Vehicle-roadside communication systems for traffic regulation;
- Onboard software executing control strategies for driver information.

Different sensor technologies were studied by the participating car companies:

- Multibeam IR sensors (Daimler-Benz, Opel, Volvo, Volkswagen);
- Single-beam IR sensor (PSA);
- CCD-based telemetric sensors (Matra);
- Microwave radar (Jaguar);
- IR laser scanner (Renault);
- Transponder (Saab, Volvo).

Range, distance, and angular accuracy, as well as robustness to environmental conditions, were evaluated for the September 1991 Turin BMM demonstration, where nine vehicles from the above listed car companies were entered in a common dynamic AICC presentation. Other actuators and sensors are under study, provided by electronics suppliers industry members such as Bosch, Hella, SIM, Leica, and Lucas. Further endurance tests and traffic safety and efficiency evaluation are to be conducted jointly with the extended intelligent cruise control (EICC) and MRP applications in cooperation with the DRIVE TESCO project (see Section 9.3.4).

Emergency Systems

Another cooperative driving application, using vehicle-to-infrastructure communication, may be introduced on the market in the near future. If the roadside beacons are equipped with red and yellow warning lights emitting in the driver direction when receiving warning information from a vehicle, EW can be performed through interbeacon communication. The Companion demonstrator (developed by BMW with active cooperation of Basic Research Partners in Communication and Traffic Engineering, the Universities of Aachen, Munich, and Stuttgart) is an EW system, completed by emergency call (an automatic call for rescue operation). Emergency system installation requires the following technologies:

- Accident and/or crash sensors;
- Geographical position determination;
- Vehicle-roadside communication;
- Interbeacon communication;
- Link to rescue/traffic management center.

Cooperation Within PROMETHEUS

Telecommunication and traffic engineering experts from basic research groups take part in most of the cooperative driving tasks. Feasibility studies and evaluation are frequently carried out by the PROMETHEUS working groups in the fields of sensors, actuators, MMI infrastructure-based communications, and intervehicle communications. Close cooperation has been developed by PROMETHEUS members who have developed company demonstrators in the cooperative driving area.

- ISIS (Interactive road sign System) provides road sign information directly relayed to vehicles through IR vehicle-to-roadside and interbeacon wire communication. Automatic vehicle control may be activated (PSA).
- COMPANION provides immediate warning to approaching vehicles and call for rescue (BMW).
- MUSIC (MUlti-Sensor Intelligent Control) is an AICC demonstrator with longitudinal and lateral control (Daimler-Benz).
- CAROSI provides roadside information (speed limits and so on) using the COMPOSE (COMmunication and POSitioning Equipment) transponder system (Saab, Volvo).
- AUTOCRUISE is an AICC demonstrator using COMPOSE (Saab, Volvo).

9.3.4 Future Developments

Medium-Range Pre-information—Medium-Term Implementation

Cooperative Driving MRP applications have been specified by the CCTF in 1991 (see Section 9.3.1 and [12]). The applications include:

- Speed recommendation;
- Poor visibility warnings;
- Dangerous road surface warnings;
- Heavy traffic density warnings;
- Dangerous climatic condition warnings;
- Traffic regulation (curved road, speed limit, stop sign, and so on);
- Emergency warning.

MRP conditions may be detected by vehicle speed, acceleration, foglamp, and windshield wiper status and crash sensors. MRP information may be received by one beacon and transmitted to others before transmission to the vehicle.

EW information is usually given by direct vehicle-to-vehicle communication; however, it may also be received by roadside beacons and relayed to others through the wired roadside network. Communication with beacons is necessary for all Cooperative Driving applications when the communicating vehicle crosses a specific area with transmission disturbances (hilltops, transmission obstacles, and so on).

For most of the MRP communication systems, directionality is required. It allows a good range of accuracy (spatial and temporal) for MRP information validity, especially when the application is implemented without an absolute reference frame.

Common European EICC and MRP Demonstration

This PROMETHEUS BMM demonstration should take place in 1994. It aims at demonstrating the feasibility of integrated solutions (with high-level MMI like dashboard integrated screen, medium-head display, or head-up display) for Cooperative Driving applications using SRC systems satisfying ATT recommendations (CEN/TC 278). These SRC systems represent the first and second steps in the introduction of Cooperative Driving applications in the market. Both the 5.8-GHz frequency directional vehicle-to-roadside communication systems and the 63- to 64-GHz frequency general purpose intervehicle communication systems will be used. Demonstrated applications will include ICC and traffic regulation MRP scenarios, and will be performed in realistic traffic conditions including nonequipped vehicles.

This demonstration is prepared in cooperation with the DRIVE TESCO project. Roadside beacons will be installed at the Nardo test track (ELASIS, SASN), and vehicles will be provided by Matra, PSA, and Renault for endurance testing. These limited field trials in a highly controlled environment will be completed by microsimulation (SCANeR and SPEACS [15]) to analyze and extrapolate trial results for the European highway network. Driver acceptance will be evaluated using SCANeR. The BMM demonstration, to be held in Paris, will include a dozen vehicles with the participation of Jaguar, Matra, Opel, PSA, and Renault. Among the electronics supplier candidates for vehicle-roadside or intervehicle SRC systems are Bosch ATN, GEC-Marconi, and Thomson Composants Micro-ondes (TCM). This demonstration should convince the invited road authorities and transportation ministers of the well-proven technical and industrial feasibility of the first Cooperative Driving applications, particularly MRP systems.

9.3.5 Communication Systems

Communication Standardization

RTI services in a general way, and Cooperative Driving applications in a more specific way, have to be based on standardized European specifications [18] for high effectiveness in the introduction and acceptance of services. This implies the concept of one single multiapplication system. In this way, cost-effective solutions may be implemented for Europewide use. Future microwave communication systems have to respect the European frequency recommendations of the CEPT.

- Vehicle to roadside: 5.795 to 5.805 GHz;
- Additional subband (specific local requirements): 5.805 to 5.815 GHz;
- Vehicle to vehicle: 63 to 64 GHz;
- Vehicle radar: 76 to 81 GHz.

Consequently, the PROMETHEUS 1994 BMM Cooperative Driving demonstration will use single communication systems in the 5.795- to 5.805-GHz and/or the 63- to 64-GHz frequency band. The ISO CEN/TC 278 is responsible for road transport and traffic telematics. Up to now, there has been no working group in the CEN/TC 278 dealing with Cooperative Driving. MRP applications, which are already available at the prototype level

(Bosch ANT, GEC-Marconi, TCM), are proposed to be integrated in working group WG4 (Individual Traffic Information).

Vehicle-Roadside Communication

General requirements have been defined by the CCTF [19] defining a bidirectional communication link between the vehicles and roadside beacons. The requirements include a road infrastructure interconnection link. The first requirements for MRP/EW applications are the following.

- Frequency: 5.8 GHz;
- Message size: 200 bits maximum;
- Data rate: 100 kbps to 1 Mbps;
- Message lost ratio: 10^{-3} maximum;
- Transmission range: 10m to 30m;
- Transmission: read/write.

Bosch ANT, GEC-Marconi, and TCM have already presented prototype solutions at the Second Cooperative Driving Workshop, held in Paris in May 1992.

Intervehicle Communication

Communication architecture requirements have been defined by the CCTF [20]. In order to develop and evaluate Cooperative Driving communication systems, which would allow a wireless dynamic local-area networking, research has to be carried out in the fields of channel characteristics, modulation techniques, protocols, and antennas. Communication systems from Bosch, Marconi, Thomson, and Matra have been or are under evaluation by the CCTF. For the 1994 Paris BMM demonstration, Matra's MANET (Matra Network) system is proposed with the following transmission characteristics:

- Frequency: 2.45 GHz (1992) to 5.8 GHz (1994);
- Data rate: 2 Mbps;
- Transmission range: 500m to 1,000m;
- Cycle time: 100 ms;
- Message size: 256 bits;
- Access control: dynamic time division multiple access.

9.3.6 Introduction of Cooperative Driving Systems on the Market

Cooperative Driving applications may predict and avoid collisions and serious accidents and also increase driver comfort and traffic efficiency, reduce travel time, decrease fuel consumption, as well as provide passive and/or active driver support. Among the first applications, AICC and MRP systems may be introduced in the near future on the market (see Sections 9.3.1 and 9.3.4 and [12]).

AICC does not rely on intervehicle communication and does not require other vehicles to be equipped. This autonomous distance warning system, providing the driver with a better safety and comfort level, is a first step towards intelligent cruising systems. Intelligent maneuvering and intersection control would arrive later in a stepwise introduction.

The simplest way to provide the driver with information about the overall traffic is the RDS-TMC one-way communication concept, which is already available in several European countries. Dedicated SRC systems make it possible to implement most of the above described MRP applications and may be used for intervehicle communication in some limited ICC application cases. Combining AICC or ICC with SRC-provided MRP systems will allow the achievement of an important part (EICC) of cooperative driving applications (see Figure 9.17). The corresponding driver information and/or support devices should be available for product development within the next few years.

This introduction should be facilitated by the availability of toll payment or ADS technologies, which should be easily modifiable for MRP multiapplication systems. Then

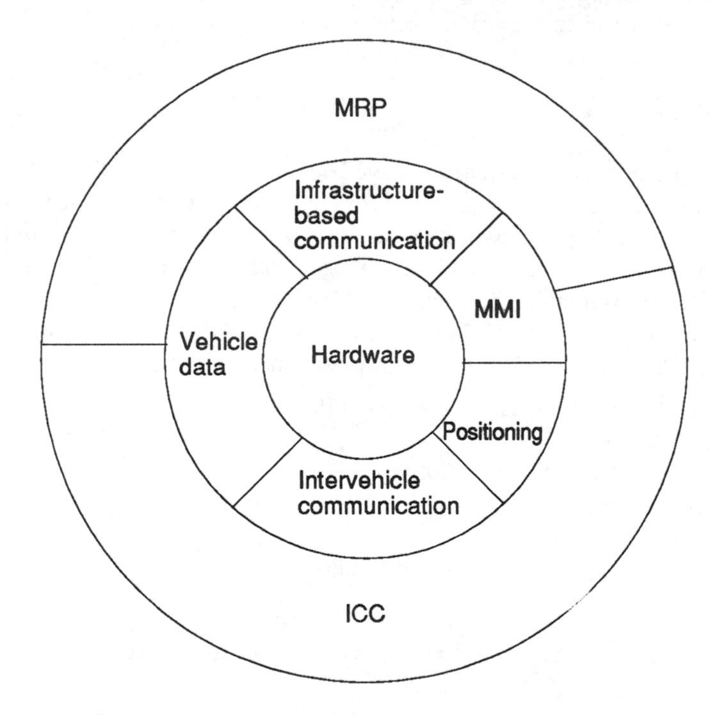

Figure 9.17 The common European EICC and MRP demonstration. ICC = based on intervehicle communication; MRP = based on infrastructure communication; EW = common layer using the two types of communication.

the improvement of existing Cooperative Driving applications may be carried out by enhancing or completing AICC and SRC systems to achieve IMC and IIC applications. At the same time, new absolute and/or relative positioning systems will be developed, as ICC, IMC, and IIC applications require higher position accuracy [21], which must be permanently available. Cooperative Driving, thanks to PROMETHEUS, will help drivers to drive progressively more safely and efficiently through active intervehicle and driver cooperation.

9.4 DUAL-MODE ROUTE GUIDANCE*

9.4.1 Introduction

In road vehicles, drivers reach their destination by following a route through the network of roads and streets. This task consists of three subtasks:

- *Route planning* for selecting a route according to specified criteria;
- *Navigation* for finding and following the selected sections of the network;
- *Replanning* during the trip, because the basis for the initial plan is no longer valid due to incidents or congestion.

The technical system supporting these three activities is called a *Route guidance system.* The classical means of route guidance are road and street maps, road signs, and familiarity with the surroundings. In fact, the benefits of advanced route guidance systems are sometimes questioned, since about 90% of drivers are familiar with their local area. Route guidance can be autonomous (performed entirely in the vehicle) or infrastructure-based (performed centrally and transmitted to the vehicle). This section will argue that a dual-mode approach, combining both autonomous and infrastructure-based modes, is the optimum solution from both the technical and the economic points of view.

9.4.2 Need for Route Guidance

The need for route guidance does not only arise from driving through unfamiliar areas. In the future, we have to expect denser road traffic in Europe. Forecasts indicate a growth of vehicle mileage of 20% to 40% by 2010, with only minor extensions of the road network. In a macroscopic view, this will lead to longer travel times and higher fuel consumption due to more congestion on the roads. Experience has shown that congestion (expressed by queue length integrated over time) grows three to five times faster than mileage. In this context, route guidance has to improve the efficiency of road transport by supporting better planning, taking into account average traffic conditions. For the same reason, it has to support navigation by avoiding detours and blocked roads.

*This section was written by P. Häußermann and H.-G Zimmer.

At the individual level, drivers will try to minimize the loss in efficiency associated with congested roads by better route planning and more frequent replanning. Every modification due to actual traffic conditions needs additional support in navigation. For best performance according to their personal criteria, drivers need detailed information on the network, giving not only the length of route, but also the duration of the journey calculated from average impedances along the different sections, and, in the future perhaps, the variations with time or according to weather conditions. It is simply no longer reasonable to read all data out of a map, especially during driving. The computer selecting just the required data from mass storage (e.g., CD-ROM) and presenting them in a clearly arranged form is now the optimum tool for this task.

In the future, however, the static data of the network has to be complemented by dynamic traffic information for appropriate reaction to the current situation. If this information is accurate and complete, drivers would use it to their advantage, thus perhaps violating spheres of public interest, such as driving through residential areas. In order to balance public and private interests, route guidance information by traffic management centers has to be filtered. But it will still be the user optimum under restrictions imposed by society.

In the past, bad experiences with traffic information was primarily due to the deficiencies of traffic data collection, processing, and distribution. For technical reasons, traffic management centers could not meet the requirements of real-time control. Progress in information technology and mobile communication allows us to base planning and navigation not on expectations but on information.

All attempts to maintain efficiency in denser traffic increase the driver's workload and thus the potential to cause accidents. It is the general opinion that denser traffic is prone to more accidents. With respect to the accident rate (i.e., the number of accidents with injuries per million vehicle kilometers), statistics do not support such a statement. Only in a very few cases is it possible to identify a single cause of an accident or its avoidance. In order to be useful in traffic, any route guidance system has to be supportive without being distracting. It is very difficult to give just the required information at the right moment. Therefore, the design of the MMI is the crucial point in the development of guidance systems. There is no single solution, because of the variability of human behavior.

PROMETHEUS traffic engineers have estimated the effect of a traffic-responsive route guidance system in Europe. The numerical results depend on the communication system between the infrastructure and the vehicles. Broadcasting (e.g., by RDS-TMC) has a smaller effect than bidirectional communication via short-range mobile communication systems. Assuming the necessary equipment in all road vehicles, the estimated benefits for the Western European countries in the year 2000 are:

- Reduction of accidents with injuries by 2.5% to 6%;
- Reduction of travel time by 3.5% to 9%;
- Reduction of fuel consumption by 4.0% to 10%.

It should be noted that these figures refer to a ''normal'' development of the traffic infrastructure, as in the installation of more variable-message signs. Therefore, these figures describe the benefits to road traffic that the individual can contribute by using a modern route guidance system. At first glance, these figures may not be impressive. But read in a different way, they clearly say that in the future it will be detrimental to safety and efficiency of road transport not to use a route guidance system.

9.4.3 Autonomous and Infrastructure-Based Route Guidance Systems

The main difference between these two systems is the place where the route planning process is performed, and therefore where the data of the road network is stored. In an autonomous system, it is in the vehicle (e.g., with data on CD-ROM). In an infrastructure-based system, the database is in a network of traffic management center computers, and the route planning is done there. Both principles have comparable features, but quite different advantages and disadvantages.

Autonomous Route Guidance Systems

Autonomous route guidance systems are designed to work independently of support by external roadside equipment, except for broadcasted traffic messages received through the car radio. Therefore, a digital road map is stored in the vehicle and the route optimization process, if any, is also performed on board in a fully autonomous manner. Vehicle location is done by dead-reckoning navigation and map matching. Combining the results of both route optimization and vehicle location, precise guidance information from any starting point to any destination point can be generated for driver assistance. Figure 9.18 indicates the basic architecture of autonomous route guidance systems.

Examples of autonomous systems under development in Europe are Travelpilot (Bosch), CARIN (Philips), CARMINAT (Renault/ Philips) and ROUTENRECHNER (Daimler-Benz). For technical details, see [22]. All systems are planning to integrate RDS-TMC to upgrade static route guidance to a dynamic, traffic-responsive guidance system. RDS-TMC is able to transmit 50 to 100 bps (i.e., about 50 messages per minute) of digitally coded traffic information as an inaudible signal via the ordinary FM radio broadcast channel.

Another initiative to generate and transmit traffic information is called SOCRATES. It is based on the GSM Cellular Radio Network and proposed by a consortium including Philips, Bosch, British Telecom, and Siemens. The concept is to use a single channel of the cellular radio network in each direction. The downlink from the base station to the vehicle is operated in a broadcast mode for disseminating traffic information. The uplink to the base station allows multiple access by floating cars in order to collect travel time patterns. The advantages over RDS-TMC are higher data rates (9.6 kbps) and traffic data collection by bidirectional communication. For details, see Chapter 6 of this book.

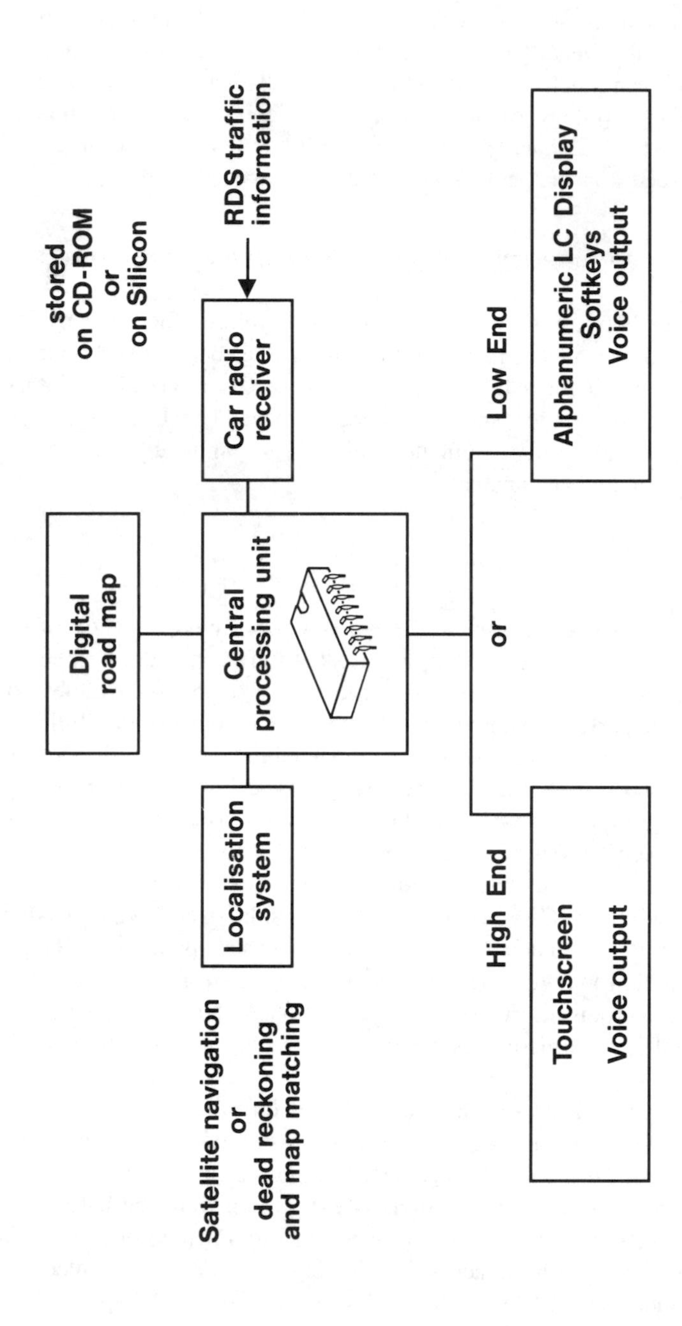

Figure 9.18 Autonomous route guidance systems.

Autonomous systems have medium equipment costs, which have to be paid directly by the users. They can be introduced to the market soon and without serious problems, but have only a limited capability to react to actual traffic situations. There are advantages in certain conditions, especially on highways, where relatively few data are needed to provide dynamic guidance. The planning process in the vehicles can take into account the special wishes and needs of drivers. Therefore, the results are appropriate for them, but cannot be influenced by traffic management authorities. The authorities claim planning sovereignty, since only central planning and traffic control can take factors like air pollution, noise reduction, and so on into consideration.

Infrastructure-Based Systems

Infrastructure-based route guidance systems consist of a simple dead-reckoning navigation device and a transmitter-receiver unit as vehicular components, and of a roadside beacon network connected to a central computer system in the traffic management center. Figure 9.19 shows the system components. With precise knowledge of the road network and the actual traffic situation, the central computer system performs the route optimization process. The traffic situation will be described by the travel times needed to drive from one beacon to another within the beacon network. The result of route optimization is a recommendation of how to reach a destination from the respective beacons. The information will be sent to the beacons, which transmit it to the passing cars. While passing a beacon, cars transmit their travel times and receive route recommendations to all possible destinations, together with the position of the beacon. The position data are used to update the navigation system in the vehicle. An onboard device selects the appropriate route towards the desired destination, which has been given by the driver at the beginning of the journey and stored in the device. With the vehicle's position (calculated by the navigation device) and the selected route, precise guidance information can be generated and displayed. LISB and EURO-SCOUT are systems of this type (LISB is a predecessor of EURO-SCOUT). A detailed description is given in Chapter 4 of this book.

Infrastructure-based systems offer low-cost equipment in vehicles and fully dynamic route guidance, but need roadside infrastructure. The installation of an infrastructure for acquisition, processing, and distribution of traffic data will be expensive and time-consuming. Therefore, such systems can only be introduced gradually, thus creating a number of equipped islands in an otherwise unequipped network. This procedure unfortunately restricts the benefits of the system during the long introduction period.

Infrastructure-based systems are designed as a means of a collective route planning process. The algorithm will be defined by the traffic management authorities according to their needs. Drivers might fear that the information is biased against their individual preferences. They might be suspicious of the system tracking their car, although this is by no means the intention today. Their hesitation may reduce the acceptance of the system and therefore the desired influence on traffic efficiency.

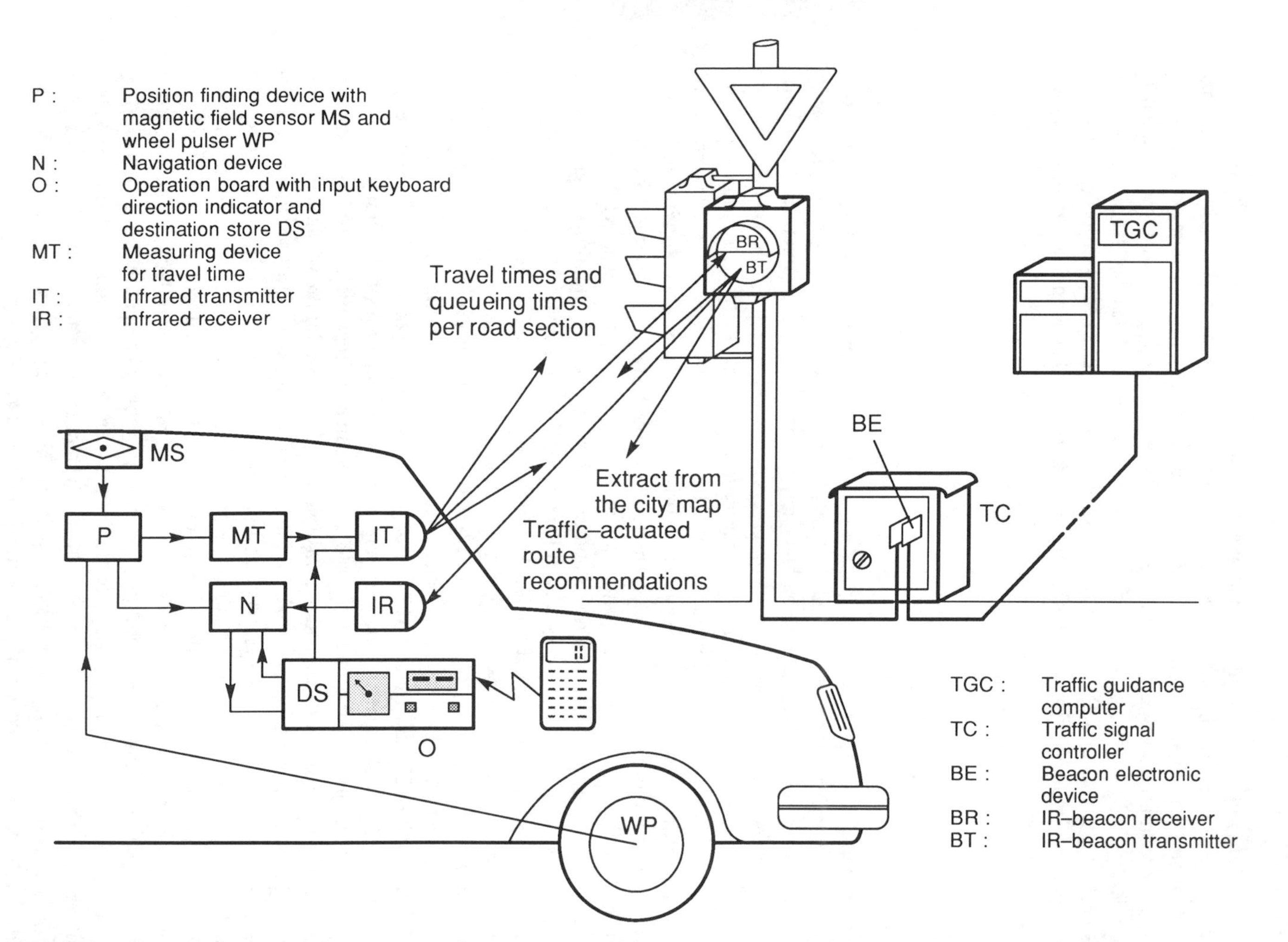

Figure 9.19 System components of infrastructure-based route guidance systems (diagram courtesy of Siemens).

9.4.4 Dual-Mode Route Guidance Systems

The concept of dual-mode route guidance systems has been generated by the question "Which of the two basic architectures described above should the automotive industry recommend to their customers?" Their inherent limitations do not permit the selection of just one of them. But the introduction of different route guidance systems in the same car and eventually for the same purpose will create problems of user acceptance and operation by unskilled users. Three arguments support the integration of both approaches into one system.

- It provides incentives for individual acceptance by being autonomous, if needed, in addition to being responsive to traffic.
- It paves the way for general acceptance of collective guidance recommendations by comparing them with static onboard information.
- Finally, it facilitates the gradual introduction of traffic-responsive guidance systems before the required infrastructure covers the whole network.

In order to promote the concept, demonstrate the technical feasibility, and implement it in road transport, PROMETHEUS has defined a CED 9 called *dual-mode route guidance system*. This project is the framework of the car manufacturers for a consensus on the vehicular components of the system, the necessary standards and interfaces, as well as a strategy for system implementation. The work is coordinated at the system level by PROMETHEUS, leaving room for individual solutions by the participating companies within the margins of the specifications agreed on.

System Components

According to its basic concept, a dual-mode route guidance system consists of three major components: vehicular guidance equipment, a traffic management center, and a communications network. Communication interfaces facilitate the communication between these components. Figure 9.20 shows the components and their interconnections.

As in autonomous route guidance systems, the vehicular components consist of a digital road map, a location system, an external communication interface, and an MMI, all of which are connected to a central processing unit. In contrast to autonomous systems, the digital road map can be limited to the main road network of an area. Guidance within areas not covered by the onboard map will either be performed by simple dead-reckoning navigation or assisted with the roadside infrastructure. The external communication interface has to support RDS-TMC, GSM, or SOCRATES, as in autonomous systems, and also bidirectional communication with beacons in equipped infrastructure.

The roadside infrastructure for traffic-dependent collective route guidance consists of a beacon network connected to a computer system at the traffic management center. At first, it will be installed in areas with normally dense traffic, such as in inner-city areas. The central computer performs a collective route optimization, taking into account

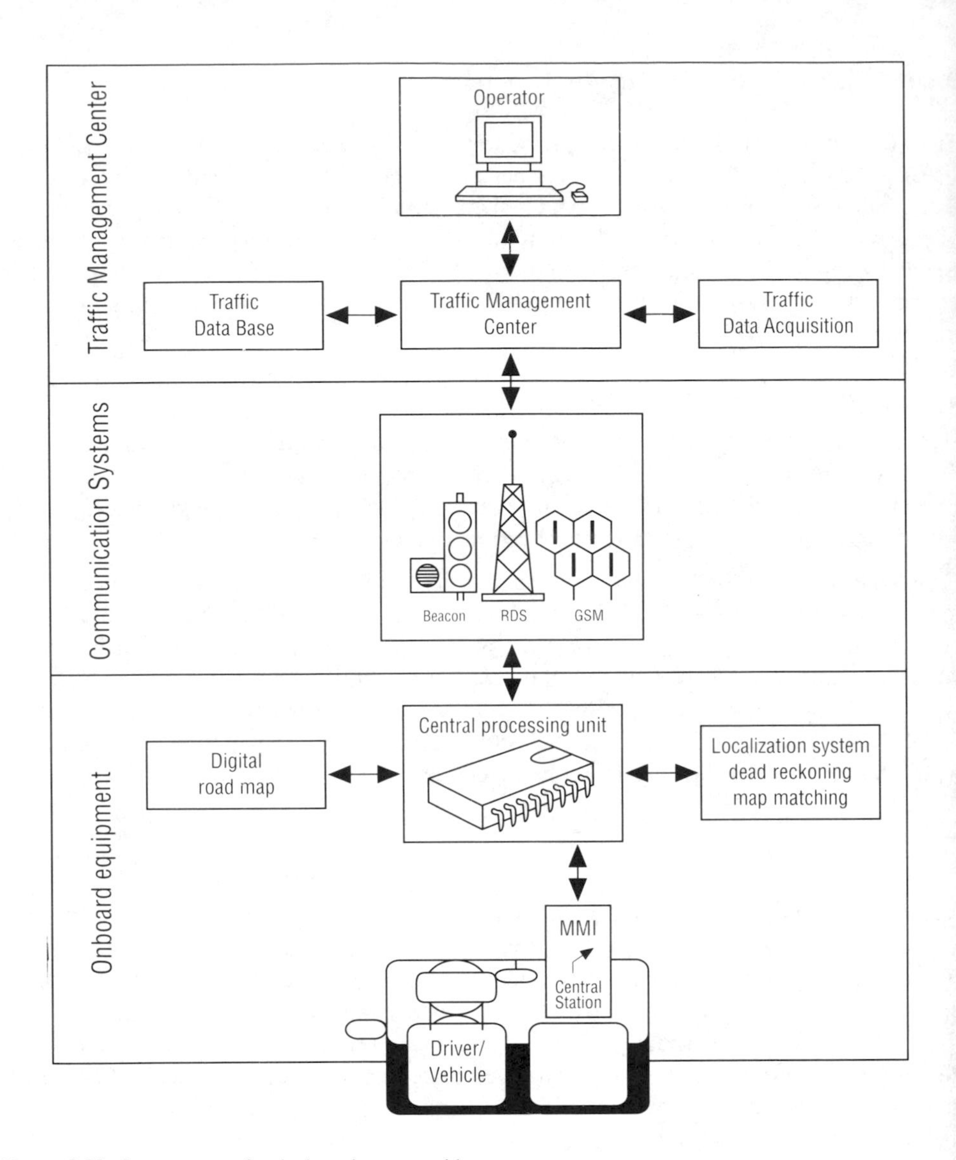

Figure 9.20 Components of a dual-mode route guidance system.

the current traffic information within the network covered by the beacons. The traffic data are acquired either by conventional means (e.g., loop detectors or beacons collecting travel times from floating cars). In principle, it does not matter whether the beacons communicate with the vehicles via IR or microwave. Practical experience with IR exists from the LISB field test in Berlin. Microwave communication offers good opportunities for integration with other RTI services, such as automatic debiting. There will be no problems installing the infrastructure step by step in accordance with public requirements, starting with the most important and crucial areas. The autonomous parts of the vehicular components are fully operational, perhaps with reduced features on roads not contained in the digital road maps on board. Each new beacon network "island" will improve the performance of the whole system.

In addition to the beacons, the public communication network is necessary to provide traffic information in areas not covered by a beacon network. In Europe, RDS-TMC is regarded as a basic source of traffic information. In the future, it might be superseded by digital audio broadcasting, which could provide better services with the same principle. Bidirectional communication systems like GSM or SOCRATES will improve route guidance with new services, such as commercial information on parking facilities, hotels, service stations, and so on. An essential problem has not been solved yet: the consistency of the information from different sources. Dual-mode route guidance cannot function properly if traffic information by RDS-TMC is inconsistent with the traffic information used by the beacon system. The field trials for RDS-TMC and the POLIS initiative will be used to address this problem. Of similar importance is the consistency of the road maps used in vehicles or in traffic management centers.

Onboard System Architecture

The components of a dual-mode route guidance system are just a composite of those of autonomous and infrastructure-based systems. But the architecture of the vehicular guidance system is not just beacon communication added to an autonomous system or vice versa. The essential new item is another level of software, a central route management system, which in principle controls the autonomous and the infrastructure-based subsystem, both running parallel. This software controls the priorities for the subsystems, checks the consistency of their results, facilitates the smooth transition from one subsystem to the other, and informs the driver in an unambiguous manner. The architecture of a dual-mode route guidance system is shown in Figure 9.21. This architecture exemplifies the basic principle of the PROMETHEUS approach: higher benefits and versatility by the integration of several subsystems combined with reduced operating efforts. Besides that, the architecture demonstrates the need for precompetitive cooperation of all participants involved in order to obtain an early consensus on those items that ensure the consistency of the whole system.

9.4.5 Demonstrations of Feasibility

The first demonstration of dual-mode route guidance systems was given at the PROMETHEUS BMM in Torino in September 1991. The aim there was to show the technical feasibility by "gluing together" existing laboratory equipment with special interfaces and ad hoc developed software. The Fiat test track La Mandria was the network. A course of

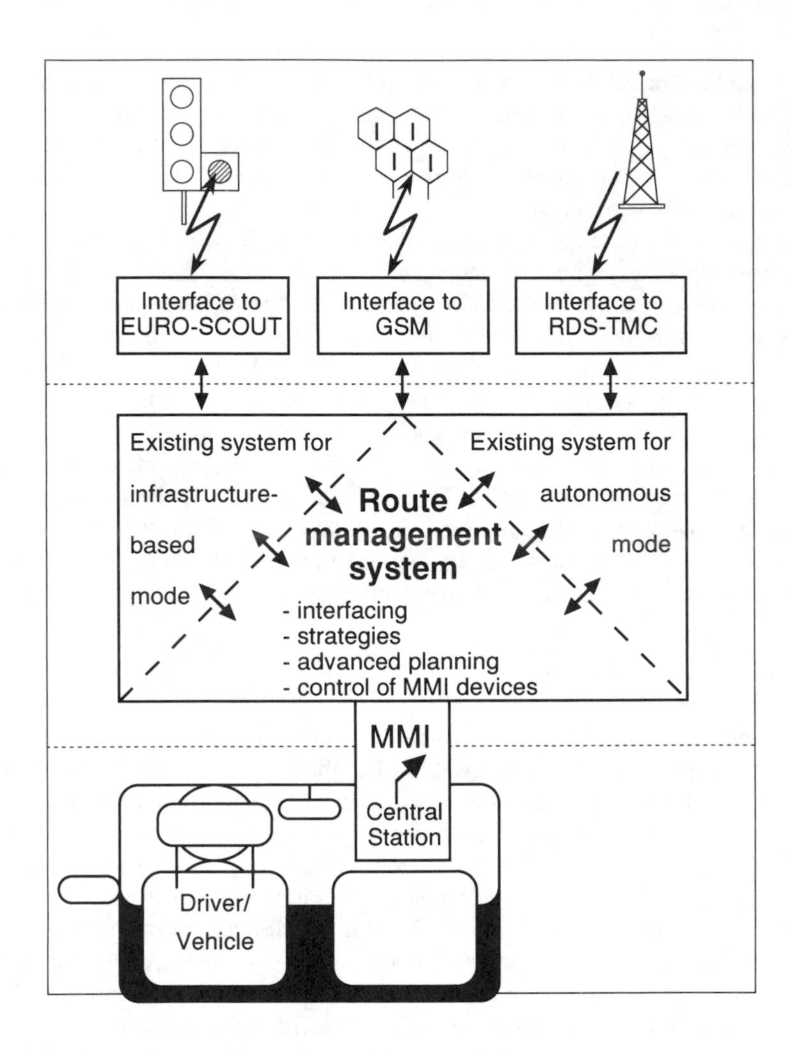

Figure 9.21 Onboard system architecture of a dual-mode route guidance system.

about 10 km was available for tests. A number of crossings and junctions provided different tours between origin and destination of trips. The environment allowed the interpretation of specific areas as a highway, rural roads, and urban streets. A personal computer acted as the traffic management center and simulated incidents or unexpected road construction work requiring deviations from normal routes. Traffic-related information was available via ALI-SCOUT beacons, the GSM-based SOCRATES system, and RDS. Two types of dual systems were demonstrated:

- ALI-SCOUT together with Travelpilot (Daimler-Benz, MAN, Opel, Peugeot);
- SOCRATES together with CARIN (BMW, Ford, Renault, Saab, Volvo).

In addition, RDS-Radio (not yet RDS-TMC) was integrated with the systems demonstrated by Daimler-Benz and Ford. The road map had been digitized and stored on a CD-ROM. Several types of acoustic and visual outputs to the driver were demonstrated by the participating companies, ranging from head-up display to alphanumeric readout. Figure 9.22 shows the display used in the Daimler-Benz demonstration. La Mandria demonstrated that dual-mode route guidance:

- Can offer different routes for one origin-destination pair;
- Switches smoothly between infrastructure-based and autonomous mode without confusion over the correct position;
- Selectively transmits dedicated warnings;
- Reacts properly on wrong route choices by the driver;
- Has benefits due to the integration of different principles (e.g., updating the map matching process or comfortable handling of the driver's mistakes);
- Offers a human-machine interaction that is easy to use and easy to understand.

In short, the message was that although the theory and the technology behind it might look quite complicated, there are already cars available, and everybody is able to use them with obvious benefits and without difficulties.

Figure 9.22 Display unit for route guidance used in the Daimler-Benz demonstration of dual-mode route guidance on the La Mandria test track in September 1991.

9.4.6 Future Work and Implementation

The work for the Torino demonstration confronted the engineers in the automotive industry and their partners in the electronics and suppliers industry with many problems of technology and especially system engineering. Thus, it provided plenty of experience as a basis for a common specification, which has to be delivered in 1994—the scheduled end of the current phase of PROMETHEUS. With regard to the vehicular part of the system, the following items require detailed specifications, consensus on the principle, or the establishment of standards.

- The human-machine interaction;
- Routing management (i.e., switching between modes);
- Interfaces between autonomous or infrastructure-based subsystems and the central routing management;
- Interfaces to the public communication network and to the communication network within the vehicle.

This type of work can and will be done by PROMETHEUS working groups. But even with respect to the autonomous subsystem, the results depend on progress of activities beyond PROMETHEUS. The problem of establishing, maintaining, and marketing digital road maps or the questions related to pan-European coding of traffic messages and the responsibility for their content are just two examples. Infrastructure-based systems can only be specified in cooperation with traffic managers. Here, the European policy framework for road transport becomes relevant for technicians. But it has not yet been formulated in an explicit manner and will never be final. Nevertheless, there is now a broad consensus in Europe that mobility and transport efficiency cannot be maintained without bringing advanced transport informatics into action. In the framework of the EC program ATT, several implementation or field trial initiatives have been started. Relevant to dual-mode route guidance are tests in Athens, Barcelona, Cologne, Gothenburg, Munich, Stuttgart, and Torino. A detailed description of the trial in Stuttgart is given in [4]. For a general overview, see Chapter 8 of this book.

9.4.7 Conclusions

Dual-mode route guidance systems are much more than "high-tech." First of all, they manifest the commitment of the automotive industry for cooperation with traffic management in the implementation of real-time traffic control. They connect individual vehicle control strategies with collective traffic control strategies. This way they improve individual acceptance and efficiency of collective control as well. They allow for a gradual introduction of a system that finally will incorporate the direct cooperation between drivers and traffic managers for the benefit of all of us. There is no unique technical solution for dual-mode route guidance systems, but there is a unique approach by the partners of the

PROMETHEUS program towards a European system that can be developed into different products with the same basic functions in vehicle and traffic control.

REFERENCES

[1] ''Safe and Effective Mobility in Europe,'' issued by PROMETHEUS Office for BMM'91, Torino, Sept. 1991.

[2] Hipp, E., ''Integrierte Konzepte für ein Flottenmanagement im Güternah- und Fernverkehr,'' *VDI-Berichte 915*: Mobilität und Verkehr—reichen die heutigen Konzepte aus? VDI-Verlag Düsseldorf 1991. (Engl. trans.: ''Concepts for an Integrated Fleet Management in Short- and Long-Distance Goods Transport,'' *Proc. VDI-Berichte* No. 915: Mobility and Traffic—Are the Existing Concepts Sufficient?)

[3] Cooperative Transport Management for the Greater Munich Area; issued by Free State Bavaria et al., Munich, 1991 (available from BMW AG, Munich).

[4] Häußermann, P., ''STORM—Integriertes Regionales Verkehrsmanagement in der Region Stuttgart,'' *VDI-Berichte Nr. 915*: Mobilität und Verkehr—reichen die heutigen Konzepte aus? VDI-Verlag Düsseldorf, 1991, pp. 167–183. (Engl. trans.: ''STORM—Integrated Regional Traffic Management in the Stuttgart Area,'' *Proc. VDI-Berichte No. 915*: Mobility and Traffic—Are the Existing Concepts Sufficient?)

[5] Cremer, M., ''An Integrated Architecture for Future Freeway Information and Control Systems,'' *Proc. Engineering Foundation Conf. on Traffic Management Issues and Techniques*, Palm Coast, Florida, 2–4 April 1991.

[6] "Functions or How to Achieve PROMETHEUS Objectives,'' issued by PROMETHEUS Office, Stuttgart, July 1989.

[7] Fontaine, H., and G. Malaterre, ''Driver Needs and Safety Effects of PROMETHEUS Functions,'' *The XIIIth International Technical Conf. on Experimental Safety Vehicles*, Paris, 4–7 Nov. 1991.

[8] Kemeny, A., ''PROMETHEUS—Design Technics,'' *Proc. Int. Congress on Electronics in Transportation*, SAE, Vehicle Electronics in the 90s, Detroit, Oct. 1990.

[9] PROMETHEUS Cooperative Control Task Force, ''Cooperative Control Application Specifications,'' *CCTF Deliverable*, Paris, 2 Oct. 1990, 121 pages.

[10] Kemeny, A., and J. M. Piroird, ''A Simulator for Cooperative Driving,'' *Proc. DRIVE Conf.*, Brussels, 4–6 Feb. 1991, pp. 930–942.

[11] PROMETHEUS Cooperative Control Task Force, ''Introduction of Cooperative Control Systems on the Market,'' *CCTF Deliverable*, Paris, Jan. 1991.

[12] PROMETHEUS Cooperative Control Task Force, ''Cooperative Driving: Medium Range Pre-information, Application Specifications for Short Term Implementation,'' *CCTF Deliverable*, Paris, Feb. 1992.

[13] Augello, D., R. Havas, H. G. Metzler, and E. Schubert, ''Traffic Flow Harmonisation by Cooperative Driving,'' *Proc. 3rd Int. Conf. ATA*, Firence, 8–9 April 1992, pp. 1889–1898.

[14] Pons, A., and A. Kemeny, ''Network Topology Regulation for Communication Load Control—First Results,'' *Proc. 4th PROMETHEUS Workshop*, Compiègne, 9–10 Oct. 1990, pp. 302–318.

[15] Broqua, F., G. Lerner, V. Mauro, and E. Morello, ''Cooperative Driving: Basic Concepts and a First Assessment of Intelligent Cruise Control Strategies,'' *Proc. DRIVE Conf.*, Brussels, 4–6 Feb. 1991, pp. 908–929.

[16] Zackor, H., and X. Zhang, eds., ''Ad-hoc Assessment of Integrated Systems,'' PRO-GENERAL, Steierwald, Schönharting und Partner GmbH, Stuttgart, Feb. 1992.

[17] PROMETHEUS Cooperative Control Task Force, ''Evaluation Procedures for the First Cooperative Control Demonstrator Communication System,'' *CCTF Deliverable*, Paris, Jan. 1992.

[18] Blume, F., M. Ohler, and K. Zurmühl, ''An Implementation Strategy for RTI Services,'' *Proc. 2nd Cooperative Driving Workshop*, Paris, 18 May 1992, 4 pages.

[19] PROMETHEUS Cooperative Control Task Force, ''Requirements for Vehicle-Roadside Communications in Cooperative Control, *CCTF Deliverable*, Paris, Jan. 1991.

[20] PROMETHEUS Cooperative Control Task Force, ''Communication Functionalities and Requirements for Cooperative Control,'' *CCTF Deliverable*, Aachen, Oct. 1990.
[21] PROMETHEUS Cooperative Control Task Force, ''Requirements Analysis of Positioning Systems for Cooperative Control,'' *CCTF Deliverable*, Paris, Oct. 1990.
[22] Häußermann, P., ''Route Guidance Systems—Combination of Autonomous Systems for Main Road Networks With Infrastructure-Based Systems for Urban Areas,'' *Proc. PROMETHEUS Presentation at the SITEV'90*, issued by PROMETHEUS Office, Stuttgart, May 1990, pp. 91–112.
[23] Dumoulin, E., ''Strategies for the Introduction of MRP/RTI Applications on the Market,'' *Proc. 2nd Cooperative Driving Workshop*, Paris, 18 May 1992, 12 pages.

Chapter 10

IVHS America: A Public-Private Partnership

Lester Lamm and James Costantino

10.1 INTRODUCTION

A national effort to bring the Intelligent Vehicle Highway System (IVHS) to fruition in the United States is well under way. This chapter examines significant historical events; describes IVHS America, a unique public-private organization whose aim is to promote, foster, and accelerate the deployment of IVHS in the Unites States; surveys the current status of the U.S. IVHS program; and highlights the recently published *Strategic Plan for IVHS in the United States.*

10.2 BACKGROUND

It has become clear that the enormously successful interstate highway program in the U.S. now requires the integration of information technologies into the existing physical infrastructure in order to achieve measurable improvements in mobility. Although a number of tentative initiatives have been taken in this direction during the last 20 years, no organized national program to integrate information and computer technologies into the existing infrastructure emerged. Rather, isolated instances of state and local programs were developed to meet the mobility challenge. Notable among these were a variety of contemporary studies and demonstrations pursued by the California Department of Transportation (CALTRANS) and the University of California at Berkeley to explore alternatives to demonstrably inadequate highway transportation and its severe environmental effects. Other states, universities, and the Federal Government became interested in the possibilities presented by the new technologies as the problems of highway congestion, safety, pollution, and international competitiveness increased, while the alternative of large-scale expansion of highway mileage grew less viable for political, environmental, and societal reasons.

The Intelligent Vehicle Highway Society of America, or IVHS America, had its genesis in an informal group of volunteers from industry, government, and universities concerned with the mounting surface transportation dilemma. This group, named Mobility 2000 by its members, focused its efforts on worsening urban traffic congestion and how technology could help solve it. The interest of Mobility 2000, however, went beyond the mobility crisis to the development of a future surface transportation system using advanced technology to reduce congestion, minimize environmental effects of surface transportation, and improve safety, productivity, and energy efficiency.

Mobility 2000 held major meetings in San Antonio in 1989 and in Dallas in March 1990. Other meetings over a two-year period were held at various locations throughout the country. The purpose of these meetings was to focus attention on the issues and opportunities for using advanced technology for highways. Mobility 2000 sought to provide coordination and an exchange of information, and define a national cooperative program to advance the development of highway technology. Over a period of three years, the group identified preliminary R&D goals, the operational testing programs needed, and implementation strategies to ensure the earliest national availability of useful technology to address major problems of traffic safety, traffic congestion, and air pollution.

The work of Mobility 2000 was also stimulated by the awareness of international competitiveness with both Japan and the European community, who had a number of IVHS projects well under way. Japan had three major programs, designated as the Advanced Mobile Traffic Information and Communication System (AMTICS), the Road-Automobile Communication System (RACS), and the Vehicle Information Communication System (VICS). In Europe, a number of individual projects were coordinated throughout the EC under the names of DRIVE and PROMETHEUS. A major U.S. effort was necessary to address its unique transportation needs and to seek solutions that would require the development of new U.S. technology, adapting existing foreign technology, or some combination of the two.

Mobility 2000 was not designed to be a permanent organization; rather, it was intended to be the precursor of a formal, national, public-private organization that would coordinate IVHS research, development, operational testing, and implementation. At an IVHS National Leadership Conference in May 1990, called by the U.S. Department of Transportation, the Highway Users Federation for Safety and Mobility (HUFSAM), and the American Association of State Highway and Transportation Officials (AASHTO), the concept of a public-private coordinating organization was discussed. It was at this meeting that IVHS America was conceived.

It was also decided at the leadership conference that IVHS America was to be a public-private partnership that would seek nonprofit status from the Internal Revenue Service and be incorporated under the laws of the District of Columbia. Official bylaws and articles of incorporation were drawn, and on August 15, 1990, IVHS America was incorporated, and on November 14, 1990, a 501(c)(3) nonprofit determination for the new society was issued by the Internal Revenue Service.

IVHS America began its operations in earnest in late 1990. The Congressional House Appropriations Committee, perceiving the need for just such a coordinating mechanism, indicated in the 1991 Appropriations Act that "the committee is concerned about the apparent lack of a nationwide public-private coordinating organization to guide the complex research and development activities in the IVHS area" (Committee Report on H.R. 5229-U.S. DOT Appropriations for FY 1991). With the legal impediments removed and funding mechanisms in place, a functioning, nonprofit partnership, the Intelligent Vehicle Highway Society of America, came into existence.

IVHS America is primarily a focal point for organizations involved in IVHS. State and local government agencies, academic institutions, associations, and private companies all pay annual membership dues to support the operations of IVHS America; these contributions are augmented by funding from the federal government for performing designated tasks. For IVHS America, the challenge lies in the diversity of IVHS. The technology is highly interdisciplinary, ranging from physics to psychology. The institutional arena is equally diverse, demanding new working relationships among all levels of government. New public-private partnerships have been formed. Legal issues such as product liability and privacy are being addressed. Many participants in IVHS compete for resources and customers; many have objectives and constituencies at odds.

If IVHS is to succeed, however, this diversity must generate concerted action—a coherent national program of technical exploration and testing leading to deployment across the U.S. Research must be planned, executed, and coordinated. Institutional and legal barriers must be addressed and their effects mitigated.

In December 1991, President Bush signed the Intermodal Surface Transportation Efficiency Act (ISTEA), a watershed in U.S. transportation history. ISTEA signaled a major shift in transportation investment. With the interstate highway system substantially completed, the federal government shifted its concentration to new transportation priorities. IVHS is one of those new priorities. With the aim of deploying proven technologies, exploring longer term, high-payoff technologies, and establishing mechanisms to clear the institutional hurdles, ISTEA established a six-year, $660 million national IVHS program. ISTEA made the concept of a national IVHS program official.

10.3 IVHS FUNCTIONAL AREAS

A wide array of technologies makes up IVHS, including electronics, computer hardware and software, control, and communications. Five functional areas have been identified in which these technologies are applied. All five functional areas are overlapping and can be applied to rural areas as well as urban.

10.3.1 Advanced Traffic Management Systems (ATMS)

ATMS is the basic building block of IVHS. All other functional areas will use the information provided by ATMS. ATMS will integrate management of various roadway functions, including freeway ramp metering and arterial signal control. In more sophisticated implementations, ATMS will predict traffic congestion and provide alternative routing instructions to vehicles over wide areas in order to maximize the efficiency of the highway network and maintain priorities for high-occupancy vehicles (HOV).

ATMS will collect, utilize, and disseminate real-time data on congestion on arterial streets and expressways, and will alert transit operators of alternative routes. Dynamic traffic control systems will respond to changing traffic conditions across different jurisdictions and types of roads by routing drivers around delays where possible. Rapid detection and response to traffic incidents will be especially effective in reducing congestion on expressways.

10.3.2 Advanced Travel Information Systems (ATIS)

ATIS provides a variety of information that assists travelers in reaching a desired destination via private vehicle, public transportation, or a combination of the two. Onboard navigation systems are an ATIS building block. In future systems, these will be augmented by information from the ATMS. The information will include locations of traffic incidents, weather and road conditions, optimal routes, recommended speeds, and lane restrictions. While such information will be used in vehicles, it could also be used for pretrip planning at home, in the office, at kiosks, or even by owners of portable or palmtop computers.

10.3.3 Advanced Vehicle Control Systems (AVCS)

AVCS enhances the driver's control of the vehicle to make travel safer and more efficient. Accidents could be avoided, as opposed to just having their consequences mitigated. AVCS includes a broad range of concepts that will become operational on different time scales. Collision warning systems would alert the driver to an imminent collision. In more advanced systems, the vehicle would automatically brake or steer away from a collision. Those systems are autonomous in the vehicle and are likely to be developed by the automotive industry and its suppliers. They should offer substantial benefits by improving safety and reducing accident-induced congestion, justifying public sector funding during the initial development stage.

Longer term AVCS concepts rely more heavily on infrastructure information and control that could produce major increases in roadway throughput by as much as two or three times, perhaps more. One example is limited-access automated lanes, in which the movements of all vehicles are automatically controlled while they are in the special lane. Such a system will likely require close communication between the roadway and the vehicles and between the vehicles themselves.

ISTEA calls for development and demonstration of a completely automated highway and vehicle system that will serve as the prototype for fully automated IVHS systems. The goal is to have the first fully automated roadway or test track in operation by 1997.

10.3.4 Commercial Vehicle Operations

Operators of fleets of trucks, buses, vans, taxis, and emergency vehicles have already begun adopting IVHS technologies. Their leadership role is expected to continue because fleet operators can clearly see the economic benefits. Thousands of heavy-duty trucks are already equipped with automated location systems and two-way radios that link drivers with their dispatch centers. Automated vehicle identification systems are already automating toll collection and thus improving traffic flow in New York, Texas, and Oklahoma. The benefits of electronic toll collection are not limited to commercial vehicles. Indeed, passenger car drivers are the principal beneficiaries, because increasing the number of vehicles in use that can move through electronic toll lanes reduces congestion. A number of commercial and public fleet operators use automated vehicle location systems—onboard navigation, Loran-C (a terrestrial-based location system), and GPS. With these systems, dispatchers can instantly determine the location of any vehicle.

10.3.5 Advanced Public Transportation Systems

APTS will use constituent technologies of ATMS, ATIS, and AVCS to improve operation of HOVs, including transit buses and car and van pools. ATIS will inform travelers of the alternative schedules and costs available for a trip, while ATMS will provide instantly updated information. Real-time ride matching is another application that gives car and van poolers new flexibility in planning trips.

Smart cards will enable consumers to board transit vehicles, as well as pay tolls and parking fees, all without cash. In addition, preferential measures (such as selective traffic-signal timing) for HOVs are included in APTS.

10.4 CURRENT STATUS

A number of projects and operational tests of IVHS are ongoing, funded from various public and private sources. See Table 10.1. New projects and tests are continually being announced and implemented.

Table 10.1
Current U.S. IVHS Projects and Operational Tests

Project and Location	*Participating Sponsors*	*Focus*
PATH Berkeley, CA	CALTRANS University of California Ford Motor Company FHWA	Integrated traffic management and traveler information Automated freeways Roadway electrification Multimodal traveler information
GUIDESTAR Minneapolis, MN	Minnesota DOT University of Minnesota FHWA	Traffic data collection and distribution Autoscope video imaging
INFORM Long Island, NY	New York DOT FHWA	Integrated systems Freeway management Variable-message signs
TRANSCOM Northern NJ metropolitan, NYC	New York DOT New Jersey DOT Other TRANSCOM member agencies FHWA	Incident management Automated vehicle identification Vehicle probes
SMART Los Angeles, CA	Los Angeles County Transportation Commission CALTRANS California Highway Patrol City of Los Angeles FHWA	Highway advisory radio Changeable message signs Emergency response Coordinated interagency traffic management
FAME Seattle, WA	Washington State DOT Washington State Transportation Center FHWA	Incident management Integrated systems Ramp metering
Integrated System Project Anaheim, CA	CALTRANS City of Anaheim FHWA	Incident management Institutional coordination Traffic operation center
Incident Management & Integrated Systems Demonstration Minneapolis/St. Paul, MN	Minnesota DOT FHWA	Traffic information Incident response Information systems Heavy truck incident management
Pathfinder Los Angeles, CA	CALTRANS General Motors FHWA	In-vehicle navigation Probe vehicles Information systems
TRAVTEK Orlando, FL	City of Orlando Florida DOT General Motors AAA FHWA	In-vehicle navigation Traveler information Motorist services Real-time traffic information Traffic probes Dynamic route guidance

Table 10.1 *(continued)*
Current U.S. IVHS Projects and Operational Tests

Project and Location	*Participating Sponsors*	*Focus*
ADVANCE Northwestern suburbs of Chicago, IL	Illinois DOT Motorola Illinois Universities Transportation Research Consortium FHWA	Dynamic route guidance In-vehicle navigation Probe vehicles
FAST-TRAC Oakland County, MI	Michigan DOT Siemens Automotive Ford Motor Company Chrysler General Motors Oakland County Road Commission City of Troy FHWA	Dynamic route guidance and driver information system Beacon technology Advanced traffic management Integrated traffic management and traveler information
I-95 Intermodal Mobility Project	Pennsylvania DOT FHWA	Urban transportation corridor Satellite communication Freeway surveillance
Urban Congestion Alleviation Project I-95, northern VA	Virginia DOT Virginia Transportation Research Council FHWA	Video imaging detector system Incident detection
DIRECT Greater Detroit area, MI	Michigan DOT FHWA	Motorist advisory systems Radio data system Cellular phone Automated highway advisory radio
Urban Congestion Alleviation Demonstration Project I-95, Baltimore, MD	Maryland State Highway Administration FHWA	Changeable message signs Highway advisory radio
HELP/Crescent	DOTs of Alabama, Arizona, California, Idaho, Iowa, Minnesota, Nevada, New Mexico, Oregon, Pennsylvania, Texas, Utah, Virginia, Washington, British Columbia Port Authority of New York and New Jersey Motor Carrier Industry FHWA	Integrated heavy vehicle monitoring system Automated vehicle identification Automated vehicle classification Weigh-in-motion Urban/rural operations Onboard computers System integration

Table 10.1 *(continued)*
Current U.S. IVHS Projects and Operational Tests

Project and Location	*Participating Sponsors*	*Focus*
ADVANTAGE I-75	DOTs of Florida, Georgia, Kentucky, Tennessee, Ohio, Michigan City of Ontario Quebec Motor Carrier Industry FHWA	Motor carrier operations Urban/rural operations
Washington State Portable Traveler Information System I-90, Snoqualmie Pass, WA	Washington State DOT FHWA	Rural test In-vehicle radio receivers Road condition information
Live Aerial Video Montgomery County, MD	Maryland State Highway Authority Montgomery County Departments of Traffic and Police FHWA	Live video from aircraft to traffic management center
Live Aerial Video Fairfax County, VA	Virginia DOT Fairfax County Police Virginia Transportation Research Council FHWA	Live video from aircraft to traffic management center
Connecticut Freeway Traffic Management Hartford, CT	Connecticut DOT FHWA	Freeway surveillance and control Roadside radar detectors Closed-circuit television
Traveler Information System—Dulles Corridor Herndon, VA	Virginia DOT Dulles Area Transportation Association Town of Herndon Metro Traffic Control FHWA	Highway advisory radio Cable system Transit vehicle display
Advanced Traffic Management Systems Model Portland, OR	Oregon DOT City of Portland Metropolitan Services District Washington State DOT	Areawide system Incident management Institutional issues
Advanced Traffic Management Systems Model Denver, CO	Colorado DOT	Advanced traffic management system

Table 10.1 *(continued)*
Current U.S. IVHS Projects and Operational Tests

Project and Location	*Participating Sponsors*	*Focus*
Bellevue Smart Traveler Bellevue, WA	Metro Transit Bellevue Transportation Management Association City of Bellevue Metro Transit Washington State DOT University of Washington FTA	Dynamic ride sharing Dial-up information (Traffic Reporter) Mobile communication
California Smart Traveler Six local sites, CA	CALTRANS FTA	Real-time traveler information Videotex and audiotex traveler information Dynamic trip match, smartcards Hand-held devices (travel cards, mobile telephones)
Houston Smart Commuter Houston, TX	Texas Transportation Institute Metropolitan Transit Authority City of Houston State Department of Highway and Public Transportation FTA	Real-time traveler information Dynamic trip match Audiotex and videotex traveler information Variable-message signs Smart kiosk
Ann Arbor Integrated Smart Bus & Smart Traveler Ann Arbor, MI	Ann Arbor Transportation Authority City of Ann Arbor University of Michigan FTA	Automated customer information Multiple-use smartcard Traveler security Vehicle location Computer-assisted dispatch Advanced displays Personal travel cards
Twin City Mobility Manager St. Paul Minneapolis, MN	Regional Transit Board Minnesota DOT University of Minnesota Metropolitan Transit Commission FTA	Mobility manager Automated vehicle location technology Smart card Specialized transit services
Portland Smart Bus Portland, OR	Tri-County Metro Transportation District FTA	Audiotex and videotex traveler information Multimodal transportation operations control Fixed-route and dial-a-ride integration Route deviation Smart kiosks Personal travel card Automated customer information Geographic information systems

Table 10.1 *(continued)*
Current U.S. IVHS Projects and Operational Tests

Project and Location	*Participating Sponsors*	*Focus*
Chicago Smart Bus Chicago, IL	Chicago Transit Authority City of Chicago FTA	Service reliability Automated vehicle location Signal preemption Real-time service adjustments
Anaheim IVHS Operational Integration Anaheim, CA	City of Anaheim Orange County Transit District CALTRANS FTA	Smart kiosks Real-time traveler information Variable-message signs Transportation managment center
Rogue Valley Mobility Manager Medford, OR	Rogue Valley Council of Government Rogue Valley Transportation District Group Ride Service Ashland Senior Program Upper Rogue Community Center Call-A-Ride FTA	Single point of contact Smartcards Real-time transit information Demand-responsive transportation Geographic information systems Automated third-party billing Computer assisted dispatch Multimodal trip reservations
Baltimore Smart Bus Baltimore, MD	Baltimore MTA Westinghouse FTA	GPS AVL Computer-aided dispatch Management information system
Denver Smart Bus Denver, CO	Denver RTD Westinghouse FTA	GPS AVL Computer-aided dispatch Management information system
PIKEPASS OK	Oklahoma Turnpike Authority	Electronic toll collection (implementation)
ExpressToll	E-470 Public Highway Authority	Electronic toll collection (implementation)
TOLLTAG: New Orleans, LA	Louisiana Department of Transportation Greater New Orleans Bridge Commission	Electronic toll collection (implementation)
Grosse Ile, MI	Grosse Ile Bridge Company	Electronic toll collection (implementation)
TX	Texas Turnpike Authority	Testing of electronic toll collection devices
Buffalo, NY	New York State Thruway Authority	Testing of electronic toll collection devices
Goethals Bridge, NY	Port Authority of New York and New Jersey Triborough Bridge and Tunnel Authority	Testing of electronic toll collection devices

Table 10.1 *(continued)*
Current U.S. IVHS Projects and Operational Tests

Project and Location	*Participating Sponsors*	*Focus*
NH	New Hampshire Department of Transportation	Testing of electronic toll collection devices

10.5 THE STRATEGIC PLAN FOR IVHS IN THE UNITED STATES

Recognizing that a coherent national strategy would be key to the success of IVHS, Congress requested in the ISTEA that the Department of Transportation (DOT) prepare a strategic plan by December 1992. The DOT, in turn, asked IVHS America to prepare its own strategic plan to serve as a foundation for the congressional report. In writing its plan, IVHS America received inputs from the broad IVHS community, including federal, state, and local government agencies; industry; academia; trade associations; and consumer and public-interest groups.

The purpose of the *Strategic Plan for IVHS in the United States,* published May 20, 1992, is to guide the development and implementation of IVHS technology in keeping with the goals of safety, enhanced mobility, and improved productivity of our transportation system. The plan establishes the goals and objectives of a national IVHS program; estimates the magnitude and sources of funding required; identifies key challenges to IVHS deployment and seeks ways in which they can be resolved; suggests appropriate roles for the public, private, and academic participants and methods to help build cooperation among them; and outlines a course of action to develop, test, and deploy IVHS technology.

10.5.1 Goals

The *Strategic Plan* has identified several operational and institutional goals for the IVHS program. Table 10.2 lists these goals. While they may appear very general, achieving even a fraction of these would improve the transportation industry and society as a whole.

10.5.2 Magnitude and Sources of Funding

According to the *Strategic Plan*, IVHS will be paid for principally by the users of its products and services: consumers, commercial users (such as the trucking industry), toll authorities, transit operators, and the like. As in the case of the highways themselves, government infrastructure spending will be the foundation for growth. The development costs for IVHS will be largely paid for by the private sector in its quest to develop products for what promises to be a very large market. In addition to infrastructure spending, federal

Table 10.2
Goals of IVHS

Operational	*Institutional*
Improve safety	Create IVHS industry in the United States
Reduce congestion	Revitalize the transportation profession
Increase and improve the quality of mobility	Create new model for development and deployment of new technology
Improve environmental quality and energy efficiency	
Improve economic productivity	

government support will be needed to back long-range R&D, academic research, and essential activities that cannot be self-sufficient, such as the legal and institutional implications of IVHS.

Achieving the aims set out in the *Strategic Plan* is expected to require a public infrastructure investment on the order of $40 billion over the next 20 years. End-user spending for products and services over that same period could reach $170 billion or more, depending on market response. The public expenditure for IVHS may seem large, but it is small relative to expected total public transportation expenditures—less than 3% of the $1.6 trillion expected to be spent on surface transportation in the U.S. during the same period. Of course, market uncertainties, rapidly changing costs for evolving technologies, and other demands for development capital make it difficult to predict the program costs, especially over a 20-year period. Therefore, estimates can only be provisional. As results from operational tests become available, it will be possible to predict consumer interest and total program costs more accurately.

10.5.3 Challenges to IVHS Deployment

Successful integration of the separate technologies of IVHS requires that a number of cross-cutting issues be addressed early in the program. These include system architecture, standards and protocols, safety and human factors, and institutional and legal challenges.

System Architecture, Standards, and Protocols

IVHS will progress as advanced technology and information are integrated with the conventional infrastructure to provide an expanding set of consumer services over ever-increasing geographic areas. As development proceeds, there will be ever greater interaction among ATMS, ATIS, and AVCS. IVHS can be more than the sum of its parts, but this inherent synergy can be tapped only if it is regarded, from the start, as an integrated set of capabilities.

Integration will not only be temporal, but also spatial. Systems will be created separately in various areas of the country. These "islands" will be linked eventually to include the entire nation, much the same way that the interstate highway system grew. Phased implementation will hasten delivery of benefits to travelers and will help create public demand for further deployment.

Understanding this, the IVHS community has devoted considerable energy in the areas of system architecture and standards and protocols. In fact, the U.S. DOT will be initiating a two-year, $20 million program to develop and evaluate alternative architectures. In parallel, the development of standards and protocols is moving forward on many fronts and will proceed even more rapidly with the definition of a national system architecture.

Safety and Human Factors

It would be a mistake to forget that the consumer is principally concerned with the personal benefits of a technology, not with issues of integration or standards or possible societal benefits. In the end, consumers will determine the fate of IVHS by voting with their dollars. This suggests that very careful attention be paid to human factors in the design of IVHS hardware and software and public education programs to ease the transition to IVHS. Public agencies, which will buy a substantial amount of IVHS hardware, software, and systems are crucial customers as well.

Institutional and Legal Issues

Deployment is not solely a technical issue. Institutional and legal issues need to be addressed and solved. The institutional and legal issues identified in the *Strategic Plan* that must be addressed include:

- *Legal*—tort liability, antitrust, privacy, procurement, intellectual property, regulatory structure, and jurisdictional authority to develop traffic management;
- *Institutional*—intergovernmental/interagency coordination, changing organizational culture, public-private cooperation, and societal impacts of IVHS.

10.5.4 Roles and Responsibilities of the Participants

Implementing IVHS will require unprecedented cooperation among all levels of government, the private sector, and academia. IVHS can serve as a national model for the deployment of technology-based systems where public and private sector coordination is a central concern. The Strategic Plan outlines the consensus roles and responsibilities of the respective constituents.

IVHS America

A leading role in the design of a national program of IVHS research, development, and deployment will be played by IVHS America, which is the forum where the private and public members of the IVHS community come together to reach consensus and take action to accelerate implementation of the technology. As a Federal Advisory Committee to the Department of Transportation, it will help guide the federal government's IVHS activities and will advise the DOT on establishing program priorities. All of the other constituents described below are represented within IVHS America. More information regarding the role and responsibilities of IVHS America is provided in Section 10.6.3.

Private Sector

The private sector's role in IVHS is fundamental. Industry will make by far the largest investment in IVHS, but only in expectation of profits. The marketing of IVHS products and services is best understood by the private sector, which will develop the technology and market the wide array of products and services that will make IVHS a reality.

IVHS can be a significant business opportunity for automakers and for companies in the electronics, computer, communications, and information industries. The market is not limited to vehicles—for example, hand-held devices will provide a variety of traveler information, including bus schedules, directories of business listings, and tourist attractions. Similar information services could also be provided on home or office computers. Fulfilling IVHS infrastructure needs will also create a large market. Needs in this area include sensors and actuators, beacons, and hardware and software for electronic toll collection and areawide traffic management systems. IVHS could create new roles for the private sector. For instance, the private sector could privately finance and operate a variety of infrastructure services, such as collection of traffic data, if it received a franchise from the appropriate public agencies.

Federal Government

The federal government will provide a national perspective on IVHS. Federal spending, as exemplified by the ISTEA, will be required to catalyze private and local spending. The DOT has the key responsibility for encouraging and coordinating the development of the technology in conjunction with state and local governments, private industry, and academia. The DOT will commission research, fund demonstrations and operational tests, ensure uniformity of evaluations, encourage implementation, and ensure nationwide compatibility of systems when required. The Federal Highway Administration (FHWA) has been designated as the lead agency for the DOT's program. The office of the secretary, as well as other DOT administrations, will also play key roles consistent with their primary responsibilities. Those other key DOT administrations are the National Highway Traffic Safety Administration (NHTSA), the Federal Transit Administration (FTA), and the Research and Special Programs Administration (RSPA). Other federal agencies will also be involved in aspects of IVHS. These include the Federal Communications Commission, the Department of Energy, the Environmental Protection Agency, the Department of Justice, the Department of Defense and the Interstate Commerce Commission.

State and Local Governments

State and local governments are responsible for building, operating, and maintaining surface transportation systems, and for managing traffic. This makes their participation in IVHS crucial to its success. If IVHS is ignored or rejected by local government, it will fail. State governments own the interstate highways, U.S. highways, and state roads. Local governments own arterial highways and local roads. Many transit systems are owned by either state or local government or multijurisdictional agencies. State and local governments will install, maintain, and operate the IVHS infrastructure, or they will possibly contract these functions out to the private sector. Carrying out such programs will require extensive Federal assistance. ISTEA emphasizes the importance of metropolitan planning organizations (MPO) in coordinating regionwide transportation systems. State and local governments in neighboring jurisdictions must find new ways to cooperate in order to develop and deploy IVHS. Moreover, when systems that reach across jurisdictional boundaries are installed, cooperation will be required to operate them—coordinating transportation control operations is just one example of such a requirement. Local governments may also want to use IVHS to promote other transportation-related social, political, or economic objectives.

Academia

Universities must develop new academic programs that will educate a new type of transportation professional, one schooled in the disciplines and concepts fundamental to IVHS. These include, for example, communications, computer science, systems engineering, and institutional studies. Academia must develop new concepts and knowledge germane to IVHS and must integrate new academic disciplines with transportation. The traditional civil engineering transportation program taught in most universities will be simply inadequate to the demands of IVHS. Academia will also help implement and evaluate IVHS, assessing the current state of likely technological improvements and performing basic and applied R&D and operational tests.

Professional Societies

Many professional societies and other organizations will be involved in IVHS. Societies will be primarily responsible for setting standards and protocols and disseminating information through journals and conferences to educate their constituents on IVHS.

10.5.5 Course of Action

As a strategic plan should, the *Strategic Plan* lays out not only what is to be accomplished, but also sets a course of action that will enable the partnership to accomplish it. Table 10.3 summarizes the major near-term actions that will enable the IVHS community to achieve its objectives.

10.6 IVHS AMERICA

As described in Section 10.5.4, IVHS America is the institutional embodiment of the entire community interested in bringing IVHS to the U.S. This section will further highlight IVHS America, how it is organized, and what it is doing to implement the goals and objectives of the *Strategic Plan*.

10.6.1 IVHS America Mission

''Coordinate and foster a public-private partnership to make the U.S. surface transportation system safer and more effective by accelerating the identification, development, integra-

Table 10.3
Near-Term Actions

R&D Through Deployment	*Integration*	*Organizational Program*	*Education and Training*	*Planning*
Provide consistent, dedicated public funding Provide resources for research and development Deploy advanced transportation management centers Test and deploy a prominent set of services and applications Conduct operational tests for vehicle fleet systems	Create well-defined procedures for operational tests and establish tests sites Develop a system architecture Promote standards and protocols Define RF spectrum needs and get appropriate allocation	Address key institutional issues Seek resolution of key legal issues and procurement procedures Pursue international cooperation	Establish university-based IVHS research and education centers Develop the human resources needed to support IVHS Inform the public about progress	Update the *Strategic Plan* and provide advice to DOT Make program recommendations to DOT

tion, and deployment of advanced technology.'' These words were crafted carefully. The notion of *accelerating* the process acknowledges that advanced technologies will continue to become available to the surface transportation field, but that their development and acceptance need to be quickened and coordinated if full benefit—increased mobility, productivity, safety, and energy efficiency—is to be realized. While technology identification, development, integration, and deployment might traditionally be considered issues to be handled in sequence, that approach is no longer acceptable in today's competitive world environment. Just as many U.S. organizations now realize that *concurrent engineering* is essential, IVHS America will provide *concurrent acceleration* by addressing technology identification, development, integration, and deployment issues in parallel.

10.6.2 IVHS America Organization

To perform its mission, IVHS America relies on a volunteer committee structure augmented by a small staff. This section describes the responsibilities of the various committees, as well as the role of volunteers (IVHS America members).

Volunteer Committee Structure

IVHS America has a three-tier committee structure: the board of directors, the coordinating council, and the technical committees (see Figure 10.1).

Board of Directors. Overall direction of IVHS America is vested in the board of directors, elected by the membership. The board deals with broad issues of organization mission and scope, and membership requirements and fees. The board has established three committees: administrative policy and finance, policy planning, and membership. Other ad hoc committees, such as nominating and bylaws, are established as needed. In addition to guiding the business aspects of the society, the board sets the overall strategic policy of the organization and approves and transmits official recommendations to the U.S. DOT.

Coordinating Council. The coordinating council, subject to board approval, defines the strategic objectives and necessary technical activities of the society. Subcommittees of the coordinating council deal with broad issues of concern to the entire membership. The three subcommittees currently in operation are strategic planning, international liaison, and clearinghouse and editorial review.

A major role of the coordinating council is to oversee and coordinate the activities of a varying number of technical committees. These committees are established on an as-needed basis and can be disbanded or integrated into other committees when they have accomplished their objectives. Although referred to as *technical committees,* the scope of these groups is not restricted to strictly technical issues. The chairperson of each of the technical committees serves as a member of the coordinating council. The functions of the coordinating council include:

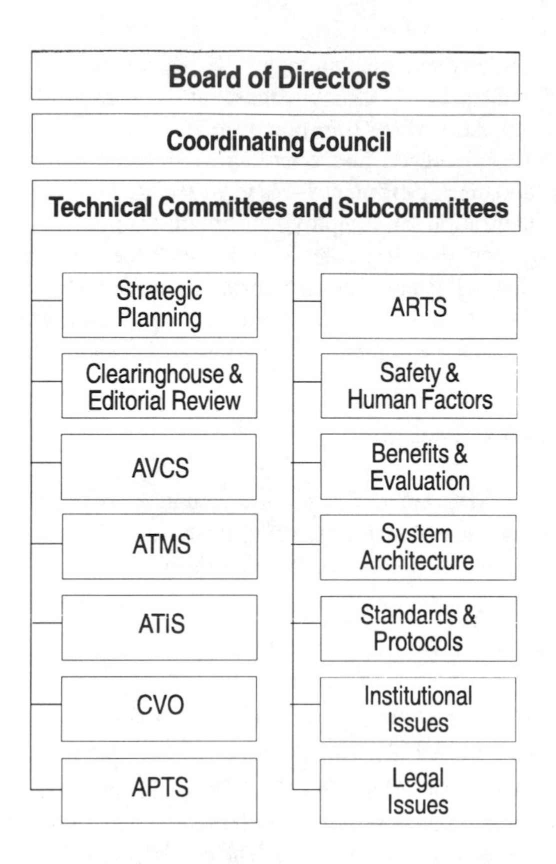

Figure 10.1 IVHS America volunteer committee structure.

- Guides technical committee and subcommittee activity, including:
  - Ensuring that each committee has a clearly defined function and meaningful milestones,
  - Minimizing redundancy and overlap in committee activities, and
  - Ensuring that each committee meets its milestones and responsibilities;
- Recommends Board of Directors' approval of IVHS America consensus resolutions in areas including:
  - Advice to the DOT and
  - Communications with outside organizations (e.g., standards-setting bodies);
- Coordinates activities with other groups, including Technical societies, Trade associations, and Foreign groups.

Technical Committees. Much of IVHS America's value as a public-private partnership is due to its technical committees. Participation in these committees is open to any IVHS America member, from any of the following constituencies: public sector (state, federal and local entities), private sector (individual companies and associations), or universities. Most committees include members from all three types of organization. Each technical committee serves to accelerate the national program by recommending action in their area of expertise, providing feedback on top-down related activities, such as the *Strategic Plan*, and serving as a forum to allow exchange of information and ideas among the IVHS community, which indirectly accelerates IVHS implementation.

The technical committees are reviewed every three years to determine if they should be continued, and, if so, in what form and with what responsibilities. IVHS America currently has 20 technical committees. Each of these committees is composed of volunteers who share an interest, personal, or organizational, in the objectives of the respective committees. Grouping committees according to area of interest has the benefit of enhancing the awareness of individuals across the U.S. of technological solutions to our surface transportation challenges, and motivating committee members, since they are pursuing tasks that they feel are important.

The current set of committees fall into three categories: (1) functional areas, committees that address technologies by logically grouped sets of applications (ATMS, ATIS, AVCS) and/or by specialized user bases (APTS, CVO); (2) cross-cutting, committees that deal with issues of needs and benefits, integration, and deployment that cut across all of the functional areas; and (3) task forces, groups that are shorter in term and concerned with issues requiring specialized attention. Committees in this category are the Evaluation/Benefits Committee, Safety and Human Factors Committee, System Architecture Committee, Standards and Protocols Committee, Institutional Issues Committee, and Legal Issues Committee.

University and Industry Fellows, Loaned Volunteers

To obtain skill and expertise that would not otherwise be possible, IVHS America utilizes university and industry fellows to the greatest extent possible and draws loaned volunteers from the partnership as needed to accomplish specific tasks. Six such volunteers, in addition to regular IVHS America staff, were used to author the *Strategic Plan*. Since IVHS America is an international organization, an exchange of fellows with Europe and Japan is an integral part of the IVHS America program.

10.6.3 Federal Advisory Committee

IVHS America has been chartered by the DOT as a utilized federal advisory committee (FAC). This relationship provides for IVHS America to formally provide advice and recommendations to the DOT regarding national IVHS program needs, goals and objectives, plans, and progress. In this capacity, IVHS America provides a forum for discussion and recommendations on IVHS activities, including the areas of system architecture, standards, human factors, institutional issues, and program priorities. It also assists in ensuring that DOT activities are coordinated with similar activities being conducted outside the DOT. Meetings of IVHS America that wholly or in part are intended to perform as a FAC must meet certain legally established requirements. For these purposes, scheduled meetings of the executive committee and the coordinating council are considered to be FAC meetings unless a specific prior determination is made.

10.6.4 IVHS America Activities

To fulfill the mission described in Section 10.6.1., IVHS America focuses its efforts in the seven areas listed below. Depending on the area, responsibility for program accomplishment lies with either the volunteer committee structure, the IVHS America staff, or a combination of both.

- Program planning;
- System architecture;
- Standards and protocols;
- Institutional and legal;
- National IVHS Information Clearinghouse;
- International liaison; and
- Public awareness and education.

Program Planning

As part of its role as a utilized FAC for the DOT, IVHS America coordinates the planning efforts of the national IVHS program. Each year IVHS America submits a planning report to the DOT. The *Strategic Plan* will be updated biannually. As noted in Section 10.5., the *Strategic Plan* sets out the long-range vision and strategy for identifying technological solutions to our nation's surface transportation problems and challenges and identifies the institutional and legal issues that must be addressed to implement these technologies. A single plan is needed so that new technologies will work within a well-thought-out national infrastructure rather than in piecemeal fashion. The updated *Strategic Plan* will reflect current events and allow the IVHS community to continue to use the *Strategic Plan* as the framework of the national program. In addition, ''tactical'' program recommendations will be submitted to the DOT annually. The tactical plan, based on the current strategic plan, will provide recommendations for federal IVHS research, testing, and deployment programs for the next two fiscal years. This schedule will ensure that these recommendations are available during the DOT's internal planning stages and that this planning can benefit from the expertise represented by IVHS America.

System Architecture

The IVHS America Board of Directors has passed a resolution recommending that the DOT initiate a two-year, approximately $20 million program to develop a national IVHS system architecture using multiple consortia. The DOT began such a program at the end of 1993. A factor driving the recommendation for a consortia approach is that the path taken to develop a sound, open national architecture will be as important as the technical content of the architecture itself. Any architecture must deliver tangible benefits to the users and operators of the surface transportation system. Thus, to achieve both the desired societal (top-down) and user (bottom-up) benefits, the architectural definition process must consider IVHS from both top-down and bottom-up. The traditional domain of system architects and engineers is top-down. In addition to advising on the top-down technical and policy issues, IVHS America will ensure that the bottom-up focus is adequately considered and that the users and operators are involved throughout the program.

Standards and Protocols

IVHS-related standards and protocols are needed to ensure mutual compatibility of systems and subsystems and to speed the development and deployment of new technologies. Such standards are called *enabling* standards. But standards must be developed carefully and methodically to ensure that they do not stifle innovation or creativity. IVHS America members, through the Standards and Protocols Committee, develop recommendations on needed areas of standardization, the priority of these needs, and the preferred standards-setting organization to develop each standard or protocol. Members also actively participate in workshops in many of the areas that will need standardization. These functions are ideal for a public-private partnership in which all vested interests are represented.

Institutional and Legal

Institutional and legal issues are being identified and addressed early in the national IVHS program. Congress therefore included a provision in the ISTEA that the DOT, in cooperation with the Departments of Justice and Commerce, prepare and submit a report on nontechnical constraints by December 1993. This report must address issues of antitrust, privacy, educational and staffing needs, patent, liability, standards, and other constraints regarding the IVHS program, as well as recommend legislative or administrative actions and address ways to further promote industry, state, and local government involvement in the program. IVHS America is assisting in the preparation of this report. A process similar to the one used in developing the *Strategic Plan* may be appropriate. IVHS America serves as the venue and forum for interested parties to assemble and digest the available research and experience regarding nontechnical issues, and develop consensus recommendations for their resolution.

National IVHS Information Clearinghouse

The National IVHS Information Clearinghouse is a legislatively mandated repository for technical and safety data related to IVHS research, development, testing, and deployment.

The Clearinghouse is much more than a database for abstracts of articles and papers on IVHS technologies: it is an information and communication focal point for IVHS America members and others. When fully realized, it will be the central repository of the latest national and international information about IVHS technologies and progress. Member organizations and others (e.g., congressional staff members) will remotely access the Clearinghouse via a desktop computer. Access will be through a local modem or one of several available computer networks. Users will be able to easily browse through the database and conduct searches for information related to their areas of interest.

The National IVHS Information Clearinghouse supports electronic mail communication between IVHS America members and staff. By encouraging an open discussion of all IVHS-related issue—pro or con—the progress toward solving mobility through the application of technology will be accelerated.

International Liaison

IVHS America's primary objective is to enhance the mobility and safety of the surface transportation system in the U.S. However, the U.S. transportation industry does not exist in a vacuum: IVHS-related products and developments abroad (particularly in Europe and Pacific Rim countries) affect U.S. plans for technology development and deployment. Often, the tendency in major new industries is to erect barriers to protect and nurture a burgeoning national supplier base. The U.S. surface transportation system can benefit from the progress that has occurred in international research and development. Conversely by gaining knowledge of and access to international developments, American product and service suppliers have the opportunity to expand their markets. With open availability of foreign progress, international cooperation will also speed deployment of IVHS in the U.S. by eliminating duplication.

Public Awareness and Education

Increased public awareness of the potential for IVHS as a solution to our nation's mobility and safety problems will result in a "demand pull" for IVHS technologies and help ensure adequate funding for deployment. IVHS America is the organization charged with spearheading the public awareness challenge, because it represents all of the primary factions in the surface transportation system: Federal, state, and local transportation agencies, private companies that market or will market advanced technologies, and associations that collectively represent the primary users of our transportation system.

10.7 CONCLUSION

The creation of IVHS America was the organizational response to a national need to have a coordinating mechanism to facilitate the IVHS efforts of industry, university, and government communities. Incorporated in August 1990, IVHS America is a member-oriented organization conducting its work through a three-tiered committee structure. This structure allows for consensus building at all levels of the organization.

The technical committees and subcommittees report to the coordinating council, which oversees the technical activities of the society. The board of directors, charts the overall course for IVHS America's activities and monitors operations. The most important role of IVHS America is its FAC responsibility. As a utilized committee to the U.S. DOT under the Federal Advisory Committee Act, IVHS America responds to specific technical and institutional requests and makes recommendations to the federal government on its IVHS program. As the pace of development and operational tests increases, the coordination role of IVHS will also increase in its public-private responsibilities.

The notion of public-private partnerships to accomplish large complex technological research, development, and deployment activities in the U.S. had not been attempted on large-scale programs prior to the establishment of IVHS America. This partnership, as evidenced by the successful development of the *Strategic Plan*, is functioning as intended.

With participation from all sectors, both domestic and international, IVHS America has been able to bring many independent programs and technologies under the umbrella of a national IVHS program. But just as the initial success of IVHS America was contingent upon the desire of the public and private sectors to work together, the cooperative atmosphere must continue in order to make national IVHS deployment a reality. IVHS America will continue to coordinate and facilitate the program partnership and serve as the linchpin to make this complex technological program happen.

SELECT BIBLIOGRAPHY

Government of the District of Columbia, Department of Consumer and Regulatory Affairs, Business Regulation Administration, *Articles of Incorporation of Intelligent Vehicle-Highway Society of America (IVHS America),* Washington, D.C., August 1991.

Intelligent Vehicle Highway Society of America, *Bylaws of Intelligent Vehicle-Highway Society of America (IVHS America),* Washington, D.C., August 1990.

Intelligent Vehicle Highway Society of America, *Committee Organization and Operating Procedures,* Washington, D.C., June 1991.

Intelligent Vehicle Highway Society of America, *Strategic Plan for IVHS in the U.S.,* Washington, D.C., June 1992.

Intelligent Vehicle Highway Society of America, *IVHS America Five-Year Program Plan (1992–1996),* Washington, D.C., June 1992.

Mobility 2000 Working Group, *Intelligent Vehicle Highway Systems: Advanced Driver Information Systems (ADIS),* Dallas, TX, March 1990.

Mobility 2000 Working Group, *Intelligent Vehicle Highway Systems: Advanced Traffic Management Systems (ATMS),* Dallas, TX, March 1990.

Mobility 2000 Working Group, *Intelligent Vehicle Highway Systems: Automated Vehicle Control Systems (AVCS),* Dallas, TX, March 1990.

Mobility 2000 Working Group, *Intelligent Vehicle Highway Systems: Operational Benefits,* Dallas, TX, March 1990.

Mobility 2000, *Reports on Major Aspects of IVHS,* Texas Transportation Institute, College Station, TX, March 1990.

Office of Technology Assessment, *Advanced Vehicle/Highway Systems and Urban Traffic Problems,* Washington, D.C., September 1989.

U.S. Department of Transportation, Federal Highway Administration, *Charter: Intelligent Vehicle-Highway Society of America* (utilized as an advisory committee), Washington, D.C., March 1991.

U.S. Department of Transportation, Office of the Secretary of Transportation, *Report to Congress on Intelligent Vehicle-Highway Systems,* Washington, D.C., March 1990.

U.S. General Accounting Office, *Traffic Congestion: Trends, Measures, and Effects, GAO/PEMD-90-1,* Washington, D.C., November 1989.

U.S. General Accounting Office, *Traffic Congestion: Federal Efforts to Improve Mobility, GAO/PEMD-90-2,* Washington, D.C., December 1989.

Chapter 11

ADVANCE—The Illinois Dynamic Navigation and Route Guidance Demonstration Program

David E. Boyce, Allan M. Kirson, and Joseph L. Schofer

11.1 INTRODUCTION

In July 1991, the state of Illinois, in conjunction with the Federal Highway Administration, initiated the largest field test of an IVHS conducted thus far. The demonstration program is based on a feasibility study prepared by the principal technical participants in this program, the IVHS Strategic Business Unit of Motorola, Inc., and Northwestern University and the University of Illinois at Chicago, both operating under the aegis of the Illinois Universities Transportation Research Consortium (IUTRC) [1]. The IVHS concept has been named ADVANCE, for Advanced Driver and Vehicle Advisory Navigation Concept. ADVANCE is a public-private sector partnership. The founding partners and their primary responsibilities are listed in Table 11.1. This chapter describes the system design and the activities planned for the field test.

The six-county, 1,200-square-mile Chicago metropolitan area had a population of 7,261,000 in 1990; its outer suburbs continue to grow rapidly. The region's suburbs house 52% of its population and a similar share of its jobs. Suburban auto ownership is high and continues to increase; more than 60% of suburban households own two or more vehicles [2]. During the past decade, the suburban highway infrastructure has remained relatively unchanged. Transit services have expanded and improved substantially and ridership has increased, but the regional transit mode share is only about 4%. As a result, the burden on the roadway system has increased, leading to congestion, delays, accidents, and the consequent environmental impacts. Resources for expanding the suburban highway system are limited; moreover, in the more highly developed suburbs, where congestion is the worst, little land is available for building and expanding highways.

Table 11.1
ADVANCE Partners' Responsibilities

	Responsibilities
Federal Highway Administration	Program evaluation
Illinois Deparment of Transportation	Project management
Motorola	Mobile navigation assistants, RF data communications network
Northwestern University and the University of Illinois at Chicago	Driver recruitment, traffic information center, traffic-related functions

In search of an alternative approach, the Illinois Department of Transportatio (IDOT) and the other participants in this program initiated an exploration of IVHS as a promising option. The logic of this choice was that IVHS might enable more efficien use of the existing highway infrastructure by informing motorists of congestion and roa blockages from accidents and construction, and by helping them to select more desirabl travel choices: alternative, less congested routes, alternative departure times, and mor convenient destinations.

ADVANCE is being implemented in two phases. Phase I will deploy a 20-vehicl test fleet equipped with dynamic route guidance systems, which will interact with a preliminary version of the traffic information center (TIC) through a radio frequency (RF communications network. Phase I is scheduled to be operational by mid 1994. Phase II expected to begin in late 1994, will equip up to 5,000 privately owned vehicles wit dynamic route guidance systems.

In the design phase, FHWA is providing 50% of the funding and IDOT is providin 25%; the remaining 25% is being provided by the universities, Motorola, and other private sector participants. As of late 1992, the following organizations have joined ADVANC by contributing vehicles, equipment, time, or licenses: Nissan, Volvo, Toyota, Saab Ford, General Motors, Peugeot, Mercedes-Benz, the National Center for Supercomputin Applications at the University of Illinois, Sun Microsystems, Navigation Technologies and ETAK.

11.2 OBJECTIVES

In response to the suburban congestion problem, a route guidance concept was develope for a large geographic area served primarily by a network of arterial streets. This settin differs from those of some IVHS demonstrations in that it is not restricted to corrido or freeways. Any action to implement IVHS in this setting is necessarily experimental i nature. The risks involved in new technologies to ameliorate suburban congestion are nc small, and an experimental approach is a logical way to limit those risks. At the same time, it was clear early in our cooperative venture that this experiment would have to be large enough to test the technology in the field and to provide convincing evidence of the value of IVHS in congestion management.

IDOT is responsible for constructing, maintaining, and operating large portions of the highway system in the region. In addition, it works cooperatively with local governments, setting standards, providing funds, and contributing technical advice. Because the primary mission of IDOT is not experimentation, it became important to place the IVHS demonstration in a broader policy context. Accordingly, the following goals were set for this demonstration.

- Improve mobility for travelers in the region;
- Reduce vehicle travel times and operating costs;
- Reduce transportation infrastructure costs;
- Improve highway safety;
- Reduce transportation energy consumption;
- Reduce transportation-generated air pollution and noise.

The specific goals for the demonstration program are twofold. As an operating agency, IDOT seeks to improve traffic operations. In this case, the demonstration is being conducted to evaluate IVHS applications for congestion relief. This evaluation is strongly focused on supporting future choices about IVHS implementation. Its operational objectives are to:

- Evaluate the effect of the IVHS on the behavior and perceptions of highway users;
- Test the effectiveness of a variety of interrelated IVHS components;
- Provide a basis for making decisions about the future deployment of IVHS in Illinois and elsewhere;
- Identify and evaluate transition paths towards operational implementation of IVHS.

11.3 SYSTEM DESIGN

11.3.1 Overview of Configuration

The proposed system will transmit real-time information on the performance of the road network to a fleet of participating vehicles. Equipment on board these vehicles will use this information, along with inputs of trip destination and route preferences from drivers, to develop route guidance instructions dynamically and present them to drivers at appropriate times.

The primary source of real-time road network travel times will be the participating vehicles themselves, functioning as roving traffic probes. An onboard navigation system will monitor each vehicle's position in relation to a detailed road network map and will determine and report point-to-point travel times to a central computer. The onboard system will also include records of average travel times for the network by link and time of day.

Additional road network performance data will come from existing loop detectors on test area freeways and from additional arterial street detectors to be added as part of this demonstration. Qualitative information on short-term incidents (e.g., accidents, breakdowns, and railroad crossings) and long-term obstructions (e.g., lane closures due to construction) will be gathered from emergency and administrative communication channels.

Onboard computers will plan routes to driver-selected destinations with a heuristic operating on a database of historical average travel times by link and time of day. Updated travel times based on probe reports, fixed detector data, and other sources will be transmitted to participating vehicles and used to update their response to real-time traffic conditions. A general diagram of the system is shown in Figure 11.1.

The high-level (level 0) system architecture of ADVANCE incorporates several key concepts: distributed intelligence (all route planning is performed in the vehicle), a hierarchical road network database (for higher performance in all map-related functions), vehicles as traffic probes (for accumulating real-time information), open (nonproprietary) RF data communications protocol, and a driver interface. The system design for ADVANCE has four major components, described below.

Mobile Navigation Assistant

The mobile navigation assistant (MNA) determines the vehicle position using a combination of sensors and a GPS receiver, performs route planning based on current traffic information received via the RF communications network (COM), and provides route guidance information to the driver. It also prepares real-time travel time reports for transmission to the TIC. A single CD-ROM disk in the MNA contains the hierarchical

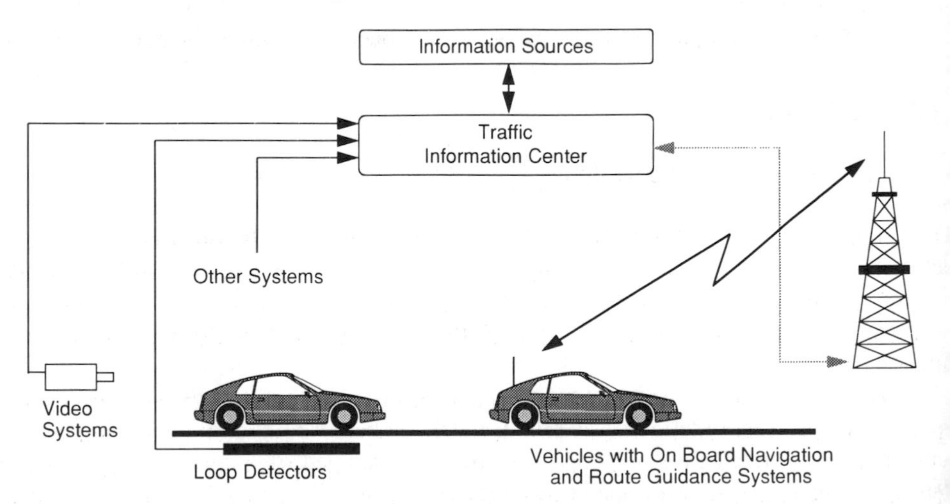

Figure 11.1 System overview (© 1991 SAE; reprinted with permission) [7].

road network database, historical average link travel time profiles, comprehensive business directory listings, and all system software. A memory card is used to accumulate travel patterns, driver behavior, and MNA operating data in real time for a 20% sample of equipped vehicles. These cards will be exchanged periodically to permit processing and archiving of data for evaluation and research.

RF Communications Network

The COM provides two-way radio data communications between the TIC and the MNAs in the vehicles. Travel time, incident, and other pertinent data are broadcast to all vehicles, and each vehicle reports asynchronously and spontaneously on its travel experience according to variable criteria which will permit the most efficient use of the RF communications capacity.

Traffic Information Center

The TIC contains the central computer facilities, the repository of all ADVANCE data, and communication interfaces with the other processes and external entities. It also provides the console system and the IDOT console operator. The traffic-related functions (TRF) described below largely reside here.

Traffic-Related Functions

TRF embodies the traffic and transportation-related data and analytic functions on which ADVANCE is based. The functions of TRF include:

1. Historical link travel time generator: Regularly updated estimates of historical link travel times by time of day, day of week, and season of year;
2. Data fusion processor: Synthesis of probe reports, traffic signal system, and other data with the historical data to provide the best estimates of link travel times for transmission to probes;
3. Incident detection: Identification of abnormal link travel times, not resulting from recurrent congestion, through various data sources, including probes;
4. Short-term travel time forecasting: Estimation of near-term travel times from recurrent patterns of flows, occupancies, speeds, probe reports, and incident information.

The interrelationships among the four components and their relations to external entities from which data are received are shown in Figure 11.2. Additional details of their design are described in the following sections.

11.3.2 Mobile Navigation Assistant

The in-vehicle navigation system performs four functions pertaining to navigation and route guidance. These are illustrated in Figure 11.3 and described below.

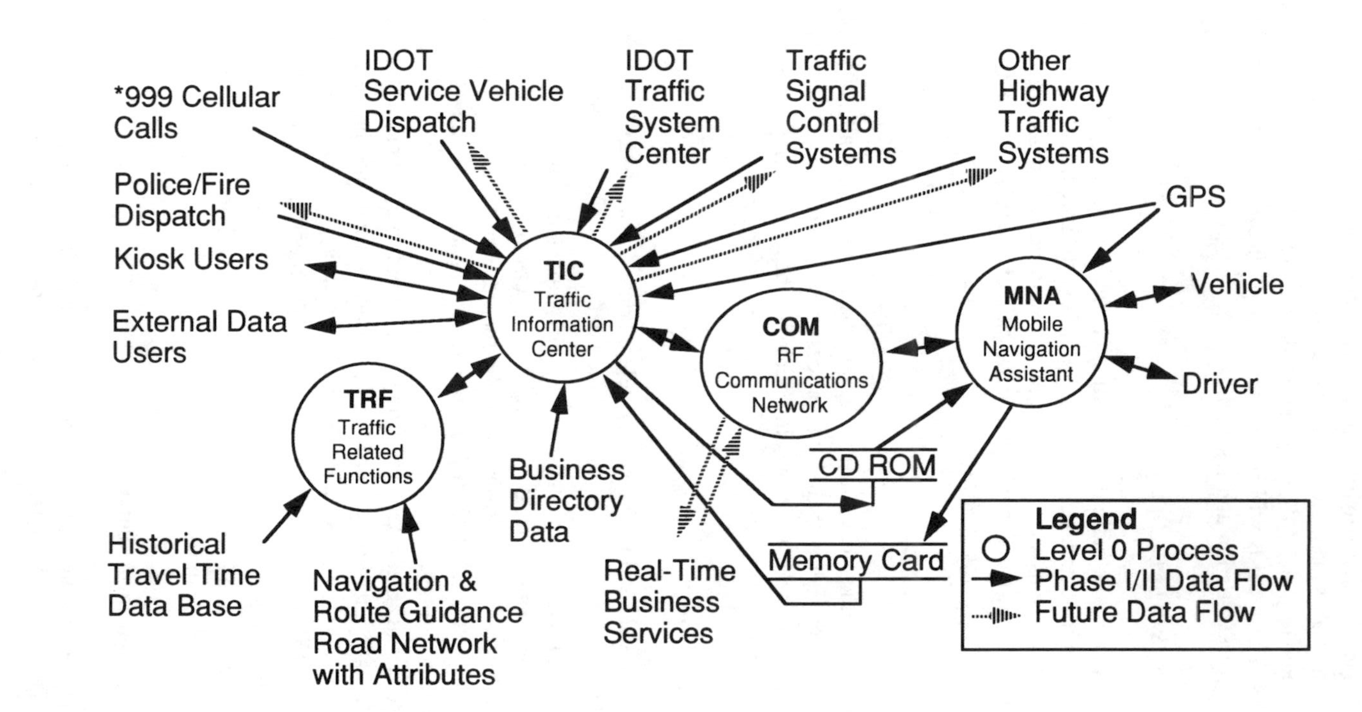

Figure 11.2 High-level system architecture (© 1992 IEEE; reprinted with permission) [6].

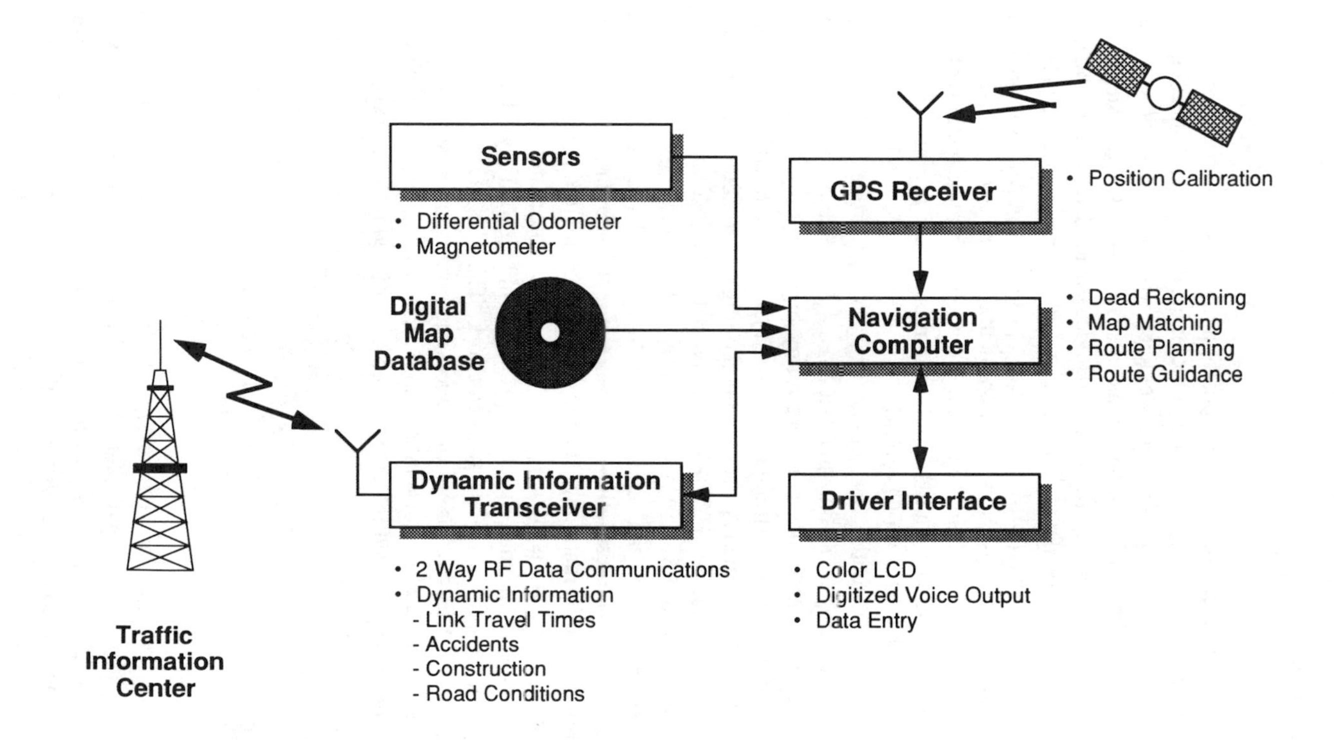

Figure 11.3 In-vehicle system (© 1991 SAE; reprinted with permission) [7].

Position and Location

The navigation system tracks the vehicle's position and location at all times. Position is the latitude, longitude, and elevation of the vehicle; location refers to the segment of the road network. Both are required, since the vehicles will travel on roadways defined in the map database, as well as on unmapped areas such as parking lots and shopping centers. Wheel speed and direction sensors provide the distance traveled, the speed, and the heading inputs used for dead-reckoning navigation calculations, which are relative in nature; based on knowledge of the current position, the new position can be estimated by vector calculations. Dead reckoning is prone to incremental errors due to roadway contours, uneven tire pressure, wheel slip, and so on. To provide an absolute calibration, additional inputs will come from the Navigation Satellite Timing and Ranging GPS receiver and the digital map of the test area on CD-ROM.

The GPS receiver provides one-second updates of latitude, longitude, elevation, speed, and heading as long as its antenna can "see" four or more GPS satellites. Since the test area is suburban and does not have many high-rise buildings, the vehicle will lose GPS signals only when in a structure such as a garage, a wooded area, or on heavily tree-lined roads. If the GPS signal is lost, dead reckoning will maintain the vehicle position and location. An advantage of the GPS input is that it is absolute and can provide a position update even when the vehicle is moved by other means (e.g., a tow-truck).

The CD-ROM contains the digital map which includes detailed information on network structure and traffic restrictions, as well as topological data required for vehicle location detection. This information will be used as another input to determine the location by assuming that the vehicle is traveling on a road and correcting the dead-reckoning calculations accordingly. The map-matching process will be used only when there is high confidence that the vehicle is on the road network. The CD-ROM will also have the capacity to store and retrieve a variety of value-added information services, such as the local business directory, tourist information, and perhaps even event schedules and prices. These services might be provided by third parties and offered to make the IVHS package more appealing to users.

Route Planning

Based on the driver's destination and current traffic conditions as provided by the TIC, the onboard navigation system will plan the optimal route, selected according to the driver's stated preferences (e.g., shortest time, shortest distance, and no expressways). A touch screen keypad and color LCD display will be used to enter the destination in terms of commonly used identifiers (e.g., street name and number), and for issuing commands to the system.

Route Guidance

Once the route has been determined, the system will provide the driver with the appropriate maneuver instructions as the trip progresses using the color display supplemented by a digitized voice output, which utters the route guidance instructions in a timely fashion. Both devices are used to alert the driver to changes in traffic conditions received from the TIC that affect the route selected and to ask the driver if a new route should be planned from the current location.

Driver Interface

The driver is provided a rich set of navigation functions and a carefully designed driver interface for effective use of the system by the novice and seasoned user alike. The interface hardware consists of a 5.7-inch color LCD display with touch screen, a dedicated set of hard keys, and voice input and output for safe and efficient operation of the system. Basic navigation functions are emphasized in simple, uncluttered screen displays, which are generally self-explanatory. Advanced features are hidden from the novice but are easily revealed to the more sophisticated user. Basic functions include an object-oriented electronic map depicting the road network and geographical and travel-related information in a range of scales, augmented with color, text, and graphics. See Figure 11.4.

The novice user specifies a destination by address, road intersection, or from a directory of businesses and other points of interest. The destination is entered by choosing, via the touch screen, from lists of valid inputs, reducing the chance for error. The user

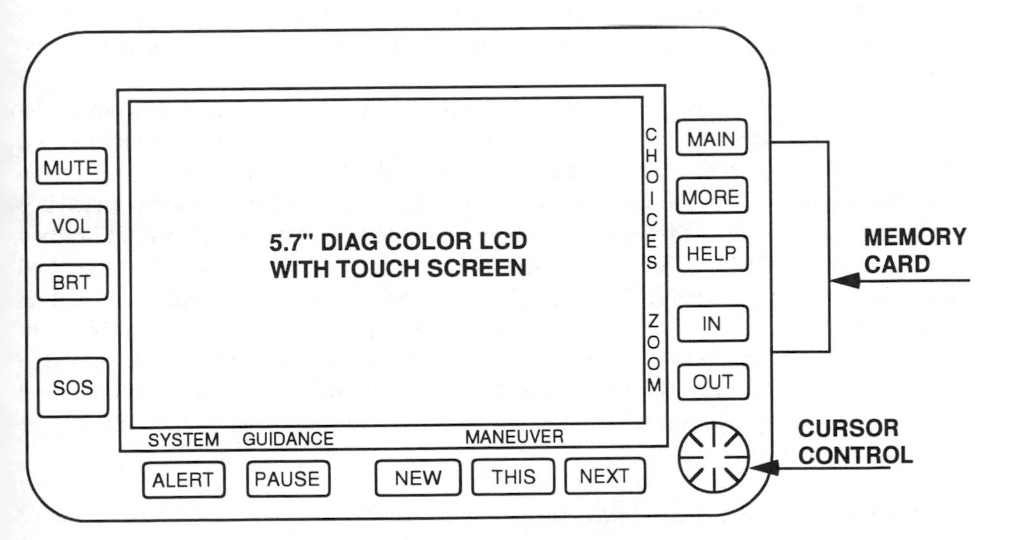

Figure 11.4 MNA driver interface (© 1992 IEEE; reprinted with permission) [6].

can preview the guidance instructions before embarking by using the THIS and NEXT hard keys, and can select one of four guidance formats, including simple abstract graphics, a head-up map, and text. If the driver leaves the prescribed route, instructions are immediately presented to guide the driver back on track. Trip status is available at any time in a display graphically depicting the elapsed and estimated remaining time and distance to the destination. In addition, an intermediate stop can be inserted into the trip at any point en route by first stopping the vehicle, entering the destination, and continuing on.

For the advanced user, a destination can be specified by selecting a point on the map, a recent destination, or an entry from a list of preprogrammed addresses (address book). The user can set up a trip with multiple destinations and save a trip for later recall. The user can specify routing requirements that require or prohibit the use of a particular road in the selection of a route. The user can also elect to avoid freeways, tollways, and particular localities. In addition to finding the fastest route, the user can specify the shortest route or the route with the fewest maneuvers. These preferences can be applied to all trips for a particular driver or to a particular leg of a trip.

The system provides two guidance modes: general and commuter. General mode provides full voice instructions along the one "best" route. In commuter mode, three dissimilar routes are calculated and presented to the driver with time and distance estimates. In both modes, traffic alerts are relayed to the driver, and route diversions are offered whenever significant travel time can be saved. The driver can then request more detail by pressing the ALERT hard key.

At any time during route guidance, the driver can press the NEW hard key to demand that the current instruction be replaced by an alternative. Such action is often necessary to avoid an obstacle, an illegal or unsafe maneuver, or some kind of database error. Of course, the driver can also simply drive off route to avoid the problem, but this action would not prevent the route planner from including the same maneuver in the recovery route.

The SOS hard key is provided on the driver interface to summon emergency assistance via the TIC. After activating the SOS, the user selects the types of assistance desired (tow, fire, ambulance, police). The request is transmitted to the TIC along with the location of the vehicle. Receipt of the message is acknowledged at the vehicle and the assistance dispatched. The design of the human interface to support the system functions described here is the result of extensive work by Motorola, American Institutes for Research, and Aaron Marcus and Associates. The design has evolved over a three-year period based on usability engineering, the testing and evaluation of computer models, and field testing of navigation system prototypes. The implementation of the software for the latest design is now under way. Object-oriented methods are being employed to provide flexibility and software reuse in anticipation of further improvement of the design throughout the course of the ADVANCE program.

11.3.3 RF Communications Network

A dedicated radio frequency communications system will support ADVANCE, receiving the dynamic link time data from probe vehicles and transmitting traffic information to them.

Inbound transmission is spontaneous and based on a contention management protocol; that is, a vehicle will attempt to transmit, and if the channel is being used by another vehicle, will wait and try again later. The outbound transmission is continuous and broadcast to all vehicles, with the data updated at regular intervals. The COM will provide two-way data communications between the computers in the TIC and the vehicles at the rate of 19,200 bps.

11.3.4 Traffic Information Center

The TIC will fuse data from vehicle probes, in-pavement detectors, verbal communications, and eventually incident detection and travel time prediction models to create outbound messages on link travel times and other roadway conditions for transmission to participating vehicles. Figure 11.5 shows a diagram of the TIC. Probe data will be received and integrated automatically, while most voice and text messages from public service agencies and other sources describing short-duration incidents, construction activities, road openings and closures, and important weather information will be entered by a console operator for use in the data fusion process. Traffic-responsive signal systems on a major arterial road will be connected to the TIC by leased telephone lines to permit real-time data acquisition.

The TIC provides all of the centralized computing resources necessary for ADVANCE. Challenges associated with TIC development include hardware configuration design and software development. In addition to the actual software development effort,

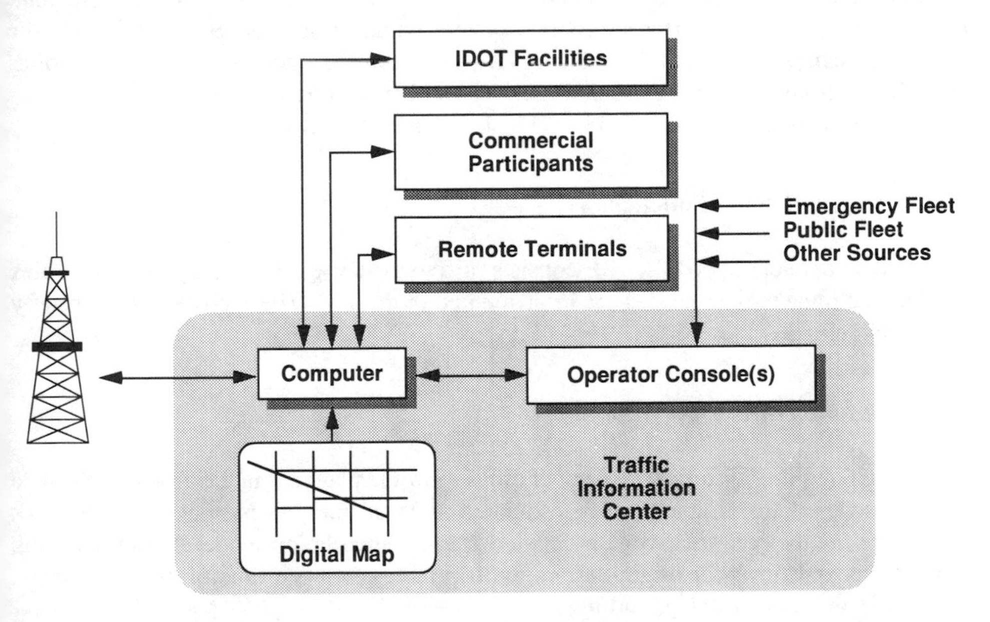

Figure 11.5 Traffic information center (© 1991 SAE; reprinted with permission) [7].

the selection of appropriate software development methods has also been an important technical decision.

The TIC hardware platform will be a high-end UNIX workstation. Primary considerations leading to this decision included price/performance ratios, scalability of computing resources, rich software development environments, software portability, ease of networking, and the availability of several UNIX hardware vendors. Sun Microsystems has been selected as the workstation vendor. Secondary considerations for selecting a UNIX workstation as the TIC platform pertain to software reuse. Although the ADVANCE TIC software is unique, the development of certain modules and components may benefit from using commercial software packages (e.g., database management systems and graphical user interface libraries). In addition to reusing commercial software packages in developing the TIC software, this hardware platform selection will more easily allow others to reuse portions of the TIC software in other ATIS demonstrations.

TIC functionality has been grouped into five categories: database(s), TIC-MNA communication interfaces, other TIC communication interfaces, user interfaces, and TIC data analysis. The TIC will contain a set of databases that will store vast amounts of ADVANCE information including current and historical probe link travel times, current and historical expressway detector data, and current and historical selected arterial detector data. In addition to traffic data, TIC databases will contain current and historical network event information (e.g., road and lane closures), a description of the roadway network, and a current fused data view of network conditions.

TIC communication interfaces include both the TIC-MNA interface and other TIC communication interfaces for transmission and receipt of data. User interfaces include functionality for both operator access and system administrative access. Additional user interfaces include providing ADVANCE partners with remote access, and later providing unequipped drivers with route planning services and current network travel time information for the ADVANCE test area using kiosks in public places.

11.3.5 Traffic-Related Functions

The TRF component of ADVANCE consists of four processes. The first process operates off line; the remaining processes are implemented in the TIC. These processes are briefly described below.

Historical Link Travel Time Generator

ADVANCE requires historical link travel times for route planning in the absence of traffic anomalies. These travel times will be estimated in an offline process that uses a network description of the test area, with a detailed static route choice model to estimate link travel times and flows for origin-destination trip tables for each time of day: a.m. peak, mid-day, p.m. peak, evening, and night.

Traffic delay functions incorporated into the model are specific to turning-movements and signal control parameters. Link travel time estimates are expected to be as accurate as can be obtained, given the state of the art of network modeling. These link times will be field-validated with data collected by probe vehicles.

Data Fusion Processor

The primary functions of the data fusion processor are as follows.

- Manage raw travel time data received at TIC from real-time sources, such as probe vehicles, flow/occupancies from freeway and closed-loop system induction loop detectors, and various anecdotal data sources.
- Provide specifications for filter and exception rates on inbound probe reports when the RF channel capacity is approached.
- Provide algorithms for fusing online and offline travel time data, with the goal of generating the expected link travel times. Fusion activities will be carried both on line and off line, with the latter aimed at updating the link profiles.
- Pass raw and processed traffic data to the incident detection and travel time forecasting algorithms in TIC.

The activity of combining and processing real-time data from different sources is called *online data fusion* and will be performed continuously 24 hours a day. Since travel times estimated by considering several independent sources are likely to be more accurate than travel times estimated from a single source [3], data fusion is critical for a traffic information processing system. Two such systems, Pathfinder and TravTek, the first two implementations in the U.S., used fuzzy logic in their implementation of data fusion [4]. This approach, although successful, nevertheless lacked the capability to recognize the interdependence of traffic flow along related road segments. Artificial neural network models are being considered for their ability to learn the interconnections between different road segments and to estimate the quality of the different data sources dynamically.

Incident Detection

The objective of the incident detection system is to identify nonrecurring, capacity-reducing incidents on the roadway network in the test area. The ADVANCE concept has three distinct components, as depicted in Figure 11.6. *Real-time data sources* will provide macroscopic flow characteristics (e.g., volume and occupancy) as well as microscopic parameters (e.g., travel times and observed traffic problems). Three *incident detection algorithms*, each for a specific data type, will independently determine the likelihood that incidents are occurring at particular locations. *Data fusion process* will integrate the information provided by the separate detection algorithms to determine overall incident likelihood at a location. Three types of real-time traffic data sources, described below, will be used for incident detection.

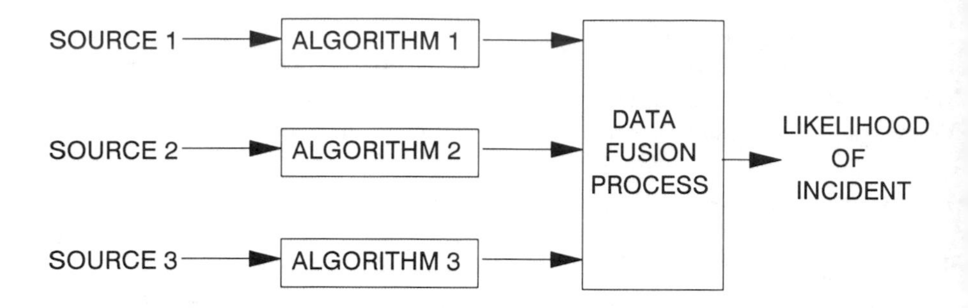

Figure 11.6 ADVANCE incident detection concept (© 1992 IEEE; reprinted with permission) [6].

- *Fixed detectors* provide periodically updated flow data for sections or points on a roadway. Fixed detectors include inductive wire loops embedded in the pavement and perhaps automated video surveillance systems.
- *Probe vehicles* are mobile sources with the potential to cover all links in the network, although the sampling rate for low-volume links may not be sufficient to provide reliable information.
- *Anecdotal sources* are eyewitness accounts of traffic problems provided by travelers or service workers. Sources of such information include emergency dispatch reports (police, ambulance, etc.), possibly through linkage with computer-aided dispatching systems; reports from cellular or roadside phones; IDOT emergency patrol vehicle reports; and construction reports and planned road closings. These sources can be descriptively rich, including the nature and magnitude of the incident.

Each incident detection algorithm will monitor data from one source type and determine incident likelihood by location. These likelihoods will be inputs to the incident detection data fusion process, which will determine an overall incident likelihood by location. Existing algorithms, such as the California family of fixed detector algorithms will be used, as they are applicable; where necessary, new algorithms (e.g., for anecdotal data) are being developed.

Short-Term Travel Time Forecasting

The MNA provides the driver with routes that attempt to minimize a function of origin-destination travel time. To compute such routes, it needs link travel times, but these times need to be for the (clock) time period when the vehicle actually traverses the link. Since desirable routes must be provided when the driver asks for them, but the computation of such routes requires travel times which occur later, it is necessary to forecast travel times.

These forecasts will have a very short horizon; that is, the most useful ones will be for no more than an hour into the future. Two types of forecasts are contemplated: static and dynamic. Static forecasts are based on historical data and make use of the observation that travel times on a link are usually similar for the same type of day at the same time of day. Dynamic forecasts use travel time information broadcast from the TIC to improve static forecasts. If for any reason dynamic forecasts cannot be provided, the MNA will default to static forecasting.

To construct static forecasts, days need to be classified by type. It appears that Sunday, Saturday, other holidays, Fridays, and other weekdays may be an adequate classification. Weather and seasons also need to be accounted for. Links, too, need to be classified. Variations of volumes on links are frequently determined by surrounding land uses. Therefore, the number of classes of links would necessarily be large. For each type of day, weather condition, and link type, link travel time information would be stored in the MNA and would provide the static forecasts.

While such static forecasts are quite good during weekends and off-peak times, their ability to predict peak period travel times is quite poor. Therefore, dynamic forecasts are desirable. In principle, future traffic conditions on any link in a network are largely the result of current conditions on upstream links, and therefore such forecasting should be possible. Various time series techniques such as ARIMA models, transfer functions, and Kalman filtering are being explored as techniques for dynamic forecasting.

A crucial problem that will be addressed as part of short-term travel time forecasting is the adjustment of forecasts for incidents. This adjustment will depend on the outcome of incident detection and will rely on predictions of when an incident would be cleared and its effects on travel times on surrounding links.

11.4 DESIGN OF THE DEMONSTRATION

The ADVANCE project will implement, test, and evaluate a large-scale route guidance system in a suburban area near Chicago. Analyses undertaken to date are concerned with the location of the test area, determination of the required number of probes, development of the driver recruitment plan, and design of the evaluation. These analyses are now briefly described.

11.4.1 Location of the Test Area

The test area for the demonstration was chosen to meet the following requirements:

- The road network should have numerous alternative routes from origins to destinations.
- Travel demand on the road network should be heavy, resulting in congestion levels for which contemporary traffic signal control systems are inadequate.
- Many trips should begin and end within the area during the peak periods, with typical journey times long enough to make route diversion a real option (e.g., 20 to 30 minutes).

- The area should be typical of modern suburban developments, with large, widely dispersed employment sites interspersed with extensive residential areas.

These criteria led to the identification of a suburban area served primarily by a high-quality arterial road network in suburban Cook County, northwest of the city of Chicago (see Figure 11.7). This area is served by a grid arterial highway system overlaid by several northwest-southeast diagonal roads, which pose challenging signal control problems. The area, which includes O'Hare International Airport, has experienced substantial employment growth since 1970 in the form of light manufacturing, office centers, regional shopping centers, and subregional government centers. Office employment expansion continues to overload an already congested road network. Most employees in the test area live in

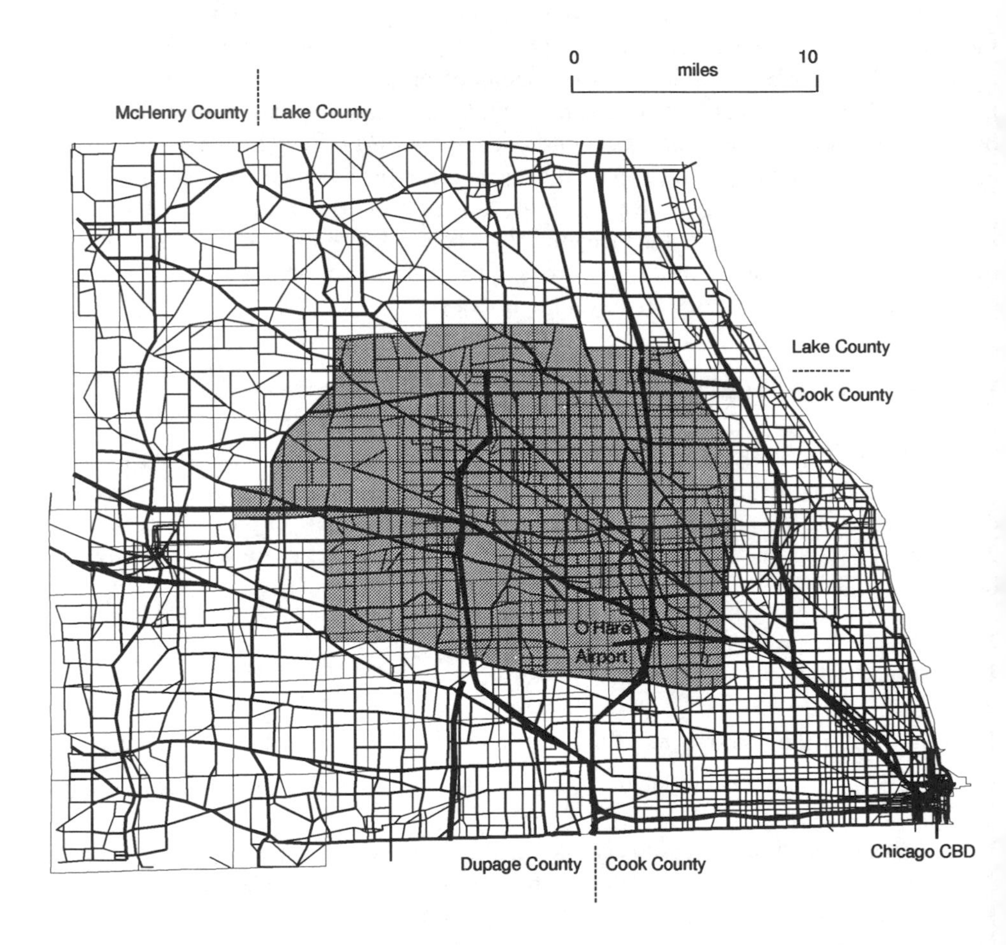

Figure 11.7 ADVANCE test area. Freeway, major arterial, minor arterial, and collector links north and west of Chicago central business district; shaded area is 280 square miles.

low-density, suburban, single-family, house and apartment developments throughout the Chicago suburbs.

11.4.2 Probe Requirements

The principal innovation of the dynamic route guidance system in ADVANCE is the use of vehicles equipped with navigation systems to monitor travel times over network links. The success of this approach depends on having a sufficient number of equipped vehicles in the traffic stream to provide reasonably timely information about conditions on the network. The number of vehicles required was estimated with network analyses of route choices of drivers over a 2,500-link network serving a 450-square-mile area from which the test area was later delimited [5].

By analyzing the pattern of peak-period travel for a typical weekday, relationships were estimated between the number of equipped vehicles and the number of links traversed by one or more vehicles in each time period of 5, 10, 15, or 20 minutes. Each curve in Figure 11.8 relates the number of equipped vehicles to an observation period of specified length for a given proportion of links traversed at least once. The number of vehicles required to monitor (travel over) a given percentage of links at least once decreases as the observation period lengthens: for example, if link travel times are to be monitored every 10 minutes, more equipped vehicles are needed than if the observation period is every 20 minutes. Similarly, more vehicles are needed to monitor 60% of the links every 10 minutes than would be needed to traverse only 30% of the links every 10 minutes.

The tradeoffs between the number of equipped vehicles (an important cost factor) and the quality (i.e., frequency and extent of coverage) of travel time data led to a judgment that between 4,000 and 5,000 vehicles will need to be equipped for this program. Excluding local streets in the test area network, analyses estimated that during a weekday peak period, at least 70% of links can be monitored every 10 minutes with 5,000 vehicles.

The probe traversal analysis also contributes to estimating RF demand. A worst case scenario for RF demand occurs when probes generate reports each time they encounter an intersection (i.e., following each link traversal). The mean link traversal per minute computed is for a typical 10-minute period for 5,000 probes. Multiplying the mean link traversals per minute times the number of links gives the number of link traversals per minute; in this case, 317 arterial link transversals per minute for 5,000 probes operating over the network. Thus, 317 arterial link probe reports per minute may be expected for this RF demand scenario. The relationship between number of links traversed per minute and number of probes reporting is shown in Figure 11.9 for arterials, freeways and ramps, and total links.

11.4.3 Driver Recruitment

The ADVANCE project will require about 5,000 drivers willing to have MNAs installed in their vehicles for the duration of the test. The recruits will comprise a mix of private drivers and commercial fleet vehicles (e.g., local delivery fleets, public service fleets such

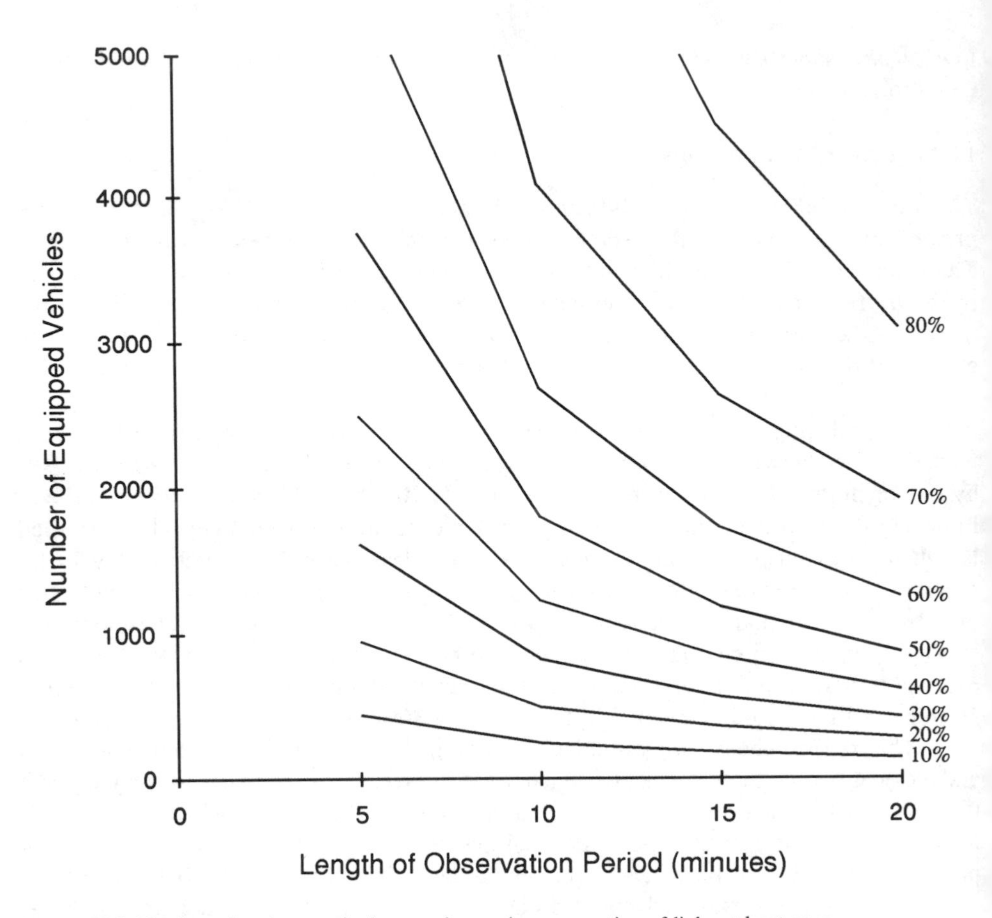

Figure 11.8 Number of probes required to monitor a given proportion of links at least once.

as police or fire, and taxis and limousines). To provide an informed basis for designing the recruitment effort, market research studies were conducted to assess the recruitability of private drivers and fleet operators.

Different recruitment processes must be defined for private drivers and fleet operators: private driver recruitment must aim at individuals, while involving fleet drivers requires the recruitment of organizations. Fleet operators have standard institutional practices, and their willingness to participate may depend on those practices. On the other hand, private driver willingness will be affected by individual characteristics and travel patterns.

Private Driver Recruitment

Private driver recruitment plan objectives are (1) to identify factors affecting driver participation in the test, (2) to design the field recruitment procedure, and (3) to contribute

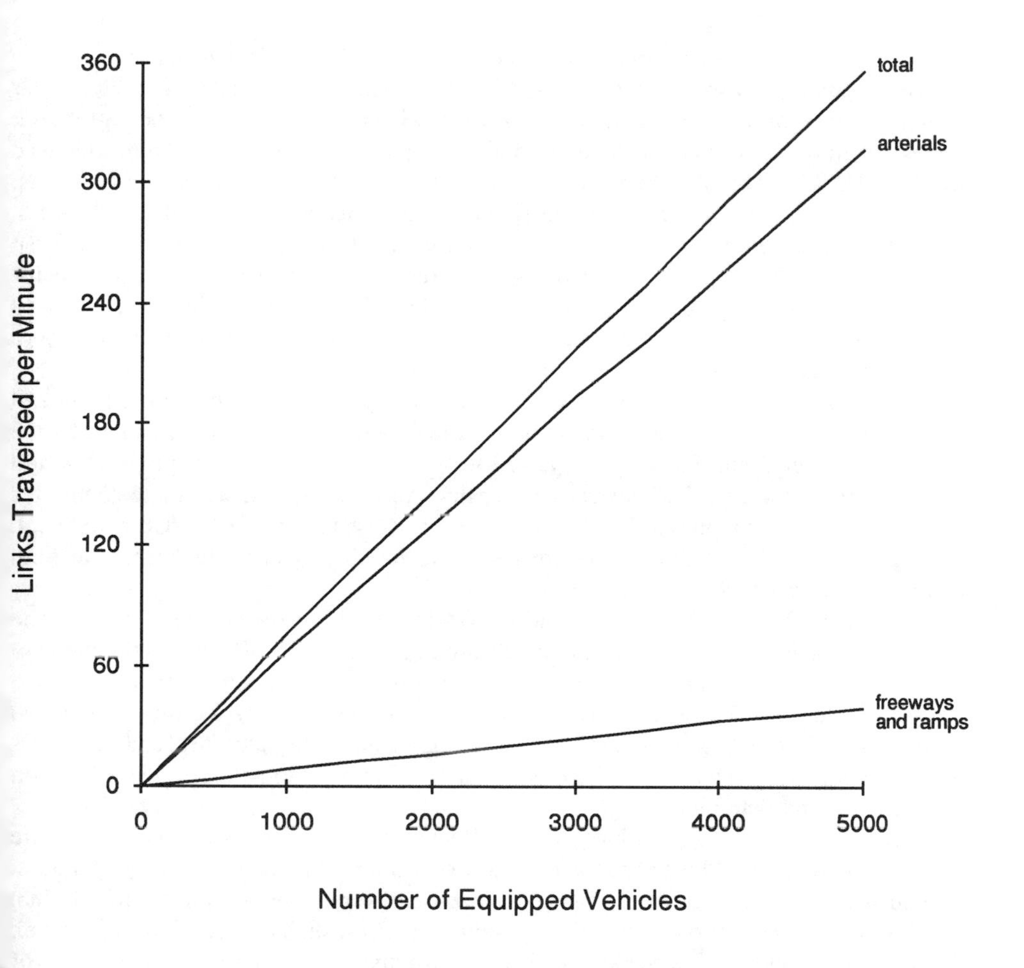

Figure 11.9 RF demand in link traversals per minute (© 1992 IEEE; reprinted with permission) [6].

to the design of the ADVANCE field test. The first step towards achieving these objectives was to conduct focus group interviews and telephone surveys to determine driver expectations of the ADVANCE concept, measure the willingness of drivers to participate in the test, explore variations in that willingness among different types of drivers, and investigate the effect of promised and potential characteristics of the ADVANCE system on that willingness.

Twenty-two persons, representing a cross section of study area drivers, participated in the focus group interviews. The major areas of discussion were driving habits, problems with traffic congestion, expectations for ADVANCE, interest in field trial participation, and responses to factors that influence the decision to participate.

Participants expressed a positive response to the ADVANCE navigation and route guidance features, but some felt that these features would not be valuable for their regular commute, since they were already quite familiar with the area and their home-to-work routes. There was a stronger positive reaction to the prospect that dynamic route guidance from ADVANCE would help them avoid unexpected delays due to traffic incidents. Participants stressed that unexpected delays have a significant impact on their schedules, and thus information that would help them avoid such delays would be a valuable benefit of ADVANCE. Participants also expressed interest in the business listing feature for identifying and locating businesses and recreational services. Some participants, primarily women, suggested that the navigation feature of ADVANCE would make them feel more secure, particularly when traveling in unfamiliar areas.

Among the negative reactions were the possibility of distraction while driving and the resulting safety risks, and the threat of electrical damage to the vehicle caused by the ADVANCE equipment. Participants wanted to know if the ADVANCE program would reimburse them for electrical failures and repairs. Another concern was the potential for increased risk of car theft and vandalism due to the presence of ADVANCE equipment. Finally, people voiced a broad concern regarding liability issues with respect to both equipment and car theft and damage.

The results of the focus group interviews contributed to the design of a telephone survey undertaken to produce quantitative information on factors affecting willingness to participate. A random sample of 1,000 study area drivers with access to cars, controlled for gender and employment status, was interviewed. The survey instrument covered individual characteristics, including sociodemographic attributes, attitudes, and travel patterns; perceptions of the ADVANCE concept; and willingness to participate as a function of incentives and deterrents.

Results show that gender has a strong effect on participation, with men being more inclined to participate. Older respondents were less willing to participate than younger ones. Individuals who held executive or managerial positions were more likely to participate than persons in other occupations. Other demographic variables, such as income and education, did not significantly influence inclination to participate. Familiarity with and use of personal computers and car telephones had a positive effect, and people who frequently listened to radio traffic reports were also more inclined to participate. Auto use and travel patterns did not affect intention to participate significantly. Individuals who were positively disposed in their beliefs about the value of ADVANCE features were more likely to be willing to participate. Figure 11.10 shows the variations in stated willingness to participate on a scale from 1, for "definitely no," to 4, for "definitely yes," across the scenarios described below.

Initial Willingness to Participate

Willingness given these requirements or incentives.

- Respond to surveys every three months.
- Bring car to central facility for service every three months.

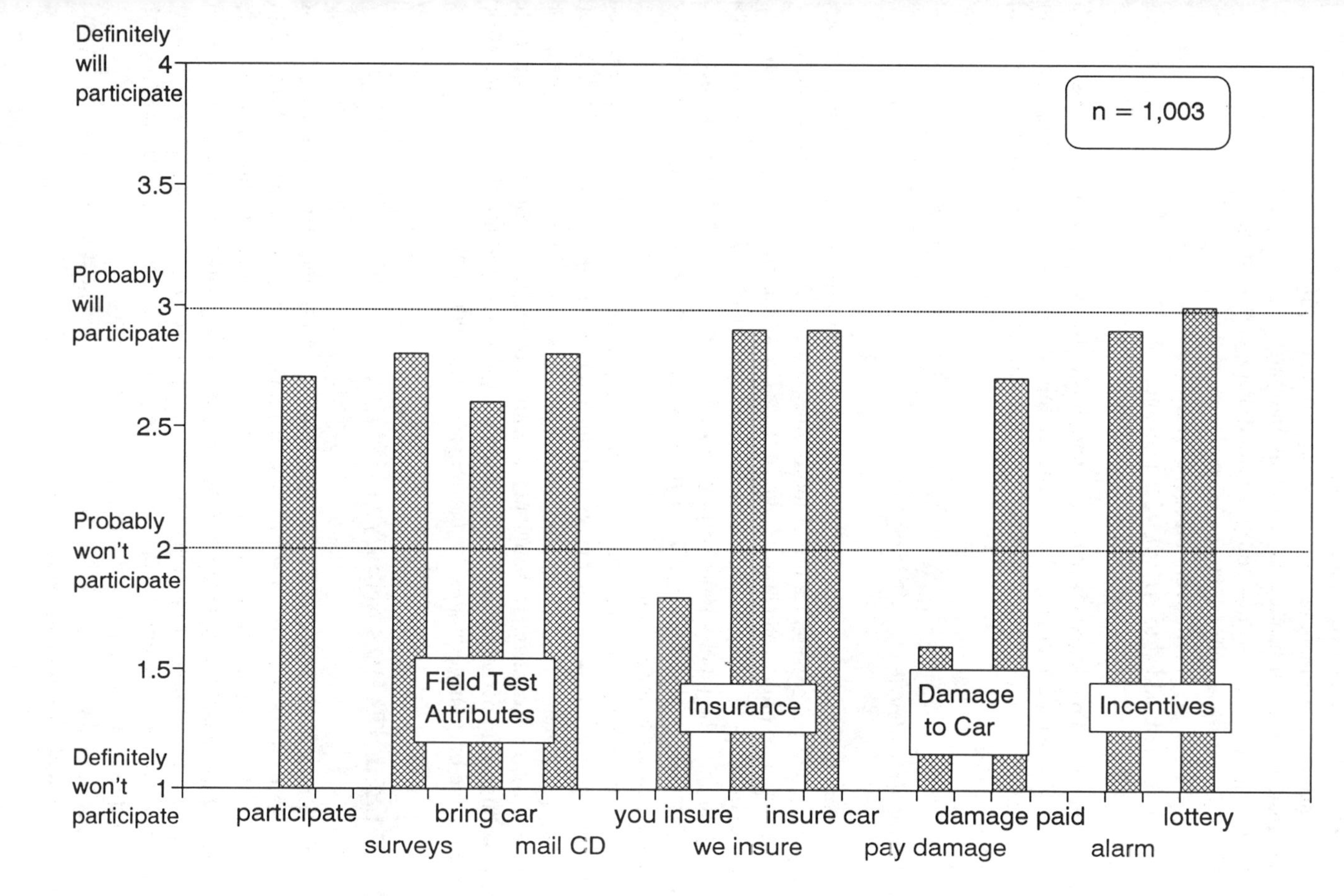

Figure 11.10 Effects of requirements and incentives on willingness to participate in ADVANCE (© 1992 IEEE; reprinted with permission) [6].

- Mail CD-ROM disk every three months.
- You insure: driver pays insurance for ADVANCE equipment.
- We insure: program insures ADVANCE equipment.
- Insure car: program insures equipment and damage risk to car.
- Pay damage: driver pays cost of electrical risk to car.
- Damage paid: program covers electrical risk.
- Car theft alarm added to ADVANCE package.
- Lottery: one in 250 chance of winning $500 for participating.

While willingness to participate is not overwhelmingly strong, it varies substantially with incentives and discouragements. The results of this survey provide a strong basis for designing a recruitment effort that will balance representativeness, network coverage, and sufficiency of fleet size.

Fleet Driver Recruitment

Fleet operators utilize their vehicles differently than most private drivers. For example, delivery, taxi, and police vehicles travel more miles per day than private cars, and so the fleet contribution to probe vehicle coverage of the ADVANCE network could be substantial. On the other hand, some of these vehicles make frequent and extended stops, which will make their probe reports more difficult to interpret. To weigh these tradeoffs, and to determine the value of ADVANCE to fleet operators, it will be important to include such organizations in the field test.

Fleet recruitment focuses on organizations rather than drivers. Criteria for selection of candidate organizations include extent and intensity of activity within the ADVANCE area, operating patterns (including stopped versus in-motion time), vehicle types, and variety of mission. Contacts are being made with public and private fleet operators to determine interest in participation, participation requirements, and limitations. This effort will then move on to negotiations for participation and recruitment.

11.5 IMPLEMENTATION AND EVALUATION

ADVANCE is a large and complex project encompassing the development and field testing of many ATIS concepts: the efficacy of probe vehicles to collect real-time data, reliance on RF communications, sophisticated onboard navigation and route planning systems, and advanced traffic analysis functions, including automated incident detection and short-term travel time prediction. The nature of the concepts to be tested mandates a large-scale field test involving 5,000 private and fleet vehicles, which in itself presents significant design, recruitment, and management challenges.

To get full value from this effort, a comprehensive evaluation plan is being devised, structured around eleven objectives, covering:

- Performance of probe vehicles as data sources;
- Usefulness of the information products produced by the TIC and MNAs;
- Effectiveness and safety of the in-vehicle human-machine interface;
- Effectiveness of the RF communications system;
- Performance of the TIC;
- Effects on driver route choice, travel behavior, and perceptions;
- Contributions to travel time and travel distance reductions;
- Benefit-cost projections for high levels of market penetration;
- Implications for learning about IVHS;
- Overall safety impact of the program.

Methods for evaluating ADVANCE against each of these objectives, and over 50 subobjectives, are being developed by the partners in cooperation with Mitre Corporation, the FHWA evaluation contractor, and Parsons DeLeuw, Inc., the ADVANCE systems integration and project management consultant.

Perhaps the greatest challenge to implementation is the integration of the parallel efforts of the four partners and their advisors to bring together a working product that will meet the route guidance needs of participating drivers and provide a strong basis on which to found future IVHS development.

ACKNOWLEDGMENTS

The authors thank the Federal Highway Administration, the U.S. Department of Transportation, and the Illinois Department of Transportation, as well as their respective organizations for the financial support of the ADVANCE project. This chapter is based in part on two papers presented at the Vehicle Navigation and Information Systems Conferences in 1991 and 1992. We wish to acknowledge the following for their contributions to this chapter through the preparation of those papers: B. C. Smith, Motorola; C. Bhat and F. S. Koppelman, Northwestern University; J. E. Hicks, K. Mouskos, P. C. Nelson, N. Rouphail, and A. Sen, University of Illinois at Chicago.

REFERENCES

[1] Boyce, D. E., J. L. Schofer and A. M. Kirson, "Scope, Feasibility and Cost of a Dynamic Route Guidance System Demonstration," Report prepared for the Illinois Department of Transportation by the University of Illinois at Chicago, Northwestern University, and Motorola, August, 1990.

[2] Prevedouros, P. D., and J. L. Schofer, "Demographics, Social, Economics and Cultural Factors Affecting Suburban Congestion, Report prepared for the Illinois Department of Transportation by Northwestern University, January, 1990.

[3] Luo, R. C., and M. G. Kay, "Multisensor Integration and Fusion in Intelligent Systems," *IEEE Transactions on Systems, Man, & Cybernetics*, Vol. 19, No. 5, 1991, pp. 901–931.

[4] Sumner, R., "Data Fusion in Pathfinder and TravTek," Vehicle Navigation and Information Systems Conference Proceedings, P-253, 71–75, 1991.

[5] Hicks, J. E., D. E. Boyce and A. Sen, ''Static Network Equilibrium Models and Analyses for the Design of Dynamic Route Guidance Systems,'' Technical report in support of the design phase of the ADVANCE Project, Illinois Department of Transportation, University of Illinois at Chicago, October, 1992.

[6] Kirson, A. M., et al., ''The Evolution of ADVANCE,'' Third International Conference on Vehicular Navigation and Information Systems, Conference Record of Papers, Catalog No. 92-CH 3198-9, pp. 516–23.

[7] Boyce, David E., Allan M. Kirson, and Joseph L. Schofer, ''Design and Implementation of ADVANCE,'' Vehicle Navigation and Information Systems Conference Proceedings, P-253, Part 1, No. 912786, pp. 415–26.

Chapter 12
The Michigan Initiative

Kan Chen, David M. DeVaughn, James G. Kavalaris, Robert E. Maki, and Kunwar Rajendra

12.1 INTRODUCTION

Because of the dominant role that motor vehicles play in North America's total transportation system, maintaining and improving highway travel safety and efficiency has been a continuing concern at all levels of government. In the United States, this concern has historically been most prevalent within southeast Michigan due to both its position as a manufacturing center and home state for America's automotive industry and its international seaway location yielding easy access to the world's major industrial and commercial markets. One-half of the United States' manufacturing activities and most Canadian economic activities (accounting for two-thirds of their gross national product) are located within 500 miles of the greater Detroit area.

Because Detroit is one of Michigan's economic focal points and one of the most heavily traversed international border crossing areas in the U.S., efficient and cost-effective transportation within the metropolitan area is critical. The recent passage of a free-trade agreement between the U.S. and Canada has heightened the importance of this area. Increasing traffic congestion problems could have a negative impact on this market's vitality.

The Michigan Department of Transportation (MDOT) reports that vehicle miles of travel (VMT) on all roads within the state has grown by over 250% since 1960. More recently, MDOT's Bureau of Transportation Planning forecasted VMT on freeways to grow 60% from 1988 to 2010, even though Michigan's population is expected to increase only slightly during this time period. This would require more than 680 additional lane miles of freeway to avoid unacceptable levels of service on much of the system if new construction was the only alternative available. (Level of service (LOS) is a qualitative rating in terms of operating conditions of the effectiveness of a highway or highway facility in serving traffic.)

It is not surprising that MDOT pioneered testing and deployment of electronics and control technologies to monitor highway traffic conditions and to convey relevant information to the driver. MDOT has continued to take action by embracing a new IVHS program using the latest methods and technologies. Starting with the Lodge Freeway Television Surveillance Project in the mid 1950s and continuing with the Surveillance Control and Driver Information (SCANDI) system in the late 1970s, MDOT has implemented inductive loop detectors, remote-controlled television monitors, emergency telephones, ramp metering, and changeable message signs (CMS) to help prevent gridlock [1]. Independent of these efforts by MDOT, Michigan vehicle manufacturers started conducting their own automated highway studies in the 1950s and have continued this research ever since, especially at General Motors.

When the most recent international IVHS movement finally accelerated in the late 1980s, there was a significant difference between it and earlier work on automated highway and electronic traffic management. The new efforts include close cooperation and coordination of related efforts between the public and private sector, with academia playing a facilitating role to provide a mutual meeting ground. *The Michigan Initiative* was born in 1987 when MDOT and the Big Three automakers agreed to become the first cosponsors of an IVHS program centered at the University of Michigan. In fact, the University of Michigan coined the term *intelligent vehicle-highway systems* to name this newly formed program and to signify its close coupling between the vehicle and highway as a total system (hence the hyphen between vehicle and highway).

12.2 THE UNIVERSITY OF MICHIGAN IVHS PROGRAM

12.2.1 Overview

Since the University of Michigan IVHS program was formally established in May 1988, over 35 organizations from around the world have sponsored its activities through financial, equipment, and professional time contributions. These include government agencies at all levels; large and small companies from automotive, electronics, and other industries; diverse user groups; and various research institutes as listed below. The asterisk indicates 1991 sponsors.

- Federal/National Government: the Federal Highway Administration,* National Highway Traffic Safety Administration, Federal Transit Administration,* and Canadian Department of Transportation (Transport Canada);
- State/Provincial Government: the Michigan Department of Transportation* and Ministry of Transportation—Ontario;*
- Local Government: the Road Commission for Oakland County, Michigan,* and Ann Arbor Transportation Authority (AATA);

- Research Institutes: the Environmental Research Institute of Michigan (ERIM);
- Users: the American Automobile Association (AAA), United Parcel Service (UPS),* and Yellow Freight;
- Automotive Manufacturers: General Motors,* Ford,* Chrysler,* Toyota,* Nissan,* Hyundai,* and Motor Vehicle Manufacturers Association,*
- Automotive Suppliers: Allied Signal, DuPont Automotive, GE Automotive, IMRA America,* Rockwell, and 3M;
- Electronics Industry: Motorola,* Matsushita,* Sumitomo,* Siemens,* Digital Equipment, ETAK,* RVSI, and Trimble;*
- Systems: Lockheed,* Martin Marietta, and Westinghouse.*

Those who pay an annual fee ranging from $5,000 to $20,000, depending on their annual revenue or budget, are involved as affiliates to help the program's planning and development. Those who pay $50,000 per year serve as members of the Industrial Advisory Board (IAB) and guide the program's basic research direction. Some large organizations, including the Michigan Department of Transportation, are both IAB members and affiliates. In addition to these sponsors' fees, the University of Michigan program also receives research contracts and education grants on a competitive basis. As a result, resources available to the program have grown from $250,000 per year in 1988 to almost $2.5 million per year in 1992.

With the advice and commitments of all sponsors, the following features, known as the *six I's*, form the foundation for the University of Michigan IVHS program.

- Interdisciplinary education and research;
- Industry (especially auto-related) involvement;
- Implementation-driven basic research;
- Incremental approach;
- International (Canada, Europe, and Japan);
- Interfaced with MDOT's field tests.

This last feature distinguishes University of Michigan IVHS activities from other, more traditional university research programs, and ensures that this program will be an integral part of the Michigan Initiative. In fact, education and implementation go hand in hand in the University of Michigan IVHS program. In addition to the above six I's, University of Michigan IVHS program activities consist of four major components: planning and development, education, basic research, and applied research.

12.2.2 Planning and Development

The planning and development activities include cooperative efforts among all program affiliates to plan their IVHS activities both internally and externally. This was typified by a Delphi survey (a method that employs a group of experts who make predictions on the timing, probability, and implications of a specified trend or event) to forecast IVHS market penetration in the next 20 to 40 years [2]. Much of this information has also been used by the affiliates to develop their own strategic plans for IVHS.

To help the general public, as well as the affiliates themselves, to better understand IVHS, the University of Michigan organized two IVHS technology demonstrations, one on its own campus in 1988 and the other in support of the American Association of State Highway and Transportation Officials' meeting at Traverse City, Michigan, in 1989. Additionally, much of this planning and development effort supported North America's IVHS movement through the ad hoc group of Mobility 2000, which was superseded by IVHS America in 1990.

12.2.3 Education

The education initiative was taken on the advice of the program sponsors who saw a need for immediate continuing education for IVHS, as well as for the longer term training of the next generation of highway and automotive engineers to develop and design IVHS. As the first, and perhaps the only program of its kind in North America, if not in the world, this interdisciplinary IVHS education component has had to deal with a number of unusual issues for it to exist and thrive in the traditional university setting [3].

This component is, therefore, structured as an interdisciplinary cooperative effort from four engineering departments (electrical, civil, mechanical, and industrial), with a number of nonengineering schools and programs (law, economics, business, and urban planning) providing both traditional university and continuing education. Key new initiatives include (1) a graduate certificate in transportation studies—IVHS, (2) an engineering summer conference, and (3) an executive education symposium.

12.2.4 Basic Research

Since the University of Michigan's basic research structure has been influenced by the incremental approach to IVHS implementation, which stressed the need for the Michigan researchers to keep the driver as a prominent element in the IVHS being considered, along with the vehicle and the highway, in the foreseeable future [4]. As shown in Figure 12.1, the top layer of the structure consists of three areas, each representing the interaction between two of the three elements. The other blocks in Figure 12.1 represent the cross-cutting areas involving all three elements and system integration, the latter stemming from the belief that many of the relevant modular technologies for IVHS are already available, and that the research challenge lies in their integration, as well as in the further development of each isolated technology.

The specific focuses of the Michigan research program have been chosen to capitalize on the relative interests and strengths of the sponsors and to complement the research activities undertaken elsewhere in the U.S. This has resulted in the emphasis on ATIS and on the active safety technology, which is the first phase of AVCS.

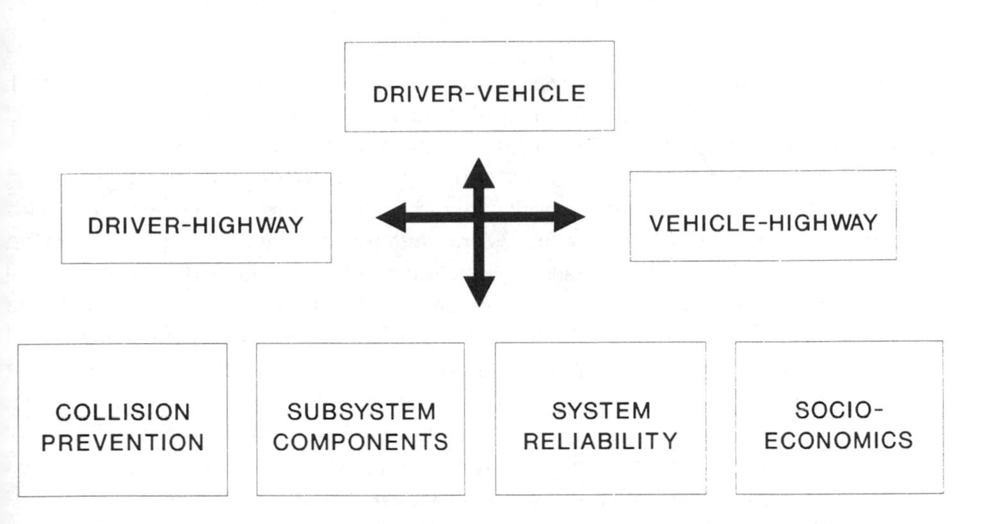

Figure 12.1 Research structure.

Within ATIS, since autonomous navigation systems are already in the marketplace, the initial basic research projects have been focused on anticipatory route guidance, which differs from the traditional dynamic route guidance in that, in the former, traffic conditions in each link of a road network are predicted for the time a vehicle is expected to arrive at that link and are then used in an algorithm for determining the optimum route. This contrasts with the latter, where only the current link times are used for guidance, even though they may change by the time a routed vehicle gets there [5]. This initial effort has since been extended to include coordination between route guidance and adaptive signal controls (i.e., coordination between ATIS and ATMS). Moreover, basic research on intermodal route guidance has begun to optimize route choice for transit and commercial vehicles.

The work on anticipatory route guidance has provided an important basis for categorizing IVHS system architecture, contrasting low-cost early programs with full-fledged, powerful systems, and contrasting vehicle-based with infrastructure-based approaches to the implementation of route optimization. To shed light on the debate between the two latter approaches, a social decision analysis methodology has been developed for IVHS design and evaluation in general, and has been applied to route guidance systems in particular. Social decision analysis provided a framework for rational comparison of IVHS design and architecture that takes into account the multiple attributes and multiple parties involved in broad system considerations. The methodology has been illustrated by its application in investigating the conditions under which dual-mode guidance can be superior to both vehicle-based and infrastructure-based approaches [6].

Fundamental work on human factors has also been centered around ATIS. Low-cost laboratory tools have been developed for human factors research, such as recording eye fixation, and experiments have been conducted to examine how (in which format) in-car traffic information should be represented so that it is easy to use. Basic research has also been done to understand the spatial information processing in the human mind and its implications in the prediction of human spatial behavior in route choice.

In the area of active safety technology, basic research began with the development of an approach to acquire basic data for describing the vehicle motion environment. This approach has since been adopted by the federal authority to support a substantial effort in actual data acquisition [7]. For lateral vehicle control, a lane-departure warning and control system is being developed that will combine the information of the previewed roadway, projected route of the vehicle, and the driver status model. For longitudinal control, basic research has been conducted to use vehicle speed and headway controls for traffic management. In such a system, the traffic management center would communicate appropriate values of speeds and headway to the vehicles equipped with near-term control technologies for the prevailing traffic conditions, so that traffic flow would be improved not only with regard to uniformity, but would also have less chance of rear-end collisions and possibly greater throughput.

Recognizing that nontechnical issues are at least as challenging as technical issues in IVHS implementation, the basic research program at Michigan has also included a socioeconomic component. Over the past few years, research on legal liability in IVHS has concluded that the problem is not critical in ATIS/ATMS, but would be increasingly important as driver control of the vehicle is diluted by technology [8]. Recent work on both legal and institutional issues has suggested procurement in IVHS public-private partnerships to be an important problem, and various means for overcoming the barriers are being investigated. Basic research has also been done on congestion pricing, resulting in the innovative idea of combining a fee for IVHS service with an economic incentive for drivers to divert from congested routes. In other words, it is suggested that negative road pricing may be a more practical way to accomplish the objective of traditional road pricing without the practical problem of political acceptability [9].

12.2.5 Applied Research

The applied research component consists of several thrusts, one of which is research on the socioeconomic aspects of IVHS, including policy issues, market projection, user acceptance, social benefits, legal liability, and impacts on urban development—all of which are deemed important for practical IVHS implementation. A set of six papers dealing with these socioeconomic aspects of IVHS has appeared in a special publication of the Society of Automotive Engineers [10] and was selected as a special compendium to the proceedings of the first annual meeting of IVHS America [11]. While the above work emphasized American public sector policy issues, a complementary worldwide effort was also subsequently launched for investigating organizational responses to IVHS in both the public and private sectors of Europe, Japan, and North America [12]. By improving the understanding of both the things in common and the differences in organizationa responses to IVHS around the world, these studies can help form future public policies and corporate strategies for IVHS.

Another cluster of IVHS applied research in the Michigan IVHS program is a set of research contracts awarded by the U.S. DOT, including human factors of in-vehicle displays, safety-related applications of IVHS, and IVHS enhancements for transit operations. These projects represent the breadth of Michigan research interests corresponding to the missions of the three major branches of U.S. DOT: the FHWA, the NHTSA, and the FTA. However, perhaps the most important single focus of IVHS applied research in the Michigan program has been the support for MDOT at the state level in its development and implementation of the concept of the Metropolitan Transportation Center (MTC).

12.3 THE MDOT IVHS PROGRAM

12.3.1 Metropolitan Transportation Center

Michigan's $6.2 million MTC evolved from discussions between MDOT and the University of Michigan regarding the need for an IVHS field laboratory to evaluate various IVHS technologies in the real traffic environment. With consideration for the needs of private industry in real-world evaluation of IVHS initiatives, the idea of an IVHS implementation committee representing academia, private industry, and city and state government became a reality in late 1989 to guide development of the MTC and related IVHS activities. Input from the private sector was supplied by representatives from Chrysler, Ford, and General Motors, and from various component manufacturers.

The MTC has emerged as a permanent, national resource, which is administered by MDOT's transportation systems staff. MTC's mission is to:

- Create and maintain an infrastructure enabling the participation of qualified public and private organizations in field experiments and demonstrations to "prove out" IVHS concepts so that prudent decisions can be made on building surveillance and communications infrastructures and on developing products for both the wayside and in-vehicle markets.
- Create, maintain, and operate an infrastructure supporting advanced services to the motoring public on behalf of improved efficiency and safety (including services such as advanced traffic management, driver information, and vehicle control functions for supporting vehicle operations that use technologies that have reached a suitable state of readiness).
- Provide a permanent home for MDOT's Detroit Freeway Management section's SCANDI operations center, since it, and its predecessor, the Lodge Freeway Television Surveillance Project, had been using leased facilities to coordinate freeway operations since its beginnings in the mid-1950s.

The new MTC serves this mission and provides a central facility for operational field test sites that are being established in cooperation with FHWA. This facility, which was officially opened in January 1992, is located on the second floor of a new Greyhound intercity bus terminal near the Lodge freeway (M-10) in downtown Detroit. It contains nearly 16,000 square feet of space used as office, traffic laboratory, control room, and computer room space. The MTC is the hub of an infrastructure that is distributed over metropolitan Detroit's road network. This network is about to be expanded and will be used not only as an ATMS, but also as a test-bed for developing, testing, and evaluating IVHS technology.

12.3.2 Expansion of Detroit's Existing Advanced Traffic Management System

This project will extend surveillance and driver information coverage from 32.5 miles to 250 miles of freeway in the greater metropolitan Detroit area. This system, when its five segments are complete within seven to eight years, will have the ability to respond quickly to incidents and manage diversion onto alternate routes using advanced technology for traffic surveillance, data collection, and the conveyance of real-time traffic information to the driver. While complete financing for this approximately $90 million expansion has yet to be finalized, MDOT recently awarded a contract for preliminary engineering and early deployment of the ATMS expansion. This contract includes provisions for evaluating the new technologies, evaluating system architecture needs and computer configuration, and programmatic issues and operational economies for early deployment of the ATMS measures. Also included is the development of an incident management plan for a 25-mile section of the freeway system. This plan will serve as the prototype for developing incident management plans for the entire Detroit metropolitan freeway system.

In addition to the ATMS expansion, the older portion of existing ATMs is being upgraded. A contract to replace nine aging CMSs with twelve flipped disk CMSs, one fiber-optic CMS, and one light-emitting-diode-type CMS was awarded (the fiber-optic and light-emitting diode (LED) signs are technologies that are to be evaluated for use by MDOT). Technicians at the MTC have brought the existing system up to peak performance levels.

12.3.3 DIRECT

The first major initiative emanating from the new MTC is the $8 million DIRECT (driver information radio using experimental communication technologies). DIRECT's objectives are to:

- Support MDOT's commitment to ATMS/ATIS by establishing an operational IVHS test-bed under the MTC's control in order to determine the technical feasibility of large-scale, real-time information systems;
- Compare alternative means of communicating motorist information;
- Evaluate user acceptance and selection of communication methods and technologies;
- Assess program impacts on traffic and driver effectiveness.

DIRECT targets 21 miles of I-94 between downtown Detroit and I-275 for testing different communication technologies for transmitting relevant (and only relevant) information to the motorist from the roadside and MTC to roadside. Funding for this project is through a public/private partnership agreement between the FHWA (50%), MDOT (25%), and several automobile and electronic component manufacturers (25%). This is a major link between downtown Detroit and Detroit Metropolitan Airport and is a major industrial corridor. Approximately 150 trucks per hour use highway the roadway. Average daily traffic varies between 84,000 to 150,000 vehicles along the route (1991 data). In the eastern half of this roadway section, the LOS varies between C and F [13]. The DIRECT project consists of two components: MTC-to-roadside, and roadside-to-motorist. The technologies in the following section will be tested and evaluated.

12.3.4 MTC to Roadside

Spread Spectrum Radio Systems. The Hughes Network Radio (HNR), which uses a low-power spread spectrum transceiver and an embedded microcontroller, is proposed for use. The HNR supports data messages and compressed video communications at 128 kbps with the ability to activate one site per subnetwork. The HNR is thus designed to transmit data to the MTC and return command and control to the remote network controllers. The radio requires a one-time equipment certification, and the Federal Communications Commission (FCC) does not require site licensing.

Digital Trunking Radio. Provided by the private partner G. E. Ericsson, this system operates in the 800-MHz bandwidth and requires licensing by the FCC. The system uses three channels to convey the ''transmit Message XX'' command to the roadside transmitters and ad hoc digitized voice messages.

12.3.5 Roadside to Motorists

Low-Power Highway Advisory Radio With Flashing Signs. A conventional radio from which motorists, upon noting a flashing sign advising them to tune in to a station, can receive localized AM transmissions from the roadside. Pinpoint delivery of traffic information will be achieved by linking together limited-range transmitters.

Automatic Highway Advisory Radio (AHAR). A special radio that operates on the AHAR transmission, using localized (roadside) transmissions of a frequency-modulated signal at an FCC-approved frequency. There will be one transmitter per message reception zone. The special feature of AHAR is the automatic preemption of the entertainment system in the car.

Radio Data Systems. An FM receiver with voice and text-data functions, combined with subsidiary communications authorization (SCA) subcarriers on an existing FM radio transmission (DIRECT will evaluate both in-vehicle and roadside RDS receiver applications). Additionally, feasibility of a secondary audio program (SAP) on a broadcast TV signal to be used with the field test is being evaluated, since apparently SAP could be available relatively more easily than RDS-SCA.

Cellular Call-In. Using a cellular phone (home, office, or mobile) for calling a semiautomated terminal, the public will be able to receive advisory messages with number-code specificity linked to intended route or current location on the highway.

Initial testing will involve the use of 30 special communications-equipped vehicles provided by Chrysler, Ford, and General Motors. Drivers will be provided traffic advisory information, by exception. *By exception* means that motorists will only receive information on conditions that affect their anticipated driving situation (''messages will be broadcast to unique zones spaced approximately three miles apart, with eastbound and westbound traffic in the same area having separate message zones'' [13]). These messages will include updates on traffic congestion, weather conditions, road conditions, and parking constraints. For example:

> When an incident is detected at the MTC, a traffic advisory message will be formulated and presented to an operator for review and approval.* This advisory message data-packet will then be delivered through the Infrastructure Communications Subsystem (ICS) to remote sites where it will be broadcast to affected drivers. Finally, in-vehicle equipment will determine whether this message was actually broadcast, and this status information will be sent back to the MTC for verification [13].

Eventually, motorists will be provided advice on alternate routes and estimated travel times both at the present and in the relevant future time span.

Evaluation of the test is an extremely important component, which will be completed under contract with the University of Michigan, Ann Arbor. In addition to the task of designing the test driver characteristics, this element is proposed to cover the evaluation of message context, delivery, technical system performance, and reaction of test drivers. As part of this effort, vehicle location technology known as *Teletrac* will be used to pinpoint the detours or routes taken by test drivers upon receiving the incident message.

One of the strong features of the DIRECT project is the diversity of private industry partners. Noteworthy in this regard are General Motors, Ford, and Chrysler Corporations, contributing ten vehicles with RDS radio equipment and cellular phones; G.E. Ericsson, contributing Digital Trunking Radio, Pactel, the Vehicle Location Technology equipment; in addition to detectors from Whalen Co.; and significant cash contributions from the Auto manufacturers Michigan Bell and AAA. Significant interest has been shown by several others to be part of the program in different ways.

*Design phase research is evaluating the costs and operational characteristics of a video image detection system as compared to loop detection for speed and reliability of incident detection, incident verification, queue length prediction and estimation, incident cause assessment, and operational flexibility. Methods to fuse this data with information from direct human surveillance for transformation into useful traffic flow assessments and effective traffic advisory messages are still being designed [14].

12.3.6 Oakland County's FAST-TRAC

The FAST-TRAC (Faster and Safer Travel Through Traffic Routing and Advanced Controls) project involves a cooperative effort between MDOT, the Road Commission for Oakland County, the Federal Highway Administration, the University of Michigan, Oakland University, and several automobile and electronic component manufacturers. FAST-TRAC targets Oakland County, a high-growth area of over one million people north of Detroit and the site of two-thirds of all office construction in Michigan since 1986, for a comprehensive, $53 million operational field test of communications, data sources, and software development for the world's first large-scale network to combine ATIS and ATMS. In addition:

> By taking advantage of hardware, software, and systems concepts which have already been field proven, FAST-TRAC will be better able to avoid the risks and time lags commonly associated with completely new programs, thus promoting faster deployment of an operational field test environment [15].

FAST-TRAC's objectives are to determine:

- How applicable IVHS technologies are for resolving the mobility crisis that is having an impact on this nation's congested suburban areas (Oakland County's 5,000-mile road network is subjected to over 10 billion miles of driving each year);
- How these technologies can be used by road organizations at all levels of government, from small villages to major metropolitan areas;
- How these systems can be implemented across multiple jurisdictions (Oakland County has 61 local units of government within its boundaries);
- How these technologies will alter a local government's staffing requirements and their staff's needed level of expertise;
- How this system can be implemented across functional classes of roads from local streets to major metropolitan freeways;
- How effective this system is in reducing traffic accident frequency and severity;
- How a system such as this can be adapted to northern weather conditions.

The ATMS system will provide dynamic areawide traffic control for arterial roadways and freeway access by combining the SCATS demand-responsive computer control network with the Autoscope video image processing system (an alternative to inductive loop detectors), and by providing supplementary sensory information to the ATIS system. This portion of the FAST-TRAC program is called TEKLITE.

The ATIS portion of the system will consist of a second-generation ALI-SCOUT system that provides dynamic route guidance for vehicles using an infrared beacon infrastructure that can transmit route guidance information to the driver via both voice messages and a simple navigational display (see Chapter 4 for a full discussion of ALI-SCOUT). The ALI-SCOUT technology also allows vehicles thus equipped to be used as traffic probes, which facilitates real-time traffic monitoring and adaptive signal control.

Phase 1 is to involve 60 vehicles equipped with ALI-SCOUT's in-vehicle units (IVU) traversing a 36-square-mile network within the city of Troy, Michigan, which includes 95 traffic signals linked to an ATMS and ten infrared beacons linked to an ATIS. Phase 2 is projected to expand the number of IVU-equipped vehicles to 1,000, to expand the number of linked traffic signals to 200 (all signalized intersections in Troy), and to expand the number of infrared beacons to 100 such that approximately 150 square miles would be covered. Finally, within a five-year implementation window, Phase 3 is projected to increase the number of IVU-equipped vehicles to the range of 3,000 to 5,000, to expand the ATMS system to 27 additional communities outside of Troy, such that over 800 signals throughout the county would be linked, and to double the number of ALI-SCOUT beacons to 200, such that the ATIS would encompass 250 to 300 square miles. Efforts have been made to link Oakland County's Traffic Operations Center to MDOT's MTC so that freeway ramp controls, variable message signing, and other freeway operational improvements can be integrated with the surface street ATMS/ATIS to guarantee optimal performance throughout the overall highway system.

FAST-TRAC will expose key industry officials to the benefits of IVHS by providing them with a nearby test-bed that will fulfill many of the operational test objectives detailed in IVHS America's Strategic Plan, including human factors considerations and productivity gains related to commercial, public service, public transit, and private vehicles [15].

12.3.7 MDOT/FTA Project

In accordance with MDOT's goals to develop IVHS technology with both public transit and highway interests in mind, a meeting was held at MDOT's Detroit Freeway Operations Center (DFO) in November 1990 with representatives from southeastern Michigan's major public transit agencies and private transit providers in order to solicit ideas for public transit involvement in future IVHS initiatives and to brief everyone on the various IVHS projects MDOT was considering. As a result of this meeting, a project was developed to provide a means of transmitting DFO's graphical traffic flow status on Detroit's freeway system to the Detroit Department of Transportation (D-DOT), Suburban Mobility Authority for Regional Transportation (SMART), Greyhound bus terminals (downtown Detroit) UPS, and the Commuter Shuttle Co. at Metro Airport.

This graphical display system consists of a mainframe computer at the MTC, which collects real-time data from ATMS and outputs them to UNIX workstations at these remote locations. Graphical software on the workstations translates these data onto a map of the freeway system that is color-coded according to levels of congestion. These workstations are linked to the MTC by modems and leased telephone lines. Maps are updated every 60 seconds. Dispatchers can either view the entire freeway system or use the (workstation) mouse to highlight areas on this map and receive very detailed information on specific sections of the freeway. This information on traffic flow allows dispatchers to choose alternate routes, thereby significantly reducing the time drivers spend in congestion.

This will provide a significant savings in operating costs and better on-time performance for system operators. Because the same information can provide benefits to commercial vehicles as well as public transit, this project also serves as a commercial vehicle operations pilot project to demonstrate IVHS applications for metropolitan Detroit fleet operators.

12.3.8 Advantage I-75

MDOT joined the Advantage I-75 program as a full partner in their efforts to develop an advanced highway and vehicle technology system for reducing congestion, increasing efficiency, and enhancing the safety of motorists and other users of I-75 from Florida to Michigan. Originating at a June 1990 conference attended by 135 individuals representing motor carriers, national and state trucking associations, the six states and two provincial governments that are within this corridor (Florida, Georgia, Tennessee, Kentucky, Ohio, Michigan, Ontario, and Quebec), the U.S. and Canadian national governments, equipment suppliers, and others, this program's inaugural project is the application of AVI technology to facilitate motor-carrier operations by allowing transponder-equipped and properly documented trucks to travel at mainline speeds on any segment along the entire length of I-75, with only minimal stopping at enforcement stations.

> As currently envisioned, each transponder-equipped truck entering the corridor would be weighed at the first open enforcement station and operating credentials would be checked by computer. Roadside inspection would be performed only on those trucks having been selected for inspection in accordance with the state's normal sampling plan. Necessary trip-specific information (truck identification, axle weights, etc.) would be immediately transmitted in a basic data packet to the next downstream station. Upon reaching that station, the truck would be identified by AVI equipment and, if pre-cleared, would be directed to bypass the station. The basic data packet would be updated with the time of passage before being transmitted by computer to the next downstream station to repeat the process. The examination of operating credentials, when necessary for pre-clearance at the downstream station, would also be accomplished by computer [16].

When fully implemented, this program will benefit motor-carrier operators by making the borders between states more transparent, thus enabling faster delivery time, lower operating costs, and enhanced fuel savings; it will benefit mainline motorists by reducing congestion and enhancing safety near enforcement stations; and it will benefit state/provincial agencies by reducing costs while increasing the effectiveness of their truck-monitoring activities through reduced paperwork and increased uniformity. In addition, Advantage I-75 accomplishes its goals without creating any additional centralized bureaucracies to handle enforcement. This program's success lies in its ability to implement future technological advancements by creating partnerships and facilitating critical dialogue between various existing state and provincial agencies who will retain their role in monitoring truck movements and in enforcing motor-carrier regulations within their own boundaries. The enrollment of 4,000 commercial vehicles during the test program has been proposed following a carefully designed criteria for selection. Additionally, adding main-line weigh-in-motion (WIM) equipment to the project appears to a strong possibility at the present time.

12.3.9 International Border Crossing Study

In a joint 50-50 partnership with the Ministry of Transportation in Ontario, Canada, MDOT is currently involved in a project to identify the institutional barriers to developing transparent, seamless and nonstop borders between the U.S. and Canada by application of U.S. technologies. This phase is followed by design, and then deployment at the Detroit-Windsor and Port Huron-Sarnia borders is not long in the future.

12.3.10 Metropolitan Detroit Incident Management Coordination Efforts

The Metropolitan Detroit Incident Management Coordination Efforts (MDIMC) Committee, which consists of representatives from MDOT, state police, county road commissions, FHWA, AAA, and over 20 other agencies, is playing an aggressive role in developing and implementing policies for an efficient incident management program for Metropolitan Detroit. Incident data fusion at MTC and electronic communication links between various law enforcement and response agencies is helping the efforts to move into the age of IVHS and high-technology deployment. An unprecedented momentum currently exists to organize eight different task forces on subjects like quick removal, motorist information, jurisdictional matters, and budget to custom design the blueprint for action in this regard for the needs of metropolitan Detroit.

12.3.11 National Incident Management Conference

With these varied programs under way, MDOT took the leadership to sponsor a national incident management conference in November 1991 for encouraging greater communication between all levels of government, industry, academia, and various citizen groups. Specific conference objectives included:

- Creating an awareness of incident management problems and needs, particularly among those whose responsibilities would be essential to the implementation of a successful action program;
- Clearly defining the basic elements of an effective incident management program, the principals to be involved, resources required, and specific recommendations for the steps necessary to effect an areawide, coordinated incident management program;

- Establish a clear charge to conference participants and outlining the next activity to be undertaken in developing a workable action plan.

By encouraging everyone to communicate and cooperate towards a common goal, this incident management conference helped to strengthen the foundation for IVHS by increasing the confidence among all the organizations involved, so that everyone would have enough confidence in each other to continue preparing for the future by actively participating as a team within this growing transportation systems movement.

12.3.12 Other Interests

Other interests currently being pursued in the state of Michigan include the Automated Highway System, the Advanced Rural Transportation System (ARTS), and the Smart Cruise Platform, which utilizes automated cruise control.

12.3.13 MDOT's Transportation Systems Operation Paradigm

It is through these various projects and academic endeavors that MDOT's Transportation Systems Operation Paradigm has become a working reality. Initiated while staff professionals were independently developing plans for IVHS and freeway reconstruction programs, the realization and conviction arose that operating techniques are neither frills, which may be added to physical road construction if budgets allow, nor are they low-cost substitutes for physical construction [17]. Rather, it was decided that integrating an ATMS infrastructure with a responsive incident management plan would:

- Optimize available capacities on parallel routes to minimize main-line delays during construction;
- Retain capacities gained during construction by minimizing delays due to nonrecurring incidents.

Through an extensive brainstorming process, transportation system deficiencies were first categorized as either related to the driving environment (i.e., driving comfort, safety, surface/base structural integrity) or to various capacity-reducing incidents (recurring or nonrecurring, temporal or nontemporal). By categorizing in this manner, opportunities were provided both to select from an array of solutions, ranging from very low to very high technological content, and to include all potential countermeasures to these deficiencies so that traditional responses that might not otherwise be evident could be developed within their own contextual format, including IVHS. For example, a deficiency identified as being associated with *just-in-time delivery* (which has effectively turned many freeways into moving warehouses for the automotive industry) could lead to potential solutions of either varying manufacturing schedules to better integrate with traffic patterns, or varying the work schedules of others in the traffic stream to better fit production schedules.

12.4 CONCLUSION

Michigan's IVHS initiative has been launched with worldwide participation by a tripartite consortium of government, industry, and academia, even though specific field-test areas are necessarily focused in Michigan. Since these various test areas cover both dense urban sections of freeways and surface streets, as well as semirural portions, including the high volume of motorists who access Detroit's Metropolitan Airport, MDOT hopes to establish southeast Michigan as a major national test-bed, utilizing this state's "critical mass" of technologies. By providing a centralized location for evaluation of alternative detection and surveillance technologies, as well as high-technology communications between the control center and the roadside, Michigan's new MTC, MDOT's DIRECT, Oakland County's FAST-TRAC, and the various other IVHS activities previously mentioned, can all help stimulate Michigan's growing high-technology base. These concerted IVHS activities have created an opportunity for MDOT and the other agencies involved to cultivate a positive image by providing leadership and management to solve a problem that has an impact on a very large percentage of the population. In addition, it is anticipated that these projects will provide information that will ultimately lead to developing transportation management programs that are more effective and less costly than the methods commonly employed. For example, as southeast Michigan's freeway system developed, more and more traffic used these faster and safer facilities to reach their destinations. However, in many instances, as freeway traffic volumes increased, the old surface arterials have actually become faster and safer, such that with proper driver education and updated information on traffic conditions, they could successfully be used as alternate routes.

In the face of severe budget deficits, rising fuel prices, and reductions in operating revenues, transportation policies for the future must be both cost-efficient and cost-effective, thus making the best use of limited resources. IVHS meets these criteria and is an affordable, efficient, and effective method for relieving traffic congestion, improving safety, and improving mobility. MDOT is committed to relieving congestion problems without spending large amounts of taxpayer money.

Michigan industry, MDOT, and the University of Michigan have long recognized the potential benefits of IVHS initiatives and have been active proponents for advancing these technologies through their leadership in Mobility 2000 and IVHS America. With various unique public-private partnerships integral to the Michigan Initiative, this state can continue to help lead the IVHS movement by bringing together expertise from industry, academia, government, and various citizens groups into a synergistic union for improving the driving environment.

REFERENCES

[1] Maki, R. E., "Intelligent Vehicle Highway Systems: Opportunity for Technology Development in Michigan," Michigan Technology Update, March 1991.

[2] Underwood, S. E., K. Chen, and R. D. Ervin, "The Future of Intelligent Vehicle-Highway Systems: A

Delphi Forecast of Markets and Sociotechnical Determinants,'' Transportation Research Board paper no. 890804, 1989.

[3] Chen, K., B. A. Galler, and T. B. Reed, ''The University of Michigan IVHS Education Program,'' *Record of the 2nd Vehicle Navigation and Information Systems Conf.,* IEEE and SAE, 1991.

[4] Chen, K., and R. D. Ervin, ''Developing a Program in Intelligent Vehicle-Highway Systems in North America,'' *Proc. 20th Int. Symp. on Automotive Technology & Automation,* 29 May–2 June 1989, pp. 1103–1113.

[5] Chen, K., and S. E. Underwood, ''Research on Anticipatory Route Guidance,'' *Record of the 2nd Vehicle Navigation and Information Systems Conf.,* IEEE and SAE, 1991.

[6] Chen, K. and T. B. Reed, ''Social Decision Analysis for IVHS,'' paper presented at the 3rd Annual Meeting of IVHS America, April 1993.

[7] Ervin, R. D., C. C. MacAdam, and K. Gilbert, ''A Measurement and Processing System for the Vehicle Motion Environment,'' paper presented at the 3rd Annual Meeting of IVHS America, April 1993.

[8] Syverud, K., ''Legal Constraints to the Research, Development and Deployment of IVHS Technology in the United States,'' paper presented at the 3rd Annual Meeting of IVHS America, April 1993.

[9] Stafford, F. P., and K. Chen, ''Economic Aspects of Public-Private Partnerships for the Provision of Roadway Services,'' TRB Paper No. 930148, 72nd Annual Meeting of the Transportation Research Board, Jan. 1993.

[10] ''Automated Highway/Intelligent Vehicle Systems: Technology and Socioeconomic Aspects,'' Special Publication SP-833, SAE, 1990.

[11] IVHS America, *Proc. First Annual Meeting,* Reston, VA, 17–20 March 1991.

[12] ''IVHS and Vehicle Communications,'' Special Publication SP-877, SAE, 1991.

[13] Gilbert, R. K., S. E. Underwood, and L. E. DeFrain, ''Comparison of Alternative Driver Information Systems,'' *Record of the 2nd Vehicle Navigation and Information Systems Conf.,* IEEE and SAE, 1991.

[14] "Final Report,'' Michigan Department of Transportation Contract MDOT89-2330DAB, May 1991.

[15] Grubba, J. L., ''A Proposed Deployment of Intelligent Vehicle-Highway Systems in Oakland County, Michigan,'' testimony before the U.S. House of Representatives Committee on Appropriations' Subcommittee on Transportation, 1 May 1991.

[16] Advantage I-75 brochure, Kentucky Transportation Center, University of Kentucky, Lexington, KY, 1990.

[17] Orne, D. E., and R. E. Maki, ''The Michigan Department of Transportation System Operation Paradigm,'' *Proc. 24th Int. Symp. on Automotive Technology & Automation's Dedicated Conf. and Exhibition on Road Transport Informatics/Intelligent Vehicle-Highway Systems,* Florence, Italy, 20–24 May 1991.

Chapter 13
Overview of Japanese Development and Future Issues

Hironao Kawashima

13.1 INTRODUCTION

In Japan, the number of road traffic deaths reached 16,765 in 1970. This gave rise to a large amount of social concern, and comprehensive safety programs were conducted by ministries. As a result, the installation of road facilities such as traffic signals, traffic signs, and guardrails was accelerated. Moreover, the equipment and facilities for traffic surveillance and control were systematically installed in large cities. Although the number of road traffic deaths decreased to half the highest value within a few years, it has gradually increased recently, and in 1988 the number rose above 10,000 and is still rising. The number 10,000 has been considered as another critical level requiring a further discussion on the nationwide safety program.

On the other hand, during the last decade, convenient door-to-door parcel delivery services have been welcomed by consumers, and the demand for such services is still growing. Moreover, in the field of modern mass production and distribution systems, structural changes were evident in the last two decades. In particular, the concept of production was shifting to the small-lot-size production of a diversified variety of goods, and the concept of physical distribution was changing to small-volume, high-frequency delivery of goods. In other words, the *just-in-time* concept is considered to be the key to cost reduction and market strategy.

Although the effort to improve road facilities, which began in the 1970s, is continuing, it seems that the effect of the measures adopted has already been saturated, or that the traditional measures cannot cope with the recent problems generated by the structural or qualitative changes in physical distribution systems.

In the 1970s, improving the installation of equipment and facilities was not recognized as a procedure for introducing the concept now called IVHS or RTI. However, the legacy of the efforts in the 1970s became a very large driving force for the realization of RTI in the 1980s. In that sense, the achievements in the 1970s can be seen as the introduction of the preliminary stage of RTI.

The in-vehicle information systems that use mobile communications to receive information from traffic control centers use a wide variety of methods. Drivers can obtain or select different information according to their request. Multiple functions of in-vehicle information systems can also be considered as potential tools for road administrators to conduct more advanced or sophisticated traffic management. Because the preliminary stage of RTI has been accomplished in Japan, the integrated use of RTI is considered and expected to be a practical method of lightening road transport problems.

The first part of this chapter deals with the present status of information in road transport. In particular, various roadside facilities to provide information on congestion, traffic accidents, and travel time are explained in Section 13.2. Special attention is focused on the graphic information board that shows the location of congestion in innercity expressways. The reactions of drivers to the graphic and travel time information boards are outlined based on the questionnaire surveys conducted by the road administrators. In Section 13.3, recent developments of in-vehicle information systems in Japan, that is to say, navigation-based systems, are explained. A model to clarify the possible forms of using mobile communications in road transport is proposed, and the relative relationships of various systems in Japan as well as in Europe and U.S. are shown. In Section 13.4, the reactions of drivers who used the navigation system with map display are discussed, and the importance of human-machine interface problems is stressed.

The latter part of the chapter deals with the future issues for the realization of advanced informatics in road transport. In Section 13.5, topics related to future R&D are discussed. The first topic is about the discussion on the introduction of the dynamic route guidance system based on the navigation systems with map displays. The second topic is about R&D projects on more advanced systems. The ideas examined by the Advanced Road Traffic Systems (ARTS) Research Committee and Super Smart Vehicle System (SSVS) Research Committee are explained. In Section 13.6, more general issues for the realization of informatics in road transport are discussed.

13.2 ROADSIDE INFORMATION AND TRAFFIC MEASUREMENT SYSTEMS

In this section, a brief sketch of the state of installation of facilities for traffic control and measurement is given. Examples are the roadside facilities providing information to drivers and traffic measurement systems for traffic surveillance and control. The installation of systems using digital picture processing is increasing in Japan, and typical and recent examples are shown. Moreover, special attention is focused on the driver's reactions to travel time and graphic information boards.

13.2.1 Facilities in Urban Networks

As shown in Table 13.1, traffic surveillance and control centers are installed in 74 cities, which include 47 prefectural capitals and major cities with populations over 100,000. The installation of centers was a part of the comprehensive safety program started in 1970 and took 15 years to complete. The plan to install small-scale traffic surveillance and control centers for cities, which have a population over 30,000, has been in operation since 1985, and 80 control centers have already been installed. Control centers accumulate data obtained from detectors (mostly ultrasonic detectors), and the degree of congestion is estimated. Finally, all the necessary information is illustrated and visually represented on the graphical panel in the control center. Every five minutes the data on the graphical panel are updated.

In the R&D phase, attempts to estimate travel time of vehicles are conducted and the method of applying travel time data to traffic management is considered. In order to estimate the travel time, a number plate recognition system that uses digital picture processing is developed and tested. In addition to the low recognition rate of number plates due to optical conditions and the existence of overlapping views, the matching rate is very low, since only the last four letters of the number plate are recognized by the system in order to protect the privacy of drivers. However, since travel time is generally a very easily understandable quantity, describing traffic conditions for drivers and road administrators, improving the methods to measure travel time and the integration with other measurements are under consideration.

On the other hand, efforts to automate the generation of messages for roadside broadcasting systems are being realized. For example, a system that uses fuzzy logic to generate messages automatically is already in use [1].

Table 13.1
Road Traffic Surveillance and Control Centers
and Traffic Information Facilities in Japan
(March 1991)

Type of Facility	*Number*
Control center	74
Control subcenter	80
Signal unit	131,629
Detector-based area-controlled signal units	40,549
Vehicle detector	57,537
TV camera for surveillance	974
Traffic information board (free pattern type)	1,478
Highway radio equipment	130
Travel time measurement equipment	19

13.2.2 Facilities in Expressways

All the expressways are toll roads, and drivers are sensitive to the degree of congestion on them. One purpose of providing information to drivers is to announce the present traffic situation of the expressways so that drivers can decide the shortest travel time route of the expressway, or can take the nearest exit to use different roads or can even be mentally prepared for the congestion to come. Another purpose is to provide information off the expressway so that drivers can decide whether or not to use the expressway before they enter the toll gate.

As shown in Table 13.2, a large number of detectors and television cameras are installed along the expressway to monitor the condition of traffic 24 hours a day. The detectors (mostly ultrasonic) are used to measure mean velocity, time occupancy, and traffic volumes; various indicators of traffic conditions such as degree of congestion and occurrence of incidents are estimated. In order to show drivers a macroscopic view of the network, graphic information boards are used on innercity expressways. In order to provide more sophisticated information to drivers and to obtain more useful data for road traffic administrators, various R&D efforts are being conducted by electric and electronic companies under the supervision of expressway administrators.

One such example is an attempt to provide information on travel time. On the innercity expressway, detectors are installed every 300m to 500m. Using the time mean velocity value, the travel time of the corresponding section is derived and added up to form the travel time of the interval, which is 5 to 10 km. Theoretically, the actual mean travel time of vehicles is not equal to the travel time derived from the detector using the method just mentioned, unless the vehicles are cruising at a uniformly constant speed.

Table 13.2
Traffic Information Facilities of Japanese Expressways

	Intercity Expressways (March 1990)	*Tokyo Metropolitan Expressway (March 1991)*	*Hansin Expressway (January 1991)*
Total length (km)	5,335	220.0	152.8
Mean number of users (millions/day)	4.5	1.1	0.77
Detectors	793	1,748	1,203
TV camera for surveillance	1,607	570	109
Traffic information board	3,735	380	292
Graphic information board		18	3
Traffic information board on street		195	
Traffic and graphic information board on street		6	
Highway radio	33	2	23
Traffic information terminal for drivers	5	7	2
Travel time information board			56

However, by adjusting various parameters, the accuracy of travel time obtained from detectors is satisfactory for all practical purposes. In particular, the accuracy of travel time was examined by introducing a system that recognizes the number plates of vehicles. In this case also, only four letters are recognized. On the expressways, the inflow and outflow only occur on ramps, and therefore the matching rate of number plates is higher than the rate in urban areas. However, the performance of this system still depends on the time of day, weather, and the distribution of headway time.

Another application of digital picture processing is a system to determine the vacancy situation of parking areas, which is installed in the service area of an intercity expressway. The parking area consists of four blocks, and the total capacity is 603 cars. Using images from 16 TV cameras and sophisticated digital dynamic picture processing, the existence and the movements of vehicles entering and exiting parking lots are determined. Since the TV cameras can cover approximately 50% of the parking area, the estimation algorithm to determine the vacancy situation of the whole parking area is developed by introducing a learning algorithm based on the neural network. The results are displayed on the information boards of the service area in order to guide drivers to the block where parking is available [2].

13.2.3 Reaction of Drivers to Travel Time and Graphic Information Board

The reasons for selecting these two topics are not only that these information boards are important measures in present road traffic management of expressways, but also that the possible influence on future design and developments of in-vehicle information systems should be considered. The travel time information boards (which provide travel time) are installed on the Hanshin Expressway, and 56 boards are presently in operation in 1991. The boards are installed at toll gates and the nearby streets linked to the toll gates. The estimated travel time from the toll gate to major points of the expressway network, such as junction points of ring roads, is indicated on the board. The distances to the major ring road points of the network are 5 to 10 km (see [3]).

After implementing the first systems in 1989, a study to examine the reaction of drivers to the travel time information boards was conducted. The questionnaire survey was designed, and it was distributed at six toll gates during the time periods of 7 to 9 A.M. and 9 A.M. to 5 P.M. Out of 1,000 drivers, 174 drivers answered the questionnaire, which covered driver's sex, age, area of residence, type of vehicle, purpose of journey, and frequency of using the expressway. According to the study, 84% of drivers almost always look at the travel time information board, and 86% of drivers think that if the difference between actual travel time and the travel time indicated on the board is less than 5 minutes, they can ignore the difference.

The graphic information boards, which are composed of LEDs, have been installed on both the Metropolitan Expressway (since 1987) and the Hanshin Expressway (since 1989). The size of a typical graphic information board on the Metropolitan Expressway is 45m high by 6m wide by 1m deep (see Figure 13.1). The board is installed by the expressway just before the junction of the ring roads. The board indicates the condition of congestion by the color illumination of the link. For example, if the mean velocity of vehicles is between 20 to 40 km/h, orange illumination is used; below 20 km/h, red illumination is used; if an accident occurs, a blinking red cross is indicated at the place of the accident [4].

The questionnaire to examine their reactions was distributed to 36,000 drivers, of whom 4,973 mailed back the sheets, which covered driver's sex, age, occupation, vehicle type, frequency of using expressway, and purpose for using the expressway. Although 95% of drivers recognized the graphic information board, the results become slightly different if drivers are classified by the frequency of using the expressway. For example, 17% of drivers who use the expressway less than once a month did not recognize or notice the existence of those information boards.

The format of the network used in the graphic information board is quite favorable to drivers, but again the familiarity depends on the frequency of using the expressway. In particular, 69% of drivers answered that the format was easy to understand, 27% of drivers answered that some part of the format was difficult to understand, and 3% of drivers answered that they could not understand it at all. If we look at the drivers who

Figure 13.1 Example of graphic information board on Tokyo Metropolitan Expressway.

use the expressway less than once a month, 53% could not or could only partly understand the graphic information board.

On one hand, the first survey shows that travel time is useful for drivers to decide the traffic condition and route selection. The favorable reaction of drivers is accelerating the introduction of similar systems on other expressways. On the other hand, although the graphic information board contains complicated information, the research study reports that most drivers, especially experienced drivers, think that it is a good information source to support their decision. When the vehicle is cruising at 60 km/h, drivers have only a few seconds to see and recognize the board. However, drivers sometimes feel it is beneficial to see the macroscopic view of the traffic situation in the network.

13.3 IN-VEHICLE INFORMATION SYSTEMS

13.3.1 Basic Configuration of Japanese Systems

The development of in-vehicle information systems, or more precisely, navigation-based systems, began in the mid 1980s. The basic configuration of the systems consists of a mobile communications unit, sensors, microprocessors, a display unit and a large-volume memory device (sce Figurc 13.2). In Japan, CD-ROM is used as the large-volume memory device, and a digital road map database is implemented. The latter is the key element for navigation systems and for integrating various functions, such as traffic information (congestion, road works) and motorist information (location of hotels, restaurants, and gas stations).

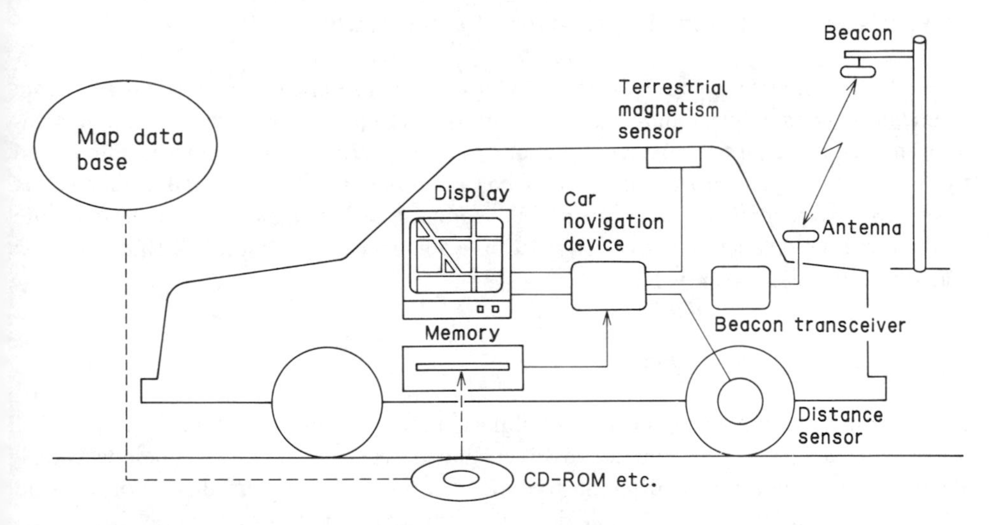

Figure 13.2 Typical configuration of in-vehicle information system.

The establishment of the standard for the digital road map database began about 1989. It is designed to meet diversified needs, such as vehicle navigation, road management, publication of road maps for various purposes, and other public and private services using road maps. The database contains accurate road configurations, location information, and road attributes. The graphical information is collected from 1/25,000- or 1/50,000-scale topographic maps. A 10-year program to complete a 1/25,000-scale digital road map covering all the basic roads and all other roads with a 3m or greater roadway width has been started [5].

Common display units used in the present in-vehicle information systems are CRT (cathode ray tube). Not only are road maps and traffic information displayed, but so are the key indices to retrieve digital maps and the menus to operate in-vehicle information systems. The use of a head-up display is also being considered, and a prototype model to display route guidance indications and names of expressway exit ramps was demonstrated.

Typical sensors used in in-vehicle information systems are distance, direction, and magnetic sensors. A model that uses sophisticated sensors, such as a gas rate gyroscope, is already on the market. The development of new types of gyroscopes is very active, and models using an oscillation gyroscope or a fiber-optic gyroscope are expected to be on the market soon.

The microprocessor is a basic element for controlling and integrating information and data from the communications unit, sensors, and database. It also controls the display unit to generate information and images for drivers. Therefore, a high-performance microprocessor is required, and an in-vehicle information system that uses a 32-bit microprocessor equipped with 1 MB of memory will appear on the market soon.

13.3.2 Classification of the Use of Mobile Communications

The total function of an in-vehicle information system depends heavily on the basic character of the mobile communication system. An attempt to classify mobile communication links with regard to realizable functions in road traffic management was introduced by Jeffery [6]. The approach in this text has a similar intention, but more attention is devoted to the technical features of mobile communication links, which determine the amount and the characteristics of information exchanged between the roadside facilities and vehicles and between vehicles.

Type I Mobile Communications

In this group, the main idea in using mobile communication links is to provide traffic information and parking information to drivers and to assist them in making their decisions. Therefore, the idea is not so different from the concept motivating installation of roadside information systems such as information boards, highway radios, and so on. Moreover, based on the improvement of facilities that began almost 25 years ago, the adoption of type I mobile communication links is the most practical and realizable strategy to appear in RTI for Japan.

However, the main difference between the functions realized by the facilities in the preliminary stage of introducing RTI and the functions realized by in-vehicle information systems is the great freedom one can acquire to process, convert, and provide various information to drivers inside their vehicles. In particular, if type I mobile communications is combined with a navigation system, traffic and parking information can be overlaid on the map information. This configuration will offer drivers the freedom to choose the information they need and a macroscopic view or background information on the traffic condition in the network. Table 13.3 shows some features of type I mobile communication links and the characteristics inherent in this type of communication. AMTICS and a practical version of RACS of Japan belong to this group [7–11]. Various systems using RDS-TMC also fall into this category [12]. For example, CARMINAT, which is one of the projects in EUREKA, uses RDS-TMC and a digital map database [13].

Type II Mobile Communications

This type of mobile communications is designed as a two-way communication system which also has a simulcasting mode. Some realizable functions in road transport are, for example, route guidance, parking management, traffic control, and emergency calls. Although a detailed discussion of the design of the route guidance system using type II mobile communications will be shown in Section 13.4, thorough discussions of the other realizable functions are beyond the scope of this chapter and will be omitted. See Table 13.3. ALI-SCOUT, which uses an IR communication system, and SOCRATES, which uses next-generation cellular radio system GSM, both belong to this category [14,15]. The Individual Communication System tested in the RACS Integrated Experiment was designed to have a simultaneous downlink part and an individual uplink part [8,16].

Type III Mobile Communications

This type of mobile communications is designed to exchange ID codes by two-way transmission and realizes individual type communication such as message and/or data transmission in a dialogue fashion. The realizable functions depend on the amount of data transmission designed for the mobile communication link. Examples are automatic vehicle identification (AVI), automatic vehicle management (AVM), and fleet control of trucks, debiting, and interactive motorist information services. Type III mobile communications can be designed to include the functions of both type I and II mobile communications. However, the characteristics of communication are different between type I and II, and in some cases type III mobile communications can be implemented independently of the realization of type I and II mobile communication systems. See Table 13.3. The satellite two-way communication system OmniTRACS belongs to this group, and the system is

Table 13.3
Type I, II, and III Mobile Communication Features

Type	Direction	Mode	Information	Characteristics	Communication Zone		Realizable Functions
					Wide	Small	
I	G → V	Simulcast	Traffic, parking, travel time	Amount of information, transmission time	Large, update cycle (10 min)	Small, zone passage (1 sec)	Navigation, traffic information, parking information
II	G → V	Simulcast	Traffic, parking, travel time, guide table for route guidance	Amount of information, transmission time	Large, update cycle (10 min)	Small, zone passage (1 sec)	Dynamic navigation, route guidance, parking management, traffic flow control, network traffic control, emergency call
	V → G	Individual	Travel time	Number of subscribers, collision of communication	Limited by communication capacity, quite probable	Unlimited, very rare	
III*	G → V	Individual	ID code, turning direction, messages	Number of subscribers, collision of communication	Limited by communication capacity, quite probable	Unlimited, very rare	Interactive route guidance, fleet management, message (character, image) exchange, emergency call, automatic debiting
	V → G	Individual	ID code (OD information), travel time, messages	Continuity of communication	Continuous	Intermittent	

Note: V = vehicle; G = ground.
*Vehicle-to-vehicle dialogue communication through the use of ground facilities are included in Type III, as is connection to ISDN.

used mainly by road freight transport industries [17]. In CACS (Comprehensive Automobile Traffic Control System), the dynamic route guidance system was tested and communication system developed belongs to this group [18–20]. A full-scale model of the Individual Communication System tested in the RACS Integrated Experiment also belongs to this category. It was designed to transmit messages, voice messages, and image data such as facsimile by using newly developed microwave beacons [8,9,10,16,21].

Type IV Mobile Communications

The modes realized by this type of mobile communications are vehicle-to-vehicle communications, vehicle-to-ground communications, and combinations of these two. Type IV mobile communications is in the research phase, and feasibility and performance are not yet clear. Type IV mobile communications is considered to be the key element to controlling vehicles in nonautonomous automated systems design to realize functions such as autocruise, collision avoidance, and convoy/platoon. As a result, the specification of communication will be quite different from ordinary digital, time sharing, packet communications. Therefore, it seems that the realization of Type IV mobile communications is independent of the status of other types of mobile communications. Some functions realizable by type IV are listed in Table 13.4 [22–24].

Table 13.4
Type IV (Vehicle-to-Vehicle) Mobile Communication

Direction	*Realizable Functions*
V → V → . . . → V → V	Exchange of vehicle motion data for convoy system, collision avoidance system, and autocruise system Message from patrol car Message from/to vehicles Message from/to vehicles in the opposite lane
CN → R → V → V → . . . → V V → V → . . . → V → R → CN	Emergency call Traffic information Message from/to vehicles Message from/to vehicles in the opposite lane
V V ⋮ ↘ ↗ ⋮ V → R → V ⋮ ↗ ↘ ⋮ V V	Exchange of vehicle motion data for convoy system, collision avoidance system, autocruise system, and system that displays the relative position of vehicles Message exchange by electronic mail

Note: V = vehicle; R = roadside equipment; CN = communication network.

13.4 SOME ASPECTS OF HUMAN-MACHINE INTERFACE

When drivers need traffic information, such as congestion and road construction, there are several advantages of using the in-vehicle information systems compared with looking at variable-sign boards or listening to highway radio. Actual functions that drivers can use depend on the design of each in-vehicle information system. However, generally speaking, we can assume that the following functions can be realized without any special operation from the driver's seat. It is obvious that these functions cannot be realized by traditional ways of providing traffic information from the roadside.

- Drivers can acquire the information when necessary.
- Drivers can reconfirm the information.
- Drivers can obtain the information and only the information requested.

On the other hand, the flexibility of in-vehicle information systems may, in the end, provide too much information to drivers. The situation of information overload might be more serious for older drivers, although the in-vehicle information systems can be designed for and specially adjusted to suit the elderly [25].

Therefore, human-machine interface problems are very important, and suitable guidelines for the design of systems for different sorts of people (e.g., young and old, experienced and inexperienced) are urgently needed. However, although it is easy to state the purposes of design such as user-friendly systems or easily recognizable systems, problems exist in the fact that these purposes or concepts are very vague and difficult to specify quantitatively. Moreover, human beings are usually very adaptable to new situations and it is therefore difficult to analyze system design characteristics by simple stimulus-response types of approaches.

13.4.1 Questionnaire Surveys in CACS

In the CACS route guidance system, while the indication by arrows was technologically the best choice in the 1970s, the validity of guiding drivers by simple indication of arrows became a controversy among the people who had driven the equipped vehicle. The drivers who knew the route and traffic situation especially did not like to be guided by the indication of arrows.

During and after the CACS experiment, several questionnaire surveys were conducted to analyze the reactions of drivers as a part of the CACS project. In one survey, which asked 353 people who visited the test site their impression of CACS, 84% of the people responded that they would like to purchase the in-vehicle unit if the price was reasonable. On the other hand, in a different survey, which asked 627 professional and nonprofessional drivers about the validity of route guidance in the context of traffic management and control, nearly 60% of the drivers answered that they did not want to obey the route guidance indication.

The reaction of drivers in the second survey can be interpreted in two ways. One is that they do not like to be controlled by authorities. Another point is that when they were guided by the CACS route guidance system, they feel uneasy because the system did not tell drivers the whole perspective of the route, so they could not be well prepared for the next situation. This type of reaction was more evident with professional drivers or drivers who knew the area very well.

13.4.2 Evaluation of Navigation System

A second example of the difficulty of analyzing human-machine interface problems can be found in a study conducted by the author's group [26]. The study was intended to evaluate driving performance with or without a navigation system which is on the market. The navigation-equipped vehicle and nonequipped vehicle were prepared, and when drivers use nonequipped vehicles, an ordinary paper map was handed out. The drivers' reactions were recorded by video cameras. For practical reasons, the driving performance of five young drivers were recorded and analyzed. The course was set in the Yokohama area, where all drivers were unfamiliar with the course. Moreover, all five drivers had never used the navigation system before.

In Figure 13.3(a), the error rates based on the shortest distance versus actual distance traveled are illustrated. The results show that the navigation-equipped vehicles have a more stable performance than the nonequipped vehicles, although the differences among the driving ability of drivers should be taken into account. By analyzing pictures from video recorders, the eye movements of drivers were traced and the proportion of time that the drivers fixed their eyes to the front view was derived. Figure 13.3(b) shows the results of five drivers, and it is obvious that when drivers use navigation-equipped vehicles, they look at the navigation system frequently, so that the time ratio of watching the front view is less than with the drivers using nonequipped vehicles.

However, from verbal protocol analysis of the video tapes, the items to which the drivers paid attention and those they tried to identify by name or place were counted. The items were road signs, signal names, intersection names, buildings, names of bus stops, and sign boards of shops. The normalized counts are shown in Figure 13.3(c). The results show that when drivers use paper maps, they have to see the outside view more carefully, since they cannot identify the location of their vehicle easily.

From these examples, it can be deduced that if the location of the vehicle is displayed on the map, then the driver can check the location whenever needed and can concentrate on driving. As a result, the driver feels very secure and sometimes can even rely on the system. These mental factors are not directly related to driving safety, but they should be taken into account. Moreover, these discussions imply that the time ratio of watching the front view by the driver cannot be the only measure used to evaluate the merits or defects of using in-vehicle navigation systems.

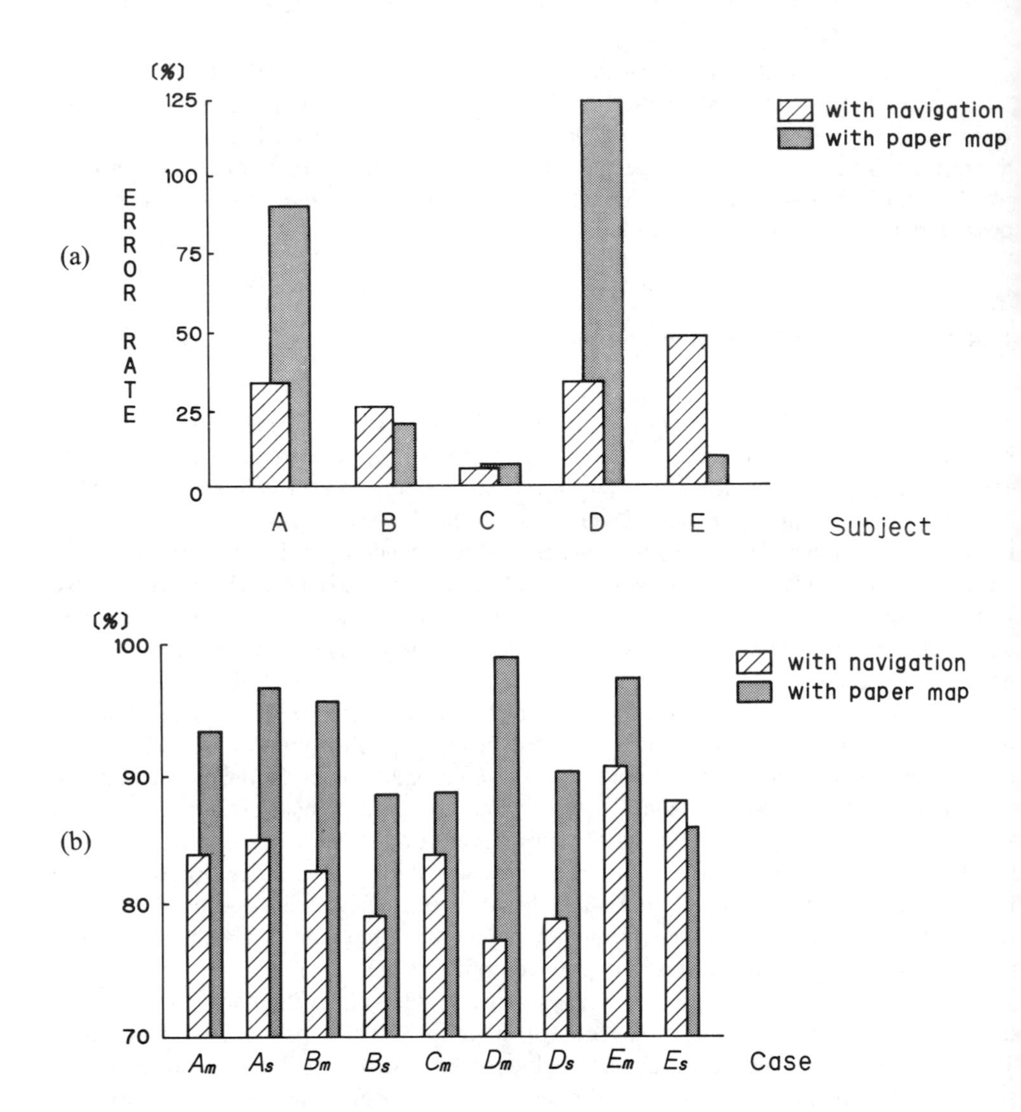

Figure 13.3 (a) Error rate with or without navigation. (b) The time ratio of watching the front view. A_m = subject A on major road; A_s = subject A on street. Case C_s was not available.

13.4.3 General Framework for Analysis and Design

Based on our daily experiences and from the various examples mentioned above, it seems natural to make a hypothesis that the drivers are conducting two kinds of decisions when making a journey (see Figure 13.4). One part is based on instantaneous decisions mainly related to acceleration, steering, lane changing, and maneuvering. For this purpose, short-

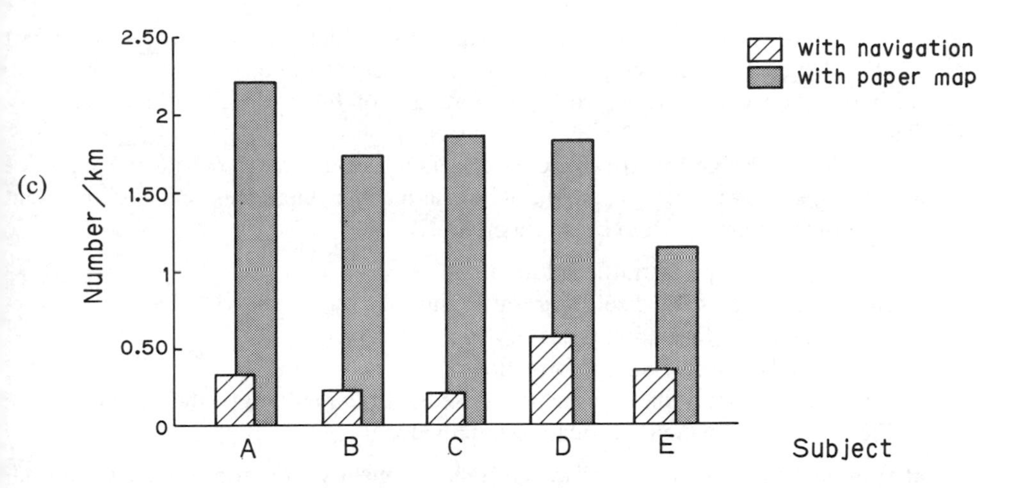

Figure 13.3 continued. (c) Number of information sources the subject watched while driving. Information sources include: road sign, name of signal, name of intersection, building, name of bus stop, and board of shop.

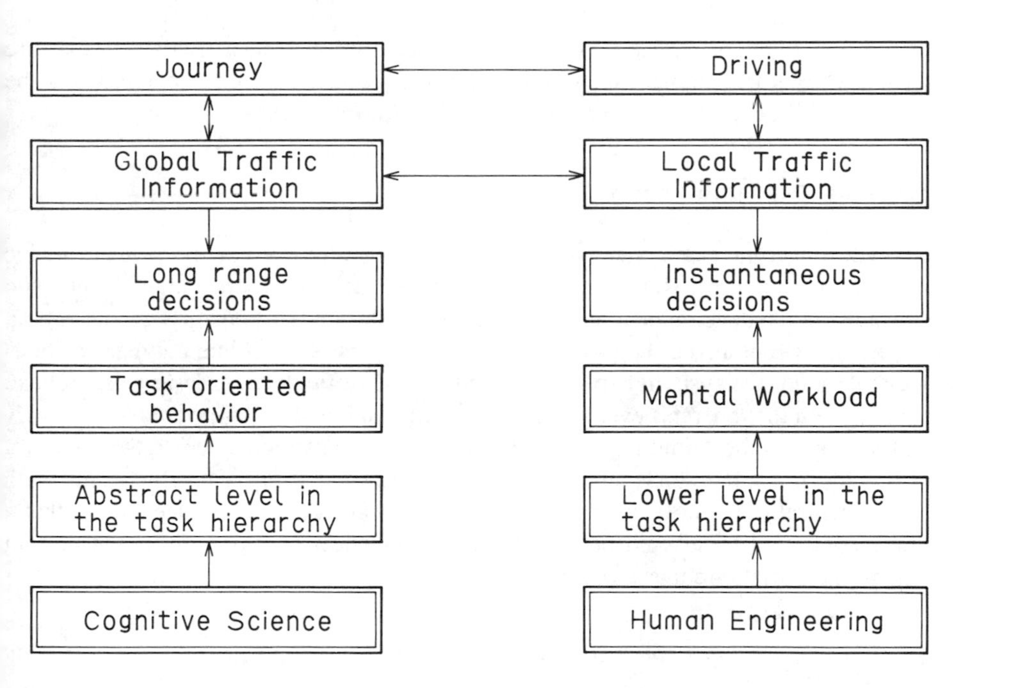

Figure 13.4 Basic structure of human-machine interface of in-vehicle unit.

range information such as the information around the vehicle is necessary. Another part is based on longer term decisions such as decisions about route selection. In this case, traffic information about the network and forecasts of future situations are necessary [27,28].

In order to design an in-vehicle information system that handles two kinds of information, the software design in terms of human-machine interfaces becomes important and the following items need to be considered.

- The scope and type of traffic information;
- The range of areas for displaying traffic information;
- The content of information necessary to assist drivers;
- The methods of expressing information;
- The timing of providing information linked with the motion of the vehicle;
- The sequence in which information is provided.

In other words, the design of the information management system for in-vehicle information systems and the relationship with the human capability of understanding this information are and will be very important research objectives to be dealt with [29].

13.5 FUTURE ISSUES OF R&D

In this section, two topics related to the future perspective of R&D activities in Japan are discussed. One is the problem of introducing route guidance systems in Japan and the other is the projects related to more advanced road traffic systems.

13.5.1 Route Guidance System

The CACS route guidance system successfully demonstrated the new horizons of traffic control and management. However, at the same time, the researchers and engineers who are involved in the development have recognized the difficulty of designing, conducting, and operating a centralized, large-scale sociotechnological system like a dynamic, interactive route guidance system. Especially noted are the difficulties of designing a robust, fail-safe system that operates even when the penetration rate of equipped vehicles is very low. Therefore, while admitting that the total cost of constructing centralized control systems with simple in-vehicle units is lower than with sophisticated in-vehicle units with minimum centralized control systems, most of the researchers and engineers think that a centrally controlled route guidance system is not practical in Japan under the present situations and social circumstances [9].

Scenario of Introducing Route Guidance System

The strategy Japan adopted was to introduce sophisticated navigation systems at a very early stage of penetration. Now, more than 6,000 autonomous navigation systems with map displays (some equipped with GPS) are sold per month, and this indicates that the marketing strategy has been supported by the market. Within a few years, models using traffic information from type I mobile communications, such as AMTICS and RACS, will appear on the market. This will be the second phase of penetration.

As was mentioned previously, Japanese in-vehicle information systems are equipped with digital road databases. This implies that a high-performance microprocessor is also installed in the vehicle. Using the microprocessor, along with travel time information, computation of route selection can be carried out within the vehicle. At the stage of adopting type I mobile communications, the travel time information is obtained from digital picture processing systems and from estimation systems using detector data. Therefore, real-time, historical, or even predicted travel time information of a particular road network, such as innercity expressways, are all that will be available at this stage. The result of route selection can be displayed on the map so that the background traffic conditions and macroscopic view of traffic conditions in the network can be provided to drivers at the same time. Moreover, the indication of turns based on the selected routes determined by the in-vehicle microprocessor can also be generated on the CRT. These types of systems are also called *dynamic navigation systems* [30].

At the third stage of penetration, the next scenario is to introduce two-way communications. In this case, accurate travel time data can be obtained from the data transmitted by each vehicle. Although centralized route guidance such as CACS can be constructed using two-way mobile communications, it seems the Japanese systems will have a different system configuration, since the first step of introducing RTI was to realize navigation systems with map displays (see Figure 13.5).

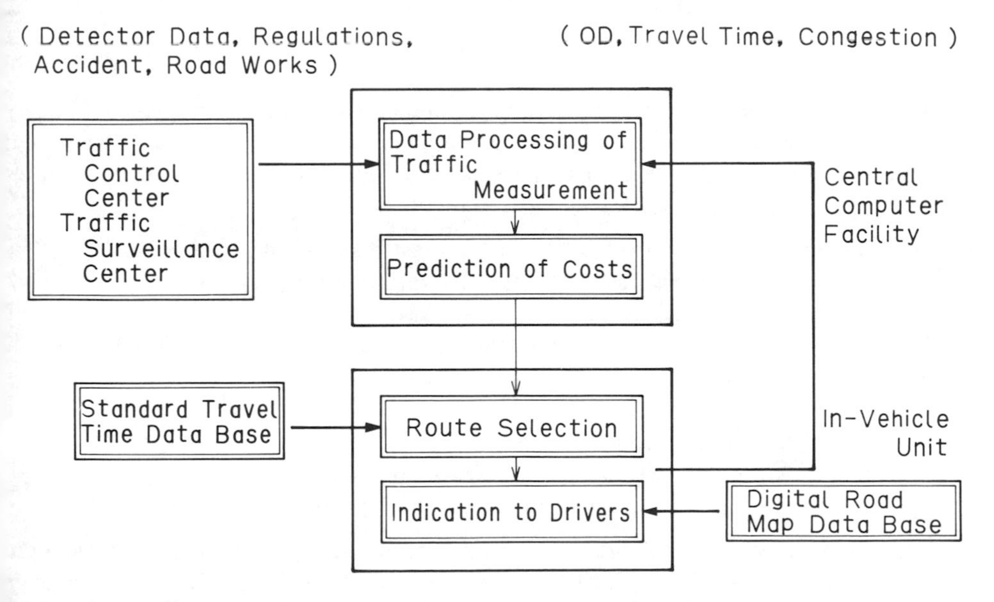

Figure 13.5 System configuration of route guidance system based on navigation system.

In Figure 13.5, the central facility accumulates travel time data, determines the cost data based on travel time, and distributes the cost data by communication links so that each vehicle can compute a desirable route. Here, the cost data are determined by travel time, prediction of travel time, and the modification of travel time data in the sense of Ben-Akiva and others, only in a different situation [31]. In other words, the central facility never guides the vehicles, but just gives various cost data to drivers. As the penetration rate increases, the cost data will achieve a certain accuracy and drivers' decisions will begin to rely on these data. Although the onboard calculation of route selection is adopted in the system configuration, the control of vehicles is expected to be sufficiently attained by the control and modification of cost data. If a road pricing scheme is introduced based on the cost data just defined, then the control aspects of the proposed system becomes more obvious.

In the final stage of penetration, the integration with signal control and the realization of traffic assignment by using type II two-way mobile communications will be introduced. At this stage, the dynamic models used to describe traffic flow in the network are expected to exist, since travel time data and OD information are available by using type II mobile communications. This is also an area where basic and integrated research is needed.

Advantages of Onboard Route Selection

There are several advantages of introducing onboard route selection, even when a two-way communication link is established and travel time data are available.

Flexibility of Route Selection

Route selection is the area where the driver's preference comes in. Each driver, consciously or not, has his or her own objective functions based on taste. (Ben-Akiva and others used similar ideas for analyzing the route choice behavior of drivers [31].) Several examples of objective functions for determining an optimum route are:

- Guide to major roads and staying on the same road as long as possible;
- Guide to the route that has stable, small variance in travel time;
- Guide to the route where there is no congestion;
- Guide to the route that passes through as few intersections as possible;
- Guide to the shortest travel time route;
- Guide to the shortest distance route;
- Guide to the cheapest route;
- Guide to the route where number of turns is the minimum;
- Guide to the route that avoids going through a certain area of town.

In the proposed system configuration, drivers can choose their own objective function and the system becomes more flexible as a whole. On the other hand, if a route guidance system is designed to give various kinds of recommended routes that are calculated in he central facility of the route guidance system, then the whole system becomes very complicated. The routes recommended by the central facility of a route guidance system would eventually become standardized, and personal choices, such as the last two objective functions listed above, would not readily be considered. As a consequence, some drivers or probably many drivers would not like to be guided by the standardized route the central facility recommends. Therefore, the effect of a route guidance system as a tool for traffic management would diminish.

Reduction of Computational Load

f all of the OD pairs in the network or in some kind of aggregate network are considered n calculating the optimum route in the central facility of a route guidance system, the computational load becomes very high. In CACS, one-third of the 15-minute cycle time was considered to be too long in order to keep up with the dynamic behavior of traffic ituations in Tokyo. Therefore, if the number of OD pairs is large and the cycle time is determined to be 5 minutes or 1 minute (which are the standard cycle times of the traffic monitoring systems in Tokyo), the computational load in the central facility becomes normous, even if supercomputers are introduced for calculations. This implies that the operating cost of traffic management by interactive route guidance systems becomes very xpensive.

On the other hand, if the optimum route is calculated by the in-vehicle unit, only one pair of ODs needs to be considered, and this makes computational loads extremely mall. Therefore, even with an ordinary personal computer, the optimum route can be alculated within a satisfactory period of time. Moreover, the driver can even calculate he *k*th optimum route and compare it with the actual routes on the map generated on the CRT display.

The results of the CACS pilot test imply that the difference in travel time between he first and third shortest time routes are small, and in urban areas, these difference become relatively smaller as the trip length increases [32]. Therefore, it would be more practical to show each driver both the alternative routes and estimated travel time costs on the same screen, so that the final decision could be made by the driver.

3.5.2 Current R&D Programs

n Japan, several programs have begun recently, and new programs are expected to begin soon. The status of these programs is very progressive, and it is therefore not appropriate o describe in detail the current activities.

Advanced Road Traffic Systems

To cope with future traffic demands, there are various research activities being undertaken by the Ministry of Construction. Some examples of the research are the development of information technology for the management of the new expressway from Tokyo to Kobe, and a feasibility study to construct a new underground logistics system. ARTS aims at making further use of road-vehicle communication capabilities on ordinary highways, expressways, and future expressways. In December 1989, a research committee was formed by researchers from universities, 17 private corporations from the electronics and automobile industries, and two government organizations. The following two systems are examples that have been thoroughly examined (see [11, 33] for recent developments).

Road-Vehicle Communications by Leakage Coaxial Cable

According to the feasibility study for the newly planned expressway from Tokyo to Kobe, which is called the *Second Tomei*, approximately 25% of the road will be constructed in tunnels due to environmental issues and the high cost of land. In spite of the technical difficulties involved in communication between vehicles and roadside facilities in tunnels, the need to exchange information exists, such as for hazard warning, safety issues, and preventing a decrease in speed when vehicles enter tunnels. In such a situation, the use of leakage coaxial (LCX) cable as the means of ordinary communication and assisting driving by automated cruising systems using LCX communication links seems to meet the necessary requirements.

To begin with, the research committee determined that the potential capabilities of existing communication systems are not suitable to realize nonautonomous automated systems, such as autocruise, collision avoidance, and convoy/platoon. In order to realize a real-time, continuously linked, highly reliable type IV mobile communication system, a new idea of using LCX cable as the means of communication is proposed. The feasibility study was conducted using the LCX communication system for the control of vehicles in the direction of movement. In this study, the block size of the cable used in the communication is tentatively determined at 1 km. The specification of cable layout and protocols for road-vehicle communications and the type of information needed to conduct the control of vehicles are examined. The viability of this technology will be checked by simulation studies and field experiments (see Figure 13.6).

Road-Vehicle Lighting Integration System and Guidelight System

The road lighting system is activated by using the road-vehicle communication link or a roadside vehicle sensing system. Improvement in the quality of lighting is another research objective of the system. Since two sources of light are better than one in enhancing the three-dimensional appearance of objects on the road, the research to acquire the best

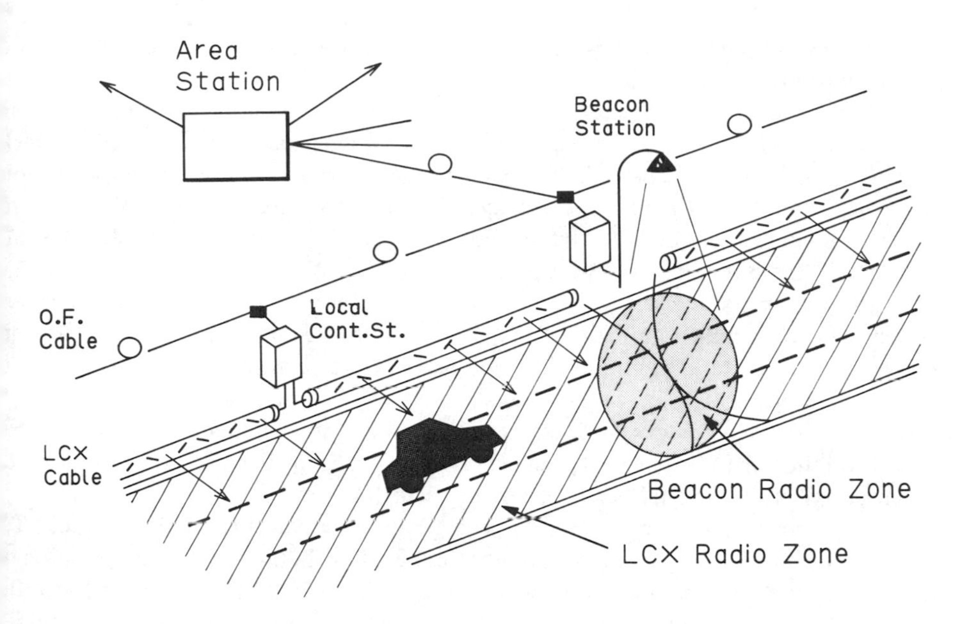

Figure 13.6 Concept of road-vehicle communications by LCX cable.

pattern for obstacle recognition is an example that falls into this category. This system apparently saves energy in comparison with the ordinary lighting system on roads with the appropriate traffic volumes. Moreover, the system is expected to be economical in the long run. Cost-benefit analysis and technological feasibility studies are now being conducted.

The Guidelight System is an idea to prevent accidents by providing visual information to the driver directly on the road infrastructure. Light-emitting devices, embedded in the road surface (or along the roadside), light up ahead of a speeding car. The length of the area lit is determined by the speed of the vehicle and by road friction. The system is expected to have a substantial effect on drivers. More basic studies on road pavement materials, analysis of driver's reactions, and the MMI of the system are needed [34].

Super Smart Vehicle System

MITI coordinated a two-year preliminary study program called *Super Smart Vehicle System* in August 1990. The members of the study program were from universities, national institutes, and more than 30 private corporations from the electronics and automotive industries. The purpose of SSVS is to create a vision for advanced vehicular systems that is highly harmonized with people and their society. Moreover, the key concept of the vision is to recognize automobiles as a cooperative system and not as independent systems.

A more practical purpose is to establish guidelines for R&D to realize the vision and t extend the study to a national R&D project [24].

Prior to SSVS, the concept of vehicle-to-vehicle communications (type IV mobil communications) has been studied since 1981. Small-scale experiments using IR and UH radio were carried out. The protocols for exchanging information on the driving conditior of vehicles while cruising are under consideration. The potential capability of vehicle-tc vehicle communications and integration with road-vehicle communications were consic ered in the framework of SSVS (see, e.g., [22–24]). On the other hand, some of th technologies of image analysis, photo sensors, and computer architecture for image analys were listed and examined for the applications to road traffic management and the autonc mous vehicle control system (see [35] for recent developments). After two years c preliminary study, MITI has not yet launched SSVS as a national project like CAC Basic studies on vehicle-to-vehicle communications and the autonomous vehicle contr system, originated from Personal Vehicle System (PVS), will be jointly continued b organizations related to MITI and the private sector.

Although ARTS is targeted for the technology of 10 years from now and SSVS targeted for the technology of 20 to 30 years into the future, both programs have a commc perspective on R&D: that the infrastructure and vehicle should be coordinated in ord to realize the functions of intelligent vehicles. The difference is that SSVS aims for vehicl oriented systems and ARTS aims for infrastructure-oriented systems. The difference com from the characters and the jurisdiction of the supervising ministries.

13.6 CONCLUDING REMARKS

In this section, the perspective and future problems in the field of informatics in roa transport are discussed.

13.6.1 Need for Comprehensive Study on Human-Machine Interface Problems

The importance and difficulty of human-machine interfaces were stressed in the previo sections, and some facts that are different from the common knowledge of eye movemen and visual perception were illustrated. To the author's knowledge, no standard methc of evaluating the phenomena treated in the chapter exists. In view of this point, tl methodologies developed in cognitive science might give us a hint to solving these kin of problems [27,28]. However, this approach is new in analyzing drivers' behavior, ar its applicability to actual design problems is still open to discussion.

13.6.2 System Engineering Approach to Computer Network Design of Route Guidance System

The system configuration explained in Section 13.4.1 can be characterized as the distribut process of route calculation. From the system engineering point of view, the configuratic ems to be resistant to random errors inherent in large-scale systems. Moreover, the onfiguration discussed in Section 13.4.1 will avoid becoming complicated and inflexible y adopting the centrally controlled route guidance system. At the third or fourth stage f penetration, each vehicle has a database of its own, and the central facility possesses huge database on cost data. These databases are linked by two-way mobile communicaons. In such a case, the whole design of computer networks will be very challenging search to conduct. As was pointed out in Section 13.3.3, the architecture of microprocesors in the vehicle should be designed based on the human capability to understand formation. At the same time, the design of the computer network and information flow each in-vehicle unit conditioned by the scope, the amount of information, and the ning of transmitting the information should be governed by integrated design concepts.

3.6.3 International Collaboration and Standardization

om the examples and discussions given in this chapter, it is clear that required characteris s of RTI are heavily connected with the characteristics of the traffic situation in the twork. As urban traffic control policies differ from city to city, the design of RTI could different in each city. International standardization of hardware and software is a cessary procedure to popularize the system in the world, and people are beginning to scuss this. Examples currently exist in human-machine interfaces, the design of computer chitecture in vehicles, and linkage with communication systems. However, standardizan should be discussed based on the recognition that the traffic situation, and social, nancial, and legal constraints are different among countries and cities.

The necessity for international collaboration exists in the fact that the realization RTI brings about high cost and high risk. The main difficulty is that basic research d application of technology have to proceed at the same time. Moreover, in scientific d engineering work, a trial-and-error approach, which we usually do not dare to adopt, sometimes inevitable in order to develop a new system. However, the problem is that we install a particular system in a city, we cannot test multiple systems at the same ne. Obviously, cost and organizational problems are the main reasons for not adopting e multiple approach. Therefore, it is usually very difficult to identify which of the merits the introduced system are specific to the technology, to the traffic situation of the test ld, or to the organization operating the system.

For example, as we mentioned previously, the researchers and engineers have a gative opinion of the immediate introduction of dynamic, interactive route guidance stems in Tokyo based on their experiences in the CACS experiment. However, the periences in CACS might have been specific to Tokyo or to the manpower and the ganizational structure adopted to conduct the experiment. Conversely, the experiences CACS and probably of LISB might be very informative for the design of a route idance system in other cities (probably small cities) in Japan or in any city in the world.

In this sense, the mutual exchange of information is very important to the countries 10 have an interest in introducing new systems, since, for the practical reasons mentioned above, only a few systems can be tested in one country. This characteristic will be more apparent with highly risky projects like SSVS and ARTS, which Japan now has, and projects such as PROMETHEUS in Europe and IVHS in the U.S.

13.6.4 Social Acceptance of Information and Road Transport

In the society of the market economy, the final index in measuring the social acceptance of traffic information provided by in-vehicle information systems is the number of units sold on the market. This is the feature that did not need to be taken into account in the installation of roadside information facilities. Only the budgets of public sectors determined the extent of installations.

From the general technological aspect, there are several constraints that seem to be inherent in and specific to informatics in road transport. One constraint is that the in-vehicle information systems must be located around the dashboard, which has limited space, bad heat conditions, and vibrations, and the size and the arrangement of the display unit are limited. Therefore, it seems that redesign of the dashboard and console is necessary in the near future.

Another aspect is the limitation in understanding of the traffic situations in a network. The traffic situation in a network can be considered as a randomly changing phenomenon and to construct a precise measurement system is very costly. Additionally, it is difficult to conduct maintenance of the system. Large numbers of intervals or links in the network should be considered. As a result, only the aggregate variables such as time mean or space mean values can be provided to drivers at some constant time intervals. In the route guidance system, for example, this implies that the difference in mean travel time of two routes becomes meaningless if the standard deviations are large compared with the time difference [36].

When the scale of the network is very large and a large number of vehicles are involved in the route guidance system or traffic information system using Type II mobile communications, the behavior of the system contains random elements which cannot be avoided. It seems that after introducing the system, the drivers and the road administrators need some time to get used to the characteristics of the information that the system can provide, and a period of social learning seems to be necessary. Although the system would be designed balancing the complexity of the system, the quality of information, and the cost to construct and conduct the maintenance of the system, some kind of trial-and-error approach is necessary to introduce a sociotechnological system such as a route guidance system or a traffic information system using type II mobile communications.

The third point is the need to integrate with other traffic management measures. For example, in order to construct a parking information and management system, there should be enough parking area to divert the vehicles. In order to guide vehicles, multiple alternative routes should exist. Moreover, in order to manage the demand for road transport, other modes of transportation should be ready for use. Therefore, it is clear that social acceptance of informatics in road transport is not independent of the realization of noninformatic traffic management measures, and a policy to integrate the measures for traffic management and control is needed. Especially in Japan, the development of in-vehicle units has gone ahead of other methods of realizing traffic management, and the consideration of the balance among the methods to provide traffic information seems to be necessary in the near future.

REFERENCES

[1] Oda, T., ''Application of a Fuzzy Algorithm for Traffic Information Transmission Systems,'' *IFAC/IFIP/IFORS Symp. CCCT*, 1989, pp. 473–478.

[2] *Ashigara Service Area Parking Availability System (Image Processing Type)*, Tokyo: Japan Highway Public Corporation, 1991.

[3] Matsuo, T., ''Traffic Control System on Expressways,'' *OECD RTR Seminar*, Chiba, Japan, 4–6 June 1991.

[4] Inokuchi, H., ''Traffic Congestion and Its Countermeasure of Metropolitan Expressway,'' *OECD RTR Program Seminar*, Chiba, Japan, 4–6 June 1991.

[5] Kamijo, S., Okamura, K., and Kitamura, A., ''Digital Road Database for Vehicle Navigation and Road Information System,'' *IEEE VNIS'89*, pp. 319–323.

[6] Jeffery, D., ''Driver Route Systems: State of the Art,'' *Telematics—Transportation and Spatial Development*, H. M. Soekkha, ed., VSP, Ultrecht, 1990.

[7] Tsuzawa, M., and H. Okamoto, ''Advanced Mobil Traffic Information and Communication System (AMTICS),'' *IEEE VNIS'89*, pp. 475–483.

[8] Shibata, M., ''Development of Road/Automobile Communication System,'' *Transportation Research*, No. 23A, 1989, pp. 63–71.

[9] Kawashima, H., ''Japanese Perspective of Driver Information Systems, *Transportation*, No. 17, 1990, pp. 263–284.

[10] Kawashima, H., ''Two Major Programs and Demonstrations in Japan,'' *IEEE Trans. on Vehicular Technology*, Vol. 40, No. 1, 1991, pp. 141–146.

[11] Kawashima, H., ''Present Status of Japanese Research Programs on Vehicle Information and Intelligent Vehicle Systems,'' *DRIVE Conf.*, 4–6 Feb. 1991.

[12] "Specification of The Radio Data System RDS for VHF/FM Sound Broadcasting,'' Brussels: European Broadcasting Union, Document Tech. 3244, 1984.

[13] "CARMINAT Leads the Way,'' press document, October 1990.

[14] Sparmann, J. M., ''LISB Route Guidance and Information System: First Results of the Field Trial,'' *IEEE VNIS'89*, pp. 463–466.

[15] Catling, I., F. op de Beek, C. Casimir, R. Mannings, F. Zijderhard, W. Zechnall, and J. Hellake, ''SOCRATES: System of Cellular Radio for Traffic Efficiency and Safety,'' *Proc. DRIVE Conf. of Brussels*, Vol. 1, Elesevier, Amsterdam, 4–6 Feb. 1991, pp. 28–43.

[16] Kawashima, H., Y. Ishii, and R. Fukui, ''Discrete Minimal Radio Zone Communication System in RACS Project and Its Performance Evaluation,'' selected papers from *IFAC/IFIP/IFORS Symp. CCCT 1989*, 1990, pp. 19–26.

[17] Kerver, T., ''Mobile at Ku Band Paying Off,'' *Satellite Communications*, June 1989.

[18] Fujii, H., ''The CACS Project and Now-Dynamic Route Guidance as the Final Target,'' *65th Annual Meeting, Transportation Research Board*, 1986.

[19] Fujii, H., ''The CACS Project: How Far Away Are We From the Dynamic Route Guidance System?'' *Transportation for the Future*, D. F. Batten, and R. Thord, eds., Berlin: Springer-Verlag, 1990.

[20] Yumoto, N., H. Ihara, T. Tabe, and N. Naniwada, ''Outline of the Comprehensive Automobile Traffic Control Pilot Test System,'' *Trans. Res.*, Rec. 737, Nat. Acad. Sci., pp. 113–121.

[21] Kawashima, H., ''Integrated System of Navigation and Communication in Japan,'' selected papers from *IFAC/IFIP/IFORS Symp. CCCT 1989*, 1990, pp. 257–264.

[22] Aoki, M., and H. Fuji, ''An Intervehicle Communication Technology and Its Applications,'' *Proc. 22nd ISATA*, Vol. 1, 1990, pp. 127–134.

[23] Tsugawa, S., S. Murata, T. Yatabe, and T. Hirose, ''Vehicle Following System Using Vehicle-to-Vehicle Communication—Its Concept, Control Algorithm, and Communication System,'' *Proc. ASME/ISCIE USA-Japan Symp. Flexible Automation*, 1989, pp. 6621–662.

[24] Tsugawa, S., and S. Murata, ''Velocity Control for Vehicle Following Through Vehicle/Vehicle Communication, *Proc. 22nd ISATA*, Vol. 1, 1990, pp. 343–350.

[25] Rumar, K., ''In-Vehicle Information System,'' *Int. J. Vehicle Design*, No. 9, pp. 548–556.

[26] Daimon, T., H. Kawashima, and M. Akamatsu, ''A Study of Drivers' Characteristics When Using In-Vehicle Information System,'' *Japanese Journal of Ergonomics*, Vol. 29, No. 3, 1993, pp. 157–165.

[27] Michon, J. A., ''On the Multidisciplinary Dynamics of Traffic Science,'' *IATSS Research*, No. 11, 1987, pp. 31–40.

[28] Takasaki, G. M., and P. F. Wasielewski, ''Research in Vehicle Information Systems at General Motors,'' *IEEE VNIS'89*, pp. 250–254.

[29] Godthelp, H., and F. op de Beek, ''Driving With GIDS; Behavioral Interaction With the GIDS Architecture,'' *Proc. DRIVE Conf. of Brussels*, Vol. 1, Elesevier, Amsterdam, Feb. 4–6, 1991, pp. 351–370.

[30] Yumoto, N., ''Status of Advanced Driver Information Systems in Japan,'' *70th Annual Meeting Transportation Research Board*, Washington, D.C., 15 Jan. 1991.

[31] Ben-Akiva, M., M. J. Bergman, A. J. Daly, and R. Ramaswamy, ''Modeling Interurban Route Choice Behavior,'' *9th Int. Symp. Transportation and Traffic Theory*, 1984, pp. 299–330.

[32] Tsugawa, S., K. Kitoh, H. Fujii, K. Koide, T. Harada, K. Miura, S. Yasunobu, and Y. Wakabayashi, ''Info-Mobility: A Concept for Advanced Automotive Functions Toward the 21st Century,'' *SAE Int. Congress and Exposition*, 25 Feb.–1 March 1991.

[33] Kawashima, H., M. Shibata, T. Matsumura, and H. Tsunomachi, ''Advanced Road Traffic Systems (ARTS): Surface Transportation and the Information Age,'' *Proc. IVHS America Annual Meeting*, Newport Beach, California, 17–20 May 1992, Vol. 1, pp. 42–49.

[34] Tsuda, H., K. Yamada, T. Honda, and T. Ishikawa, ''Road Vehicle Lighting Integration (ROVELI),'' *24th ISATA*, Florence, Italy, 20–24 May 1991.

[35] Tsugawa, S., N. Watanabe, H. Fujii, and M. Hirayama, ''Research and Development Projects for Info-Mobility Technologies,'' *Proc. IVHS America Annual Meeting*, Vol. 1, Newport Beach, California, 17–20 May 1992, Vol. 1, pp. 50–57.

[36] Tsuji, H., R. Takahashi, H. Kawashima, Y. Yamamoto, ''A Stochastic Approach for Estimating the Effectiveness of a Route Guidance and Its Related Parameters,'' *Transportation Science*, Vol. 19, pp. 333–350.

Chapter 14

RACS and IVCS

Hiroshi Tsunomachi, Yutaka Miyata, and Yasuhiko Kumagai

14.1 ROAD-AUTOMOBILE COMMUNICATION SYSTEM (RACS)*

14.1.1 Preface

RACS is a system of IVHS-RTI jointly developed in 1984 by the Ministry of Construction (MOC) Public Works Research Institute with cooperation from HIDO (Highway Industry Development Organization), private sector automobile producers, and electronics manufacturers. The development of RACS from the technological side attained its goals, and it was decided to aim at an early realization of the system in 1991 by integrating other systems (e.g., AMTICS) that share the same technological domain with RACS to create a comprehensive system called VICS (Vehicle Information Communication System) described in (Section 14.2). At this time, RACS is becoming realized as a beacon system as a part of VICS. In this section, we will introduce the concept of RACS, its outline, and the history of its development, taking into consideration that this system also covers a part of the history of VICS.

14.1.2 Development of RACS

14.1.2.1 Background of the Development of RACS

The development of RACS has been promoted by the following conditions.

- In spite of recent rapid growth in the volume of automobile transportation, infrastructure (such as roads) has not been developed correspondingly. Therefore, increasing traffic congestion and accidents have emerged as important social problems.

*This section was written by Hiroshi Tsunomachi.

- Although we now have access to a great deal of information in our offices and homes, automobiles have been isolated from this development. As a result, drivers want more information for such things as avoiding traffic congestion.
- Along with the rise in ownership of automobiles by households, there has been an increase in the number of drivers lacking knowledge about geography and roads and who thus desire useful information.
- Businesses need to know the arrival time of people or cargo more accurately in order to increase the efficiency of production and of other aspects of business. For this purpose, they are expecting the implementation of communications between drivers and offices or transportation control centers, as well as the provision of accurate traffic information.
- Recent developments in electronic communications and information processing technology have made it possible to design mobile communication systems to satisfy these requirements.

14.1.2.2 Points of Consideration During the Development of RACS

In developing RACS, we plan to overcome the problems and make it possible to satisfy drivers' needs and desires. Current measures to provide road traffic information include road signs for providing static information, along with variable-message boards, highway advisory radio services, and so on for providing dynamic information, as well as radio and TV for spreading information over a wide area. However, these measures have a limited capacity in terms of the volume of information and with regard to the content of information, because such information is targeted for a large number of unspecified drivers.

In addition, the Japan Road Traffic Information Center provides road traffic information by telephone. However, the coverage of information is not sufficient in terms of either quality or quantity. Moreover, the information is usually obtained by the driver before the trip, so it cannot help the driver to respond quickly to the current traffic situation (for example, in order to change routing to avoid a traffic jam).

Drivers are not satisfied with uniform information. They desire accurate and high-quality real-time information according to their specific destination and situations, including information covering both wide and local areas. However, systems ot collect such information have not been fully developed. For example, sensors to monitor the actual traffic situation must be improved in terms of density and area covered, but it could require a huge investment to develop such an infrastructure using past techniques. Therefore, it is desirable that we develop a system that not only satisfies the current information requirements of the drivers, but can also be used to collect information.

14.1.2.3 Position of RACS in the Development of IVHS-RTI Technologies in Japan

The first IVHS-RTI technology project in Japan was CACS, researched and developed from 1973 through 1978. It was a large project, conducted in collaboration with universities, government ministries, and private sector firms. CACS utilized advanced communications and computer technologies and integrated the traffic control system and the traffic guidance system. It produced significant technological achievements.

However, this system needed to receive the destination code from each vehicle, to process the dtae, and then to transmit the most appropriate directions to each car. Consequently, in spite of the relatively small amount of equipment required by the system, it could not be developed for practical application because it required provision of a massive amount of ground infrastructure.

After this experiment, in the 1980s automobile manufacturers and electronics companies took the initiative in the development of onboard equipment that was operable without the need for ground infrastructure. Such developments include directional and distance sensors, digital road maps coupled with CD-ROM for storing the data, and GPS, which performs position location by satellite. With these developments, a technological foundation for so-called *static navigation* was established for enabling drivers to recognize their own position and destination with an onboard display of the digital road map.

As a consequence of this situation (both the infrastructure and onboard technologies have been considerably researched and developed), the Road Automobile Communication System Study Group was established in 1984 with the aim of developing a system that meets drivers' requirements and can be practically implemented through the gradual spread of onboard equipment and the development of infrastructure. The basic concept of the system is as follows.

- A large quantity of real-time information is provided according to the location of each vehicle. This has been accomplished as a result of rapid technological advances in the fields of communications and onboard microcomputers.
- The onboard equipment stores and selects the information and couples it with the information in the large-capacity CD-ROM to provide the processed information to the driver.
- The ground center provides other individual information on request by each driver.

In this system, both the ground and onboard systems are operable individually, and each system works together to provide information. This system can fully utilize the technological merits of both infrastructure and onboard equipment independently to provide the desired information, as contrasted with conventional systems, which require full development of both types of equipment as an inseparable unit.

14.1.2.4 History of the Development of RACS

The development of RACS was initiated with the establishment of the Road-Automobile Communication System Study Committee (chairman: Professor Takaba of Tokyo University), an organization established under HIDO in 1984. This committee studied the development concept and determined the outlook for development. Since 1986, development has been performed with the collaboration of the MOC and 25 automobile manufacturers and electronics companies in the private sector. In this collaboration, development has been conducted towards three phased targets.

In the first phase in 1986, the correction of actual position by means of the beacon was successfully performed, and the effectiveness of the navigational function was confirmed. In the second phase in 1987, the following points were confirmed.

- Introduction of the map matching technology can reduce the density of the installation of beacons.
- The information supply function covering traffic jams and trip times can be coupled with the digital maps for drivers to find the most appropriate routes to the destinations using the onboard equipment. The display of parking information (such as locations, fees, and availability) is likewise possible.

In the third phase from 1988 to 1989, the possibility of (automatic vehicle monitoring) (AVM) and AVI by means of bidirectional communication and individual communication by facsimile was studied. And in the Tokyo area, comprehensive trials of each function were performed to confirm the technological feasibility as a conclusion to the project.

In 1990, technological development was concluded, and experiments began to put the accumulated technological achievements into practice. Before commencing the actual operation, we assumed the following.

- A frequency range of 2.5 GHz;
- One-way communication by the beacons to the cars;
- A transmission speed of 64 kbps.

More than 100 beacons were also installed in the metropolitan areas of Tokyo, Osaka, and Nagoya in order to perform transmission experiments. Based on these experiments, we are now creating a manual for roadside installation of the beacons. In 1991, we installed more beacons to provide quasipractical static information. This experiment has allowed us to find points to consider in creating practical data.

14.1.3 Outline of RACS

14.1.3.1 Outline of the System

As is shown in Figure 14.1, RACS consists of (1) beacons which are installed along the road in order to communicate by radio with the cars, (2) system centers, which are connected to the beacons by wire to control the content of the information and regulate communication, and (3) onboard equipment, which displays the information in the car and transmits driver commands to the beacon. The beacons will be installed along the roadside at intervals of 2 to 10 km. They communicate digitally at a high speed (the targeted transmission rate is 64 kbps, which is equivalent to 8,000 Japanese characters per second) at frequencies between 1 and 3 GHz to cars within 70m from the beacon. Several system centers will be constructed according to the quantity of information and

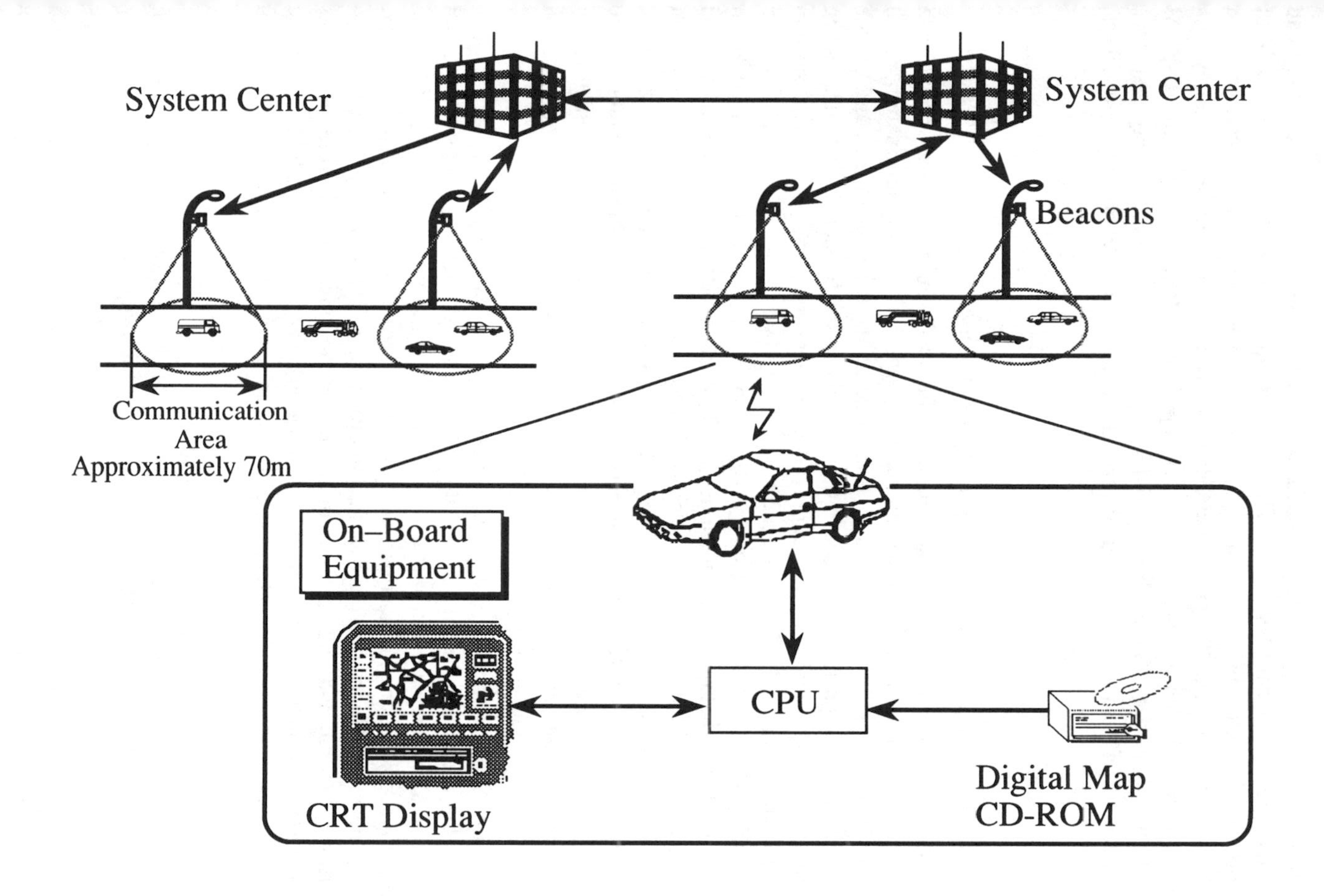

Figure 14.1 Overall structure of the system.

the processing method. They will be linked with the beacons by means of existing road dedicated lines or optical-fiber cables. The onboard equipment will receive the bulk of information transmitted by the beacon to display on the CRT display or to produce sound information. At this stage, the driver may obtain more useful information by applying a digital road map, which has already been developed and is being marketed in CD-ROM form, to the equipment. The method of displaying information and its safety assurance largely depend on the design of individual car manufacturers and electronic device makers.

14.1.3.2 Function of the System

The functions of RACS can be generally classified as follows.

Navigation Function. Navigation function in its broad meaning includes various road traffic information services, including intersection signs and parking information, but in this case it is limited to the navigation system based on the digital road map and has the position correction and road guidance functions. There are frequent divergences when vehicle location is inferred on the digital map by matching with on-vehicle sensors (direction and distance). Position correction is performed when the car passes the beacon. The actual position of the car is detected by the onboard sensor, which locates its position on the digital map, but the obtained data might not be accurate. Road guidance based on static information, including the shortest possible way to the destination, may be obtained with the conventional combination of digital maps and the onboard CPU. But RACS enables such types of guidance as the fastest possible way to the destination and dynamic road information based on the real-time and comprehensive road information from the beacon. In the future, this road guidance function may be developed to perform functions such as dynamic control of the flow of traffic.

Information Service Function. The static information we can provide in this category includes the actual position of the car, the route name, the name of the locality, and information about the intersection (such as its shape), which way to go according to the destination, explanation of regulations, and guidance information, such as major facilities, parking areas, and landmarks. The dynamic information includes road traffic information covering both local and wide areas (regulations, traffic jams, and trip time as well as information on accidents and road work), information regarding the availability of service areas and parking areas, and much more. Drivers can select any of this information when desired.

Individual Communication Function. Compared to the previous two functions, which are communicated only from the beacon to the car, bidirectional communication can dramatically expand functionality. For instance, the following communication or supply of information might be possible.

- Emergency communication (information to police or emergency hospitals in case of accident or other emergency);

- General calls, business communication (with offices or clients, or operational directions provided by the operations manager of bus, taxi, or truck fleets);
- Inquiry, reference, and reservation (for information providers, travel agents, etc.);
- Information about automatic tolling (individual vehicle number);
- Information about the vehicle conditions, vehicle ID, vehicle position (automatic vehicle monitoring);
- Collection of road traffic information (traffic jams, trip times, accidents, abnormal road conditions, etc.);
- Direction of routes and route guidance (on request, drivers can be provided with information on routing at intersections or the way to destinations).

Regarding the collection of road traffic information, each car passing the beacon automatically provides its ID number and the actual time to the center through the beacon. The center manages and processes the data in order to obtain the required travel time between any two given points. With this function, each car can be considered to operate as a sensor of traffic conditions. In addition, this function can make possible faster response times to accidents or abnormal road conditions by information relayed through the center by the first vehicles to discover such accidents or conditions.

14.1.3.3 *Characteristics of the System*

RACS has as its base an intermittent miniature zone system with microwaves. The technological characteristics are as follows.

- Since there is no interference between zones, a single frequency can serve the entire country.
- Since propagation of the radio signals is not much influenced by the topography or the surrounding buildings, reception conditions remain stable and the propagation path can be secured with little error.
- The high carrier frequency of the system permits high-speed data communications.
- The low electric power (10 mW) and relatively long wavelength employed by the system allow the ground stations and onboard equipment to be made smaller and cheaper.
- Because the communication is intermittent, communication cannot be provided outside of the zones, and continuous communication is not possible.
- The functions and information provided can always be changed to correspond to the point of installation. In other words, information can be produced about the local area. The system can also flexibly respond to any future expansion of the functions.
- Density of zone installation can be determined flexibly. Therefore, it would be possible, for example, to install the system with a low density all over Japan in the

first stage, then to gradually increase the density according to demand. Also, it i possible to install the system at higher densities in urban areas and lower densities in rural areas.

- The number of users can be increased without limit by increasing the number of zones.

14.1.3.4 Outline of the Beacons

The beacons function to convert hard data programmed into their internal memories and dynamic information received via cable from the centers into a radio frequency format and transmit microwave radio signals. They are constructed as shown in Figure 14.2. A comparative study was made between inductive radio and microwave beacon types. The inductive radio type has been used in mobile communications experiments by other research organizations and are also being used in practice in bus-location and railroad transmission systems. However, there is a limit to the data transmission capacity for large volumes of data. The use of microwaves is immature, but has the advantages of allowing high-speed communications and small-sized reception antennas. Also, with a view from radio frequency administration, they are expected to be allocated for mobile communications use. Thus, the microwave system was selected. Also, an AM reverse phase modulation method is used for the position indicators and for the detection of travel direction from microwaves received from the beacons. By reading the changes in the phase relationships in the AM signals, the automobile-mounted signal reception equipment can detect the beacons perpendicularly and determine the travel direction. The principle of this method is shown in Figure 14.3. Experiments have confirmed that the error of position detection using this method is extremely satisfactory at within 2m or 3m. The general specifications for VICS to be implemented initially are listed in Table 14.1.

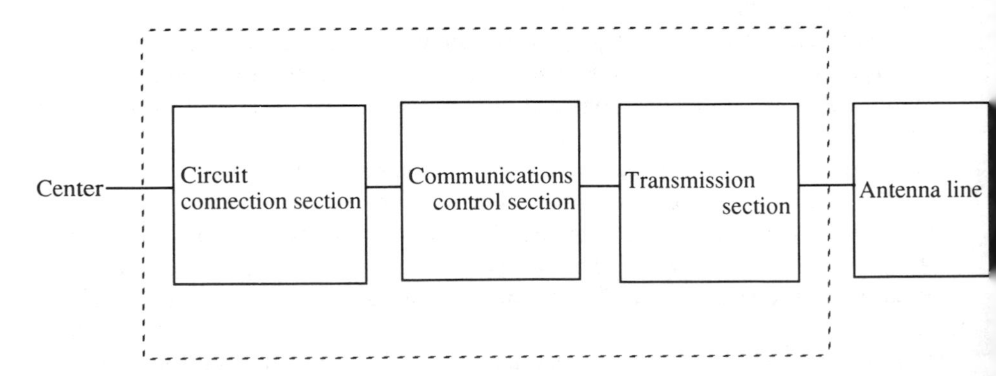

Figure 14.2 Structure of the beacons.

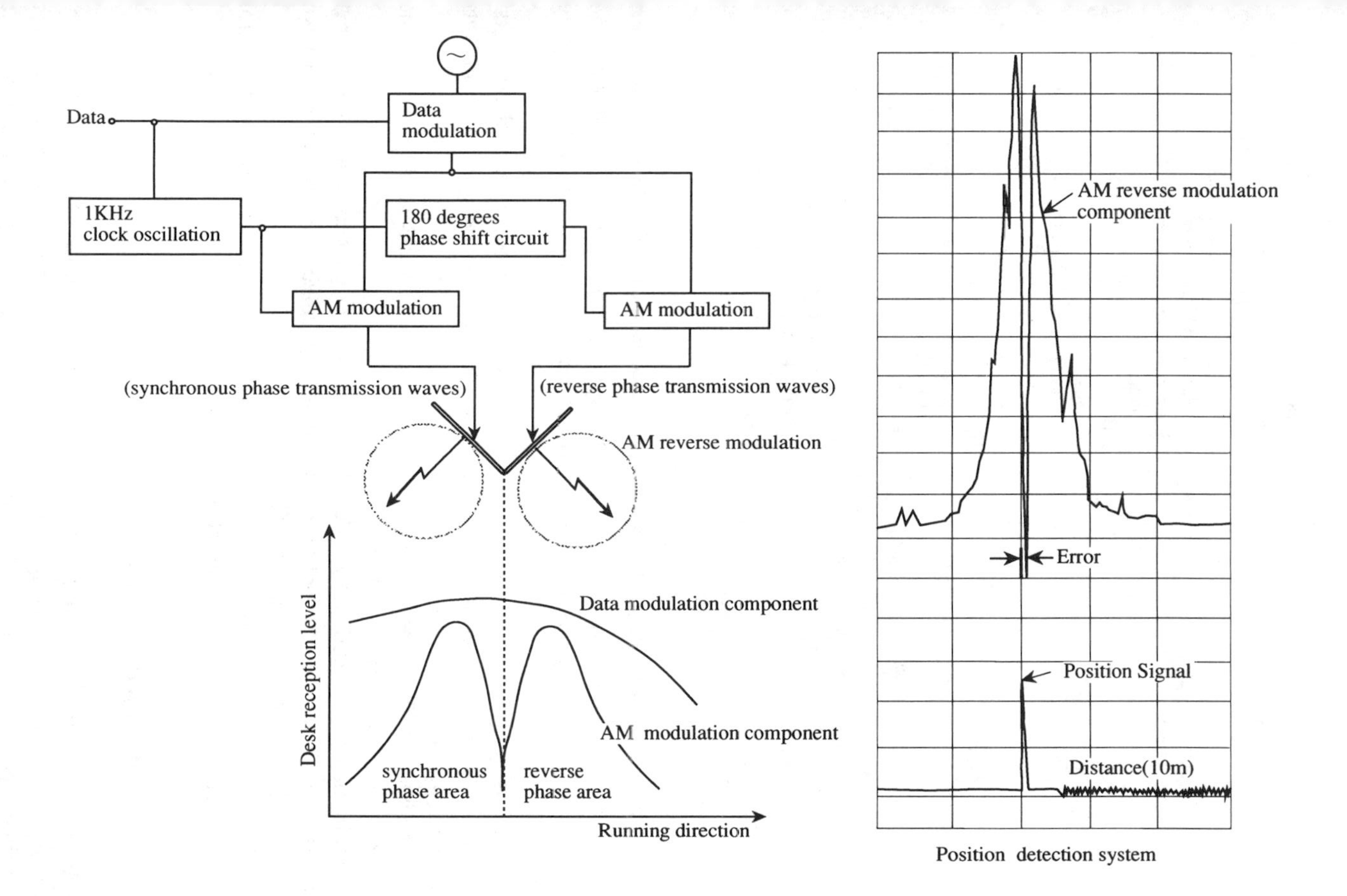

Figure 14.3 AM reverse modulation method.

Table 14.1
VICS Specifications

Item	*Specification*
Operating frequency	2.5-GHz-band single wave
Signal method	Single frequency, one direction communication
Type of radio wave	D1D
Signal transmission rate	64 kbps The allowable deviation of the signal transmission rate is plus or minus 50 × 10E-6 for 64 kbps
Code type	NZR
Modulation method	GMSK (Gaussian-filtered minimum shift keying)
Location detection/direction sensing signal modulation method	AM
Location detection/direction sensing signal modulation type	1-kHz square wave synchronized with the data frame
Antenna power	20 mW (10 mW × 2)

14.1.3.5 Summary of the Data Form

The data is transmitted from the beacons to the automobile-mounted receivers as follows.

- A segment of data is sent cyclically. The system is designed so that when an automobile containing a receiver passes by the beacon, it will receive at least three cycles.
- A cycle is designed to be easy to process by the automobile-mounted receivers. Thus, all data are divided into fixed lengths (called frames) and are sent in packets containing multiple frames.
- The number of frames per cycle varies according to the beacon, the time, and the amount of dynamic information.
- Each frame contains coding that identifies the coding of contents and confirms that the correct frames are supplied to the automobile-mounted receivers. This is known as a cyclic redundancy check (CRC).
- Each frame has a fixed length of 128 bytes and is divided into a transmission control section, header section, and actual data section.

14.1.3.6 Outline of the Vehicle-Mounted Receivers

The automobile-mounted receivers contain position detection, direction determination, data restoration, and data processing functions, as shown in Figure 14.4. However, there are also simplified versions that do not contain a vehicle-mounted position sensor and a

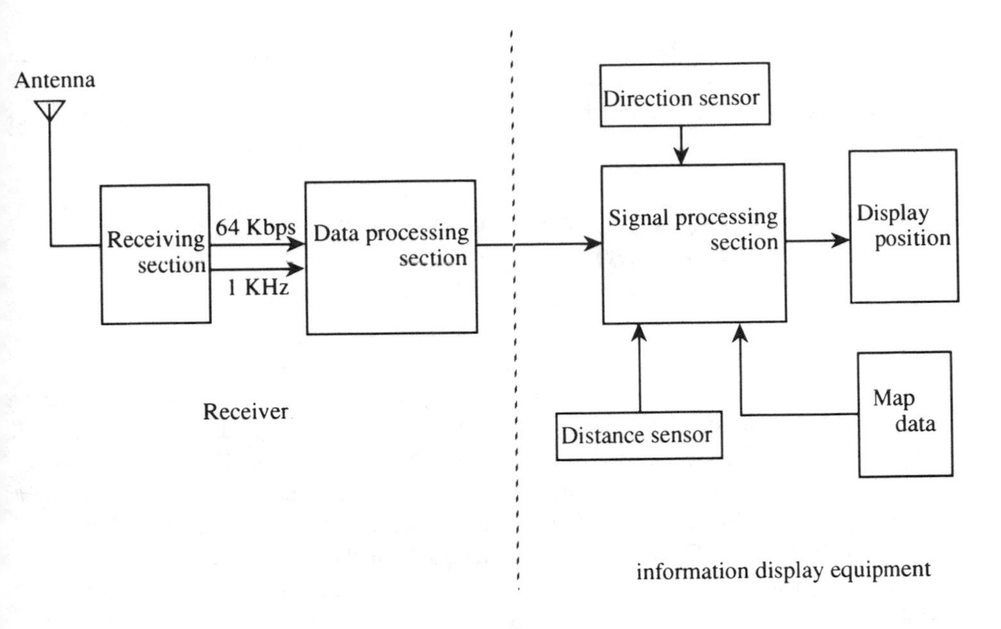

Figure 14.4 Structure of automobile-mounted equipment.

CRT display. The vehicle-mounted antennas directly receive the broadcasts in an oblique upward direction from the beacons, which are located along the road at a height of 5m to 7m. In contrast, because the reflective waves and dispersed waves from surrounding vehicles, buildings, the road surfaces, and so on come from lateral and downward directions, the aerials for the vehicle-mounted receivers are given an upward orientation and a wide orientation forward and backward in the direction of travel of the vehicle.

14.1.4 Future Outlook

As mentioned earlier, there was a goal of implementing in the autumn of 1991 a single directional information function as a beacon system as a part of VICS, which would be coordinated with other media. Taking into consideration (1) the complementary relationship of simultaneously utilizing the features of, for example, FM multiplex broadcasting and those of the beacon broadcasting method, (2) the infrastructure provision policy, and (3) clarifying the policy of response from the automobile-mounted equipment side together with each type of media from information sources through data processing, it is necessary to construct a single, consistent system, and the unified efforts of both the public and private sectors are necessary.

On the other hand, regarding the parts not introduced by VICS (i.e., the various functions made possible by bidirectional communications), the technological feasibility of such functions was confirmed by the comprehensive HIDO experiments in 1989, but consultation and adjustment are necessary by public sector bodies and other groups in order to implement it as a social system.

HIDO is conducting research toward the goal of implementing this as a social system.

14.2 LATEST MOVEMENT OF VICS—VEHICLE INFORMATION AND COMMUNICATION SYSTEM*

14.2.1 Introduction

In Japan, several systems have been developed by different authorities with the idea of reducing traffic congestion and accidents in the field of ATIS. The Public Research Institute of the MOC had proceeded to develop RACS, working with 25 private companies since 1986. In the meantime, AMTICS was set up by the Japan Traffic Management Technology Association with private companies under the supervision of the National Police Agency in 1987. Those two systems had almost the same functions, giving real-time traffic information on in-vehicle displays to indicate the proper route for individual destinations with different transmission media. AMTICS adopted the Teleterminal system for broadcasting communications in its pilot test in 1989 and 1990. In the meantime, RACS was developing the Beacon system for the microzone communication method. Through pilot tests it was shown that most technical problems had been solved.

In 1990, three governmental agencies, the National Police Agency, Ministry of Posts and Telecommunications, and MOC, proposed to unify those two projects into a new project called VICS. In addition, three public sectors and seven major private companies wanted RACS and AMTICS to work together to promote VICS, and the VICS Promotion Council was established in October 1991. This section describes these activities in general and emphasizes the recent progress at the VICS Promotion Council.

By the censensus of the ten promoters who met on 3 September 1991, the Preparation Office for the establishment of the council was formed. The ten promoters were the presidents of two car manufacturers, five electric/communication manufacturers, and representatives of three public sectors:

- Toyota Motor Corporation;
- Nissan Motor Co., Ltd.;
- Sumitomo Electric Industries, Ltd.;
- Oki Electric Industry Co., Ltd.;
- Hitachi, Ltd.;
- NEC Corporation;
- Matsushita Communication Industrial Co., Ltd.;
- Japan Traffic Management Technology Association;

*This section was written by Yutaka Miyata and Yasuhiko Kumagai.

- Research & Development Center for Radio Systems;
- HIDO;

The representative of the ten promoters was Mr. Shoichiro Toyoda, the president of Toyota Motor Corporation. The inaugural meeting was held in October 1991. At the meeting, several topics, such as the structure of the organization and its rules, were discussed.

The council will proceed with the development of the new road traffic information systems, paying attention to the efficient utilization of valuable radio frequencies and the integration of the systems that have been researched and developed in related fields. Some committees are already launched and have proposed various activities. This section will give a general description of each committee and some committees' activity reports.

14.2.2 Objectives of the VICS Promotion Council

The objective of the council is to promote the adoption of VICS into practical use within a reasonably short period of time. To achieve this, the comprehensive plan includes: (1) conducting investigations, research, and development aimed at putting VICS into practical use; (2) activities to spread the use of VICS; and (3) other activities necessary in achieving the council's objective.

14.2.3 Road Traffic Information in VICS.

A VICS Operating Body will be established to operate the VICS Center (tentative name), which is expected to gather source data collected by road and traffic authorities, JARTIC, and others and to send them to the media centers in order to make accurate road traffic information available to automobiles. As for data transmission, beacon, FM multiplex, and teleterminal methods are now under consideration. The beacon is a high-speed data communication device that uses a quasimicrowaves through antennas installed on the roadside in order to transmit information to vehicles passing those points. FM multiplex is the transmission method for frequency-modulated sound and data in which digital signals are multiplexed onto existing stereo sound signals using VHF waves. Teleterminals are two-way, large-capacity, and high-speed data communication devices using packet radio communication on a multichannel access system between the terminals and a radio station.

14.2.4 Outline of the Organization of the VICS Promotion Council

The roles of the three committees under the steering committee can be summarized as follows.

Commerce Committee

This committee studies practical uses of VICS, conducts research on various issues necessary for the projects, and inquires into various subcommittees, as well as coordinating three subcommittees. The system subcommittee researches the project range of VICS, types of projects, and systems. The safety subcommittee researches safety of drivers with VICS terminals installed in vehicles. The database subcommittee researches required data specifications for VICS information.

Research Committee

This committee is expected to investigate various kinds of media necessary for VICS. There are also three subcommittees under this committee. The beacon subcommittee researches technical conditions of transmitting road traffic information using beacons. The FM multiplex subcommittee researches practical methods of using frequency modulation and multiplexing. For road traffic information, the teleterminal subcommittee researches technical conditions for transmitting road traffic information using teleterminals.

Experimental Committee

The activities of this committee will be carried out soon after their purpose, content, and period of experiments are decided.

14.2.5 Current Activities of the Steering, Commerce, and Research Committees

Some committees and subcommittees have had meetings and have approved general operation plans, as follow.

Steering Committee

This first meeting was held in November, 1991. Twenty-nine members of the steering committee and representatives from the National Police Agency, the Ministry of Posts and Telecommunications, and the MOC participated in this meeting. The following subjects were discussed and approved:

- Organizations and policies of the steering committee;
- Membership of committees and subcommittees of the steering committee;
- Public relations activities of the council and the organization of the secretariat.

Except for the experimental committee, members were recruited from a maximum of 50 companies and organizations for each committee, and from 20 companies and organizations for each subcommittee. The members of committees and subcommittees were selected from as many industries as possible to broaden the viewpoints of the committees and subcommittees. Their reasons for participation corresponded to the activities' goals and aims. In addition, outlines of the roles of committees and subcommittees were discussed and approved.

Commerce Committee

This committee mainly investigates items, such as the following, to realize the VICS:

- The structure of organization that will spread the use of VICS;
- Systems and networks that develop social infrastructure for the future;
- Careful consideration given to the safety of VICS.

In December, the first meeting was held with 49 companies and organizations and representatives from three authorities, with the aim of starting various subcommitte activities. The basic concept of VICS was reviewed. The second meeting was held in January 1992. Matters to be investigated, time schedules, and organizations of the committee and subcommittees were discussed. Regarding the schedules, a decision was made to consult with the steering committee.

Since the first commerce committee meeting, three subcommittees have been working on VICS concepts, specifically in terms of organization, funding, and systems architecture. The system subcommittee studies aspects of the VICS Operating Body, such as business prospects, funding, income, and expenditure are under investigation. Technical aspects of VICS Center System (tentative), such as VICS information processing computer systems and communications network, are being discussed. The safety subcommittee focuses its activities on investigation into safety of the in-vehicle information system. Items being discussed are equipment criteria, safety guidelines, displays, operation standards, and others. The database subcommittee mainly investigates VICS information, user needs, information service items, formats, and unification of information from a variety of sources. Regarding information services, the following items are under consideration:

- Traffic congestion: section and level of congestion;
- Temporary regulation: section, time, and causes;
- Traveling time: traveling time between major points;
- Parking: location and its availability;
- Others.

Research Committee

This committee mainly investigates the VICS communication media and coordinates subcommittees. In December 1991, the first meeting was held with 50 companies and organizations, as well as representatives of the three authorities, to start various activities of subcommittees. The basic concept of VICS was reviewed and matters to be discussed were adopted. The second meeting was held in January 1992. Matters to be investigated, schedules, and organizations to promote research programs were discussed and approved. After that it was decided to consult with the Steering Committee about the decision on plans for the committee. Three subcommittees have also been working to specify applications, information to be transmitted, system configurations, and others. The beacon subcommittee is investigating the application of the beacon communication system's information service in VICS media for practical use. The FM multiplex subcommittee is evaluating FM subcarrier communication and its data format for practical use in VICS media, as a subordinate working group to the Telecommunication Technology Council of Japan. The teleterminal subcommittee is studying application of teleterminal system to VICS media for practical use, featuring two-way communication capability of the teleterminal system.

14.2.6 Conclusion

The VICS Promotion Council was established on October 25, 1991. Two hundred and five companies and/or organizations, including overseas companies, belong to this Council. The steering committee was formed and has decided on the directions of the activities in the council. The organization of the council and directions of activities in each committee and subcommittee were approved, and they have started various activities to realize VICS. The VICS Operating Body was established in late 1992 after careful planning of VICS's safety, cost performance, and social infrastructure for the future. In order to start information services during 1993, each committee and subcommittee, except for the Experiment Committee, has approved its time schedule and has proceeded energetically with study and research into the practical use of the system.

This section was written in the early 1992. The time schedule has been changed, and the optical beacon has been under consideration as an additional communication medium. The VICS Promotion Council is now forwarding the demonstration experiment; its public demonstration is scheduled to be held in Tokyo in November 1993.

SELECT BIBLIOGRAPHY

Takada, K., Y. Tanaka, and Y. Kitamura, ''RACS: Result of the First Overall Field Trial,'' *24th ISATA*, May 1991.

Tanaka, M., T. Kuroda, and O. Yamada, ''Transmission Performance of FM Multiplex Broadcasting for Mobile Reception (in Japanese),'' *ITEJ Technical Report*, Vol. 16, Jan. 1992.

Okamoto, H., ''Evaluation of The 2nd AMTICS Pilot Test in Osaka,'' *24th ISATA*, May 1991.

VICS Promotion Council, ''VICS Newsletter,'' 1991, 1992.

Chapter 15

Onboard Equipment

Nobuo Yumoto

15.1 DYNAMIC ROUTE GUIDANCE

In CACS, which was investigated from 1973 to 1978 in Japan, the ground system calculated an optimum route for each origin-destination pair based on the traffic condition, and sent the turning direction to the vehicle on receipt of its destination code when it passed over a loop antenna at the entrance of an intersection. The onboard system depends on the ground infrastructure. It is difficult to start the installation of the ground infrastructure before the wide use on onboard systems is ensured.

To avoid the chicken-and-egg effect, the combination of navigation system and roadside radio was proposed. It was suggested, firstly, to let the navigation system, which works without the ground infrastructure, become popular, and then to start the radio transmission of traffic information to navigation-system-equipped vehicles [1].

Onboard equipment for dynamic navigation comprises a transceiver, a router with a display, and a locator with sensors and a map memory, as shown in Figure 15.1. The locator tracks the position of the vehicle by integrating the displacement vector measured by the distance and direction sensors. The router calculates an optimum route based on traffic data received by the transceiver and on the road network stored in the map memory. It determines the turning direction at an intersection knowing the position of the vehicle and the neighborhood geometry.

The roadside equipment may also send the position data to correct any navigation error and receive travel time data from the vehicle. As an alternative to onboard route calculation, the route can be calculated by the ground system and a guide table sent to the vehicle. The elements necessary to implement the dynamic navigation system are (1) traffic information source, (2) ground-vehicle communication media, (3) navigation-system-equipped vehicles, and (4) digital map database.

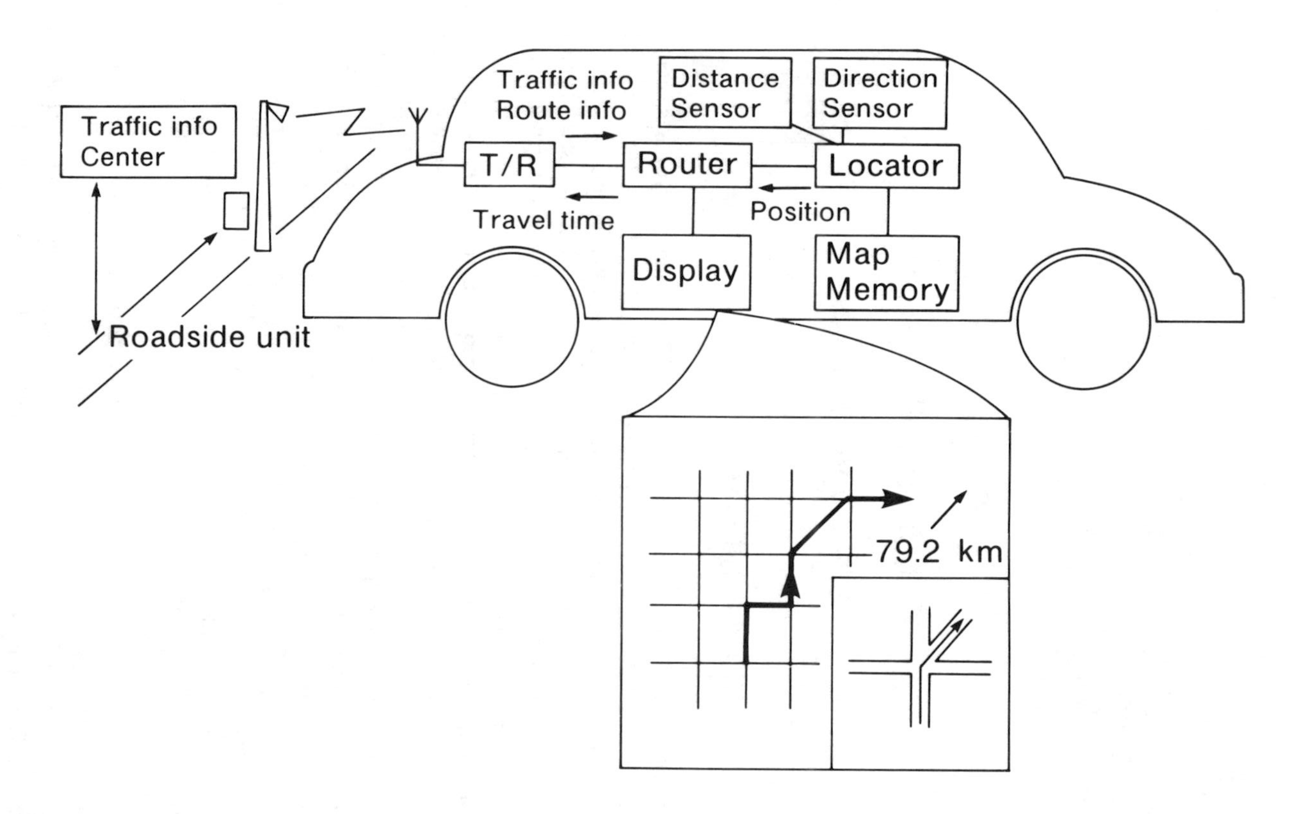

Figure 15.1 Dynamic navigation.

Route guidance can be implemented by the following procedures (Figure 15.2): (1) The optimum route for an OD is calculated based on the map and the travel time of each link. (2) The turning direction is determined from the route and the position of the vehicle. The position can be obtained with the navigation function based on the map and the displacement.

There are variations in route selection and display, as shown in Figure 15.3. Initially, there will not be enough vehicles equipped with the dynamic navigation unit to measure and report travel time. Computer calculation of an optimum route will be difficult because only information such as the degree of congestion is available. Therefore, route selection should be left to the discretion of drivers with course information shown on the map display.

When the quality of travel time data is improved by an increase in the number of equipped vehicles, computer calculation of an optimum route becomes reasonable. The choice is whether to do the route calculation at the ground facility or on board. In the former case, such as ALI-SCOUT or AUTOGUIDE, the guide table is sent to the onboard computer, which gives turning directions to the driver [2,3]. This makes the onboard equipment more compact because the map ROM is not necessary and the display is simple. Drivers, however, cannot be informed of the background traffic conditions. In the latter case, traffic information is sent to the vehicle and the onboard computer calculates the route. Besides the turning instructions, the background traffic condition can be displayed. An onboard map ROM is needed, but a map display helps the driver inform the computer of the destination. Turning selection can be performed by the ground by use of bidirectional interactive communication, as in CACS [4].

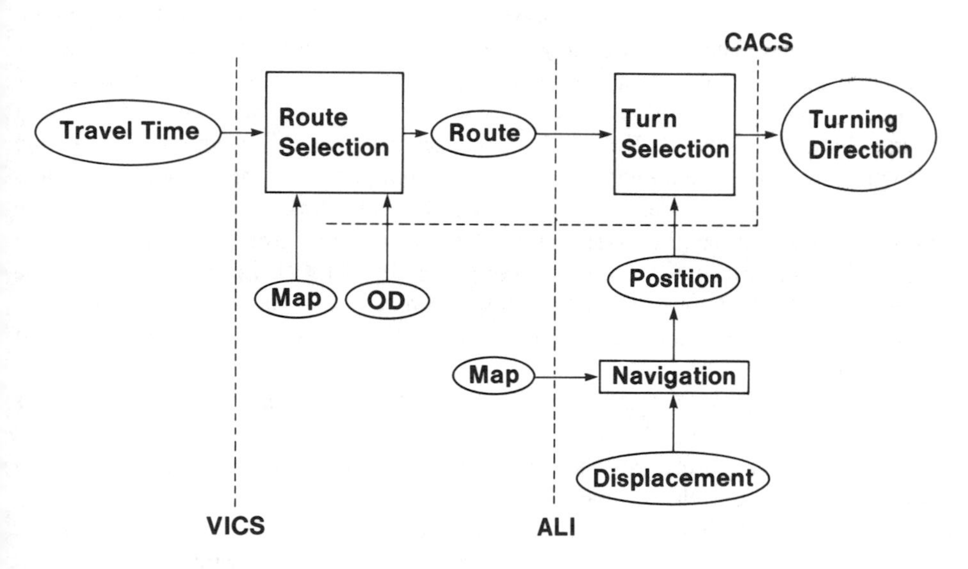

Figure 15.2 Route guidance.

	Ground ➧ Vehicle	Vehicle ➧ Driver	Route Selected by
I	Congestion	Map + Congestion	Driver
II	Travel Time	Turning Direction Map + Congestion	Vehicle
III	Guide Table Local Map	Turning Direction	Ground

Figure 15.3 Route selection.

15.2 A BRIEF HISTORY OF NAVIGATION SYSTEMS

The first navigation system was sold by Honda and fitted in its Accord model in 1981 using a gas rate gyroscope as the direction sensor [5]. In 1987, Toyota Electro Multivision was installed in its Crown, the first car to use a CRT to display the map [6].

Navigation techniques have been investigated in the author's group with the dynamic navigation in mind. The map matching technique [7], in which the measured route is correlated with the map to compensate for the accumulated error of the sensors, was developed. In 1987, a contract for a police car location system was awarded by Aichi Prefecture Police Department. For this system, a precise digital map with a 1:2,500 scale was digitized and calibrated. Each police car was equipped with a navigation system and transmitted its position to the headquarters via the radio link. Because these cars are monitored 24 hours a day, this system provided a severe test ground for the navigation technique. This technique was adopted in the Drive Guide for Nissan's Cedric and Cima in 1989 as the world's first map matching navigation system installed at an assembly line [8,9]. It also featured guidance for such places of interest as railway stations, hotels, golf courses, and stores.

Car models equipped with the navigation system have been increasing: Mazda's Eunos Cosmo (GPS) [10], Mitsubishi's Diamante (map matching) [11], and Honda's Legend (improved gas gyroscope). Pioneer and Toyota announced GPS navigation systems for the "after" market. Nissan released new 1991 models of Cedric and Cima with a fiber-optic gyroscope (FOG). Suzuki announced a navigation system with LCD on the Alto, a minicar model. Table 15.1 shows features of navigation systems on board recent car models.

Table 15.1
Navigation Systems

Manufacturer	*Model*	*Release*	*Supplier*	*Sensor*	*Map for Positioning*	*Display Map*	*Others*
Honda	Accord	1982	Honda	Gas rate gyro		1:100,000 or less	(Film map)
Toyota	Crown	1987	Nippondenso	Earth mag. Steering wheel		1:75,000 or less	
Nissan	Cedric Cima	1989	Sumitomo Electric	Earth mag., diff. odometer	1:2,500 (SEI)*	1:25,000 or less	
Mazda	Cosmo	1990	Mitsubishi Electric	Earth mag., diff. odd. GPS	1:25,000 (DRMA)**	1:12,500 or less	
Mitsubishi	Diamante Sigma	1990	Sumitomo Electric	Earth mag., diff. odometer	1:2,500 (SEI) 1:25,000 (DRMA)	1:12,500 or less	
Honda	Legend	1990	Honda	Gas rate gyro	1:25,000 (DRMA)	1:25,000 or less	
Toyota	Soarer Crown	1991	Nippondenso	Earth mag., diff. odd. GPS	1:25,000 (DRMA)	1:10,000 or less	CDCRAFT, route indicator
Nissan	Cedric Cima	1991	Sumitomo Electric	Earth mag., fiber-optic gyro	1:2,500 (SEI) 1:25,000 (DRMA)	1:12,500 or less	CDCRAFT, beacon receiver
Suzuki	Alto	1991	Sumitomo Electric	Earth mag., diff. odometer	1:2,500 (SEI) 1:25,000 (DRMA)	1:17,000 or less	CDCRAFT
Mitsubishi	Gallant	1992	Sumitomo Electric	Earth mag., vibration gyro	1;2,500 (SEI) 1:25,000 (DRMA)	1:12,500 or less	CDCRAFT, route indicator
Toyota	Mark II	1992	Matsushita Electric	Earth mag., fiber-optic gyro	1:25,000 (DRMA)	1:10,000 or less	CDCRAFT, route indicator

*SEI: Sumitomo Electric Industries, Ltd.
**DRMA: Japan Digital Road Map Association

15.3 CONFIGURATION OF ONBOARD EQUIPMENT

The control switches, including touch-sensitive switches and the audio-visual equipment including a CRT are shared among navigation, telephone, and CD audio. Figure 15.4 shows the configuration in Nissan's 1991 new model Cedric [12]. The system uses a FOG instead of the differential odometer. The FOG is included in the electronic control unit (ECU). A pair of separate CD-ROM drive units are equipped, one for the map database and the other for the audio and CDCRAFT (CD and CAT Applied Format). The CD-ROM drive interface board is mounted on the ECU, which is installed in the rear trunk. Two fiber-optic data links are used to transmit data from the CD-ROM drive units to the interface board. The keyboard consists of mechanical function keys and touch-sensitive switches which use infrared. The microcomputers used in the system are:

1. Locator
   - CPU: 16-bit CPU and a floating point processor;
   - Memory: 256K program ROM, 576K work RAM, 8K EEPROM;
   - Sensor interface: 12-bit analog-to-digital converter.
2. Display controller
   - CPU: 16-bit CPU, 8-bit 1-chip microprocessor, and a graphic controller;
   - Memory: 512K program ROM, 768K work RAM, 288K video RAM;
   - Display interface: 16 out of 4,096 colors palette IC.

15.4 MAP MATCHING

Dead-Reckoning Navigation Function. The position is obtained by accumulating the distance and direction traveled from the previous position (dead reckoning). The distance the vehicle traveled is obtained from the count of the pulses from the wheel sensors. The direction is determined by correlating the accumulated direction change obtained from the difference of the counts between the left and right wheel sensors, and the direction measured by the geomagnetic field sensor. The differential odometer using the wheel sensors offers good precision over a short time period, but the directional error accumulates with time, and an error also tends to be introduced due to tire slip. The geomagnetic field sensor is also subject to errors introduced by geomagnetic variation and magnetic interference. Using both sensor types and checking and comparing their output, it is possible to obtain the required precision, which would be difficult with a single sensor. The chassis magnetism and the magnetic field interference are estimated and compensated for by comparing the measured direction with the map data. To estimate the chassis magnetism, the output of the geomagnetic field sensor before and after turning is compared with the turning angle obtained from the differential odometer. This system has been able to keep the positioning error caused by the directional error to within 5% of the distance traveled.

Map Matching Function (Basic Model). In areas where a detailed map is available, the map matching method is used to obtain the precise location. The accumulated error caused

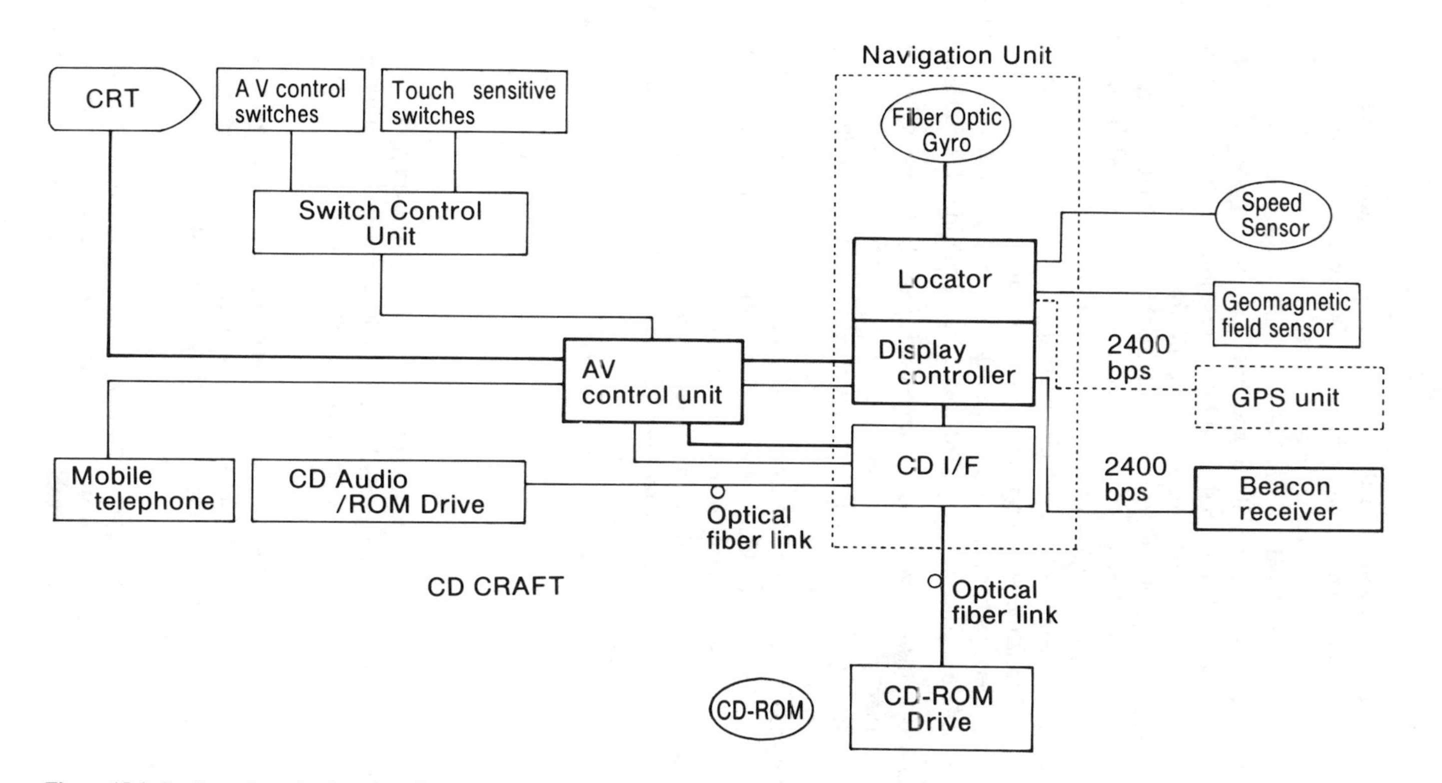

Figure 15.4 Configuration of onboard equipment.

by the sensing cannot be avoided in the dead-reckoning method. However, it can be compensated for by using map matching in which the correlation between the vehicle path obtained from the sensor data and the road network pattern stored in the digital map memory is statistically calculated. The locator selects all possible links when the vehicle encounters a branch or intersection. All the candidate links are compared with the measured path recognized by dead reckoning and given the correlation coefficient (vehicle existing coefficient). If the dead-reckoned path diverts from a link, the correlation coefficient of that link becomes smaller, and if it drops below a threshold constant, the link is removed from the candidates. Once a link enters the candidate list, all possible branches are traced and checked. Since a large volume of data is obtained whenever the vehicle turns at a corner, the chance of identifying the vehicle location is biggest at corners (Figure 15.5). By obtaining the correlation between the path of travel by dead reckoning and the map network, errors of dead reckoning can be canceled. The road network data used for this purpose were made by encoding every road wider than 2.5m in a 1:2,500-scale map.

Improvement of Map Matching Method. With the basic model map matching method, it is not easy to correct positioning error on a continuing curve with a very long diameter. The model may lose the correct location when driving a long distance on the expressway. A new system was developed to solve this problem. When it becomes difficult to correct the location by the basic method, the locator switches to the new map matching method automatically. The locator searches the location by obtaining the correlation between the shape of the long path of travel and the road network over a very wide area. It can correct the error of the initial position setting within 100m with 85% probability. Even if it fails to correct the initial position at a given time, there are successive chances. As a result, correction of the location will be done almost completely. The location error is less than 80m with 99% probability if the basic method is combined with the new method, even without the FOG.

15.5 SENSORS

Geomagnetic Field Sensor. A pair of flux gates are usually used as the geomagnetic sensor. A geomagnetic field sensor is easily affected, in principle, by disturbing magnetic fields outside the vehicle and magnetization of the vehicle itself, and is accurate to only 10 deg.

Differential Odometer. The difference of counts between the left and right wheel rotation sensors can be used to measure the rotation of the vehicle. This is called a *differential odometer.* The differential odometer tends to introduce error due to tire slip. This is also used to compensate for the magnetic field disturbance.

Gas Rate Gyroscope. A gas rate gyroscope consists of a piezoelectric vibration pump, a nozzle to jet helium gas, and a pair of hot-wire flow sensors to detect deflection of the gas flow, which occurs when the vehicle rotates. The deflection is measured by the

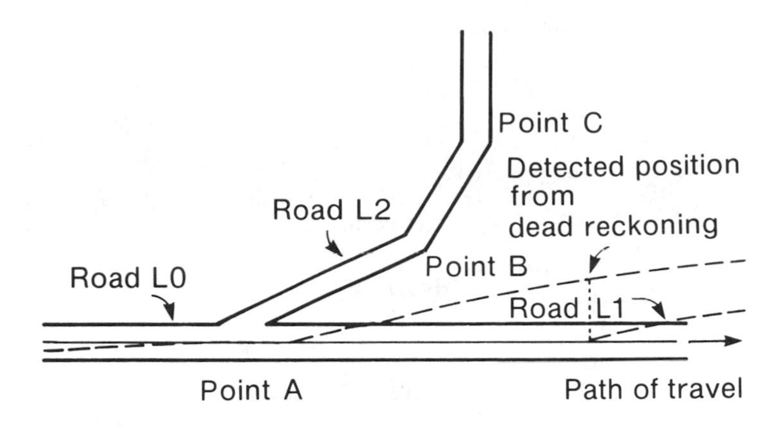

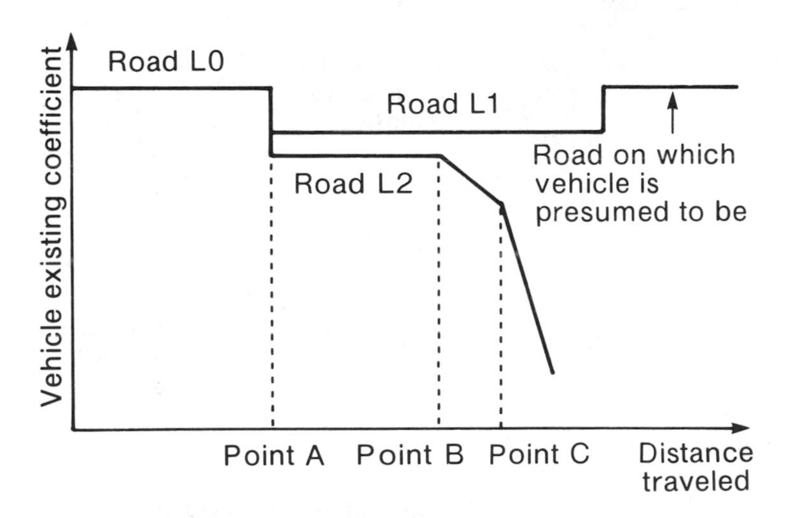

Figure 15.5 Map matching: the road network and vehicle path (top) and the change of vehicle existing coefficient (bottom).

temperature difference between a pair of the electrically heated sensing wires. See Figure 15.6.

Vibration Gyroscope. A vibration gyroscope uses the principle of the Coriolis force. The rotation around the z-axis of a piezoelectric ceramic beam induces a vibration in the y-direction when the beam is vibrated in the x-direction. See Figure 15.7.

Fiber-Optic Gyroscope. At the moment, the FOG is the most stable and accurate rotation rate sensor for automotive use and can achieve a comparatively low cost with sufficient

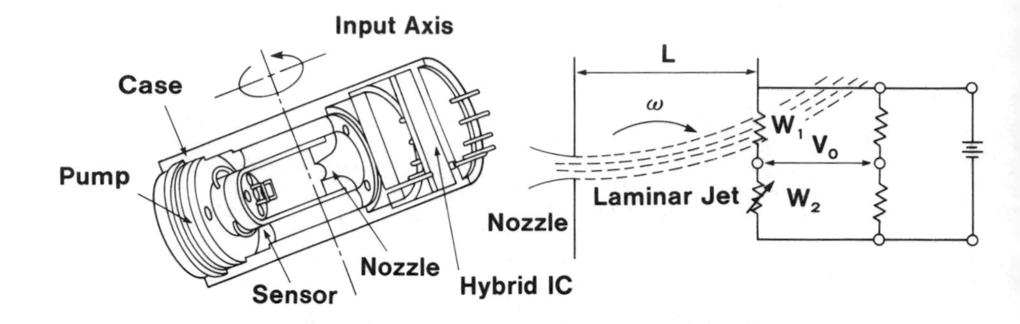

Figure 15.6 Gas rate gyroscope.

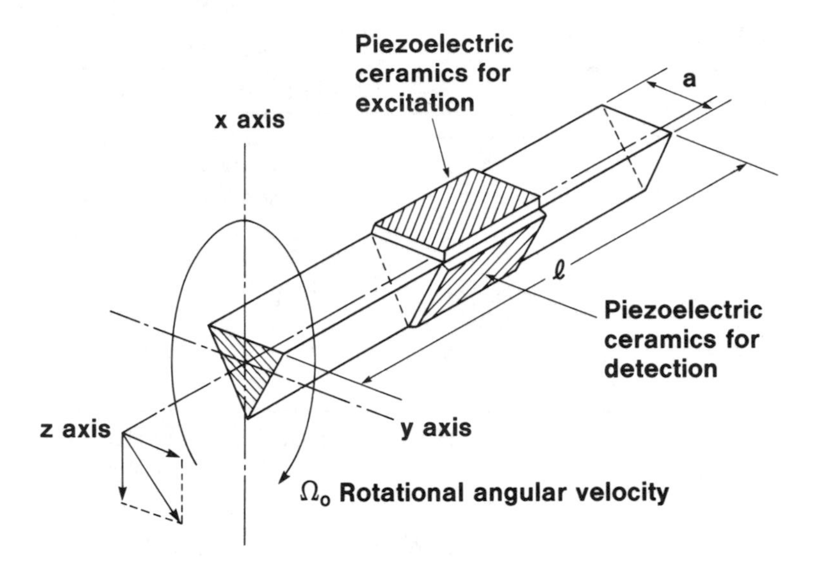

Figure 15.7 Vibration gyroscope.

accuracy for the map matching. A small error can be canceled by the map matching process, and the ECU can correct an offset drift error by checking the output of the FOG while the vehicle is not in motion. The operating principle is shown in Figure 15.8. The light propagates in both the clockwise (CW) and counterclockwise (CCW) directions. When the optical paths rotate, the time the CW light takes to travel differs from the time the CCW light takes for the same span. The FOG measures the rotation rate by detecting the phase difference between the CW and CCW light. The FOG is designed to be resistant

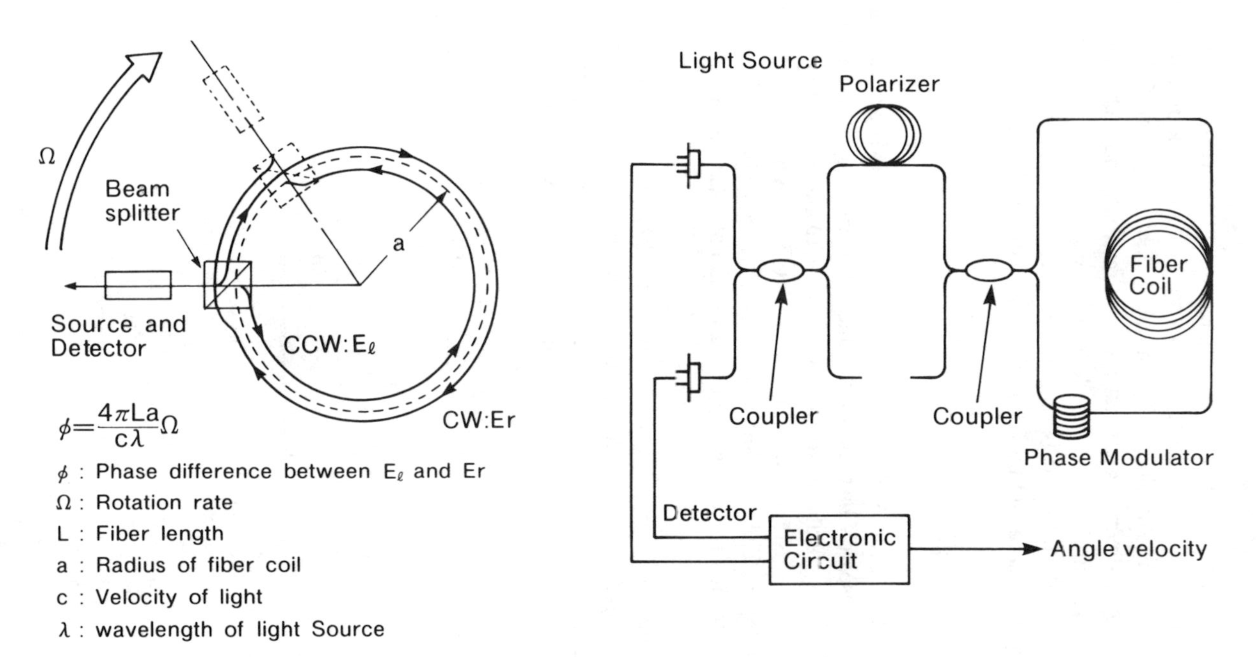

Figure 15.8 Fiber-optic gyroscope: (a) operating principle (Sagnac effect); (b) configuration.

to vibration and humidity by producing all the optical elements with optical fibers. Table 15.2 shows its primary specifications [13].

Absolute Location Detector. A sign post, a beacon, or GPS can be used as absolute location detectors, so the driver does not need to set or correct the initial location even after traveling by ferry boat. Absolute location data as obtained from GPS may have an error of more than 50m (sometimes several hundred meters), and a careless adoption of the absolute location data may adversely reduce the accuracy of location detected by the map matching method. Therefore, it is only used when the difference of the locations detected by the map matching and by GPS exceeds a certain threshold.

15.6 DIGITAL MAP

DRMA. The Digital Road Map Association (DRMA) was established under the initiative of the Public Works Research Institute of the Japanese MOC in 1988. The association supplies digital road map databases to the member companies on magnetic tapes [14]. The Geographical Survey Institute publishes the 1/25,000-scale topographic maps series, which covers all of Japan. The 1/50,000-scale maps are derived from the 1/25,000-scale maps. The graphic information for the digital road map databases is collected from either of these.

SEI. The author's group, Sumitomo Electric Industries (SEI), has developed 1/2,500-grade digital road map databases for the ten major metropolitan areas based on the maps published by the municipal governments. We use the 1/2,500-grade maps for map matching and display, which gives us a very accurate positioning capability and a clear display. We use DRMA's 1/25,000- and 1/50,000-grade maps for map matching in sparsely inhabited areas and for the route selection and display in all areas. Figure 12.9 shows the coverage of the maps. (DRMA's 1/25,000-grade areas include SEI's 1/2,500 areas.)

Table 15.2
Specifications of the FOG

Item	*Specification*
Noise	0.05 deg/s
Offset drift	0.1 deg/s/10°C
Scale factor drift	±1.5% at −10~60°C
	±3.0% at −20~70°C
Linearity	1% at full scale
Response	1Hz
Maximum input rate	~90 deg/s
Warm-up time	1s
Temperature range	−20~70°C
Dimensions	150 × 210 × 25mm
Weight	850g

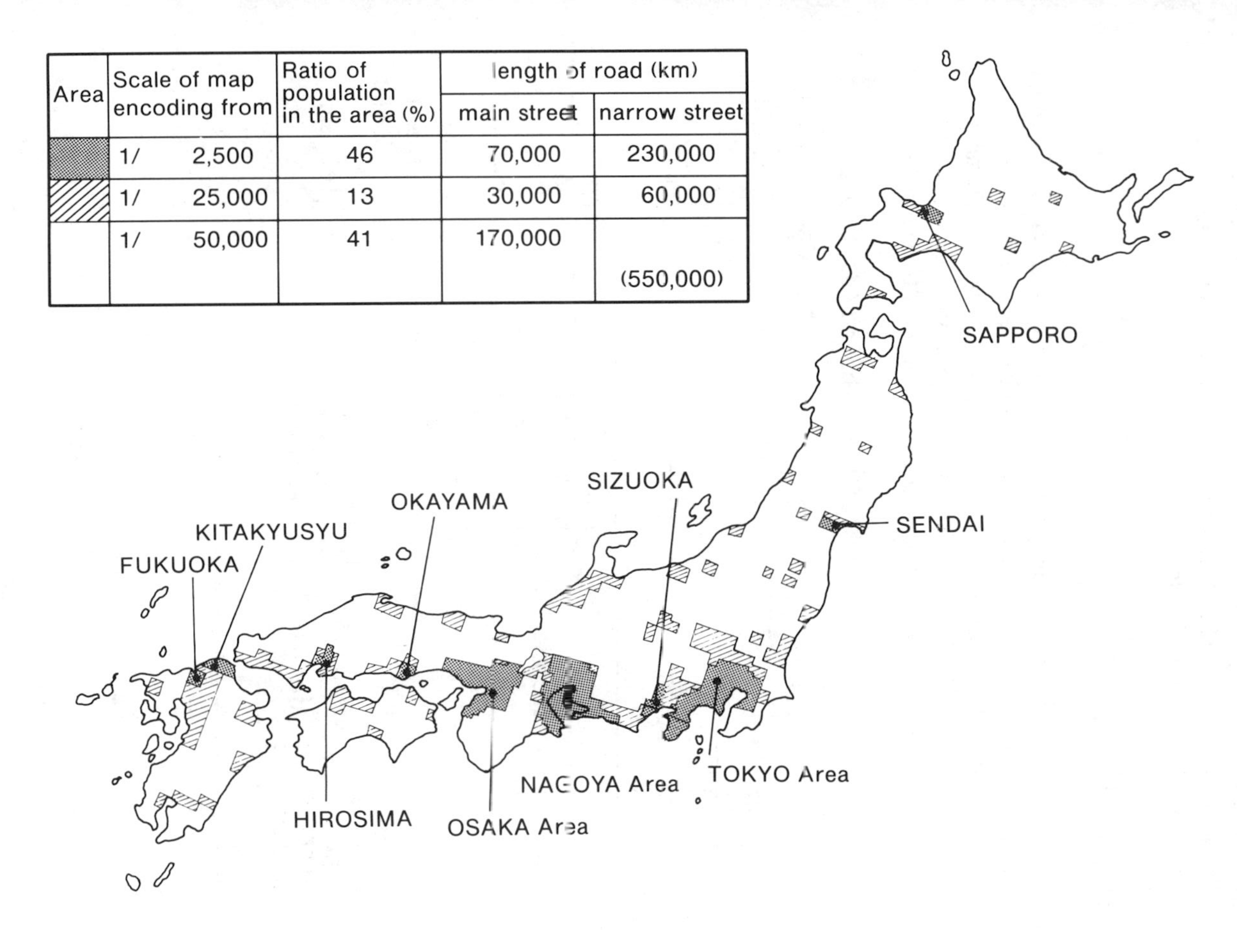

Area	Scale of map encoding from	Ratio of population in the area (%)	length of road (km)	
			main street	narrow street
	1/ 2,500	46	70,000	230,000
	1/ 25,000	13	30,000	60,000
	1/ 50,000	41	170,000	
				(550,000)

Figure 15.9 Map database.

Facility Reference. Some navigation systems have a reference to facilities such as railway stations, hotels, department stores, amusement centers, museums, car dealers, and golf clubs. The locations, addresses, and telephone numbers are stored in the map CD-ROM. The driver can select these as destinations.

15.7 CDCRAFT

CDCRAFT (Figure 15.10) has been proposed by Toyota Corporation, Nissan Motor Co., Ltd., Nippondenso Co., Ltd., and Sumitomo Electric Industries, Ltd., as a common standard of CD format and application program for automobile navigation and entertainment using CD and CRT display [15]. This standard enables application programs by third-party software vendors to be executable on navigation systems of different make.

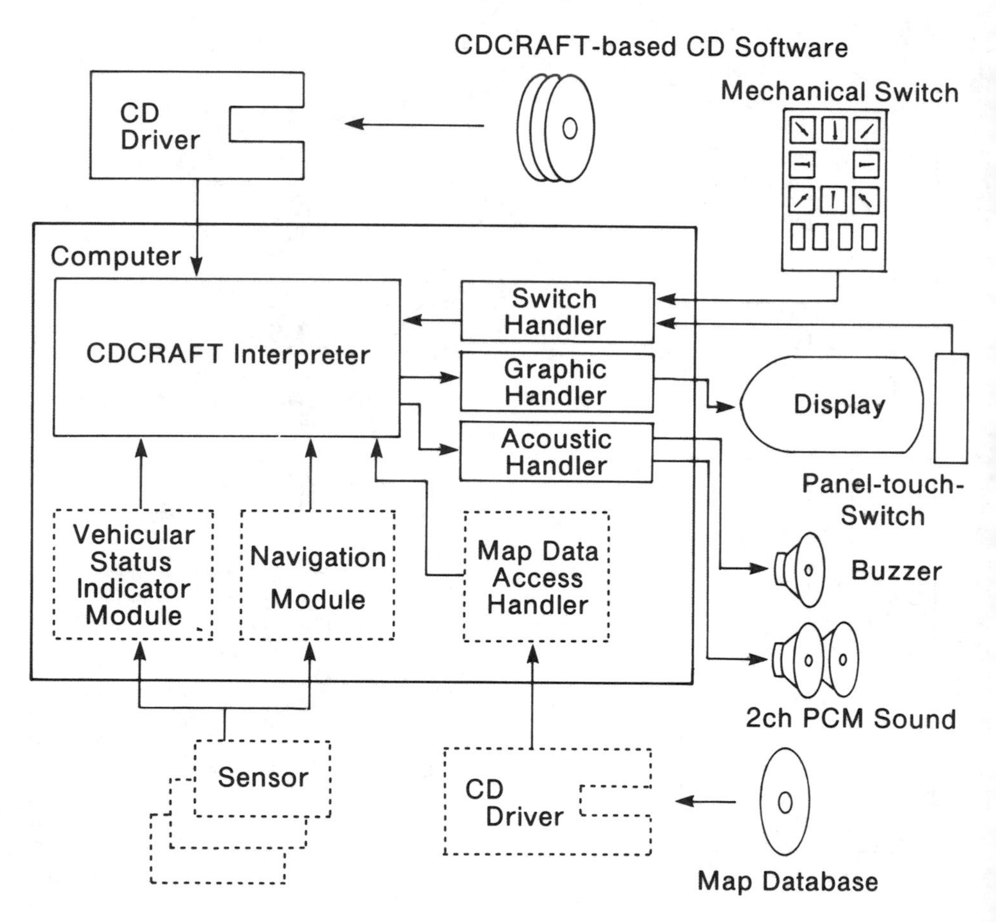

Figure 15.10 CDCRAFT.

The program stored in the CD-ROM is executed by an interpreter program that is installed in the ECU, which also takes into account differences between navigation systems. The CD-ROM stores programs, data, and also PCM-encoded audio data. It is possible not only to display pictures, but also to present audio sounds at the same time. By using the commands that interface with the navigation system, the CDCRAFT application program can retrieve the map from the system, receive current location information, and then set the destination data. Software vendors can develop application programs that would allow information retrieval of tourist resorts and route guidance using voice and illustration maps.

15.8 COMMUNICATION MEDIA

Teleterminal. A pilot experiment was carried out in Tokyo in 1988 using Teleterminal, a new mobile data cellular radio in the 800-MHz band with a 9,600-bps transmission rate. One channel was dedicated to broadcasting the traffic information. A larger scale experiment was started for demonstration during the International Garden and Greenery Exposition in Osaka in 1990. Such information as congestion, regulation, road works, and parking vacancy is displayed on board with the vehicle position superimposed. Teleterminal is now in operation in Tokyo.

Sign Post. The sign post sends a 250-byte position code to the vehicle at a 16-kbps transmission speed as the vehicle passes through the communication zone. At the same time, it detects the presence and speed of vehicles. See Figure 15.11. Table 15.3 shows the specification of the sign post [16].

Beacon. A bidirectional microzone communication system using quasimicrowave (1 to 3 GHz) was developed [17]. A pair of antennas are fed in phase with a phase-modulated signal to obtain a larger zone (60m), and fed differentially with an AM carrier to get a sharp cutoff just under the antenna. See Figure 15.12. In a small-zone system, the amount of data required to be sent is smaller than in the case of a wide-zone system, because detailed data are needed only for nearby places; the further away the places are from the beacon, the more approximated the road network can be. A transmission test in preparation for practical use has been carried out since the summer of 1990. One hundred and three beacons, which transmit data to vehicles at 64 kbps, were installed in the Tokyo, Nagoya, and Osaka areas. Table 15.4 shows the specification of the beacon. Figure 15.13 shows the receiver for the beacon. Recently, a bidirectional IR beacon has been developed which has the capability of detecting vehicles, too. This type of beacon is also put to trial use throughout the country.

FM Subcarrier. Use of an FM subcarrier for broadcast of traffic information has been investigated. In a wide-zone system such as FM broadcasting, more data needs to be sent because the data must be of uniform detail throughout a wider service area. On the other hand, the updating cycle time can be fully used for transmission, unlike in the small-zone

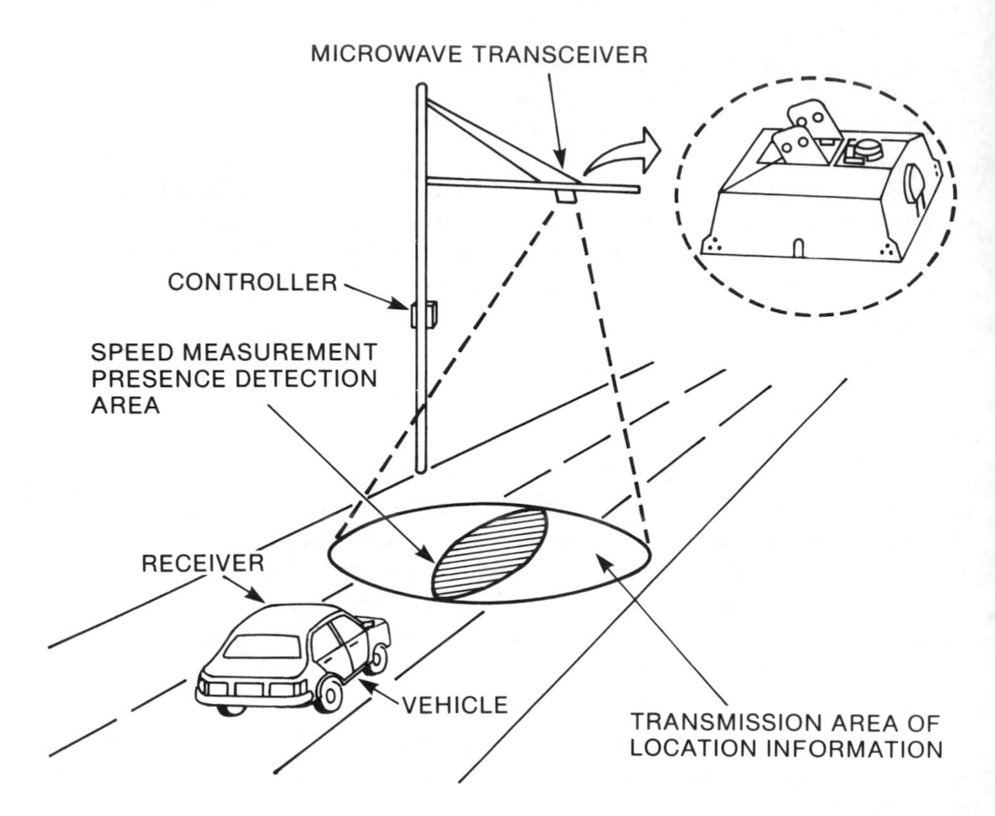

Figure 15.11 Sign post.

system, where data must be sent within the short time during which the vehicle passes through the small zone.

15.9 FUTURE DEVELOPMENT

The fundamental technologies for navigation systems have been developed. Static navigation systems that work without the ground information are now rapidly penetrating throughout Japan. The number of navigation-equipped cars has exceeded 400,000. Communication systems for the dynamic navigation system have been tested in the field and partly in trial use. These activities are to be integrated into VICS (see Section 14.2), which is expected to accelerate the penetration of the navigation system remarkably and improve the traffic situation. A considerable growth of multimedia information systems combined with the navigation system is anticipated, as is a commercialization of simpler, lower cost versions.

Table 15.3
Specifications of Sign Post

Item	*Specification*	*Remarks*
Frequency	13 GHz	
Output power	30 mW	
Microwave projection angle	45 deg to 75 deg (downward from horizontal)	
Installation height	5m to 6m above the road surface	
Modulation	Pulse amplitude modulation	
Modulation rate	16 Kbps	
Location information supply area: width	3 lanes or more	Minimum receiver sensitivity: –65dBm
Location information supply area: direction of travel	3m or more	
Speed measurement range	4~120 km/h	
Speed measurement accuracy	±10%	10km/h or greater
Vehicles to be detected	Compact car and larger	
Output	Speed, presence of vehicle	
Power consumption	~ 25 VA	

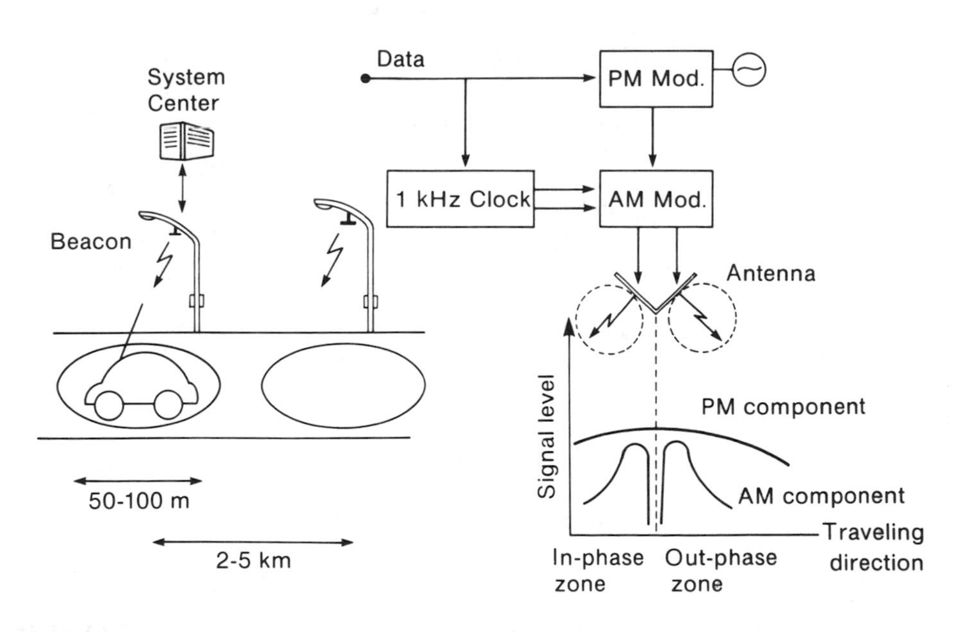

Figure 15.12 Beacon system.

Table 15.4
Specifications of Beacons

Item	*Specification*
Carrier frequency	2.5-GHz band
Transmission mode	One-way transmission
Modulation for data	GMSK
Modulation for positioning and direction detection	AM (1-KHz-square signal)
Data transmission rate	64 Kbps
Transmission coding	N R Z
Positioning and direction-detection	Phase comparing between AM 1k-Hz-square signal and data frame (see figures)
Error correction	CRC

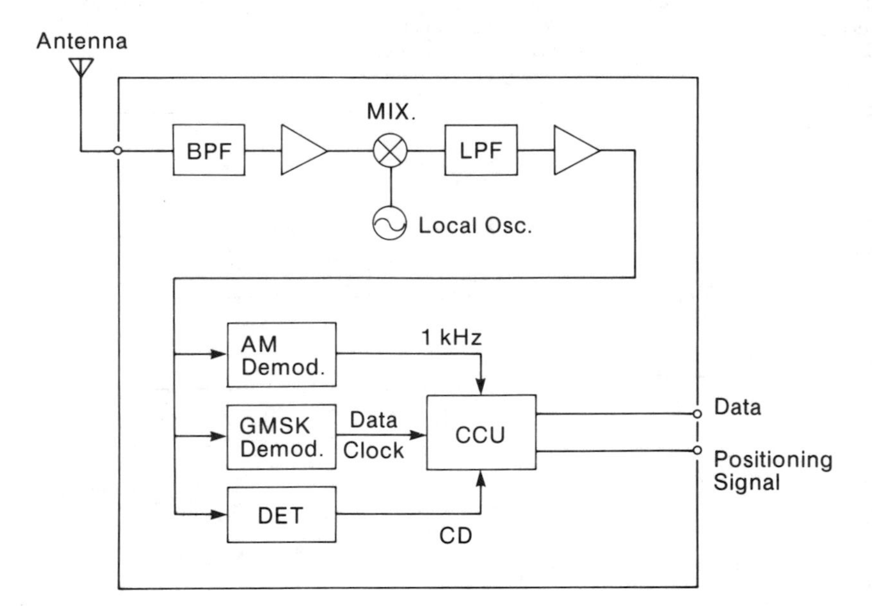

Figure 15.13 Beacon receiver.

REFERENCES

[1] Yumoto, N., ''Status of Advanced Driver Information Systems in Japan,'' *TRB 70th Annual Meeting, 1991.*

[2] Hoffmann, G., J. Sparmann, R. Tomkewitsch, and W. Zechnall, ''Guidance and Information System Berlin,'' *Proc. Int. Road and Traffic 2000 Conf.,* Berlin, 6–7 September 1988.

[3] Belcher, P., and I. Catling, ''Electronics Route Guidance by AUTOGUIDE; The London Demonstration,'' *Traffic Engineering and Control,* London, November 1987.

[4] Yumoto, N., T. Tabe, H. Ihara, and M. Naniwada, ''Outline of the CACS Pilot Test System,'' presented at 58th Annual Meeting, Transportation Research Board, Washington, D.C., January 1979.

[5] Tagami, K., T. Takahashi, and F. Takahashi, ''Inertial Navigation System for Use in Automobiles, 'Electro Gyrocator,' '' *J. Society of Automotive Engineers of Japan,* Vol. 36, No. 5, 1982.

[6] Shoji, Y., T. Horibe, and N. Kondo, ''Toyota Electro Multivision,'' Paper 880220, *SAE Int.,* Detroit, Michigan, 1988.

[7] French, R. L., and G. M. Lang, ''Automatic Route Control System,'' *IEEE Trans. on Vehicular Technology,* Vol. 23, No. 2, May 1973.

[8] Mitoh, K., ''Multi-AV System for Nissan's Automobiles,'' the Session for Update on International Development in Intelligent Vehicle-Highway Systems, *TRB 69th Annual Meeting,* January 1990.

[9] Itoh, T., S. Tsunoda, K. Hirano, and J. Tanaka, ''Navigation System With Map Matching Method,'' Paper 900471, *SAE,* 1990.

[10] Kakihara, M., ''Mazda Car Communication System,'' *24th ISATA,* 910005.

[11] Matsuda, Y., et al., ''Man-Machine Interface and the Control Software for Automobile Navigation System,'' SAE Technical Paper 910060, March 1991.

[12] Ikeda, H., et al., ''Sumitomo Electric's Navigation Systems for Automobiles,'' *VNIS,* 1991.

[13] Nishihara, Y., et al., ''Compact Fiber Optic Gyro,'' *Sumitomo Electric Technical Review,* No. 30, 1990.

[14] Kamijo, S., K. Okumura, and A. Kitamura, ''Digital Road Map Database for Vehicle Navigation and Road Information Systems,'' *VNIS'89,* Toronto, September 1989.

[15] Tuzimoto, K., et al., ''CD Software Specification for Vehicle Information Display System CDCRAFT,'' *1990 IEEE Workshop on Electric Applications in Transportation* (IEEE Cat 90th 310-3).

[16] Uetakaya, K., and H. Fukui, ''Microwave Vehicle Detector,'' *24th ISATA Int. Symp. on Automotive Technology and Automation.*

[17] Shibano, Y., T, Noricane, T. Iwai, M. Yamada, and S. Tsurui, ''Development of Mobile Communication System for RACS,'' *VNIS'89,* Toronto, September 1989.

[18] Nakahara, T., N. Yumoto, and A. Tanaka, ''Multi-Criterion Area Traffic Control System With Feedback Features,'' paper No. 3.9, *IFAC/IFIP 1st Int. Symp. on Traffic Control,* Versailles, June 1970.

[19] Inose, H., H. Okamoto, and N. Yumoto, ''A Multi-Computer System, Metropolitan Tokyo Traffic Control and Surveillance System,'' *2nd Int. Symp. on Traffic Control,* 1974.

[20] Sakai, K., et al., ''In-Tunnel Traffic Flow Measuring System Using an ITV Camera,'' *Sumitomo Electric Technical Review,* No. 29, Jan. 1990.

[21] Rosen, D. A., F. J. Mammano, and R. Favout, ''An Electronic Route Guidance System for Highway Vehicles,'' *IEEE Trans. on Vehicular Technology,* Vol. VT-19, 1970. pp. 143–152.

[22] Takada, K., Y. Tanaka, A. Igarashi, and D. Fujita, ''Road/Automobile Communication System (RACS) and Its Economic Effect,'' *VNIS'89,* Toronto, September 1989.

[23] Kawabata, T., K. Fujita, T. Fukumitsu, T. Asai, M. Yoshii, and H. Watanabe, ''Advanced Mobile Traffic Information and Communication System,'' *Sumitomo Electric Technical Review,* No. 29, Jan. 1990.

[24] Tsuzawa M., and H. Okamoto, ''Advanced Mobil Traffic Information and Communication System—AMTICS,'' VNIS'89, Toronto, September 1989.

Glossary

AAA	American Automobile Association
AAAS	American Association for the Advancement of Science
AASHTO	American Association of State Highway and Transportation Officials
AATA	Ann Arbor Transportation Authority
ACEA	European Automotive Manufacturers Association
ADS	automatic debiting system
ADVANCE	Advanced Driver and Vehicle Advisory Navigation Concept
AHAR	Automatic Highway Advisory Radio
AICC	Autonomous Intelligent Cruise Control
AMTICS	Advanced Mobile Traffic Information and Communication System
ANSA	Advanced Network Systems Architecture
APPLE	Advanced Pilot Project for London and Europe
APTS	advanced public transportation system
ARQ	automatic retransmission request
ARTHUR	Automatic Radiocommunication system for Traffic emergency situations on Highways and Urban Roads
ARTS	Advanced Rural Transportation System
ASN.1	Abstract Syntax Notation.1
ATIS	advanced traveler information system (U.S. and Europe)
ATIS	Advanced Traffic Information Service (Japan)
ATMS	advanced traffic management system
ATT	advanced (road) transport telematics
AVCS	advanced vehicle control system
AVI	automatic vehicle identification
AVL	automatic vehicle location
AVM	automatic vehicle monitoring

BMM	board member meeting
CACS	Comprehensive Automobile Traffic Control System
CALTRANS	California Department of Transportation
CAN	controller area network
CANDI	Surveillance Control and Driver Information
CASE	computer-aided software engineering
CCD	charge-coupled device
CCITT	Consultative Committee in International Telegraphy and Telephony
CCTF	Cooperative Control Task Force
CCW	counterclockwise
CDCRAFT	CD and CRT Applied Format
CDPD	cellular digital packet data
CEC	Commission of the European Communities
CED	common European demonstrations
CEN	Comité Européen de Normalisation
CEPT	European Conference of Ministers of Post and Telecommunication
CITIES	Cooperation for Integrated Traffic Management and Information Exchange Systems
CITRA	Corridor Initiative for Transit Route Through the Alps
CMS	changeable messages sign
COM	RF communications network
COMFORT	Cooperative Management for Urban and Regional Transport
COMPOSE	Communication and Positioning Equipment
CRT	cathode ray tube
CSEE	Compagnie de Signaux et d' Equipements Electroniques
CVO	commercial vehicle operation
CW	clockwise
D-DOT	Detroit Department of Transportation
DAB	digital audio broadcast
DFO	Detroit Freeway Operations
DI	driver information
DIRECT	Driver Information Radio Using Experimental Communication Technologies
DNT	DRIVE normalized transmission
DOT	department of transportation
DRG	dynamic route guidance
DRIVE	Dedicated Road Infrastructure for Vehicle Safety in Europe
DRMA	Digital Road Map Association
EC	European Community
ECMT	European Conference of Ministers of Transport

ECU	electronic control unit
ECU	European currency unit
EDI	electronic data interchange
EFTPOS	electronic funds transfer at point-of-sale
EICC	extended intelligent cruise control
EID	Empresa de Investigacao e Disenvolvimento de Electronica
EPHOS	European Procurement Handbook for Open Systems
ERIM	Environmental Research Institute of Michigan
ERP	electronic road pricing
ERTICO	European Road Transport Informatics Implementation Coordination Organization
ETSI	European Telecommunications Standards Institute
EW	Emergency Warning
FAC	Federal advisory committee
FAST-TRAC	Faster And Safer Travel through Traffic Routing and Advanced Controls
FCC	Federal Communications Commission
FEC	forward error correction
FHWA	Federal Highway Administration
FIR	far infrared
FOG	fiber-optic gyroscope
FPLMTS	future public land-mobile telephony systems
FS	feasibility studies
FTA	Federal Transit Administration
GDF	Geographic Data Format
GMSK	Gussian-filtered minimum shift keying
GOSIP	Government OSI Profile
GPRS	general packet radio service
GPS	Global Positioning System
GSM	Global System of Mobile Communication
HAR	Highway Advisory Radio
HDLC	high-level data link control
HIDO	Highway Industry Development Organization
HNR	Hughes Network Radio
HOV	high-occupancy vehicle
HUFSAM	Highway Users Federation for Safety and Mobility
IAB	Industrial Advisory Board
IATSS	International Association of Traffic and Safety Sciences
IBC	integrated broadband communications
ICAD	Intelligent Computer Aided Driving
ICC	intelligent cruise control
IDOT	Illinois Department of Transportation

IHT	Institution of Highways and Transportation
IIC	intelligent intersection control
IMC	intelligent maneuvering and control
IP	Internetwork Protocol
IR	infrared
IRTE	integrated road transport environment
ISA	Integrated Systems Architecture
ISDN	integrated services digital network
ISIS	Interactive Road Sign System
ISO	International Standards Organization
ISTEA	Intermodal Surface Transportation Efficiency Act
IUTRC	Illinois Universities Transportation Research Consortium
IVHS	intelligent vehicle-highway systems
IVU	in-vehicle unit
KP	kernel projects
LCX	leaky coaxial cable
LED	light-emitting diode
LLAMD	London, Lyon, Amsterdam, Munich, and Dublin
LQ	linear quadratic
MANET	MAtra NETwork
MCSS	Motorway Control and Signaling System
MDIMC	Metropolitan Detroit Incident Management Coordination Efforts
MDOT	Michigan Department of Transportation
MELYSSA	Mediterranean-Lyon-Stuttgart Site for ATT
MMI	man-machine interface
MNA	mobile navigation assistant
MOC	Ministry of Construction
MOSI	Mobile Open Systems Interconnection
MoU	Memorandum of Understanding
MPO	metropolitan planning organization
MRP	medium-range preinformation
MTC	Metropolitan Transportation Center
MUSIC	Multi-Sensor Intelligent Control
NHTSA	National Highway Traffic Safety Administration
NIR	near infrared
OBU	onboard unit
OD	origin-destination
ODP	open distributed processing
OSI	Open Systems Interconnection
P&R	park and ride
PAMELA	Pricing and Monitoring Electronically of Automobiles

PIN	personal identification number
PM	program management
POCSAG	Post Office Code for Standardization Advisory Group
PP	pilot projects
PROMETHEUS	Program for a European Traffic With Highest Efficiency and Unprecedented Safety
PSPDN	public switched packet data network
PTPIS	public transport passenger information system
PVS	Personal Vehicle System
RACE	Research into Advanced Communications for Europe
RACS	Road-Automobile Communication System
RCS	roadside charging station
RDS	Radio Data System
RDS-TMC	radio data system traffic message channel
RF	radio frequency
RHAPIT	Rhein-Main Area Project for Integrated Traffic
ROSA	RACE Open Services Architecture
RRL	road research laboratory
RSPA	Research and Special Programs Administration
RTI	road transport informatics
SACTRA	Standing Advisory Committee on Trunk Road Appraisal
SADT	Structured Analysis and Design Technique
SAP	secondary audio program
SCA	subsidiary communications authorization
SCANeR	Simulator of Cooperative Automotive NetwoRk
SCATS	Sydney Coordinated Adaptive Traffic System
SCOOT	split, cycle, and off-set optimization technique
SEI	Sumitomo Electric Industries
SMART	Suburban Mobility Authority for Regional Transportation
SMS	short-message service
SNRA	Swedish National Road Administration
SP	supporting projects
SRC	short-range communication
SSVS	super smart vehicle system
TACS	Total Access Communication System
TC	technical committee
TCM	THOMSON Composants Micro-ondes
TCT	transport, computers, and telecommunications
TEMS	third-generation mobile systems
TETRA	trans-European trunked radio
TIC	traffic information center
TIGER	Travel Information and Guidance for European Roads

TMC	traffic message channel
TORG	Transport Operations Research Group
TRACE	Transport Application Coding for Europe
TRF	traffic-related function
TRL	Transport Research Laboratory
TRRL	Transport and Road Research Laboratory
TSAP	transport service access point
UDP	User Datagram Protocol
UMTS	universal mobile telephone system
UPS	United Parcel Service
UTC	urban traffic control
UTEP	urban, technical, and environmental planning
UV	ultraviolet
VICS	Vehicle Information and Communication System
VMS	variable-message signs
VMT	vehicle miles of travel
WIM	weigh-in-motion

About the Authors

Ian Catling, Ian Catling Consultancy. Mr. Catling is a computing and transportation consultant with 23 years of professional experience in government, the computer services industry, and consultancy. Since forming the Ian Catling Consultancy (ICC) in 1983, he has established a worldwide reputation as an expert in RTI, ATT, and IVHS. ICC is prominent in the DRIVE and PROMETHEUS programs, and Ian Catling is currently the overall project manager for two major projects: SOCRATES, which is developing RTI systems based on cellular radio, and the LLAMD Euro-Project, which is implementing linked field trials in five cities.

Mark Andrews, Porsche AG. Mr. Andrews' first experience of vehicle design was when the team from his school, King Edward VI Grammar School, Chelmsford, entered British Petroleum's Build-a-Car competition in 1978. In 1982 he graduated with honors in electronic engineering from Liverpool University, having been sponsored by the GEC English Electric Valve Company, Ltd. He later joined Jaguar Cars, Ltd., and was responsible for the development, together with GenRad, of the world's first total vehicle electrical system diagnostic computer. This was launched worldwide in 1987 coinciding with the launch of the then new XJ65 model. After moving as a manager to the research department, his involvement with the EUREKA program PROMETHEUS provided an opportunity to move to Porsche in Germany. Mr. Andrews is a chartered engineer and member of the IEE, but also sees himself as one of the new generation of "European" engineers.

Michael G. H. Bell, University of Newcastle. Mr. Bell has been deputy director of the Transport Operations Research Group (TORG) at the University of Newcastle upon Tyne since May 1992. Prior to that, he completed eight years as a New Blood lecturer in transport operations in the Civil Engineering Department, during which time he initiated or was involved in 17 TORG research projects funded by the Science and Engineering Research Council, the EC, and industry. In addition to his teaching and research activities, he is involved in publishing as an associate editor for Transportation Research B and as an editor for the Research Studies Press series of books on traffic engineering. Dr. Bell is the acting director of TORG for the academic year 1992–93, during the period of Professor Peter Hills' presidency of the Institution of Highways and Transportation (IHT).

Philip T. Blythe, University of Newcastle. Mr. Blythe graduated with an honors degree in electrical and electronic engineering in 1985. He then worked for a joint academic research team at Newcastle Polytechnic and Newcastle University, developing microwave communications systems for vehicle-to-roadside data communications. At the end of 1988, Mr. Blythe was appointed project coordinator for the DRIVE I project PAMELA on behalf of the prime contractor, the University of Newcastle upon Tyne. In addition to this, his research interests lie in many fields, including automatic debiting, communications systems, road-use pricing, and integration of RTI technologies. He has participated in a number of working groups in the DRIVE I and II programs dealing with standardization issues, such as frequency allocation (CEPT), container identification and AVI (British Standards Institute (BSI) and ISO), smart cards (CEN/TC224), RTI (CEN/TC278), and automatic debiting (coauthored the HADES I and CASH specifications). He has also been appointed chairman of the task force dealing with European issues of communications for transport applications. Mr. Blythe has been largely responsible for the definition and formation of the ADEPT consortium and has subsequently been appointed overall project coordinator of the ADEPT project. He also represents the university in the CASH project, and is the only expert on the team who is not from a road administration or the Ministry of Transport. He has been appointed chairman of one of the seven DRIVE II-ATT program areas of operational interest, "Area 1 Demand Management," and is also the chairman of the task force on "Communications Interfaces." He was project coordinator of the consortium awarded a contract by the U.K. Department of Transport to critically review road-use pricing technologies and their applicability to a London context, and of the consortium awarded a similar study contract for the New Zealand Ministry of Transport. Mr. Blythe has published over 50 chapters, articles, and papers in the fields of transport technology and road-use pricing. He is also currently pursuing research for a Ph.D. in the field of integration of RTI techniques.

David E. Boyce, University of Illinois at Chicago. Mr. Boyce is director of the Urban Transportation Center and professor of transportation and regional science at the University of Illinois at Chicago. He is coordinator of the activities of the Illinois University Transportation Research Consortium for the ADVANCE project. Dr. Boyce has worked for the last 18 years on the implementation and testing of network equilibrium models of travel choice. He is leading the development of a large-scale network model with realistic traffic delay functions for the estimation of link travel times by turning movement for the ADVANCE project. Prior to coming to the University of Illinois, Chicago, in 1988, Dr. Boyce was a faculty member at the University of Pennsylvania, Philadelphia, and the University of Illinois at Urbana-Champaign. He has served as president, secretary, and international conference coordinator of the Regional Science Association International. He is an associate editor of transportation science and a member of the Editorial Advisory Committee of Transportation Research.

Kan Chen, University of Michigan. Mr. Chen was born in Hong Kong, grew up in China, and came to the United States to attend college. After getting his bachelor's degree from Cornell University in 1950 and doctor of science degree from MIT in 1954, all in electrical engineering, he worked for Westinghouse Corporation for 12 years, the last few as system technology R&D manager. Between 1966 and 1970, he was with Stanford Research Institute as a program director, with a joint appointment at the Engineering-Economic Systems Department of Stanford University. In 1971 he became professor of electrical engineering and computer science at the University of Michigan, doing teaching and research in technology planning and assessment, and in social decision analysis. Between 1980 and 1987, he was director of the interdisciplinary Ph.D. program in urban, technical, and environmental planning (UTEP) at Michigan, and conducted research in sociotechnological systems. Dr. Chen has been a cofounder and codirector of the Michigan IVHS program since 1987, responsible for the education and basic research components of that program, which has had over 35 American and international sponsors from industry and government agencies at all levels. Dr. Chen spent his sabbatical leave during 1990–91 in Europe and Asia, visiting over 50 IVHS projects in those continents. Having been a core member of Mobility 2000, the predecessor of IVHS America, Dr. Chen served the latter organization on a number of its committees, including its Coordinating Council, International Liaison Committee, Information and Clearinghouse Subcommittee, and University R&D Issues Subcommittee. He also chaired the Technical Program Committee for IVHS America's second annual meeting in 1992. Dr. Chen is a fellow of IEEE and of the American Association for the Advancement of Science (AAAS). He has published seven books and over 120 articles in professional journals, including 20 on IVHS.

James Costantino, IVHS America. Mr. Constantino is executive director of IVHS America and has an extensive background in transportation research, development, education, and policy in government, industry, and academia. Previously, Dr. Costantino was a professor of transportation engineering at George Mason University and an associate dean and professor of engineering at George Washington University. He was also the executive vice president and chief operating officer of the Free Congress Research Foundation, managing partner of the Charles River Group, and executive vice president and chief operating officer of JAYCOR, Inc. In his Federal Government career, Dr. Costantino held senior positions at the Federal Aviation Administration, the National Aeronautics and Space Administration, and the Department of Transportation. His most recent Federal position was as Director of the Volpe National Transportation Systems Center in Cambridge, Massachusetts. He is a registered professional engineer, a director of the National Society of Professional Engineers and IVHS America, a fellow of the American Association for the Advancement of Science, and a member of the advisory boards of several engineering and transportation organizations. He received degrees in mechanical engineering from the University of Massachussetts, in engineering administration from George Washington University, and in business economics from American University.

David M. DeVaughn, Michigan Department of Transportation. Mr. DeVaughn has a B.S. in agricultural economics, focusing on public policy analysis, and an M.S. in civil engineering, focusing on transportation engineering, both from Michigan State University, where he is a Ph.D. candidate in civil engineering. He is also currently working as a transportation engineer in the Transportation Systems Section of the Traffic & Safety Division of the MDOT. He has coauthored several papers on IVHS and served as coeditor of the Guideline for ATMS, published by IVHS America. Prior to joining MDOT, Mr. DeVaughn worked ten years in the construction industry.

Peter Häuβermann, Daimler-Benz, AG. Mr. Häuβermann received his master's degree in engineering (Dipl. Ing) in 1979 from the Technical University of Stuttgart, Department of Electronic Sciences, where he specialized in theoretical communication technology and microprocessor systems. He then joined Daimler-Benz Research as a research engineer in the field of automotive electronics. In 1984 he developed the Daimler-Benz route guidance system, and in 1986 he was responsible for Daimler-Benz PROMETHEUS PRO-ROAD activities. In 1990 he became manager of Daimler-Benz PROMETHEUS activities, where in 1992 he became senior manager responsible for traffic research.

Peter J. Hills, University of Newcastle. Mr. Hills is professor of transport engineering and director of the Transport Operations Research Group at the University of Newcastle upon Tyne. He began his professional career as a member of the working group on the Buchanan report *Traffic in Towns*. After leaving the (then) Ministry of Transport, he spent nine years as a lecturer at Imperial College, London, and was engaged in numerous consulting studies. In 1972, he was appointed assistant director of research at Leeds University in the newly formed Institute for Transport Studies.

In 1977, Professor Hills moved to Newcastle University to take up his present post, where he is responsible for a large research group with about ten current projects in the fields of urban traffic control, public transport operations, freight movement, traffic safety, and road traffic informatics. In addition to *Traffic in Towns*, he coauthored the book *Motorways in London* and many other publications in the transport field. Over the period 1970 to 1981, he was associate editor of the international quarterly journal *Transportation*. From 1983 to 1986, he directed the team that produced *Roads and Traffic in Urban Areas* for the IHT. This was published jointly with the Department of Transport in October 1987. From 1985 to 1989, he was appointed by the Secretary of State for Transport as a Visitor to the TRRL (Safety and Transportation Group).

In 1988, Professor Hills formed a consortium of European partners (including Newcastle University/Polytechnic, Philips U.K. and Sweden, Philips Components in Germany, Compagnie de Signaux et D'Equipments Electronique-Péage (CSEE) in France, and Empresa de Investigacao de Electronica SA (EID) in Portugal) to bid for an EC research contract through the DRIVE program. The bid was successful and led to the PAMELA project in DRIVE I. The consortium has now enlarged in DRIVE II and is developing an automatic two-way communications system between moving vehicles and the roadside, using microwave communications and smart card technology (the ADEPT project). This project, coordinated from Newcastle, will have many important Europewide applications in, for example, automated toll collection, fleet control, route guidance, online parking information, and road-use pricing.

In July 1992, Professor Hills was inaugurated as the president of the IHT for the year 1992–93. He has been invited by the EC to act as a technical auditor to the DRIVE program in October 1990, and again in 1991 and 1992. He has accepted invitations by the U.K. Department of Transport to serve as a member of the Standing Advisory Committee on Trunk Road Appraisal (SACTRA) in 1989, and to act as special advisor in research into network management (in 1992).

James G. Kavalaris, Michigan Department of Transportation. Mr. Kavalaris has a B.S. in civil engineering from Michigan State University. Currently a graduate student in civil engineering at Purdue University, Mr. Kavalaris is working as an engineer in the Traffic & Safety Division of the Michigan Department of Transportation. He has coauthored several papers on IVHS and has served as coeditor of the Guideline for ATMS published by IVHS America.

Hironao Kawashima, Keio University. Mr. Kawashima received B.S., M.S., and Ph.D. degrees in administration engineering from Keio University, Yokohama, Japan, in 1968, 1970, and 1974, respectively. Since 1972, he has been with the Department of Administration Engineering, Keio University, where he is now a professor. From 1974 to 1979, he participated in the CACS project of MITI to design data processing software and to evaluate the performances of route guidance systems. From 1984 to 1990, he was chairman of the Individual Communication Subcommittee of the RACS project. He is now a member of various research committees of public and private joint projects related to traffic information and management systems such as SSVS and ARTS. Since 1989 Dr. Kawashima has been the chairman of the Scientific Export Group of OECD RTR, called Advanced Logistics and Communications in Road Freight Transport Operations and a member of the group Evaluative Study of Road Vehicle Communication Systems. He is a member of the Information Processing Society of Japan, the Operations Research Society of Japan, the Society of Instrument and Control Engineers, Human Engineering Society of Japan, the Japan Society of Traffic Engineers, and the International Association of Traffic and Safety Sciences (IATSS).

Hartmut Keller, Technical University, Munich. Mr. Keller was educated at the University of Berlin and the University of California, Berkeley, and has been a professor of transportation planning and engineering at the Technical University of Munich since 1978. He combines his teaching with an active and influential role in European ATT research, and has played a leading role in several key projects throughout the DRIVE program. He chairs three national committees dealing with traffic control and theory, and has carried out a number of influential studies around the world.

Andras Kemeny, Renault. Mr. Kemeny received his M.S. in applied mathematics at the University of Paris IX Dauphine in 1979 and his Ph.D. in applied computer science at the University of Paris XII Creteil in 1983. From 1984 to 1987, Dr. Kemeny worked for

Thomson CSF, Simulators Division, in Paris/Osny, where he was manager of visual software research and development and was responsible for technical design of the VISA 4 (Thomson's 3D image generator) software (graphics database) and modeling and real-time database management. From 1988 to the present, he has worked for the Renault Research Center in Paris, where he is programs manager of European projects (DRIVE, PROMETHEUS); technical manager of automotive electronics research programs in the fields of simulation, telecommunications, and traffic systems engineering; coordinator of a European collaboration in these fields with research institutes, automotive companies, and electronics suppliers in Germany, France, Italy, Sweden, and Great Britain. Dr. Kemeny has responsibility, on behalf of Renault, for the development of an onboard intervehicle communication system (15p) in conjunction with a test-car demonstration program. He was also responsible for the conception of RENAULT's SCANeR simulator, a network of driving simulators, and for the technical direction of the realization, including the telecommunication and localization interfaces, the dynamics model, and the man-machine interface of the onboard system. In addition to his various lectures and publications in the fields of computer graphics and automotive electronics, Dr. Kemeny has lectured on applied computer graphics and simulation at the Institut Superieur de l'Informatique et de l'Automatique, Sophia Antipolis, France, between 1989 and 1992. He has also organized the first and second PROMETHEUS Cooperative Driving Workshops in Paris in 1990 and 1992. He is a member of the Association of Computer Machinery (ACM), IEEE, and the International Society of Stereology (ISS).

Allan M. Kirson, Motorola, Inc. Mr. Kirson received his B.S. in electrical engineering at the Technion, Israel Institute of Technology, in 1968, and continued with three years of postgraduate studies in electrical engineering and computer science at the Technion. Over the past 23 years, he has accumulated extensive experience in the design and implementation of real-time monitoring and control systems for industrial and automotive applications. He joined Motorola in Toronto in 1977, and transferred to Motorola headquarters in Chicago in 1986. In April, 1989, he joined the newly formed IVHS strategic business unit as director of technology and led a team in the design and implementation of an in-vehicle navigation system with dynamic route guidance and associated subsystems. He has been Motorola's lead technical representative in the ADVANCE project in Northeastern Illinois and is now leading a group of scientists and engineers in the application of new technologies to IVHS and in the development of next generation systems. Mr. Kirson holds two patents in the IVHS field and has numerous patents pending.

He is a member of SAE and IEEE, and serves on the following committees:

- Intelligent Vehicle Highway Society of America—System Architecture, Standards and Protocols, and Advanced Traveler Information Systems Committees;
- SAE IVHS Division—Chair of the Navigation Working Group; member of the System Architecture, Interfaces, International Traveler Information Interchange Standards Working Groups, and the Map Database Standards Committee;
- Transportation Research Communications Committee.

Yasuhiko Kumagai, VICS Promotion Council. Mr. Kumagai graduated in 1969 from Osaka University in with a degree in electrical engineering, and in 1971 received his master's degree. He joined Sumitomo Electric Industries, Ltd., and in 1973 he worked on CACS and specialized loop communication method. In 1978 he worked on the traffic control system at the expressway, specializing in hardware design. In 1989 Mr. Kumagai became general manager of the System Development Office, and in 1992 he became chief engineer of the Development Initiative & Manufacturing Division, Systems & Electronics Group. He is a member of IEEE and SAE.

Lester P. Lamm, IVHS America. A civil engineering graduate of Norwich University in Vermont, Mr. Lamm completed postgraduate studies at Harvard University, MIT, and the University of Maryland. He was elected president of the Highway Users Federation, a national coalition of businesses and associations working for better highways and improved traffic safety, in March 1986 after a 31-year career with the FHWA and its forerunner, the U.S. Bureau of Public Roads. He served as executive director of FHWA, and was the agency's top career professional from 1973 to 1982, and was appointed by President Reagan as deputy administrator in 1982. He was also an incorporator of IVHS America in 1990 (a nonprofit organization founded to accelerate the application of advanced technologies to surface transportation) and now serves as its president. A noted authority on highway transportation, Mr. Lamm is a member of the Board of Governors of the International Public Works Federation, a member of the Executive Committee of the Transportation Research Board, a director of the Road Information Program, is on the Advisory Board of the Northwestern University Traffic Institute, is the president of the Alumni Association of Norwich University, and is active in many other transportation-related professional organizations.

Willy Maes, DRIVE Central Office. Mr. Maes graduated from Leuven University with a degree in electrical and mechanical engineering (electronics option) in 1971. From 1971 to 1988, he worked as a project leader in the Belgian Ministry of Public Works, where he was responsible for the design, installation, operation, and maintenance of several computer control systems for a variety of applications, such as the remote control of the public lighting on the Belgian highway network, the centralization of traffic counts on the highways and national roads, the transmission of the processed traffic information to the highway police, and the remote control of variable message signs on the Brussels-Ostend highway. Mr. Maes was a member of several international working groups in the field of RTI/ATT. He represented Belgium in the Management Committee of the DRIVE program and was a member of the ad hoc working group responsible for the preparation of the program's work plan. In October 1988, he joined the Commission of the European Communities and became member of the DRIVE and ATT programs.

Robert Maki, Michigan Department of Transportation. Mr. Maki, a registered professional engineer of the state of Michigan, is currently the division administrator for the Traffic & Safety Division of the Michigan Department of Transportation, which is responsible for IVHS activities in Michigan. He has over 20 years of experience with state government, primarily with the Traffic & Safety Division. He has published numerous papers on IVHS and other transportation issues and was a coauthor of the Guidelines for ATMS published by the IVHS America ATMS Steering Committee of which he is a member. Dr. Maki is past chairman of the IVHS America ATMS Planning Subcommittee. He is active in many national organizations, especially the TRB Freeway Operations Committee and the AASHTO Transportation Systems Operations Special Committee. Dr. Maki was very active in Mobility 2000, acting as co-chair of the IVHS Benefits Report Committee, which served as a foundation for the creation of IVHS America.

Yutaka Miyata, VICS Promotion Council. Mr. Miyata graduated in 1968 from Waseda University with a degree in politics and economics. He joined Toyota Motor Corporation, where he worked in the Planning & Research Division and Wholesale Division. In 1986 he worked in the Telecommunications Business & Research Division. In 1991 he became general manager of the secretariat of the VICS Promotion Council.

Kunwar Rajendra, Micigan Department of Transportation. Mr. Rajendra has a Ph.D. in transportation engineering from Michigan State University and has a professional engineer's license. He is engineer of transportation systems at the Michigan Department of Transportation and is responsible for IVHS programs at the statewide level, including metropolitan Detroit. He is project director of Michigan's D.I.R.E.C.T. project, is on the ATMS Steering Committee of IVHS America, and is on the policy committees of the International Border Crossing project between U.S. and Canada, Advantage 1-75, FAST-TRAC, and the North Carolina Consortium of Multi-State IVHS Commercial Vehicle Operations study.

Dr. Rajendra has been director of transportation planning in Lansing, Michigan, and has been active in the Institute of Traffic Engineers (ITE), the American Society of Civil Engineers (ASCE), and TRB. He has authored several professional reports and papers.

Joseph L. Schofer, Northwestern University. Mr. Schofer was educated at Yale and Northwestern. He is professor of civil engineering and transportation, and director of research at the Transportation Center, Northwestern University in Evanston, Illinois. He has been on the Northwestern faculty since 1970, and before that he was at the University of Illinois at Chicago. His research interests span transportation systems evaluation; behavioral analyses of operations, utilization, and safety; planning and policy analysis, and urban transportation. He participated with the coauthors of Chapter 11 in the feasibility study for ADVANCE, and serves as coprincipal investigator for ADVANCE activities at Northwestern, which include driver recruitment, incident detection, travel time forecasting, and evaluation. He has been active in the Transportation Research Board, has served as a consultant for governments and private companies, and is broadly involved in community service as a transportation expert.

Heinz Sodeikat, Siemens AG. Mr. Sodeikat graduated from the Technical University of Berlin in 1965 (Dipl. Ing) with an M.A. in electrotechnical engineering, and then entered Siemens AG in Munich. From 1965 to 1975, he was a research and project engineer in the field of telecommunication satellites, and he spent six years in Paris for the Franco-German SYMPHONIE satellite program. From 1975 to 1986, he was a sales and marketing manager and director in Munich in the fields of satellite earth stations, electronics for defense (radars), and security systems (fire alarm, intrusion detection). Mr. Sodeikat was a delegate to Siemens Rome from 1986 to 1989 for the promotion of Siemens' security systems business in Italy. Since 1989, he has been a director within the Siemens Traffic Control Division (EURO-SCOUT project). In addition, Mr. Sodeikat is secretary of the European Standards Committee CENELEC TC 114 (dealing with "Electro-technical Aspects of IVHS"), and he is a member of the German Standards Committee DKE K717, (dealing with "Interactive Dynamic Transport Management"), U.S. TRB Communications (A3A01), and of the ERTICO supervisory board.

Hiroshi Tsunomachi, Highway Industry Development Organization. Mr. Tsunomachi majored in civil engineering in the science and engineering faculty at Waseda University. From 1963 to 1990, he was involved in the surveying, planning, design, construction, and management of the national highway in the Ministry of Construction. In 1990 he entered the Highway Industry Development Organization and was in charge of IVHS/RTI as technical counselor. He is now managing director of the same organization.

Nigel D. C. Wall has worked in the telecommunications sector for over 20 years, primarily on research and development. His experience includes specification development and commissioning of satellite earth stations, development of audio and video conference systems (as a substitute for travel), and development of experimental integrated multimedia terminals and the network to support these systems. More recently, he has been developing mobile data systems, where he was project manager for the DRIVE project CIDER and an active member of the SOCRATES team. Mr. Wall was awarded an honors degree in applied physics and electronics by the University of Durham and is a corporate member of the IEE.

Nobuo Yumoto, Sumitomo Electric Industries, Inc. Since graduating from the Electrical Engineering Department of the University of Tokyo and joining Sumitomo Electric Industries, Ltd., in 1960, Mr. Yumoto has worked on instrumentation, vehicular traffic control, automotive electronics, fiber optics, and network computing systems. He was elected a member of the board of directors in 1988, and a member of the board of managing directors in 1991. Mr. Yumoto participated in the CACS project as the acting manager of the Engineering Division of the Research Association for Comprehensive Automobile Control Technology (the predecessor of JSK). He proposed the combination of roadside radio and navigation for implementation of dynamic route guidance. He is currently the vice chairman of the VICS Promotion Council. Mr. Yumoto is a member of IEEE, the Institute of Electronics and Communication Engineers, and the Robotics Society of Japan.

Hans-Georg Zimmer, PROMETHEUS Office, Daimler-Benz AG. Mr. Zimmer studied mathematics and physics in Gottingen and obtained his doctor's degree in 1959. He then became a lens designer for Carl Zeiss, with responsibilities for the automation of microscopy and image analysis by computers. In 1975 he joined the Max-Planck Institute for Experimental Medicine in Göttinger. There he did basic research on digital image processing and applied research in microphotometry for diagnostics. In 1985 Dr. Zimmer took a position at the Institute for Microelectronics in Stuttgart and became involved in organization and management of PRO-CHIP, the PROMETHEUS subprogram for microelectronics. This resulted in his move to Daimler-Benz in 1988. In the PROMETHEUS office, he was in charge of organizing the PROMETHEUS basic research and of system engineering. He is author of a book on geometrical optics and author or coauthor of 40 publications on mathematics, physics, medicine, and transport.

Index

The Artech House Telecommunications Library

Vinton G. Cerf, Series Editor

Advanced Technology for Road Transport: IVHS and ATT, Ian Catling, editor

Advances in Computer Communications and Networking, Wesley W. Chu, editor

Advances in Computer Systems Security, Rein Turn, editor

Analysis and Synthesis of Logic Systems, Daniel Mange

Asynchronous Transfer Mode Networks: Performance Issues, Raif O. Onvural

A Bibliography of Telecommunications and Socio-Economic Development, Heather E. Hudson

Broadband: Business Services, Technologies, and Strategic Impact, David Wright

Broadband Network Analysis and Design, Daniel Minoli

Broadband Telecommunications Technology, Byeong Lee, Minho Kang, and Jonghee Lee

Cellular Radio: Analog and Digital Systems, Asha Mehrotra

Cellular Radio Systems, D. M. Balston and R. C. V. Macario, editors

Client/Server Computing: Architecture, Applications, and Distributed Systems Management, Bruce Elbert and Bobby Martyna

Codes for Error Control and Synchronization, Djimitri Wiggert

Communication Satellites in the Geostationary Orbit, Donald M. Jansky and Michel C. Jeruchim

Communications Directory, Manus Egan, editor

The Complete Guide to Buying a Telephone System, Paul Daubitz

Computer Telephone Integration, Rob Walters

The Corporate Cabling Guide, Mark W. McElroy

Corporate Networks: The Strategic Use of Telecommunications, Thomas Valovic

Current Advances in LANs, MANs, and ISDN, B. G. Kim, editor

Design and Prospects for the ISDN, G. Dicenet

Digital Cellular Radio, George Calhoun

Digital Hardware Testing: Transistor-Level Fault Modeling and Testing, Rochit Rajsuman, editor

Digital Signal Processing, Murat Kunt

Digital Switching Control Architectures, Giuseppe Fantauzzi

Digital Transmission Design and Jitter Analysis, Yoshitaka Takasaki

Distributed Multimedia Through Broadband Communications Services, Daniel Minoli and Robert Keinath

Distributed Processing Systems, Volume I, Wesley W. Chu, editor

Disaster Recovery Planning for Telecommunications, Leo A. Wrobel

Document Imaging Systems: Technology and Applications, Nathan J. Muller

EDI Security, Control, and Audit, Albert J. Marcella and Sally Chen

Enterprise Networking: Fractional T1 to SONET, Frame Relay to BISDN, Daniel Minoli

Expert Systems Applications in Integrated Network Management, E. C. Ericson, L. T. Ericson, and D. Minoli, editors

FAX: Digital Facsimile Technology and Applications, Second Edition, Dennis Bodson, Kenneth McConnell, and Richard Schaphorst

FDDI and FDDI-II: Architecture, Protocols, and Performance, Bernhard Albert and Anura P. Jayasumana

Fiber Network Service Survivability, Tsong-Ho Wu

Fiber Optics and CATV Business Strategy, Robert K. Yates *et al.*

A Guide to Fractional T1, J. E. Trulove

A Guide to the TCP/IP Protocol Suite, Floyd Wilder

Implementing EDI, Mike Hendry

Implementing X.400 and X.500: The PP and QUIPU Systems, Steve Kille

Inbound Call Centers: Design, Implementation, and Management, Robert A. Gable

Information Superhighways: The Economics of Advanced Public Communication Networks, Bruce Egan

Integrated Broadband Networks, Amit Bhargava

Integrated Services Digital Networks, Anthony M. Rutkowski

International Telecommunications Management, Bruce R. Elbert

International Telecommunication Standards Organizations, Andrew Macpherson

Internetworking LANs: Operation, Design, and Management, Robert Davidson and Nathan Muller

Introduction to Satellite Communication, Bruce R. Elbert

Introduction to T1/T3 Networking, Regis J. (Bud) Bates

Introduction to Telecommunication Electronics, A. Michael Noll

Introduction to Telephones and Telephone Systems, Second Edition, A. Michael Noll

Introduction to X.400, Cemil Betanov

The ITU in a Changing World, George A. Codding, Jr. and Anthony M. Rutkowski

Jitter in Digital Transmission Systems, Patrick R. Trischitta and Eve L. Varma

Land-Mobile Radio System Engineering, Garry C. Hess

LAN/WAN Optimization Techniques, Harrell Van Norman

LANs to WANs: Network Management in the 1990s, Nathan J. Muller and Robert P. Davidson

The Law and Regulation of International Space Communication, Harold M. White, Jr. and Rita Lauria White

Long Distance Services: A Buyer's Guide, Daniel D. Briere

Measurement of Optical Fibers and Devices, G. Cancellieri and U. Ravaioli

Meteor Burst Communication, Jacob Z. Schanker

Minimum Risk Strategy for Acquiring Communications Equipment and Services, Nathan J. Muller

Mobile Communications in the U.S. and Europe: Regulation, Technology, and Markets, Michael Paetsch

Mobile Information Systems, John Walker

Narrowband Land-Mobile Radio Networks, Jean-Paul Linnartz

Networking Strategies for Information Technology, Bruce Elbert

Numerical Analysis of Linear Networks and Systems, Hermann Kremer *et al.*

Optimization of Digital Transmission Systems, K. Trondle and Gunter Soder

Packet Switching Evolution from Narrowband to Broadband ISDN, M. Smouts

Packet Video: Modeling and Signal Processing, Naohisa Ohta

The PP and QUIPU Implementation of X.400 and X.500, Stephen Kille

Principles of Secure Communication Systems, Second Edition, Don J. Torrieri

Principles of Signals and Systems: Deterministic Signals, B. Picinbono

Private Telecommunication Networks, Bruce Elbert

Radiodetermination Satellite Services and Standards, Martin Rothblatt

Residential Fiber Optic Networks: An Engineering and Economic Analysis, David Reed

Secure Data Networking, Michael Purser

Setting Global Telecommunication Standards: The Stakes, The Players, and The Process, Gerd Wallenstein

Smart Cards, José Manuel Otón and José Luis Zoreda

Secure Data Networking, Michael Purser

The Telecommunications Deregulation Sourcebook, Stuart N. Brotman, editor

Television Technology: Fundamentals and Future Prospects, A. Michael Noll

Telecommunications Technology Handbook, Daniel Minoli

Telephone Company and Cable Television Competition, Stuart N. Brotman

Teletraffic Technologies in ATM Networks, Hiroshi Saito

Terrestrial Digital Microwave Communciations, Ferdo Ivanek, editor

Transmission Networking: SONET and the SDH, Mike Sexton and Andy Reid

Transmission Performance of Evolving Telecommunications Networks, John Gruber and Godfrey Williams

Troposcatter Radio Links, G. Roda

UNIX Internetworking, Uday O. Pabrai

Virtual Networks: A Buyer's Guide, Daniel D. Briere

Voice Processing, Second Edition, Walt Tetschner

Voice Teletraffic System Engineering, James R. Boucher

Wireless Access and the Local Telephone Network, George Calhoun

Wireless LAN Systems, A. Santamaría and F. J. Lopez-Hernandez

Writing Disaster Recovery Plans for Telecommunications Networks and LANs, Leo A. Wrobel

X Window System User's Guide, Uday O. Pabrai

For further information on these and other Artech House titles, contact:

Artech House
685 Canton Street
Norwood, MA 01602
617-769-9750
Fax: 617-762-9230
Telex: 951-659
email: artech@world.std.com

Artech House
6 Buckingham Gate
London SW1E6JP England
+44(0)71 973-8077
Fax: +44(0)71 630-0166
Telex: 951-659